Transcending Gangs

Latinas Story Their Experience

THE HAMPTON PRESS COMMUNICATION SERIES
Social Approaches to Interaction, Wendy Leeds-Hurwitz, series editor

From Generation to Generation: Maintaining Cultural Identity Over Time
Wendy Leeds-Hurwitz (ed.)

The Social History of Language and Social Interaction Research:
People, Places, Ideas
Wendy Leeds-Hurwitz (ed.)

Nonprofit Organizations: Creating Membership through Communication
Trudy Milburn

Transcending Gangs: Latinas Story Their Experience
Liliana Castañeda Rossmann

Transcending Gangs

Latinas Story Their Experience

LILIANA CASTAÑEDA ROSSMANN

California State University, San Marcos

HAMPTON PRESS, INC.
NEW YORK, NEW YORK

Printed in the United States of America

Library of Congress Cataloging-in-Publication Data

Rossmann, Liliana Castañeda.
  Transcending gangs : Latinas story their experience / Liliana Castañeda Rossmann.
      p. cm. — (The Hampton Press communication series. Social Approaches to Interaction)
  Includes bibliographical references and index.
  ISBN 978-1-61289-096-8 (hbk.) — ISBN 978-1-61289-097-5 (pbk.)
  1. Female gang members—United States. 2. Hispanic American teenage girls—Social conditions. I. Title.
  HV6439.U5R67 2012
  364.106'60820973—dc23   2012016437

Photo credit: Isaac Arostigui

Hampton Press, Inc.
307 Seventh Ave.
New York, NY 10001

Contents

Part III: Applications for Practice and Theory

Acknowledgments

There are four punctuation marks in the story of genesis for this book. Two incidents in Corpus Christi, Texas—detailed in Chapter 1—that called my attention to the issue of Latinas in gangs constitute the first two punctuation marks. In the first, I mediated a dispute between two gang-impacted teenage Latinas through the Nueces County Dispute Resolution Services. The second incident occurred shortly thereafter as I conducted peer-mediation training for middle-school students, one of whom had been gang-involved and was recounting her experiences getting out of the gang. A third punctuation turn in the story came when, during a job talk that same year, I referenced these incidents as a direction I wanted to take in my research agenda. The fourth turn came years later, at a National Communication Association (NCA) conference, where Wendy Leeds-Hurwitz asked me if I had ever pursued that project. That was just another beginning. Since then, Wendy encouraged me to continue, and this book is the result of her guidance. First of all, I want to thank her for her mentorship. Her phrase "the quotidian nature of violence" made a significant impression on the quotidian nature of working on this manuscript.

Second, I wish to thank my colleagues in the Department of Communication at California State University, San Marcos; in the College of Arts and Sciences; and especially the members of the Professional Leave Committee, and the Provost's Office for granting me a sabbatical year that I spent conducting the research consultations. Thanks to Debbie Andrews, JoAnne Moran, and Ryan Urbach in the Department of Communication at CSUSM for technical and clerical assistance.

For guidance in the process of obtaining permission to conduct research on human subjects, I thank Dr. Marisol Clark-Ibánez; members of the CSUSM Institutional Review Board, Dr. Todd Astorino, and Dr. Sonia Perez; as well as Linda Collins and Brianne Larsen. For granting me Visiting Scholar privileges at the City of San José/San José State

University Dr. Martin Luther King, Jr. Library, and for other library support, I thank Jane Light, Ruth Kifer, and Ellen Swinburne. At the CSUSM Kellogg Library, I thank Judith Downey for pointing me in the right direction the times I was not heading that way. At the City of San José Parks, Recreation, and Neighborhood Services, specifically members of the Mayor's Gang Prevention Task Force, I wish to thank the following individuals: Juan Avila, Rachel Camacho, Geralyn Conway, Charlie Hall, Fernando Lopez, Mario Maciel, Betty Montoya, Esther Mota, Raul Perez, Rich Saito, and Petra Riguero. I thank Gabriela Maldonado-Montano, at the Santa Clara County Health Realization/3 Principles Services Division, for the time she took during her busy weekend to discuss her project and its fit with mine. For answering my questions about the numbers of Norteño/Sureño gang members and a myriad of other topics related to law enforcement, girls, gangs, and graffiti, I am grateful at the City of San José Police Department to Lt. Wilfredo Montano (Ret.), Sgt. Octavio Morales, and Officers Keith Cottrell, Saul Durán, Jose Rodriguez, and Eric C. Rosengren: I owe you so much more than lunch.

I extend my deepest gratitude to Roberto Rios at Victory Outreach, who singlehandedly took it upon himself to introduce me to several women who would eventually become research consultants. For their help in contacting additional research consultants, I thank the following individuals: at the Ben Wilson Center, Shawna Larson and Steve Nordseth; at the San José Unified School District, Rosa Nieto (San José Community High) and Patricia Gonzales; at Downtown College Prep, Jennifer Andaluz; at Catholic Charities, Shelly Ahn, Erica Gonzalez, Elizabeth Jimenez, Sunny Ochoa, and So'o Poumele; and at the Mexican-American Community Services Agency, Alcides Martinez, Mario Osuna-Sanchez, Olivia Sosa-Mendiola, and Ana Lilia Soto; at the FLY Program, Mel Avanesian; and at DeAnza College and the CMM Institute, Kim Pearce.

My thanks also to Sgt. Wes McBride (Los Angeles County Sheriff's Department, Ret.), with the California Gang Investigators Association, and the National Gang Center, for providing the definition of "validation"; to Dr. Pamela Brouillard for offering me the term "The Narrative of Redemption" and many more inspiring conversations; and to Vernon E. Cronen and W. Barnett Pearce for introducing me to Social Construction and the Coordinated Management of Meaning Theory (CMM): My life has never been the same. Those who always asked "How's the book coming along?" and who commented on earlier drafts include Catherine Armas-Matsumoto, Dr. Cynthia Chavez-Metoyer, Professor Kristine Diekman, Kathy Jean Holiman-Hendrix, Dr. Kit Herlihy, Dr. Gloria Höfler, Katie Ladd, Andrea Maestre, Dr. Trudy Milburn, Dr. Carmen Nava,

Lark Kellner Nordblom, Sita Scholer, Lourdes Shahamiri, and Dr. Shawn Spano. If I left anyone out, it is entirely a mistake and not a reflection of their interest or my lack of appreciation thereof. Special thanks to Victoria Scott, whose keen eye for editorial detail ensured that no "i" went undotted and no "t" uncrossed; for our bike chats and then some. At Hampton Press, I must thank Barbara Bernstein for her immense patience and Heather Jefferson for her professional, punctilious, and prompt responses as we copyedited the final draft.

My deepest thanks yet again and always to my husband Walter C. Rossmann, who read almost all the drafts, made useful comments and suggestions, helped me develop the themes, and encouraged me all the way. Nor would this book have been what it is without my children Maxx and Emilia whose questions and interest made me try harder to explain in humane terms a phenomenon that is often clouded by political posturing and budgetary battles. Finally, to the girls and women whose stories enliven this book, your reasons for sharing them with me were to keep others from joining gangs or to help them get out. As I dedicate this book to you, I hope to have fulfilled your hopes.

Series Editor's Preface

This is the third book in the series *Social Approaches to Interaction*. Social approaches investigate communication as inherently collaborative, as joint constructions of meaning, and as embedded in a particular social or cultural context. *Transcending gangs: Latinas story their experience* fits this series because it uses a social approach (qualitative interviews) in an all too real context (gangs) and asks questions based on real people interacting (in this case, questions about the relationship between a girl and her gang: what leads girls to join gangs, what has to change for one to decide to leave, and what has to happen for her to be able to stay out). In the process, this book makes a substantial contribution to our understanding of the role of narrative in the social construction of identity, and so it will be of interest not only to the obvious audience of those who work or live with the same or related populations, but also to a wide array of readers sharing theoretical or methodological concerns.

Some years ago, when Liliana Castañeda Rossmann first talked about the possibility of writing a book for this series, we discussed several potential projects. I encouraged her to work with Latina gangs rather than another topic for several reasons. First, this was a timely and important subject in need of good research. Second, this is a topic she was uniquely qualified to pursue: given her Mexican upbringing and fluency in Spanish, as well as her empathic nature, it seemed likely she could have success in reaching a difficult population. This has not been a quick and easy research project, but the results are well worth the time and effort required.

In form, this book is uncommon in the substantial space given over to individual stories of experience. For those who are new to the use of "story" as a verb, the move is designed to draw attention to the social construction of identity through narrative, to present narratives as active creations of their tellers. The stories we tell ourselves and others matter because they shape our experiences, our understandings of the past certainly, but most especially of the future. For if we can imagine no future for ourselves different than the present in which we find ourselves embedded, how could we ever make that future come to pass? These storytellers come to transcend their difficult pasts and presents by learning to tell and live a new story for their futures. Gangs are a complex social phenomenon, one that non-members often find hard to comprehend. These stories simultaneously give a voice to the girls who tell them, serve as a resource to those designing interventions, and provide a new perspective for readers having little prior knowledge of this context.

Including so many details as part of multiple stories describing experiences with gangs adds complexity, but deliberately so. One fact separating members of any group from non-members is the significance of even small differences: to non-members, all group members appear alike, but members make finer grained distinctions. Thus, to those with no personal experience of gangs, all gang members share membership in a common set. Yet, as Rossmann points out, there is a substantial difference betwen those in a gang with no intention of leaving, those who were in a gang in the past but who have now disengaged, and those who never joined, despite what may have been substantial impact on their lives. Reading about other people's lives conveys only a small part of what they learned by living it, but the considerable detail in these stories introduces readers to some of the distinctions seen as critical by group members. The young women who story their experiences in these pages want to speak to us; Rossmann has drawn them out, recorded and transcribed their stories, and now grants us the opportunity to listen to their words. What future will we story as a result?

—Wendy Leeds-Hurwitz

Part I

INTRODUCING THE CONCEPTS

1

A Story of Stories

This is a story about stories. Not just any stories, but stories that we often do not hear, tell, know, or engage with. These are the stories of girls in gangs; of girls, now women, who were in gangs; of girls and women whose identities have formed and developed from their lives around gangs; and, most important, of girls and women whose identities transcend gangs. The stories are in their words, both in English and translated from Spanish, with some analysis and commentary, preceded by theoretical moorings and charts for future voyages into our understandings of the social realities of Latinas in gangs.

These girls, some now women, story their experiences as part of a research project, so they know to put their best face forward, yet they are candid in revealing details about the brutality and pain that the gang lifestyle brings. Some, such as the younger ones, are not even aware of what lies ahead for them should they continue this path, which outsiders might see as self-destructive but which to them is just "life." Some, such as the hard-core gang members, encounter difficulties not in storytelling their past, but in being able to tell a story through which they can envision a future for themselves. Still others, such as some who have left the gangs, make it their lifework to prevent others from joining (or to help them leave) the gang lifestyle. The possibility of storytelling their past exists because of the time and distance they have from the experiences they recount; they are sufficiently detached from these experiences that they now can tell a different story about their hoped-for future experiences.

This is not just a collection of gang stories. Fortunately for the extant academic literature about Latinas in gangs, two superb treatises have recently advanced our knowledge and understanding of their life experiences to a new level (Mendoza-Denton, 2008; Miranda, 2003). The difference between these and the present study is that this study is grounded in the Social Construction movement and takes a communication perspective (Pearce, 2008). These theoretical undergirdings

3

enable me to engage with the storytellers, analyze their stories, and offer possibilities for action that can be used by those working with gang-impacted and gang-involved girls in general, and Latinas in particular, to co-create alternative social realities that would help them stay or get out of gangs. I acknowledge the complexity of the issue and realize that neither I nor anyone else can offer anything that functions as a final answer to end the problem once and for all. Ultimately, the objective is to help gang-impacted girls and women live lives of dignity and freedom, peace and unity, strength and community despite the gang presence in their lives. Getting out of the gangs is not just a matter of saying "no," going clean, or finding God. Getting out of a gang, which I refer to as *disinhabiting*, and staying out, which I call *transcending*, require the women to be able to tell different stories, with a different ending and a different moral, of their past gang experiences. It also requires that they be able to tell stories about their future in a way that recognizes the past and engages with it to propel them forward beyond mere existence and toward engagement in relational responsibility (McNamee & Gergen, 1999), beyond bounded being and into relational being (Gergen, 2009).

WHENCE GANGS FROM A COMMUNICATION PERSPECTIVE?

The genesis for this project consisted of two separate incidents in 1997 when, as a volunteer community mediator for the Nueces County Dispute Resolution Services in Corpus Christi, Texas, I was assigned to mediate a dispute between two high school girls: a senior and a freshman. The girls and their respective friends had been engaged in episodes of taunting, mad-dogging, name-calling, spraying canned soft drinks on the other's car, and so on. They were brought to mediation by their respective parents, all four of whom were very concerned about their well-being and academic standing. At one point, I asked to caucus with the girls individually so they would be able to speak more candidly about the situation: The dispute was about a boy who had been the boyfriend of the freshman, then broke up with her and became the boyfriend of the senior, but it also became clear that the girls were involved in gang activity, if only peripherally. I guided their conversation through the empowerment model of mediation (Baruch Bush & Folger, 2005), in which they were presented with opportunities for empowering themselves and for offering recognition to the other. I focused on helping them to understand the situation relationally, where they could see the connections that linked them together beyond the boy in question.

We talked about being individuals and also being members of gangs and the advantages and disadvantages that each of these brought to them. In the end, they agreed to ignore each other and to ask their friends not to entice them to fight anymore. Although my knowledge of gangs at the time was limited to what could be gleaned from the mainstream media's depictions, I believe that they were both sincere in their agreement, and that I was able to help them see their connections to each other and to the larger system of their school and community.

The second incident, a few months later, occurred when I was conducting a daylong training for middle-school peer mediators in Corpus Christi, Texas. During a break, a group of five girls stayed in the training room, and the conversation somehow shifted to one girl telling the others about leaving a gang. Loath to eavesdrop, I began to move away and signal distance by shuffling my papers, but I soon realized with surprise that she was actually turning to me, speaking more loudly, and looking in my direction. I took these proxemic codes (Hall, 1963) to mean an expression of her desire to include me into the conversation. I moved closer again, and she then described in vivid detail how, in order to leave the gang, she had to be jumped out, just as she had been jumped in (namely, beaten by her own peers), only "more worse." Her other interlocutors expressed their amazement, and, as the break ended and other trainees filled the room, the conversation ended. Yet her words echoed within me for years: Hers was an untold story. I felt that there were many more like it, and there was so little known at the time, either in academia or outside, about the experiences of young Latinas in, out, and around gangs.

THEORETICAL UNDERGIRDINGS

From these two experiences and operating under the assumption that humans engage in the ongoing process of co-constructing our social realities through communication in general and storytelling in particular, this meta-story is firmly grounded in the social sciences movement known as Social Construction. The narrative process we routinely engage in entails the essential elements that comprise our daily living. We inhabit spaces in language that situate us in dependence, independence, or interdependence from one another, within the various social configurations made up from our participation in them, such as church choirs, families, writing workshops, Yahoo© groups, book clubs, political parties, neighborhoods, rifle and pistol associations, toddler play-date groups, alumni clubs, and, yes, gangs.

Yet, what happens when we no longer derive personal or professional pleasure from participating in such groups? In some cases, where membership is secured by paying dues, one can simply stop paying dues and let the membership expire. In some cases, like health clubs, there are penalties for early cancellation of contracts. Other groups, such as families, are more complicated to disengage from, although some people estrange themselves from their families for a while or forever. Gangs are similar to secret societies in that they do not issue membership cards, and "dues" are collected in a variety of ways. Gangs have different ways of establishing membership; some do so through a ritual "jumping in" or other type of initiation ritual, such as participating in a drive-by shooting, but not all; others demand that members wear certain colors, sport specific tattoos, or perform certain tasks, such as tagging or "jumping" those they perceive as "the enemy." Because research with such inaccessible populations is difficult, especially quantitative research that would provide adequate generalizations about specific practices, there is considerable debate among scholars of gangs about methodologies, definitions, and theoretical approaches (Bursik & Grasmick, 2006). An extensive review of gang research, with reference to appropriate literature, appears in the next chapter.

Like all other human groupings, gangs cannot simply be explained as criminal enterprises, unsupervised kids, or broken-down families, or by using the "everyone wants to belong to something" argument, although this narrative has tremendous appeal in the creation, development, and maintenance of popular notions of gangs (Nash, 2011). Rather, I take gangs as complex social phenomena co-created through the process of telling stories (Pearce & Pearce, 1998) that are lived, told, untold, unheard, unknown—social phenomena that comprise all human groupings: groupings by their members and ex-members; by law enforcement; by the media; by the communities that willingly or unwillingly host them; by the people who provide health, human, and social services to gang-involved youth; and by the rest of us who think we are not affected or responsible but do not want them in our neighborhoods. This book is an attempt to access some of these stories using interviewing techniques. The next step in the process calls for their analysis by using an array of theoretical lenses best described as Social Construction and then offering them as tools for intervention by viewing them through the Communication Perspective (Pearce, 2008), which tells us that humans (re)construct cultural and interpretive resources (such as stories) through practices (such as storytelling, among many others).

METHODOLOGY, DATA, AND ANALYSIS

The data for this project consisted mainly of interviews with girls and women who are *gang-involved*, which I define as being in a gang at the time of the interview or having been in a gang in the past, and *gang-impacted*, which I define as living in neighborhoods known to have strong gang presence or having a family member in a gang— or a combination of any of these. In reality, we are all impacted by gangs: if not directly as members or indirectly as unwitting targets of gang violence, then even more tangentially as members of communities that, however remotely, witness gangs through graffiti or other property damage; increased police spending on gang surveillance, injunctions, and suppression; and decreased spending on less politically charged issues. We are also impacted by the resulting increased school attrition rates for lower income and ethnic minority populations; decreased spending on health care; and myriad other social, political, ideological, and economic interconnections between "us" and "the other." We are affected as well by those from affluent backgrounds who purchase and consume illegal drugs that are dealt by gang members, and by how some affluent youth adopt the fashion styles of gang members to experiment with their own identity development.

I met the girls and women in this book through contacts with community services agencies that serve the City of San José and Santa Clara County, California, a greater metropolitan area in the Western United States. The interviews took at least 1 hour and, with the interview consultants' permission, were videotaped and transcribed. I also was able to observe, over the course of several months, two different girls' weekly group meetings with a facilitator. The meetings had empowerment as a focus and covered such topics as self-esteem, birth control and prevention of sexually transmitted diseases, cultural understanding and pride, and gang violence. There were at times as few as 6 and as many as 14 girls at these meetings, which were not videotaped, but field notes were kept.

The reader will find that, at times, the girls' and women's stories are quoted at length; I pause briefly to insert a commentary and analysis to theorize. As I engage with gang-impacted and gang-involved Latinas during the initial contact, the consent process, and the actual interviews, I consider them as research consultants and research associates in order to facilitate their process of storying their experience. Specifically, I argue that they engage in this process to create and inhabit a space within a continuum between dependence and interdependence vis-à-vis the gang. Some of them who have left the gang inhabit "inter(in) dependence," a term I advance to theorize their transcendence from the continuum and therefore the habits of the gang.

A PREVIEW OF WHAT FOLLOWS

Immediately following this introduction is an extensive although non-exhaustive look at gang research, which tapers by detailing the afore-mentioned two volumes (Mendoza-Denton, 2008; Miranda, 2003) that have expanded substantially our understanding of Latinas in gangs. This review of gang literature in Chapter 2 also includes considerations about ethics in research, methodologies, and approaches; my own struggles with subjectivity, representation, and voice; and the role of the girls and women as research associates/consultants in my own theorizing efforts.

A theoretical framework in Chapter 3 serves to set the stage for the subsequent theme chapters in the second part of the book. This includes a review of relevant terms and concepts from the Social Construction movement and terms offered within the theory of communication known as the Coordinated Management of Meaning that allow for analytical venture, as well as methodological approaches used during research consultations, such as Circular Questioning. The aim of this third chapter is to provide a primer on how to read each of the story-telling themes in Part II.

The stories of the girls and women comprise Part II of this book. The themes discussed and the women whose words animate them are discussed in Chapters 4 through 14. Chapter 4 focuses on the theme of "Inhabiting the Gang" and is told by Lupe, Eréndira, Florencia, Margie, Olga, and Marisa. "Family Violence," in the haunting words of Florencia, Olga, Angela, Gracia, Margie, and Lucha, is discussed in Chapter 5. Gracia, Florencia, Eréndira, Teresa, Marissa, and Chakira illustrate their experiences with "Tattoos and Identity" in Chapter 6. Chapter 7 covers the themes "Of Colors and Names" voiced by Teresa, Daniela, Elisa, Chakira, Eréndira, Gracia, Marisa, and Florencia. The crazy life of the gang, "La Vida Loca," is storied by Eréndira, Angela, Lupe, Olga, Marisa, Florencia, and Margie in Chapter 8. Eréndira, Lucha, Gracia, and Margie discuss their experiences of incarceration in Chapter 9, titled "Time Served!" The unique experiences of being active in the gang while being pregnant and having children, and how this informs their storytelling, is the focus of Chapter 10, "Mother'hood," as narrated by Eréndira, Olga, Margie, Marisa, and Florencia. Stories by Florencia, Gracia, Eréndira, Angela, Margie, and Lupe illustrate the parallel and complex themes of

"Loyalty and Respect" in Chapter 11. The "Betrayal" endured by Lupe, Florencia, Gracia, Eréndira, Olga, and Chakira is storied in Chapter 12. As a result of this betrayal and as part of their process of leaving the gang, Eréndira, Marisa, Angela, Gracia, Florencia, Lupe, and Olga highlight the role that religion plays in Chapter 13: "The Narrative of Redemption."

In Part III, "Disinhabiting the Gang" is the focus of Chapter 14 and is recounted by Eréndira, Florencia, Gracia, Olga, Lupe, and Marisa. Part III also focuses on the theme of "Transcending Gangs" in Chapter 15, summarizing the storytelling processes that Margie, Elisa, Angela, Marisa, and Olga used to stay out once they got out, or what they did to avoid getting in. This comes after discussing the story of Margie, who has not transcended. All themes include extensive quotations, in their words, with some analysis and commentary. A discussion section of each of the theme chapters is dedicated to describing and analyzing the storytelling processes that characterize the theme. I utilize the Communication Perspective as well as storytelling models (Pearce & Pearce, 1998) to advance the notion of inter(in)dependence in my analysis and theory-building. The concluding Chapter 16 suggests implications for families, practitioners, and academics and also serves as a "De-Gang-ification Manual" as it outlines possibilities for action and recommendations to enhance the already extensive array of resources for practitioners working with gang-impacted girls that the Communication Perspective offers. This final chapter also includes the rest of the story of Esperanza, which begins at the end of this first chapter and is a composite account of the solitude encountered by gang-involved and gang-impacted girls and their hope for transcendence. Appendices A and B provide a background on the storytellers and a catalog of commonly used gang terms, respectively.

I make no claims to completeness or correctness when it comes to research about the gang experiences of Latina girls and women. I believe I have provided a novel and unconventional approach not just to our understanding of their stories but also to intervention and therapeutic practices designed to help them transcend the gangs. I hope you agree and find it useful. In Part II of this book, I present the stories of my research consultants. Although their names and other identifiers have been changed, the stories are hauntingly real. In the following pages, I offer a story—the Story of Esperanza—cobbled together from stories read, heard, and overheard. The purpose of telling this composite story is to exemplify some of the variety of experiences of gang-impacted and gang-involved Latinas and what might be useful to their storying transcendence from the gangs.

THE STORY OF ESPERANZA

She hears her sister moan as she awakes, only to see her crawling on the floor. "¡*Me duele!*" ("It hurts!") her sister, Soledad, cries out. Esperanza tries to help her get up, but by this time their mother has also woken up to the situation. Soledad, 10 days short of her 15th birthday, is giving birth. Their mother runs next door, where the woman everyone knows as "La Bruja" lives, because La Bruja had helped deliver Esperanza's little brother, Octavio, who was the eighth born but only the fourth still alive. In the early morning, Soledad gives birth to a boy with numerous birth defects, due at least in part to her having worked in the fields from such an early age and being exposed to the toxins found there. Without prenatal care, these fetal malformations had not been discovered. Soledad had barely realized she was pregnant and so had not told anyone. The infant boy lives a few hours and then stops breathing. Soledad stays home from school for a week, crying and refusing to eat. The father of the boy, a 17-year-old from the neighborhood, known as "El Chulo," is in jail. Soledad's father, who is in Mexico at the time of the boy's birth, never hears of the birth of his grandson.

A few days later, Esperanza is walking home from school—she has been told by her mother to try to get Soledad to eat something—when she runs into some girls from the neighborhood who have given her trouble in the past. They surround her, all asking the same question— "What you claim?"—and taunting her with names like "Scrap" and "Paisa," which mean nothing to her but which Soledad has said are insults. As she tries to escape their gauntlet, Caridad, another girl from school, turns the corner and, seeing the commotion, picks up her pace. She raises her voice so that the other girls, who are dressed like Cholas, can hear her: "There you are! I've been looking for you everywhere." Caridad is wearing a yellow sweater and has a stick-on tattoo on the back of her hand: XV. Esperanza knows tattoos are the mark of Cholos; her sister has explained how to tell the Norteñas and the Sureñas apart. This makes her hesitant to follow as Caridad walks away, looking at the Cholas with a firm gaze. She is not defiant but not submissive, either, and the Cholas seem to be, if not intimidated, then at least not challenging her to a fight. Caridad throws a sign with her arms, making a cross with her forearms and then a V, turns to Esperanza, and says to her, "We're late for Las Quince." It all happens so quickly that Esperanza hardly has time to protest. As they walk away, Caridad asks Esperanza if she has time to hang out with her friends. Esperanza is not sure if she wants to go; besides, she has to see about Soledad, so she says, "Maybe later." Caridad responds, "Here's my number. Text me when you're ready and someone will stop by your house to walk with you to El Club de Las Quince . . . and make sure you wear yellow or white so they let you in!"

Esperanza walks home and finds that Soledad is still despondent but has eaten some beans and rice their mother had brought home from work the night before. There are also two Twinkies wrappers in the garbage, a sign that Soledad has eaten her favorite breakfast food. Esperanza sits with her sister for a while, watching TV, and then says, "I'm going to Las Quince, do you want to go?" She doesn't really know what La Quince means, only that Caridad is so adamant that it seems like something she ought to do. Soledad just shrugs her shoulders, so Esperanza goes to the closet, looking for something yellow to wear, but can't find anything, so she settles for a white top and her jean shorts. She texts Caridad, who responds that someone will stop by to walk her to El Club. About 30 minutes later, someone knocks on the door. Caridad is there, with another girl, also dressed in yellow, whom Esperanza has seen in school a few times, talking to Cholas of both sides. Her name is Fe, and everyone teases her about her praying, but for the most part, they leave her alone. As they walk down a street not too far from Esperanza's house, but one she dares not take by herself because her sister tells her it is full of "Norcacas," she realizes that the kids on that street have stopped to look at the three girls but do not antagonize them. One of them, a cute boy she has seen at school and at the Wienerschnitzel wearing red from head to toe, calls to Fe and says, "Pray for me! Save me!" as the others laugh. Fe responds in a friendly voice, "I will pray for you, but I can't save you. If you are willing to be saved, I can show you how you can do it yourself!" and gives him a warm smile.

Soon they are in front of El Club, where boys and girls are hanging out. They are wearing all colors, but, as those wearing red or blue enter, they are given yellow shirts to put on. Esperanza is wearing a white tank top and Fe says to her, "You don't have to change; white is the color for Peacemakers, so maybe you can sit in their group." El Club de Las Quince is noisy and chaotic, yet everyone seems to know each other and be happy to meet there. There are girls younger than Esperanza, who is 11, and other, older ones, who seem to be in charge of something because the younger ones are mindful of them. Caridad says to Esperanza, "If you are hungry, there will be a buffet of make-your-own tostadas in about an hour. Go to the big room on the left." She says, "You'll like it here," and leaves her alone with Fe and a dozen other girls dressed in white sitting in a room furnished with sofas and big pillows on the floor. Fe spends the next hour with her, introducing her to the other girls and asking Esperanza about school; then the group facilitator gives them some women's magazines and tells them to cut out pictures of healthful foods. Fe finds out that one of her cousins had some classes with Esperanza and says that the cousin is not there today, but that she normally comes to El Club. Fe and her cousin, both 12, are in Peacekeepers and will be going through their Quinceañera together.

Esperanza asks about it, so Fe explains: The girls participate in a program that, in exchange for celebrating their 15th birthday with a traditional big dance party, like they do in Mexico, they have to perform a series of peacekeeping activities from the time they join El Club. They are required to keep their grades up to a certain level and are prohibited from wearing any Chola attire. They attend El Club every day after school for 2 hours; if they cannot come, they have to have their parents' or teachers' signature. At El Club, there are activities and classes. Las Quince Peacekeepers offers workshops on peer mediation and working through conflict, in addition to classes about nutrition, Mexican and Mexican-American history and culture, ESL if needed and Spanish, hygiene, sex education, self-defense, relationships, as well as tutoring help for math, language, science, and other middle and high school subjects. There are other activities at El Club such as Bible studies, Ballet Folklórico where they learn the traditional dances of Mexico and other Latin American countries, and a garden where they learn to grow organic vegetables and fruit, as well as a computer lab, an art studio, and a music room, for those who want to do that. Fe grows very excited when she tells Esperanza about the new video editing equipment they just received, and she says she hopes to be the first to learn to use it. She wants to make a video of the graffiti she has been painting over with a girl who was a tagger but is now a Quince. This video will be showcased at her Quinceañera, since every girl has to present a project she has worked on since claiming Quince. The other girl is now in the art studio, creating a logo for the co-op that will sell the organic vegetables from the garden, and is trying to use other colors in addition to the required ones of El Club: white, purple, and yellow.

"Why purple and yellow?" asks Esperanza. "They are the colors of Las Quince. Purple is for the girls who claimed either Norte or Sur but don't anymore, and yellow is for the girls who never claimed," says Fe. "White is for those who are in the Peacemakers training. You probably should be wearing yellow to show you back up Quince. They'll leave you alone that way, but purple, and especially white, are neutral too." Esperanza wonders how she will get the money to buy any clothes, for her mother usually gets theirs from the Our Lady of Perpetual Help church. They are not the most fashionable clothes, but they are free to them and all the other families who often work in the fields. Sometimes she finds something that resembles what the rich kids at school or the kids who shoplift wear, but for the most part, she wears what fits her. As if reading her mind, Fe says, "There is a closet behind the game room, you can go and see if there is something you like that fits you, and don't forget to sign in, because that gives you points." "Points for what?" "For your Quinceañera! What else?" Fe laughs and puts her arm around Esperanza as they walk to the tostada buffet. Esperanza feels a kinship she has not felt since she was brought to the United States from her village in Mexico by a "coyote" about 4 years ago and feels like crying.

The next day, a girl in one of her classes comes to Esperanza and, excitedly, tells her she is Fe's cousin, Franky. Esperanza has hung out with Franky before and, although she thinks Franky is somewhat conceited, she realizes that it was Franky who once broke up a fight between two Cholas who both claimed Sur. After school, Franky and Esperanza walk home, and Franky tells her about Fe. "She's kind of a Jesus-freak, but she is pretty nice about it, never makes us feel bad because we don't go to church with her. Even her parents think she's a bit too much, but they don't mind since she's not getting in trouble that way." Esperanza wishes her own sister were a bit more of a Jesus-freak and not so boy-crazy, so she asks if Soledad can come to El Club, even though she is turning 15 in a few days. Franky says, "Yes! There is a party for girls who are older in about a month, so she could come to that group. They're getting ready to put on a play about their work in the community. Your sister could make some points by joining them in the meantime."

When Esperanza gets home, she finds her sister in bed, crying in pain. Not knowing what to do, she goes to see La Bruja, who will not answer her door. She texts her mother, who says she can't leave work or she will be written up. She runs to El Club, where she finds Caridad and tells her what's happening. Caridad goes to a room that has a red cross on the door and talks to a woman named Hortencia. Hortencia grabs a bag and runs to Esperanza's house. She does what Esperanza has seen only on TV: She takes Soledad's blood pressure, pulse, and temperature and then calls 9-1-1. The paramedics arrive in about 20 minutes, and Esperanza realizes she has never seen anyone taken away in an ambulance in her neighborhood who has not been beaten, shot, or stabbed. Soledad needs urgent medical care to remove the rest of the afterbirth and stays in the hospital overnight; when she comes home, their mother is at work, but their 18-year-old brother,

Junior, has come back from jail and manages to be helpful in getting Soledad settled.

Later that week, when Esperanza brings up the upcoming party at El Club, Soledad shows no interest in Las Quince, saying they are a bunch of rankers. Junior jokes that he is getting ready to rank himself because the time he has spent in jail was not what he thought it would be and his homies are now worried he is going to snitch about the job that landed him in jail. Later, when Esperanza tells her mother about going to El Club, her mother says that, whatever the girls do, they'd better watch Octavio because he was left alone the week before and went by himself to the storage place under the freeway where the older kids hang out and smoke dope. Their mother worries that he has already been getting high, even though he is only 7. Esperanza says there is a kids' room at El Club, where boys and girls under 10 can play games after snack time, and Octavio seems to like the sound of this.

The next day, Soledad meets Esperanza on the corner closest to their two schools and says, "I'm not going to that lame club! Who cares about Quinceañeras anyway?" Esperanza's heart grows heavy, but she manages to tell Soledad that she can get help with her homework at El Club so she won't fall too far behind and won't have to go to the Community School. "I'm not wearing no stupid yellow shirt!" says Soledad. Esperanza tells her that it is not required, but that if she wears one of her usual blue shirts, it will have to be covered.

They find Octavio, who has been waiting for them at the corner of El Club, kicking it with some kids who back up Sur and who are not too much older than he is. When the boy starts to follow his sisters into El Club, the other boys start teasing him and he mocks a fight, but Esperanza tells him that if he fights, he will not be allowed into El Club and won't get to play video games and eat ice cream. Caridad is behind the desk, looking at something on a computer screen, but immediately stops when she sees them and says, "I'm glad you are here!" handing Soledad a washable "XV" tattoo. Soledad makes a face and mumbles that she is going to get jumped for it. Caridad tells her, "If you don't want it, you can put it back in this bowl. Whenever you're ready to start being left alone by the Cholas, you can come and get one." A few moments later, an older teen, wearing white, announces, "Next week, we're getting ready to train a group of girls to work in the vegetable co-op, so if you want to make some money, you have to show us your grades. If you don't qualify because they're too low, you'll get tutoring to make sure you do the next time. But now, in about 15 minutes, we're starting a salsaerobics class in the gym, and later there is a storytelling workshop in the library, so you might want to get a snack before."

Some girls, Soledad among them, follow her into the gym, but as they turn the corner, the woman named Hortencia—who is a nurse-midwife—asks Soledad to come in to her office for a minute. They spend almost 30 minutes talking about Soledad's post-partum care. Hortencia gives her a bag containing a bottle of vitamins, some herbal supplements, and some leaflets with information about safe sex and birth control, nutrition, personal care, and exercise. There are a package of sanitary napkins, a bag of condoms, as well as free vouchers for the El Club's vegetable co-op. Soledad is worried that her homegirls will think she's ranking and is sure that El Chulo won't ever wear "one of those things," but then she sees the samples of shampoo, lotion, and make-up and takes the bag. Hortencia tells her that she needs a check-up in 2 weeks and, oh, by the way, if she wants more goodies, she can get them after the check-up. Soledad leaves Hortencia's office and tries to find Esperanza and Octavio, but there is much commotion going on at El Club and she manages to make out that it is about some fight between Norteños and Sureños.

ARTYFACT: ONE STORY, MANY VOICES

This is part of the story of "Esperanza"—of one girl or of many—wanting and waiting to tell the pieces of it that are true and relevant to their lives. In Chapter 16, I revisit the story of Esperanza to discuss the learnings from this humbling experience of talking with gang-impacted and gang-involved Latinas.

The previous story constitutes what I—playing with language, as detailed in Chapter 3—call an "artyfact." This neologism takes the word "art" and the word "fact" from the English language and the conjunction "*y*" (meaning "with") from the Spanish language to arrive at the notion of a storytelling medium that combines art with fact in order to present bits and pieces of unrelated and, yes, incoherent factual information into a new, coherent, and previously nonexistent arrangement.

Why make up a story when there are so many good ones out there? Although I did not speak with anyone whose life experiences actually echo Esperanza's, these details are gleaned from my many conversations with and about gang-involved and gang-impacted girls, from situations witnessed, and from my own reading about the lives of girls in gangs and girls living in gang-impacted neighborhoods. Likewise, although some may consider this story generally and El Club de las Quince specifically a complete fabrication, I prefer to call it an "artyfact" because, by including it in this book, I aim to highlight the many and various programs dedicated to working with gang-impacted youth. "The Story of Esperanza" also evokes not only what might be possible when these programs are combined under one roof but what might occur when they receive sufficient funding to help them come to fruition. But before arriving at the stirring conclusion of this artyfact in Chapter 16, let us turn to the promised groundwork that will demonstrate how Esperanza's story may be considered, if not real, then at least tenable in various respects.

2

Relevant Gang Research

Before I embark on a focused discussion of themes about how the social phenomenon we refer to as "the gang" is socially constructed, I would like to provide an extensive although nonexhaustive look at gang literature, beginning with the earliest works, followed by research about girls in gangs, and ending with reviews of works that specifically inform this project about Latinas in gangs. In all cases, methodological and epistemological implications are addressed.

The earliest and, by many accounts, most thorough ethnography of gangs was conducted by Thrasher (1927), who supplemented his 7-year-long personal observations with court documents and census data to provide a close look at 1,313 street gangs in Chicago. From this seminal piece, fieldwork has remained one of the most effective data-gathering processes for gang researchers (Horowitz, 1990).

Gang researchers face many challenges not often present in other field research. First is the inherent illicitness and secrecy of gang activities, which makes gang members reluctant to speak. Gangs prohibit their members from speaking to any authority figures like police officers and community service agency personnel; researchers often fall in this category. Once the obstacle of lack of trust has been surmounted, the second challenge is reliability of data. Is it safe to assume that gang members are no more inclined to embellish their stories than, for example, a forest firefighter, an aesthetician, a convention-center employee, or a member of a fraternity or sorority? Do researchers have to be extra skeptical of information provided by gang members as to its veracity because they are already suspected of violating other societal norms? These questions are not unfounded (Klein, 1971; Spergel, 1990). Establishing trust through extensive contact with the gang members may be the best antidote to this deficit of trust and the presumption of reliability of data, yet the question remains as to what extent the presence of the researcher alters the communicative environment for the gang members.

In working with my research consultants, the challenges I faced began with identifying interviewees and establishing their trust. Once they agreed to be interviewed, I had to identify a time and place to conduct the interview. The women who were out of the gang were much more willing and cooperative. The young gang-impacted girls, all minors, understandably showed more caution and hesitation, despite the fact that I had been around them for 2 or 3 months, attending their group at the community services agency. My purpose was known to them, and their parents signed the consent form. In some cases, the group facilitator gave them an incentive to participate by counting the interview as the community service hours they had to accumulate. In others, the staff at the agency provided $20 gift cards as incentive.

WHO DETERMINES WHO IS AND WHO IS NOT A GANG MEMBER?

The question of definition has plagued researchers for years, and there is little consensus about a definition of *gang* or *gang member*. One definition offers this: "any identifiable group of youngsters who (a) are generally perceived as a distinct aggregation by others in their neighborhood, (b) recognize themselves as a denotable group (almost invariably with a group name), and (c) have been involved in a sufficient number of delinquent incidents to call forth a consistent negative response from neighborhood residents and/or law enforcement agencies" (Klein, 1971, p. 13). Although this definition provides a set of criteria that are useful and relevant to many research projects about gangs, there is no agreed-on definition among academics. Ruth Horowitz (1990) notes that the "variation in locally used definitions may be useful for understanding how the relationships among criminal justice personnel, the community, the gang, and the individual gang member are defined" (p. 43).

Moreover, law enforcement personnel have different criteria for determining gang membership than do academic researchers, although no single, systematic, data-driven, and reliable criterion exists for determining gangs and gang membership (Klein & Maxson, 1989). To determine gang membership, law enforcement personnel look at a "totality of circumstances," which includes two or more among these elements: having gang tattoos, such as gang names, numbers, dots, nicknames; admitting gang membership; wearing specific kinds, brands, and styles of clothing, in addition to specific colors; having certain documents on their person or certain cell phone information; carrying or being in photos with known gang members, or appearing in photos wearing gang colors or gang attire or throwing gang signs; carrying spray-paint cans or markers used for tagging; and committing a crime for, with, or against a gang. While a youth "may want to be like others—might either wear a Nebraska hat because he likes the Huskers, or because he's Norteño—unless [police officers] have personal knowledge, or if he's standing next to a shot-caller, or if he admits to being in a gang," there are few other ways to determine membership (Montano & Cottrell, personal communication, September 27, 2007).

Furthermore, the California Gang Investigators Association (Cal-Gang) defines a "gang" as "a group of three or more persons who have a common identifying sign, or symbol, or name, and whose members individually or collectively engage in or have engaged in a pattern of criminal activity, creating an atmosphere of fear and intimidation within the community" (McBride, email communication, June 7, 2008). The state of California validates gang members for inclusion in the CalGang system by using 10 criteria established by a statewide committee of law enforcement, corrections, and prosecutors:

1. admitting to being a gang member during incarceration classification procedures;

2. admitting gang membership in a noncustodial situation;

3. being identified as a gang member by a reliable informant or source (this criterion encompasses when a subject is required to register with law enforcement as a gang member by court order per Section 186.30 of the California Penal Code. The court shall be considered a reliable source);

4. being identified as a gang member by an untested informant or source with corroborative evidence;

5. being seen wearing gang-type clothing;

6. being seen displaying gang symbols and/or hand signs;

7. having identifiable gang tattoos;

8. being seen frequenting gang areas;

9. being seen affiliating with documented gang members; and

10. being arrested with known gang members for offenses consistent with usual gang activity.

Specifically:

One must keep in mind that federal law requires that there is an established criminal predicate for the individual before that individual may be placed into an intelligence file. Criminal predicate is established when a law enforcement officer can demonstrate a reasonable suspicion that the concerned subject is involved in criminal behavior or criminal enterprise. Street gangs by definition are criminal organizations due to the propensity of its members to commit criminal acts and therefore [are classified as] criminal enterprises. In California, law enforcement officers are held to the same reasonable suspicion standard; however, in addition to that standard, if the concerned subject is to be placed in the CalGang file, the officer must also meet the established CalGang criteria. (McBride, email communication, June 7, 2008)

In correctional facilities, meeting the previously mentioned criteria of gang membership results in inmates being placed in separate Security Housing Units, which some activists assert amounts to torture. For example, at Pelican Bay California State Prison, more than "1,000 prisoners are held in bathroom-size steel boxes that measures 8 feet by 10 feet. There are no bars or windows. Prisoners are not allowed educational materials or contact with other prisoners" (Revolutionary Communist Party USA, 2002). The potential controversies that this process engenders, although beyond the scope of my current work, should not be overlooked: Youth may want to look the part but not actually be associated with any gang per se or think they have to "back up" some mythical entity they perceive worthy of their loyalty. Yet as a result, strictly because of their personal appearance, they end up being classified as gang members and thus begin their often unintentional, unidirectional, and irrevocable descent into the corrections system.

Most of the aforementioned academic and law enforcement research pertains or focuses exclusively on males because they commit the majority of all the crimes, gang-related or otherwise.

METHODOLOGICAL CONSIDERATIONS IN STUDYING GANGS

Various data-gathering and analyzing traditions have been used in studying youth gangs, and each yields different consequences vis-à-vis the extant literature. In her extensive survey of the literature, Hughes (2005) finds a deep chasm between two main traditions: qualitative and quantitative approaches. These two have much to offer but so far have had little influence on each other. Among the limitations of surveys and other official reports, Hughes finds first of all that they fail to capture what is elusive about gang realities because such quantitative methods are primarily designed to ascertain data patterns that are extrapolated from naturalistic and interactional contexts. Second, regarding seldom-studied gang populations (e.g., females, Latinas), quantitative studies do not help minimize contradictions found to exist within other populations, not to mention differences in results arising from inconsistent sampling methods. On this topic, Hughes (2005) observes that official records "have been criticized for being incomplete, inaccurate, confusing, conflicting, outdated and incapable of accurately representing the fluid nature of gang activity and membership" (p. 103). Similarly, the validity of survey data and reports potentially can be compromised by intervening agents, well intentioned or otherwise; gang self-reports can suffer the same fate. Despite these limitations, quantitative methods are mostly useful insofar as researchers wish to determine general patterns of gang behavior and membership.

Qualitative studies, in contrast, have typified gang research since Thrasher's (1927) ethnography. Although some of these studies may reinforce stereotypical images of gangs, others show that crime and violence are but two of many defining characteristics in an otherwise relatively ordinary life. Using qualitative methods often results in findings that illuminate the loose structure of gangs and their lack of a comprehensive geographic presence and unity. In contrast to other groups, members of a gang are seldom all present at the same time and place, which brings up implications and concerns regarding explanations about group behavior. For example, it would be optimal when studying a group of software developers if all members were present (even if through mediated communication, such as Skype) for their interaction to approximate its natural processes. By contrast, gang participation can be much more dynamic, with members' participation in their various activities, whether legal or illegal, not necessarily predictable. Even if a researcher were able to conduct participant-observation of a gang, she or he could not really be a bona fide member of it. Moreover, the same researcher hoping to observe gang members while they pursue some of their illegal or criminal work would encounter an unimaginable ethical dilemma: should the researcher accompany the gang members or should she or he report the crime to the police before it happens? Obviously, I am making an assumption that any gang would be involved in criminal activities. Understandably, there is disagreement about whether illicit behavior is a function of the gang as a group, as between Sutherland (1934) and Reiss (1988), or whether it is possible to determine what group dynamics influence youth toward crime when data are drawn mostly from official law enforcement records, as Klein

(1969) questions. Specifically, Klein's focus is on the distinction between aggregates that he calls "contiguous individuals" (p. 67) and the group processes. A useful distinction between delinquent groups and gangs exists (Cohen, 1969), which posits that the former are unstructured, unnamed, and errant and the latter have developed hierarchies, elaborate organizational structures, particular names accepted by themselves and others, and territorial claims.

Focusing now on the main contributions to gang research by qualitative studies, these have yielded explanations such as social disorganization, middle-class opposition, a culture of lower class social structures and opportunities (or lack thereof), slum-specific social order, deindustrialization as a cause of poverty, and multiple marginalities. Qualitative approaches have also shed light on the social capital enhancement that gang life provides to would-be members and the role of membership in identity development, regardless of its risks and problems. Advantages of field research include detailed descriptions of gang life that go beyond violent and criminal activities, descriptions that can be overlooked when quantitative data are extrapolated from their respective social contexts. "Gangs and their members are hardly a wholesome bunch, yet their values and behaviors are shown in many cases to be decent" (Hughes, 2005, p. 106). The loyalty and family-like sentiment that gangs inspire in their members could belong to this category of overlooked contexts, which I explore at some length in Chapter 11, "Loyalty and Respect."

Last, from qualitative data researchers find "considerable evidence that youth in gangs will avoid delinquent and violent behaviors when acceptable alternatives are available and unlikely to call their honor into question" (Hughes, 2005, p. 107), a point that should encourage community-based organizations and social service agencies to continue providing sound and safe alternatives for at-risk youth and for which I provide some recommendations in Chapter 15, "Transcending Gangs."

Despite this wealth of postulations and the important contrasts to quantitative findings offered by the qualitative tradition, I join in lamenting the lack of a "satisfactory explication of why youth become involved in gangs rather than other types of associations" (Hughes, 2005, p. 104). Although I do not claim that my own study will provide a definitive answer to this concern, I do hope to provide some explanation that will help fill that gap through the stories offered, particularly those in Chapter 4, "Inhabiting the Gang."

To that end, the next section focuses on research about Latina/ Latino gang youth, mostly for how these theoretical assumptions inform the current study.

LATINO/LATINA-SPECIFIC GANG RESEARCH

First, the multiple marginalities perspective mentioned earlier (Vigil, 1988) emphasizes how important it is to recognize the marginal conditions of life that surround the gang-impacted youth in our understanding of gangs. In their current structure, the poor, Mexican American neighborhoods—known by their Spanish name "barrios" but often spelled "varrio" by gang members—serve to separate the youth living in them from mainstream society. At the same time, these barrios function to develop a strong sense of identity and loyalty because it is common within the population to use the notions of "barrio" and "familia" interchangeably. In some cases, gang members take the spelling variation "varrio" as part of their gang name. Poverty often accompanies social problems such as violence, joblessness and homelessness, drug and alcohol abuse, and family disintegration, so gangs readily fill voids that these predicaments create. Therefore, Vigil contends that factors such as discrimination against Mexican American youth, the poor quality of education in those neighborhoods, the dismal labor market, and the abundance of low-skilled workers bring us around to poverty, completing the circle of multiple marginalities. No study of gang-involved Latino/Latina youth should ignore these factors.

Second, it is tremendously useful to review studies that explain how gang membership functions to empower marginalized Latino youth and help them feel that they are socially competent agents. Ethnographic studies aim to show other sides of gang life and yield profound insights into a gang's organization and hierarchy. For example, Brotherton and Barrios (2004) studied the Almighty Latin King and Queen Nation (ALKQN) gang, particularly its emphasis on respect, honesty, unity, knowledge, and love, and its system of codes and rules, lessons, and philosophical underpinnings. The cohesiveness of the gang received a boost from a combination of factors that included cultural identity and confrontations with law enforcement and not so much from rival gangs. As the gang declared itself a "social movement" working on behalf of the poor, renounced violence, refused to engage in the underground economy, and made school attendance a criterion for membership, Brotherton and Barrios argue that this was an example "of urban social and cultural resistance to control and domination," especially while facing "intense counter-insurgency operations by police" (p. xvi). Their critical ethnography rejects orthodox notions of gang research and brings to center stage the following:

> All social and cultural phenomena emerge out of tensions between the agents and interests of those who seek to control everyday

life and those who have little option but to resist this relationship of domination . . . to uncover the processes by which seemingly normative relationships are contingent upon structural inequalities and reproduced by rituals, rules and a range of symbolic systems. (Brotherton & Barrios, 2004, p. 4)

Notable is their definitional model of the street organizational phenomenon. In terms of their methodological assumptions, these authors favor a collaborative mode of inquiry through which subjects are active and reciprocal participants in a "quasi-democratic relationship." This dialogical relationship works to humanize research subjects by establishing respect and trust in their community and could potentially serve social reform and social justice ends. Ultimately, the authors make a plea for adopting new theoretical foci in future gang research, as well as for reform in educational, legislative, and criminal justice policies, so that instead of being condemned by such, the marginalized will be able to empower themselves as a result of the proposed changes.

All adolescents exist within a variety of systems of knowledge, most of which take form within their families, their communities, their schools, and the groups to which they belong. These groups, which range from sports teams to church youth groups and gangs, aim to inculcate values, norms, and symbolic codes that advance their goals. Building on the notion of multiple marginalities, gangs tend to supplement or replace—albeit poorly—the missing institutions that would normally provide these symbolic meanings. In an effort to account for this dearth, the following definition of a gang proves useful to the foregoing research project:

A group formed largely by youth and adults of a marginalized social class which aims to provide its members with a resistant identity, an opportunity to be individually and collectively empowered, a voice to speak back to and challenge the dominant culture, a refuge from the stresses and strains of barrio and ghetto life, and a spiritual enclave within which its own sacred rituals can be generated and practiced. (Brotherton & Barrios, 2004, p. 23)

Moreover, the extended case study of the ALKQN modeled a particular gang's transition away from the gang habits—characterized by secret loyalty codes, intra- and inter-group violence, and underground or illegal business practices—and toward activism that included voter registration, self-help adult education, and a focus on education, K-12 and beyond. Younger members claimed to have joined the ALKQN primarily because of these expressed commitments, as the gang was the "only political force in the barrio that had not given up on the 'incorrigibles' and the 'educational failures' " (Brotherton & Barrios, 2004, p. 25). Pertinent to my discussion of disinhabiting the gang were Brotherton and Barrios's findings that many grassroots community-based organizations applauded the efforts made by the gang to turn their attention toward empowering the marginalized, but that skepticism and dismissal was the norm among members of power-broker groups (media, major merchants, politicians, law enforcement) about the avowed transformation. In the lessons learned, this skepticism is attributed to a variety of factors. These include the practice of dismissing efforts by members of the underclass or issue- and identity-based groups to redefine themselves, pervasive racism, cooptation by the media, and the existence of a "secular consumerism" predisposed to negating "history as a form of consciousness and as a guide to practice." Although short-lived, the social-movement reforms adopted by the ALKQN provided "an extraordinary testimony to the poor's collective will and to the indefatigable spirit of youth" (Brotherton & Barrios, 2004, p. 26). The conclusion advocates an alternative social-movement-based paradigm for studying gangs that could provide many more avenues for predicting future trends. Engaging and encouraging as these two aforementioned research efforts are, they focus on either males alone (Vigil, 1988) or both males and females (Brotherton & Barrios, 2004).

RESEARCHING GIRLS IN GANGS: DIFFERENT IMPLICATIONS?

Campbell (1984/1991) was the first to offer a selective focus on the role of girls in gangs. Among her many relevant contributions was the idea that girls in gangs were still considered an anomaly that contradicted the established norms for femininity. Following this, Moore and Hagedorn (2006) conducted a thorough review of concerns about girls in gangs, finding that the earlier allusions to girls in gangs relegated them to being either sex objects for the males in the gang or tomboys. Regardless, it was assumed that both of these roles were dictated by the males (J. Miller, 2000).

While the media might be drawn to portray girl gangs as horrific aberrations, the same media also highlight the notion that females are actively involved in perpetrating acts of violence—as opposed to being typically the recipients of such—and thus challenge stereotypes about their role in society. Although there is still little consensus as to what exactly constitutes a gang, gender-specific gangs such as all-girl gangs also pique the attention of the media for their presumed novelty.

Moore and Hagedorn (2006) succinctly point out that "joining a gang—regardless of the gang's structure—is a significant act for an adolescent female, often with important consequences later in life" (p. 193). Saliently, it is possible that, despite the fact that some young women might not refer to themselves as gang members, law enforcement and society might readily identify them as gang members by the way they look or carry themselves and the company they keep.

RESEARCHING WHY GIRLS JOIN GANGS: ON THE NEED FOR GENDER-SPECIFIC METHODS

For more than a quarter of a century, several researchers have attempted to answer the question of why girls would join gangs. Campbell (1984/1991, 1987) and Moore (1991) found that the main motivation is friendship and acquiring a sense of self. Members of marginalized ethnic minorities whose prospects for employment are lacking and dwindling, and who face rejection and prejudice from the mainstream, find that involvement with gangs provides much-needed income, albeit through illegal behavior such as selling drugs (Moore, 1991; Padilla, 1992). Personal interviews (J. Miller, 2000) give insight into the roles of (a) the presence of gangs in their neighborhood, (b) family problems, and (c) the influence of family members who were involved in gangs. Combined, these factors lead most girls to affiliate with or join a gang. In some cases, it is believed that the gang may present members with a dialectic where it is both rewarding and destructive to become a member, so that joining may be, at least initially, the proverbial "lesser of two evils" (Curry, 1999). Initially, it may appear more rewarding and no less destructive than joining.

On the law enforcement side, the understanding of why girls join and stay in gangs has been succinctly focused on their auxiliary role. Although there is little documented evidence of exclusively female gangs in many large jurisdictions, police departments look at the role of women in running guns and drugs. This has had the unintended beneficial consequence of an overall increase in female police officers to conduct body searches of females suspected of such crimes. Law enforcement also has turned attention to women in gangs because of their involvement in crimes such as drive-by shootings due to women's higher likelihood of possessing valid driver's licenses as opposed to the men with whom they associate. Last, the attention of police is focused on the place in the hierarchy that a woman holds within the gang depending on the "office" that her partner holds in the gang, whether in or out of prison (Rodriguez

& Rosengren, personal communication, July 1, 2008). Although investigative police officers know that the majority of crimes and assaults are committed by men, they realize the role of women in executing activities such as making money drops, ordering hits, providing a place to stay, selling food stamps illegally, or tagging to "throw intelligence" (Montano & Cottrell, personal communication, September 27, 2007).

In summary, quantitative studies can only approximate the percentages of male versus female gang involvement; the impact of gang activity on males versus females is equally inconclusive. These questions point to a need to develop research methods geared toward specific gang populations. The qualitative tradition has made significant inroads in that respect, as discussed in the following paragraphs.

THEORIZING BEYOND THE "OPPRESSED" VERSUS "LIBERATED" DICHOTOMY

Although not all the literature about women in gangs fits neatly into any typology, it can be segmented into two main camps, according to Curry (1998) and concurred to by Hughes (2005) and Mendoza-Denton (2008). The first camp contends that girls and young women suffer much more pervasively from the effects of gang membership than boys and young men do. The "social injury" they endure marginalizes them not only from the mainstream but from their own neighborhoods, by their being seen as "no good" among their own noninvolved peers because the girls made what they thought was their only choice: to join a gang. The leaders of this argument are the prolific authors Joan Moore and John Hagedorn (2006), who urge that evidence "of sexual exploitation of female gang members at home and within their gangs is one reason for considering female gang membership a serious social concern" (p. 195). The second camp characterizes female gang membership more benevolently by drawing parallels with women's liberation movements (Chesney-Lind, 1993; Harris, 1988; Mendoza-Denton, 2008; Miranda, 2003). This school of thought sees gang involvement as providing a potentially liberating effect. In this characterization, girls find or create spaces that allow them to craft alternate notions of community and the feminine ideal beyond the control of males.

Hughes's (2005) review suggests that there is much more support in qualitative data for the social injury perspective despite the fact that some scholars interpret findings in ways that give credence to the liberation hypothesis. The life experiences of girls in gangs vary much more than what is suggested by characterizing them as tomboys, sex objects, or auxiliaries to male gangs. Qualitative studies seldom describe gangs as "a panacea to the troubled lives of the girls who eventually join . . . rather, field researchers depict female involvement in gangs as a trade-off between prior problems and problems resulting from membership" (Hughes, 2005, p. 105). Girls participate in a wider range of gang types; girls in mixed-gender gangs encounter limited pressure to engage in crime and instead find alternative ways to achieve status, such as sexual affiliation with a high-ranking male gang member; they also encounter numerous other obstacles. Many girls who join gangs to escape violence and abuse in their families of origin find that they are at an increased risk of sexual and physical victimization by other gang members. Although some may join a gang hoping it will provide an escape from vexations found at home, once they join, these girls encounter enormous oppression and devaluation from their fellow gang members, from "the enemy" (i.e., rival gangs), and also from the schools, law enforcement, and society as a whole. Some of the stories presented in Chapter 6, "Tattoos and Identity," confirm these notions.

Turning to specific examples of the liberation hypothesis, Harris (1988) draws from symbolic interaction and reference group theory in applying the concepts of "significant other" and "generalized others" to understand the girls' relationships. She demonstrates "how the peer group exerts a powerful influence on the gang girl by developing norms and values of interaction and effective support," and she describes "the sanctions applied when a group member departs from those norms" (p. 189). As a Latina girl becomes a member of a gang, the "group becomes the generalized other . . . and as the gang girl takes the attitudes of other gang members, the group takes hold of her and in a large sense controls her" (Harris, 1988, p. 68). These girls actively reject the traditional roles that their culture bestows on a Latina as a wife and mother caring for her husband, children, and parents.

Taking into account the fact that Harris conducted her study in 1988, it is intriguing to see how many of her observations remain relevant or have been challenged by contemporary gang researchers who focus on the gang experiences of girls as liberating. Harris (1998) recommends approaching the study of girls in gangs "in terms of their internal relationships" because their behavior seems to be "internally supporting and identifying" (p. 184).

In order to continue discussing the position that gangs provide a liberating effect, the various dimensions of gang participation by girls must be considered. Specifically, we must acknowledge the notion that girls commit less serious offenses and, more surprisingly, the point that it is harder to distinguish between gang members and nonmembers among girls than in boys in terms of crimes committed (Chesney-Lind, 1993). This point suggests that increased media attention to crimes committed by girls—whether gang-involved or not—signifies the growing backlash against female liberation, and that this backlash has racist and sexist motivations.

To focus on the specific task of researching Latinas in gangs, I now discuss two seminal pieces that advance the "liberating hypothesis," namely, those by Miranda (2003) and Mendoza-Denton (2008). These research projects are discussed at length for two reasons. The first is to distinguish what they mean by "liberation" from my own use of the term "transcendence." I do not doubt that gang membership may bring some benefits to a girl, but I do question the cost to her and to society that such benefits require, and thus balance the "social injury" and the "liberation hypothesis" views by offering the notion of "transcendence." The second reason for focusing in such depth on the works of these two authors is to demonstrate how other researchers have met the challenges of conducting such studies by creating a space in which research associates and research consultant can insert as much of their voice as is needed in order to be heard as they wish to be heard. From the work of these two authors, I develop the notion that the role of the researcher is that of (a) facilitator of storytelling, by framing themes and by providing astute commentary and alternative readings; and (b) consultant of future possibilities, by harvesting the successes in these stories and distilling them into strategies for others involved in the process of helping girls transcend gangs.

ADJUSTING RESEARCH AIMS TO FIT THE NEEDS
OF THE RESEARCH POPULATION

Miranda's (2003) work marks a turning point in the literature of gang research in general and about Latinas in gangs in particular. Her unconventional approach began as a projected audience research study about gang girls' reactions to a commercial feature film by Allison Anders titled *Mi Vida Loca*. As the girls in her study watched the film and engaged in lively discussion with the filmmaker, they began to realize the implications of a representation that privileges some stories at the expense of others. Because the girls expressed their anger and disappointment that the film did not represent their experiences, someone in the audience motivated them to create their own film about their lives. The result was a video titled *It's a Homie Thang!* that privileged their voices: what it means to be a gang member, the importance of their concept of loyalty and solidarity, the different kinds of girls who join, and whether they see themselves as having a choice in joining the gang. The main issue they disputed with the filmmaker of *Mi Vida Loca* was that the girls in the film engaged in fights over boyfriends; this was not so in the case of *It's a Homie Thang!*

In exploring the powers and limits of ethnography, Miranda (2003) confronts the challenges of representation regarding gang members by claiming that hers is not a gang study but "a study of girls in gangs speaking on behalf of themselves" (p. 3). This syntactic move releases her from the contrivances in which field researchers must at times engage in order to organize and synthesize enormous arrays of ethnographic data. Aware of the fact that many gang studies, by definition, set the subjects in a category of "other," she shifts the research paradigm from the street to the political sphere, and thus from gang members as subjects to citizens as contributing members of and to the political discourse. In this manner, Miranda and the girls create a "co-discursive partnership," after she confronts her own reservations about her role, her privilege, and her power to shape the subjects' responses and, thus, the results in the study.

The video *It's a Homie Thang!* "serves as a primer for gang studies" because it "explains the gang through the experiences and life stories of its female members." Moreover, by presenting the girls' voices as "authorities on their own worldview," the video stands as an "experimental moment of auto-ethnographic film" (Miranda, 2003, p. 50) and as an ethnographic product for and of self-representation, addressing pressing questions about gang-involved girls, namely, how the gang became organized, how it originated, and the sources of rivalry among gangs:

> Through these questions, the young women provide their particular accounts of joining or of why the gang is important to them. The personal stories reveal nuances of gang life and different levels of commitment to the gang. [. . .] While surveying these individual experiences in the gang, the video underlines the group values, especially the value of members backing each other up. (Miranda, 2003, p. 62)

While Miranda (2003) acknowledges conclusions by other authors (e.g., J. Moore, 1991; Vigil, 1988) that Chicano/Latino gangs are mostly about fighting, what she does not clarify is why fights, and specifically those about "backing up" as a "distinct form of group solidarity that brings the particular peer group of the gang together," occur in the first place (p. 70). Noting Hughes's (2005) concern about the challenges of qualitative research, I have tried to address this dearth by eliciting responses from my own interviewed consultants about the meanings of fights, tattoos, colors and names, loyalty and respect, and, specifically, about inhabiting a gang, among other chapter themes.

Returning to Miranda (2003), despite the concern that the girls encountered more marginalization as they engaged in efforts to transform it, the video *It's a Homie Thang!* provides a medium through which to examine their everyday activities. From it, Miranda (2003) surmises, as does Besag (2006), that girls' friendships take the form of quasi-romantic relationships, where girls pair up with their friends in exclusive same-sex dyads from time to time, as though rehearsing for opposite-sex pairings later on in life. The meaning of gang membership is enacted in episodes of spending time together, exchanging comments on poetry writings, and offering advice and solidarity on relationships with family and boyfriends. Their friendship culture also is created through the writing and exchanging of poetry notebooks, which they use as a "dialogical form and a source for maintaining friendship" that brings unity to the group, rather than through fighting among themselves.

Moreover, the girls, through their aggressive attitude, androgynous look, and unfeminine linguistic patterns, are capable of developing an identity independent of sexual objectification. These same characteristics also allow them to construct notions of worth and respect that are based primarily on their loyalty to each other and on their physical strength and fighting abilities, rather than on competing for boys' attention. Their relationships with the men in the gangs also provide a basis for examining notions of respect: "All these guys call us bitches and hoochies and don't have respect for us" (Miranda, 2003, p. 34). These observations serve as a useful baseline for my own discussion of gang-impacted and gang-involved Latinas.

It seems appropriate here to revisit the observations set forth by Harris (1988) and consider whether Miranda's work bears them out, more than 20 years later: Harris argued that girls did not commit delinquent acts against the dominant society because their victims and enemies came from their own neighborhoods; that they were unaware of the existence of mainstream society or of other patterns of acting and being in the world; and that their reactions, although neither subverted to nor deviated from the mainstream, were to immediate situations and the experience of group belonging. Future research, Harris (1988) urges, should focus on internal relationships, support, and identification.

While heeding Harris's call, Miranda (2003) simultaneously challenges and expands the literature of gangs. Her work interrogates how Latinas in gangs perform race, ethnicity, gender, and class; how they engage with popular representations of gangs; and how they manage the contradictions occurring at the intersection of family and gang relationships. Her work also cautions students of gangs and barrios about the pitfalls of objectifying them and of committing epistemic violence. She ends her examination by providing a "Frequently Asked Questions" section and a springboard for action that focuses our attention on dialogic communicative processes that take difference as a point of departure toward achieving democracy. Ultimately, her concern rests with the process of negotiating identity and representation the girls engage in and with the range of political spaces in which it occurs.

LANGUAGE CHOICE AS INDICATOR OF GANG MEMBERSHIP

The extant literature, as well as the present endeavor to expand what we know about girls, and specifically Latinas in gangs, also owes much to Mendoza-Denton's (2008) most recent liberation-hypothesis contribution on Latina youth gangs. Hers is a comprehensive account of the lives of young Latinas in a linguistic analysis that covers language and speech, including language variations that signal the dynamic nature of gang affiliation. Additionally, as a cultural anthropologist, Mendoza-Denton focuses on practices ranging from notebooks of poetry and prose (like Miranda, 2003) that are circulated among and by multiple, often anonymous authors to symbolic gleanings and intentions behind the seemingly simple act of wearing make-up. Following works by Harris (1988), Chesney-Lind (1993), and especially Miranda (2003), Mendoza-Denton's (2008) work has an "underlying feminist [epistemology that tries] to bring to the forefront more of [girl gang] members' words and images" (p. 106).

Among the many interesting insights in Mendoza-Denton's (2008) analysis lies the idea that the discourse of being "muy macha" functions as gender-transgressive self-examination for a girl's future options and, most significantly, helps her sidestep the so-called social injury that often accompanies gang membership. To offer a bit of semantic clarification, "macho," the Spanish word for the male animal, is popularly used to designate a masculine, sexist, often misogynist man, whereas the words "macha" and "marimacha" are often used to describe a sanguine woman, a "tomboy," or a lesbian.

However, Mendoza-Denton's (2008) most significant contribution consists of developing the term "hemispheric localism," which she uses to describe the idea that language choice both guides and is guided by a person's gang identity. Her analysis reveals "coexisting and conflicting discourses" that different gang members produced when she asked them for definitions and distinctions between Norte and Sur, the process these youth undertake to categorize surrounding social phenomena, and the way they interpret such phenomena "through the prism of Norte/Sur opposition" (p. 97).

As the participants in her research discussed gang membership, they alluded to language, ethnicity and race, and sociocultural designations such as education and gender. These were subsumed under an overarching politicized ideology—hemispheric localism—that projects a discourse of "turf" based in the neighborhood, yet also encompasses debates about race and immigration, and modernity and globalization. She found that the definitions of Norte and Sur go far beyond gang affiliation and geographic origin:

> With a multiple indexical ability to locate its users, language becomes the loudspeaker through which emergent political consciousness can be broadcast: language will advertise one's acquaintances and their trajectories. [. . .] Young people used the shifting indexicalities of language and other symbolic modes of expression to continually, dynamically forge the nature of what they considered to be "gangs." (Mendoza-Denton, 2008, p. 104)

As a useful reference, Mendoza-Denton (2008) provides a primer on gang identification based on government, police, research, and community perspectives. Although this might fit tightly into a brochure designed to help parents determine whether their children are involved in gangs, Mendoza-Denton interrogates this as a simplistic approach that serves to further designate people as "other." I, too, would like to note that, from time to time, local newspapers will publish some handy criteria or checklist that, if used indiscriminately, could brand just about any urban teenager searching for the elusive "coolness" factor as a gang member. Yet as Mendoza-Denton poignantly observes, these categories are laden with contradictions, and that actual practice often is different from the ideologized presentation of structured differences, or, as I theorize about them, the difference between stories lived versus stories told.

Through her work, she finds that being an anthropologist from Mexico who has lived in many parts of the world and been educated in the United States (Stanford, no less!) does not necessarily bring her any advantages when it comes to getting to know the gang members, the meaning of their tattoos, or how they identify themselves as either Norteños or Sureños. Some of the participants in her research (Sureños) assert that Norteños do speak Spanish but claim not to; others say that the only way to get ahead is for Sureños to learn English and become integrated in the U.S. mainstream culture, as the Norteños presumably have. Mendoza-Denton (2008) believes that "the evaluation of who belongs in which category is made organically and dynamically by the youth involved, with each actor exercising agency and weighing different factors in their determination of membership" (p. 131), and she provides a set of eight criteria that she believes determine this process: language use, language ideology, perceived phenotype or race, performative speech acts of claiming membership in a gang, country of origin, perceived economic position, social class, and neighborhood residence. Yet, although both Norteños/as and Sureños/as articulate elaborate distinctions and differences that divide them, those in Mendoza-Denton's study sometimes come to be united against larger forces, through exclusionist policies such as California's Proposition 187 (which aimed to deny public education, social services, and health care to undocumented immigrants but was declared unconstitutional in 1998), police raids, and generalized racism against Latinos regardless of their hemispheric localism.

In some of the subsequent theme chapters, these differences and similarities come to the fore in the women's storytelling, as I argue that a girl's ability to narrate her life and to envision different endings to her story distinguishes a girl who can transcend the gang's socially constructed distinctions between "homies" and "the enemy" and a girl who cannot.

Mendoza-Denton (2008) argues that the poetry notebooks she encounters connect people in distributed cognition that constitutes a form of distributed memory. In these notebooks, knowledge about an event or an object is distributed among the various participants or makers of such an event or object. Despite the many challenges that gang girls face regarding the performance of memory work, they nonetheless manage to memorialize their experiences via these notebooks, which both Norteñas and Sureñas circulate among themselves but which belong to no one in particular. Among their many functions, these notebooks are public advice-giving and problem solving—"a non-face-threatening way to communicate questions and to give advice that may be embarrassing or difficult to deal with in direct speech acts"— and "providing an escape valve for both direct confrontation and difficult feelings" (p. 191). In my own observations, I encountered several of these notebooks; specifically, one story told by Angela described how another girl's aggressive reaction to her use of one of these notebooks galvanized her to seek gang-involved girls for physical protection and identity-development needs. Given Mendoza-Denton's assertion of these notebooks as distributed cognition, I argue that in the case of Angela, the notebook served to ascribe to her the identity of being "fair game," an identity that she came to disavow by switching schools and being a "wannabe" in a gang.

Ultimately, from Mendoza-Denton's (2008) work we learn that social memory is created, managed, and extended through distributed memory practices that are linguistic, embodied, and reinforcing of material practices. Faced with opposition, prevention, and suppression of their material culture by parents, teachers, and police, gang girls engage in discursive and literary practices that help them forge their subaltern youth identities. Mendoza-Denton's focus on language yields extraordinary insights into youth culture that could not be reached by focusing exclusively on material practices in an attempt to discover how rules emerge and eventually serve to create identity and solidarity. "That is how homegirls remember, by combining different semiotic levels, always including language and embodiment as well as commercially available, though often illicit, material culture" (Mendoza-Denton, 2008, p. 204).

In the next chapter, I provide a set of terms that helps me describe memory and identity work as ongoing processes of storytelling. Depending on the linguistic and meaning-making resources involved, these stories situate the women I interviewed along the continuum between dependence and interdependence vis-à-vis the gang; in extraordinary cases, the storytelling helps the women transcend the gang and inhabit multivocal inter(in)dependence.

3

A Primer on Storytelling and Transcendence

One of the guiding assumptions in this study comes from Ludwig Wittgenstein's (1953/2001) celebrated saying that "the limits of my language are the limits of my world." Therefore, I take it as a cue that new terms need to be invented when facing societal challenges such as transforming gang involvement into something less noxious. I take great liberties with language here, not for the sake of invention but to enlarge the limits of our social worlds, especially those of gang-impacted and gang-involved Latinas, and of those who wish they were otherwise. Rather than trying to reinvent the wheel—in this case, "gangs"—by offering yet another study of gangs, my purpose here is to transform ways of looking at how aspects of this particular wheel are made in interaction. I try to accomplish this in two steps.

First, I provide a glossary of common gang terms in Appendix B. Should the reader encounter an unfamiliar term not found in a dictionary, she or he is invited to consult the glossary for definitions that gang-impacted and gang-involved youth, law enforcement officers, and social service professionals would recognize. Therefore, I agree with Geertz (1973) that "it is explication I am after, construing social expressions [that are] on their surface enigmatical."

Second, in this chapter, I outline and define specific terms and concepts used in analyzing the themes of the chapters that follow: storytelling and storying, inhabiting and disinhabiting the gang, multivocal inter(in)dependence, and transcendence. In this second strategy to transform our ways of analyzing gangs, I also discuss the methodology I used in the research consultations, a methodology known as "circular questioning."

STORYING

The cartoon character Calvin, in *Calvin and Hobbes*, says, "I like to verb words," to which Hobbes replies, "What?" Calvin elaborates by saying, "I take the nouns and adjectives and use them as verbs. Remember when 'access' was a thing? Now it's something you *do*. It got verbed." The final frame shows the two of them walking away as Calvin retorts, "Verbing weirds language," and Hobbes observes, "Maybe we can eventually make language a complete impediment to understanding." Although I appreciate Hobbesian philosophy (both academic and cartoonish), I only agree with this cartoon strip up until the last line. I argue that verbing does weird language, but that weirded language can sometimes enhance rather than impede understanding. Aside from being an invention of cartoonist Bill Watterson, this process is known in linguistics as "verbification," or conversion of one word form into another, in this case of a noun into a verb.

All this is prologue to introducing a key word in this study: storying. I have taken the noun "story" and converted it into the verb "to story" to denote the active signifying performed by recounting and narrating, by the linguistic process of creating one's image to oneself and to the world. Storytelling is a variant of the verb, one that subsumes the story into the act of telling it. "Storying" used as a verb allows me to highlight its ongoing nature: The stories told to me by the women presented in this book emerge from remnants of the stories lived before. As these women story their experiences, they take stories previously untold, unknown, unheard, unimagined, and unthinkable and now unleash them in the interests of transforming their identity.

Another cartoon character, Billy, the oldest child in Bill Keane's *Family Circle*, tells us that "the word 'verb' is a noun." In that spirit, the "stories" the women in this book tell are nouns that I define as close representations of what they think is real, rather than as "tall tales" or "fibs." I am keen (as it were) to clarify this seemingly minor point because often when someone tells "a story," the word "story" connotatively implies a lie or an exaggeration. Here I assume neither, for I am not looking for exact correspondence between "what really happened" and "how accurately the women describe their experiences." I require no evidence that they're telling "the truth." I take their word at face value: If they say something happened, it must serve some purpose of theirs to do so—a purpose that may be obscure to me, but one that is useful in their own self-identifying process. I have no academic interest in corroborating their stories, but I am extremely interested in observing what these stories point to and how significant details in them are used as punctuating anchors in creating a story of transcendence (more on this later).

Last, I take storying as a conscious process of acknowledging past and present, and of storytelling themselves into a better future, and therefore those who engage in the process of storying their experiences are the storytellers.

STORYTELLING

For narrative analysis, Pearce and Pearce (1998) offer a model comprising a set of types of stories and four forms of storytelling. They advance the LUUUTT Model in order to help us focus our analysis on acts of storytelling by including (a) stories Lived, (b) Unknown stories, (c) Untold Stories, (d) Unheard stories, (e) stories Told, and (f) storyTelling. It may seem redundant to point out the discrepancies between how people live their lives and the stories they tell about such lives because we live our lives through our interactions with others, yet the stories we tell about those lives comprise our sense-making efforts to scribe actions into words. Consequently, the stories we live and the stories we tell about those lives lack an exact "fit," and this lack seems problematic only if the primary storytelling form we take is the literalist. One way to describe a purposeful life is to be able to story our lives in joy, peace, happiness, health, and generosity. Among the things that keep us from being able to do this are the multiverse of stories that remain somehow inaccessible to us. These include the stories that we are incapable of knowing (unknown), and thus of telling, as well as the stories that we make the conscious choice not to tell (untold). Furthermore, we all tell stories that go unheard by others who need to hear them.

Let us return to the key aspect of the model—storytelling—to highlight the process rather than the product of telling stories. Pearce and Pearce (1998) argue that this process is central to our humanity, not simply for purposes of accounting, but more specifically for making sense of experience: The richer the stories we can tell, the better our lives can be/come. Regardless of their form and richness, stories create our social worlds. Yet, one elementary aspect of stories is that they are unfinished. Events that follow the telling of a story, or those preceding it but unknown, untold, unheard, and so on, can alter its meaning, currency, purpose, and consequence.

Pearce and Pearce's four-part model provides a heuristic. The first part of the model, one that privileges facts, is the "literalist" form often found in scientific and legal texts. The second part refers to the "symbolic" form; both storytellers and story listeners who practice this form are expected to forgo a critical reading and accept otherwise unaccountable or illogical aspects of the story. Religious and mythical texts are the primary sources of the symbolic form. Third, the "social construction" form acknowledges the consequentiality of communication and privileges the interactional nature of communication and a multiverse of context-specific and emergent meanings. This form, because it is ubiquitously "made," is crucial in transforming social worlds. The fourth form of storytelling is an "all of the above" type. Labeled "transcendent," it can encompass any, some, or all of the previously mentioned forms and it can stand on its own. To be specific, transcendent storytelling includes three characteristics. The first is that it can include any, some, or all of the other three forms of storytelling, and it does so reflexively. The second characteristic is that transcendent storytelling acknowledges the advantages and disadvantages of each of these depending on the context in which they occur. Last, this transcendent form requires storytellers to observe their participation in the story in first-person awareness and simultaneously critique the story in third-person commentary.

The girls and women whose stories comprise the core of this book engage at one point or another in all four forms of storytelling, yet the stories that make up our social worlds are not all created equal. What we say and do in any context constitutes a small part of the choices participants can make in responding to that situation. Living a story is contingent on others with whom we live it, and thus it never really functions on its own in terms of our sole authorship. Nor does a story told reflect, blow by blow, the lived reality. We live stories we never tell, and we tell stories in an order we do not quite live them by. A careful focus on the gaps that separate these two types of stories brings us greater understanding and appreciation of the meaning-making process, as well as of our social worlds. In order to develop their transcendent storytelling skills, women in gangs must first differentiate between their and other people's stories, being sufficiently skilled to "live in the tension" without accepting or discarding others' stories, a relating that comes with neither agreement nor disagreement. Aware of participating in unique communicative processes that allow them to bear partial responsibility for their own stories, these women also recognize the patterns of communication that give meaning to a multiplicity of stories that, although contradictory, may coexist side by side. Pearce and Pearce (1998) would argue that this skill-building process occurs best as women join other groups already engaged in such recognition, such as religious groups.

Modeled on these three characteristics of transcendent storytelling, I would like to outline three steps that women in gangs take to generate alternative stories about the gang so as to inhabit a space of inter(in)dependence, as discussed later in this chapter. First, as the women invite self-awareness and possibility, they (re)construct from different interpretive resources to invent other stories. Second, they establish new and unconventional connections between the stories that do not exist already and their new ones. Third, their storytelling technique allows them to perform the shifts in person-position characteristic of transcendent storytelling—for example, telling now what they thought of themselves then, as the story was lived. This basic structure of forms of storytelling propitiates my analysis of the process by which Latinas story their gang experiences.

OUT OF HABIT

The expression "out of habit" has always intrigued me because it is used to explain something done *because* of habit, arising from habit, rather than being exempt from it. To clarify, in my analysis of the themes suggested by the storytellers in this volume, I use the verb "to inhabit" to mean more than just "to reside." I use it to mean a pattern of habitual actions that brings us into close contact with others engaged in similar patterns of action. Further, to inhabit here means to be inside those habits ("in the habit," so to speak) that make one group different yet similar to another, joint actions that women in gangs learn and eventually become accustomed to, while forgetting their original context. Just as a Catholic nun wears the vestments or "habits" of her religious order and takes on a new name to story her commitment to a new life within the church, so gang members inhabit their new identity by wearing the gang's colors and receiving a new name.

In his famous tome *Democracy in America*, Alexis de Tocqueville (1969) referred to the mix of traits essential to our national character as "habits of the heart." De Tocqueville's idea of heart was equivalent to the Social Construction notion of praxis, which entails that which one must know in order to get along and get on in one's social world. Using the phrase "Habits of the Heart," Bellah, Madsen, Sullivan, Swidler, and Tipton (1985) lament how far American culture has come from earning de Tocqueville's admiration due to its unrestricted focus on individualism and consumerism. Bellah and colleagues try to recapture the vocabulary that has been lost to individualism and that Americans need to make moral sense of their lives. Far from being a "habit of the heart," the gang habit resembles the mirage created by individualism and consumerism: Your life is inadequate, and the solution to its inadequacy is to join a group (of consumers or of gang members) that will make you whole. Bellah and colleagues (1985) urge that, in reconnecting with the voices of community, "we will need to see the story of our life on this earth not as an unbroken success but as a history of suffering as well as joy" (p. 295). As the women whose stories comprise this book inhabit the gang, they buy into the false sense of community—belonging through inflicting pain on others—that the gang constructs. "Disinhabiting" the gang means taking in both the suffering and the joy that life in and out of the gang entails.

To expand on this notion of inhabiting pain, Shaw (2004) writes that gang-involved girls perennially inhabit a warrior mentality, always ready to fight, and that it "is not easy for gang girls to relinquish their well-learned, much practiced habits of survival." Quoting Scott (1991), Shaw offers an alternative: the move from reacting and surviving to being liberated by our choices relies on ensuring that "habits be identified, acknowledged for their pluses and minuses, and relegated to the realm of the conscious and the chosen" (p. 9).

Inhabiting a space with gangs may mean one or more of these four types of interaction. First, by being born into a gang of family, a girl's storytelling voice depends on that context for meaning-making. Second, by joining a gang, a girl replaces her original family as a primary meaning-making context, and therefore storytelling context, with the relationships context of the gang; paradoxically, although a move to new contexts can symbolize separation and voicing independence, it can also correspond to a retreat toward dependence in the new relational context of the gang. In the third type, the girl retains some connections to her gang family, and she also uses her storytelling voice with other, legitimate activities, such as a job that gives her enough income to sustain a drug habit, so that she inhabits interdependence with the gang. The fourth and final type of interaction in inhabiting a space with gangs manifests itself when a girl or woman transcends the gang by cultivating new habits of relating that are formed because and in spite of experiences within the gang. I refer to this type as a multivocal inter(in)dependence, as discussed below.

At this end of the gang storytelling spectrum, I speak of a girl's exit from the gang not as "complete" but as an inter(in)dependence that still acknowledges the history and impact of having been in a gang. Thus, she has transcended the situation enough to lessen the negativity of that impact but remains close enough to her story lived that she can bring about positive change for those still inhabiting dependence within the gang, as explained below.

FURTHER WEIRDING LANGUAGE WITH PUNCTUATION: INTER(IN)DEPENDENCE

In this section, I describe four previous attempts to define the term "inter(in)dependence" and how each of these fits with what I am attempting to articulate about the identity development of gang-impacted Latinas, their relationship with others, and their efforts to disinhabit and transcend gangs.

An early usage and definition of "inter(in)dependence" comes from the literature of development communication, encrusted in the "multiplicity in one world" model by Servaes (1986). This model gives particular attention to the issue of culture and cultural identity within the process of development and how nations that are interindependent forge identities. All countries in the world system are simultaneously independent from and interdependent with one another; thus, they are interindependent.

A second definition of "inter(in)dependence" comes from an exploration of the "proper relationship between church and state" (Scharffs, 2004). Here three forms of individual religious freedom are identified, each of which is correlated with a different version of autonomy: separation with independence, cooperation with interdependence, and accommodation with inter(in)dependence.

Under this model, inter(in)dependence "seeks a middle ground between conceptions of autonomy based upon conditions of stark independence, as well as conceptions of autonomy based upon conditions of thick interdependence." Scharffs (2004) acknowledges the difficulty in articulating an inter(in)dependent autonomy, yet proposes that it would be helpful "to recognize that human beings are born into and raised within social contexts." As our complete dependence on our parents as infants transforms into independence, "it is evident that the possibilities available to us are in large measure defined by the social conditions within which we find ourselves. We do not create ourselves *ex nihilio*, as self-defining adults, but emerge, through education and inculcation, as members of particular families and communities." He advances four general conditions for exercising an ideal of inter(in)dependence. First, under a commitment to independence, an autonomous life must be largely created or composed by the person living it. Second, individuals who actively participate in their community enjoy "interindependent autonomy" and must not be ignored or marginalized if they are to enjoy meaningful respect. Autonomy here does not imply a complete freedom from the presence and influence of others; conversely, inclusion implies understanding and respecting others and being responsible for what our moral positions permit and prohibit. Third, autonomous agents commit to mutual respect and tolerance by helping others live autonomous lives, free from marginalization, aggression, violence, enmity, prejudice, discrimination, and lack of opportunity and access to social, political, and economic resources. The fourth and last element that constitutes inter(in)dependence is perhaps its most definitive: empowerment. For empowerment to occur, there cannot be some "ones" who have power and give it to some "others." Rather, empowerment occurs when individuals with varying degrees of being powerful engage others in such a way that they lay the groundwork for empowerment by any, some, or all of the members of the community. When individuals have access to adequate resources, and when, from among those, they choose to perpetuate the same resources for others, inter(in)dependence occurs (Scharffs, 2004).

Autonomy based on an ideal of stark independence posits that we may have nothing in common; autonomy based on an ideal of thick interdependence posits that we have everything in common, even though we may not have the good sense to realize it. Inter(in)-dependence posits a middle ground: that we share much, although not everything, in common, and that while we should cherish and nurture that common ground, we must also carve out space in which we can exercise our independent visions of who we are and ought to be (Scharffs, 2004).

Although Scharffs's (2004) view of inter(in)dependence is quite comprehensive and useful to my own theorizing, I would like to offer yet a third useful view of inter(in)dependence:

> If I wish to stay independent, others with whom I closely relate must also be independent. Since we are interlinked in the world, it becomes our inter(in)dependence—one womyn's independence maintained by the independence of another—that allows each to maintain our individuality and uniqueness. (Post, 1990)

Taking time to contrast "inter(in)dependence" with other terms, here Post (1990) reminds us that these are also necessarily a part of one's life. "Codependence," beyond the well-intentioned efforts of advocates of alcoholism recovery and the popular usage, serves as a useful concept to analyze instances of mutual dependence, yet with a detrimental or diminishing effect on the relationship and its partners. Post sees codependence to mean, for example, a relational pattern of one adult living in dependence to another; in time, and through enough instances of dependency and resentment as the "weak" gives in to the "strong," they switch roles or end the relationship. While acknowledging that dependence is "inherent in our lives," Post cautions against pathologies of dependence where one thinks one cannot live without a relationship.

As she moves on to illuminate her concept of inter(in)dependence, Post (1990) focuses on "a personal awareness of one's own power" to "have the ability to say, this is who I am without reference to anyone else and without reflection in someone else's eyes." Relationships make us who we are, and this is why they also make us unique: We must be comfortable in both worlds, with or without a partner.

The fourth view I would like to offer is a notion of inter(in)dependence as "a form of intimacy or sharing where one's autonomy and uniqueness is both valued and celebrated" (Kegan, 1982).

Culling from these four views, as I offer that the term, "inter(in)-dependence" functions in ways similar to "transcendence." I hereby articulate a concept of multivocal inter(in)dependence and apply it to an analysis of the lives of Latinas in, out, and around gangs in order to provide a richer understanding of how that space can be inhabited in transcendent storytelling. I argue that, by being able to fluidly function within and beyond the very environment that landed a woman into a gang, she inhabits a space of inter(in)dependence through the identifying process.

I believe multivocal inter(in)dependence occurs in three stages. First, the gang-involved woman realizes that she has a free choice in leaving the gang, regardless of what the gang members or gang lore may say about *por vida* ("for life") commitments. Second, inhabiting an inter(in)dependent space in her relationship with the gang means that the woman who was a gang member participates actively in social and political aspects of her community, inspiring others and paying respect by including gang members and nonmembers alike in her relations. By "including" I do not mean that the woman "forgives and forgets" the untoward actions of gang members, especially those against her, but that she maintains a connection to their humanity as a way to extend and motivate their own developmental construction of identity. Third, the gang-involved woman faces the challenge of inhabiting appropriate linguistic resources in order to develop an appreciation for others and to answer the implications that her beliefs and values, both new and old, place on her.

But meeting this challenge, while a feat in itself, does not bring the woman to inhabit inter(in)dependence. Once she has disinhabited the gang, the woman cannot just go about her own affairs as though she had never inhabited the gang in the first place. Inhabiting inter(in)-dependence also entails reaching out to help others who came after her live a life free from want, self-exacerbated marginalization, dependence, and "a bondage"—as Florencia, one of the women whose stories make up this book, calls it—to execrable violence and inhumanity, and thus to help them achieve access to, as well as helping others achieve, independence, opportunity, and societal welfare and justice.

The women who shared their stories with me all inhabit one or more of these elements of multivocal inter(in)dependence. As they engage in the process to transcend the gang, they reach the last key element—that of empowerment. Thus, as they take into account the multiplicity of voices in their experiences, their transcendent stories are determinedly multivocal. Through their storytelling acts, they realize their own power to transform their own lives as well as the lives of others. Thus begins a new relationship within a gang member's own self-concept and how she conceives its relationship with others.

TRANSCENDING GANGS

The women's gang stories exist among many, cobbled from their own set of resources to make coherence. Do their gang stories contain different markers to allow alternative readings and the crafting of alternative stories? The women as transcendent storytellers, when engaging with different resources, are able to create stories that are equally valid—or valid for their own resources. Because no story is ever "right" or the only story, the transcendent storyteller understands that the gang has resonance and "validity" within a multiverse of stories, but also that there are many other stories worth telling beyond the gang.

While the stories the women tell about their gang experiences may enjoy validity within a specific set of social practices and habits, the very act of telling them is tantamount to creating and inhabiting a space beyond dependence on them. To transcend gangs through storytelling is to create different meanings for old terms, different emotions for old experiences, and different possibilities for new ones. The practical implications of this storytelling are not just to get out of the gang but to (re)construct memory and other linguistic and interpretive meaning-making resources in contexts that do not silence but instead acknowledge without glorification the women's experiences.

GETTING THERE: CIRCULAR QUESTIONING TO FACILITATE STORYTELLING AND TRANSCENDENCE

The primary methodological tool used during research consultations is a method known as Circular Questioning (CQ). In fact, all semi-structured interviews during the research consultation phase were guided by CQ, which is the centerpiece of the Milan School of Family Therapy (Selvini Palazzoli, Cecchin, Prata, & Boscolo, 1978). These family therapists focus on the interrelationships among elements of a system in order to understand the system's dynamic properties. Based on such principles, I argue that it is possible to characterize situations such as "gang membership" differently: not as an individual's decision or condition but as one of several unique patterns of communication present in some families or some communities. Circular questions have applications beyond therapy, such as mediation (Gadlin & Ouellette, 1986/1987), and the classroom (Rossmann, 2002). In my own attempt to understand the gang as a system, in order to facilitate change for all the interview consultants, two types of circular questions were used: (a) descriptive, to elicit information to aid a new understanding of how the "gang" is systemically connected; and (b) reflective, to attempt to precipitate a change. By using CQ during research consultations, I hoped to provide more transformational possibilities than by offering opinions, prescriptions, directives, or instructions (Tomm, 1985).

In its original family therapy setting, the method contains three key components—circularity, neutrality, and hypothesizing—that allow them to be easily applied to ethnographic pursuits generally and the study of stories by gang-impacted and gang-involved Latinas specifically. The circularity of CQ results from asking questions that help the individual or group make new connections and think in new ways about certain events and acts. One way to achieve this is by facilitating linguistic shifts from first-person actor to third-person observer. For example, instead of asking linear questions such as, "Are you in a gang?" I would ask, "How do you show to others that you are in a gang?" to demonstrate that the gang habits are performed by joint actors following implicitly agreed-on rules.

Neutrality, the second component, is not about lack of bias or involvement. Rather, it shields the interviewer from cooptation into a system. In an ethnographic interview, neutrality allows the researcher to linguistically join the system in order to delve deeper into the interviewee's patterns of meaning and action. While therapists and mediators who use CQ work better in teams, this approach was not available to me, although much is to be gained from the "gossiping in the presence of others" approach famously outlined by the Milan Team (Selvini Palazzoli et al. 1978), to "take the side" of the entire system, not any one particular member of the system. In researching gangs, for example, instead of asking a Norteña, "Do Sureñas threaten you?" I would ask a general question about gangs such as, "What are the biggest challenges that gang members encounter in society?" In addition to allowing a person shift (from first-person actor to third-person observer), this question shows that, in some ways, they are not just gang members but also members of society as a suprasystem.

The third component of CQ, hypothesizing, is used to illustrate connections between parts of stories told, as well as to actions pertinent to such stories. Different patterns of connections are generated through the creation of a flood of hypotheses that focus on opposites, absence and presence, and extremes. For instance, when a practitioner is dealing with an at-risk youth's concerns about being harassed or "hit up" by gang bangers, she or he might avoid asking her for possible causes; instead she might hypothesize that at some point the student will "not be hit up" and might ask, "When you have not been hit up, what do you think others will notice about you?" or "What do you think those who hit up on you enjoy the least about it?" Systemic connections are highlighted by asking a group of youth, "What will Estela miss the most (and the least!) when she is no longer feeling hit up?" Positive connotations also facilitate these systemic connections. In terms of gang behavior, although from the outside it may seem difficult to think of anything beneficial about gangs, the young women involved in gangs may have had, on the average, very troubled backgrounds, and thus membership in a gang puts them in a situation where they experience making premature decisions about their own lives. So, in the case of gang-involved young women, a practitioner might say how courageous it was of her to become involved in gangs to find companionship when she was hit up and even neglected by her own family, despite the dangers posed by the gang lifestyle.

By using CQ, practitioners can join a system of knowledge to explore the inter(in)dependence of persons, actions, and ideas, and to help members of a given system—a gang, specifically—become aware of their patterns of being and acting in the world. This is done by presenting them with hypotheses and positive connotations to help guide them in the process of creating alternative patterns. One key move entails a rejection of the idea that meanings inside a person's head are the "cause" of problems, so practitioners can use CQ to help gain an understanding of social phenomena such as "gangs" as socially constructed enactments. Last, CQ is helpful in probing for descriptions of relationships because it helps practitioners discover "grammars" of meaning and action—in other words, the gang discourse—for the transformation of disruptive and damaging patterns of interaction, and the creation of new, empowering, engaging, generative, and transcendent stories.

PUTTING THE TOOLS TO WORK

All of this of course finds a more fertile ground when therapists, mediators, educators, and practitioners are able to engage for a period of time longer than the 1- to 3-hour research interviews I had with my research consultants, as discussed in more detail in Chapter 16, "The Story of Esperanza."

Using CQ can be instrumental in laying the groundwork for transcendence by guiding girls to invoke stories that have been lived but have remained untold, unheard, unknown, unimagined, unthinkable, unacknowledged, and unforgettable up to now. As far as turning a critical eye toward the storytelling process, the women manage to eliminate the endemic amnesia fostered by the gang as they create different ways to use language and to challenge the coherence of the stories privileged. They tell other stories beyond what the gangs want them to privilege and create a different type of memory work that may or may not include the gang, performed in different contexts, with different interlocutors, and with different results.

Part II

THEMES

4

Inhabiting the Gang
Lupe, Eréndira, Florencia, Margie, Olga, and Marisa

WHY DO GIRLS JOIN GANGS?

On the subject of identifying factors that would predict gang entry, a longitudinal study that classified risk factors into seven domains—area characteristics, family sociodemographic characteristics, parent–child relations, school factors, peer relationships, individual characteristics, and early delinquency—provides some insights (Thornberry, Krohn, Lizotte, & Chard-Wierschem, 2006). Four demographic characteristics were significantly related to the risk of joining a gang: race (African American in the Thornberry et al. sample), low levels of education by the parents, family income level below the poverty line, and living in a household where either biological parent was missing. Their sample of female respondents, due to its statistical insignificance, provided less confidence in the results. Despite this, the domain that appeared to be a more reliable predictor of gang membership was the one related to school performance and attendance, as were lower expectations of college attendance and neighborhood disorganization. For girls who began dating early, especially older males, the likelihood of gang membership increased. All in all, the best predictor for entry into a gang entails a multitude of these risk factors.

Furthermore, Miller (2006) conducted interviews and administered surveys to arrive at a similar conclusion: No single risk factor can predict a girl's entry into gangs; rather, the better predictor is an accumulation of several of these factors combined. The presence of gangs in their neighborhood; family problems, including gang-involved relatives; and family violence, often sexual and directed at the girl, were among the most common reasons that interviewees gave for joining gangs.

These studies indicate what factors might be salient. The more these factors are present in a girl's life, the higher the chances are that she will join a gang. Obviously, not everyone who joins the gang shares these experiences, but they all share some of these factors. Were there others that did not emerge from these two studies but that the women I spoke with gave as reasons for joining? Although common conceptions of gangs assume that all gang members undergo some form of collective beating or are forced or dared to perform some crime as initiation rituals, this was not the case for several of the women interviewed for this project. The focus of this chapter is not to challenge or replace the aforementioned research, but to expand on what it is that social scientific methods have helped explain. My aim is to gather the stories and collate them into coherent themes to provide alternate accounts, in the voice of the concerned. Let us now hear (Rubin & Rubin, 1995) how the voices of Lupe, Eréndira, Florencia, Margie, Olga, and Marisa discuss their own entry into the gang, not just how—or whether—their stories invoke any, some, or all of these factors but, more significantly, how they articulate their distinct processes of inhabiting their new gang identity.

LUPE

Despite that Lupe had a traditional family (married biological mother and father consistently holding working-class jobs) and despite her parents' own avoidance of drugs and alcohol, as well as their efforts to give their children a modest yet decent upbringing, Lupe and her siblings found their way into a gang.

Lupe—Today you see gangs that claim the red and the blue . . . back then it was varrios, so there was a family that came from East LA that moved into our neighborhood, so here we are a group of us from this family that are at prime age, and I think what connected us to this other family, they were also a family, they were four brothers and one sister, and as a coincidence, we were both "Lupe" . . . we had a lot in common, we had the language, they spoke Spanish, we spoke Spanish. . . .

Liliana—Were they also first generation [Mexican American]?

Lupe—. . . they were also first generation, and my brother first took an attraction to that and the guys, it was different because we wore long hair, it was the seventies and we wore long hair then. They came and they were already "Cholos" and we didn't really know anything about the Cholo lifestyle, so it was kind of like "Wow!" These guys had khakis on, they had prestige and charisma, they were already seasoned in the gang, they came from a place . . . they were already involved. Actually, we didn't even know why they were in our town. Later we found out they had been . . . they ran them out of there, they didn't want them there. So we started to connect with them, and my brothers started to cut their hair and they . . . Cholo-looking and . . . during that time there was a movie that I believe . . . it is just interesting how a movie kind of just exploited the whole scene . . . it was *Boulevard Nights*, and although we hated the movie because of the way it portrayed Latinos in the movie . . . that really . . . it took off, the way they claimed *varrios*. "Varrio VGV" I think it was, so here we started to claim this *varrio* of this family that moved in, we took on that identity really not knowing what "Vicki's Town" meant, but we started to claim that neighborhood and. . . .

Liliana—In LA?

Lupe—. . . which came from LA . . . and. . . .

Liliana—So it wasn't YOUR neighborhood that you were claiming?

Lupe—No, we kind of like, we took it on and . . . but the . . . what we were taught and what we told from the gang, it was something that, if we backed it up, they were going to be there for us . . . that we were "carnales" and we became a "familia" . . . although we had a family and we were . . . we still are . . . my family we are very tight, bonded, but we took on this surrogate family and then other friends started adding, getting added, and just being in numbers is power . . . having a name that you claim, gave us a sense of pride and dignity and belonging.

This gang was one of the most violent gangs in San José and we started to do everything that gang members do: run around town and fight and disrupt and destroy. . . . We started to use drugs, and I mean we were just really like in a destructive lifestyle, not seeing that it was really taking us downwards, instead of giving us a sense of purpose, and a lot of it was distorted. . . .

Lupe's story has aged almost 20 years from the living and the telling of it; if she waxes nostalgic for the glamour of her past gang experiences, the same could be said of anyone who tells "war stories," "football stories," or any such accounts of past exploits. The stories, while describing vividly unusual experiences, give the audience a sense that the narrator was fully immersed in the meaning system that carried forth such actions, although with the passage of time this meaning may have changed. Lupe recognizes that her gang involvement was almost gratuitously self-serving, mindless of the risks. Yet the risks, once involved, belonged in the life-or-death category. From the factors identified above by Thornberry and colleagues (2006) and Miller (2006), Lupe was mostly exposed to the forces of neighborhood disorganization and, later, gang-involved relatives. A storytelling habit—we might consider it a "risk factor" in the social science paradigm—that Lupe's story highlights is the glamour and allure that the other gang members exude, as well as the promise of belonging and protection that, among marginalized youth, can be difficult to resist.

ERÉNDIRA

In addition to allure and glamour, the storytelling devices that girls may inhabit for joining gangs are varied, and asking them directly why they joined often does not elicit a richly nuanced story. When asked instead about her meaning of Sureña, Eréndira constructed an elaborate and detailed story about place of origin, and the origins of gangs, of all things. (As a reminder, *italics* denote when research consultants and I spoke English, while the rest was translated from Spanish.)

Liliana—So, what does being "Sureña" mean to you?

Eréndira—It's respect. It's having someone who's going to tell you, if someone were to tell you something, that you have someone to help you. Like a family. If something happened to you, you'd have, you know what I mean? *You have your backup.* You'd have someone to help you out of a bind. Almost always, if there was a problem, there would be two or three people getting into it. It was never like *one on one.* Oh, let's call . . . well, three or four and they went, instead of only one person, they'd pile up. So then I said, "*All right*, if that's how they're going to be, then I can also have [backup]." And since I had cousins and all that, then it was easy for me to tell them the problems I had, and that's when I started *banging.*

It was more like it came from the family, being Sureña and choosing that. I always saw it like that, like I was raised in San José, I was born in Arizona, in Yuma, near the border between California and Mexico. Then they'd say, "Oh, you were born here, here you have to be Norteña, you are from *Northern California.*" Then I'd say, "But you don't even know me. You don't know that I was born here, that I was raised here." There are many families that don't think that way. There are many that yes, "I'm from the north, now I have to *declare* Norte." But since I was more like from my roots, *I'm Mexican.* I am Mexican and I have to be united with my people. Since it's the *Mexican Mafia*, then I said "I have to be united with my people. It wasn't like "*I can't be Norteña*," Why am I going to be Norteña? I am Mexican. And for that reason, I related more with the Sureños. Whether you believe it or not, Sureños are more . . . in their roots, based more in their . . . in other words, Mexicans or whatever, but they're more like proud, proud of where they come from. They're not like "Well, I don't speak Spanish, *I don't know*, I don't know where my mom . . . where she was born [makes face of disgust], I've never been to Mexico, and I don't know what else." But sometimes, well, those are lies. And me, it made me proud to say that my mom has worked in the fields and thanks to that she got her residency and I went every summer to Mexico. And here I was "Yes, and my granny and the pozole, and this and that." And it was "*No, well, I don't know*, I've never eaten that, I don't know what you're talking about. . . ." Do you understand me? They got on my nerves, in that sense that they negated where they came from. It was more cultural. . . .

Curiously here, when Eréndira speaks in Spanish about needing protection, she does not use the nound *respaldo* or the verb *respaldar*, which are more elaborate words but mean the same thing. Instead, she chooses the English phrase used by those who inhabit the gang, whether Norte or Sur: "*You had your backup*." Although "backup" does not fit neatly into any of the aforementioned risk factors that are precursors to gang entry, Eréndira's need for it compelled her to inhabit the gang. This compulsory need to belong to something seems consequent to poor or nonexistent family structure, as Florencia's story shows.

FLORENCIA

Florencia's home situation was abysmal, what with the violence and the partying on the part of the parents, in addition to the sexual abuse she had endured since she was 7 years old. Her older sister joined the Marines, and her brother took to the streets. She was never jumped into a gang; she didn't need to be. Her story lacks a definite date of entry and instead shows a gradual habituating into a lifestyle for which the term "gangs" provided a convenient framework.

Florencia—When I first started out in the streets, they would called me "China" because my eyes . . . the way I did my eyeliner. But as I got older into the lifestyle, it changed in the sense, when I first started out with the girls, then we had the "Brown Pride Locos," the guys started it, but we'd all stay, the girls with the girls and the guys with the guys. The majority of us were kids that came from single homes. Or our parents, some of our parents were drug addicts or alcoholics or both. Or one mom and she was always working and didn't know if you got home from school. I guess we were all looking for something and we found it in each other. We found it. In the beginning, it was fun, that loneliness was gone. That hurt that you felt was not there, when we first time into the gangs, it was fun.

It was just, we kind of run around with each other. We lived in the West side and then there was Varrio Rana, which was our enemies, the West Side's enemy. I was known as Chucho's Little Sister. Everybody knew, so I really didn't get messed with because everybody knew him and he was into gangs on that side of town. He was crazy, you know, if he was willing to kill his own father, who else wouldn't he shoot? Everybody knew him; he wasn't somebody you messed with.

(Florencia's brother, "Chucho," did not actually kill their father; one day, when the father came home drunk and started beating their mother, Chucho took the shotgun, put it to his father's head, and told him to leave her alone and to stop or he would kill him if he ever did it again. This is detailed in Chapter 5, "Violence," under Florencia.)

Florencia—But I just saw so much at such a young age. I walked . . . I remember I had a . . . the blade alone was about seven inches, and I used to carry that knife in my back pocket and walk around the streets by myself. And one time I . . . my brother had a baby with this girl, and she was a heroin addict. I went over there to visit them, just to see what they were doing, and I walked in and she had a needle hanging out of her arm and my niece was standing on a chair stirring a pot of beans that was burning. Just things like that, and driving their car and trying to drive her to the hospital. I'm nine years old and I'm trying to drive someone who OD'd, trying to get them somewhere. Just saw a lot. It just got to a point where, I think just the violence and being afraid of death just went away.

But I was determined to not just be . . . I guess in my own ways, be a victim of the circumstances of my life. I made the decision that I was going to be on top now, and I didn't care what it was going to cost me. So, I just started getting involved, getting more friends together. I started standing out, by the way I dressed. I always was a tomboy, so now I was dressing like the homeboys. I wasn't a loud person or a promiscuous girl, I had all kinds of boys, but it wasn't like that. I wanted to be the opposite of that . . . one of the boys. I didn't want to be looked at as a girl, I didn't want anybody looking at me . . . nobody knew what I had gone through, and I didn't want anybody to know, the abuse and the molestation, the hurt. I never got involved in any kind of gay relationships, I never had all kinds of boyfriends, because some girls that go through that, they end up with another woman, or they're very promiscuous.

I just wanted to be one of the guys. So everybody started looking at me like a homegirl, from the neighborhood, and where I lived we just kind of started clicking up, started getting together with more and more girls. I kind of took it over from this one girl. She was like, "We're gonna start this little club, it's gonna be called Sisterhood." I was like, "No 'Sisterhood!' We're going to be called this: we're 'Brown Pride Locas.'" That was like the first time I felt the influence I had to just take over something. She called the meeting, she got all the girls together, everybody was there, and I just walked in and took it. I felt I could do whatever I want. Loyalty was very important to me. I just said, "This is the way it's going to be, this is what it's going to be called, and I'm the one who's going to be in charge and Gata is going to be my sidekick, and when I'm not around, she's going to take care of things." We were very young, we were thirteen.

There is a term that aptly describes Florencia's process of inhabiting the gang: "Choloization," which implies "being one of the guys" (Miller, 2000), partaking of their every gang habit, and, in Florencia's case, even outdoing the homeboys. How could she possibly have avoided inhabiting the gang, given all that was stacked against her—violence in the family, severe and constant sexual abuse, alcoholic and inattentive parents, gang-involved siblings, and gang presence in her neighborhood? Another woman whose life experiences as co-inhabiting the gang took a different shape is Margie, although she did not speak of sexual abuse, but of her own sexual activity starting at the age of 11.

MARGIE

Recall that one of the risk factors identified by Thornberry and colleagues (2006) as a predictor of gang entry was early dating, especially if the girls dated older gang members. I take the term "dating"—especially in Margie's case—to be an inadequate euphemism for sexual activity. She provided precious little detail about her experiences, claiming that she could not divulge due to her still being active in the gang. She mentioned that she got pregnant at 11 and gave birth to a son at 12. When I asked about the experience, all she said was that it was not forced.

Margie—I don't like to talk about my parents because they were never there. My dad, he was in and out of prison. My mom, she was always partying. So I took care of me and my sisters. I'm the oldest of eight, two boys and I took care of all of them. . . .

Some people tell me I was too young to know at the time, but I think it started when I was seven. I was dealing dope, selling drugs, I used to keep food in the house, I kept the rent paid, I got the bills paid, I got everything paid, I made sure they had nice clothes. Basically, I was taking care of the whole family, including my mom. I used to buy her stuff all the time. I made the car payments, I made sure the car had gas and I was only thirteen at the time.

I started getting into the whole gang thing, and that took over my life. My whole family was gang related, the people I was selling to was gang related. I got jumped in at fourteen. Still now, I'm just trying to get back on my feet and I'm eighteen now.

The extraordinary storytelling power of the gang legacy is inhabited in many ways. Girls from Gangs of Family take different approaches to identifying with and inhabiting the gang. What social science researchers generally might refer to as "risk factors," and what Moore (1994) calls "the Chola life course," these women might consider the internalized reality of their circumstances, inevitable in its conspicuousness, a natural part of growing up, and a rite of passage for everyone in their circle of relatives as "just being." Clearly a member of Gangs of Family, Margie exemplifies this "Chola life course" (Moore, 1994). Despite the pervasiveness of the gang in her family, she chose to be jumped in.

GRACIA

As a force for inhabiting a gang, violence does not have to be directed at the girl, not even in the form of sexual abuse, although it often is (Moore & Hagedorn, 2006). Paradoxically, as Miller (2006) shows, girls take to the streets to avoid family violence, yet the habits of the gang often prove as violent, if not more violent, than their families of origin. Violence is thus sufficiently commonplace as a response to problems that it establishes useful, albeit violent, patterns for treating self and others. Gracia's story of forming her own gang shows the usefulness of violence.

Liliana—I would like to know how, what would a gang look like from the eyes of a young girl, a girl who is involved . . . how is this idea of being in a gang relevant or important to a girl's identity? In general, I'd like to ask you about how you came to be in a gang, if you could begin with that . . . so, you'd like to take it from there?

Gracia—I first got introduced to gangs by a family member. There was a lot of gangs and gang violence when I was growing up.

So throughout my years, I remember a lot of red and a lot of Cholos and Cholas. They was more of the low-rider style at the time that I was a toddler, and I remember a lot of low-rider cars, and my mom and my aunts dressed as Cholas and my dad and my uncles were dressed as Cholos, with the baggy pants and their bandanas. And so that's how I was first introduced to it.

Even as a young child, I was really drawn to that. That life, that kind of environment, that kind of atmosphere, that's all I knew, that's all I lived, I never knew any different, except when I went to live with my grandma, I still had uncles that were break dancers. It wasn't a violent gang, but it was still a gang, people that were break dancing, and so I still saw it as okay. So that's how I was introduced to it, by my parents.

Liliana—So . . . it was as if it was predetermined that you would follow into their footsteps?

Gracia—I would say so, because I automatically chose to hang out with the children who had the same lifestyle as me . . . that already had similarities as me, as far as being tough, being outspoken, outgoing, and someone that was going to be a fighter like me. So I already chose that crowd and so, when I chose that crowd, it made me even more so determined to be in gangs, to be a gang leader, to live that kind of lifestyle.

That's when I started . . . I started my own gang. I was the type of person who wanted to be in gangs, but I didn't want to take orders from anybody. I didn't want anybody to tell me what to do. I was tough enough, brave enough, and ready to start my own gang. I didn't want anybody to tell me what to do. I wanted to run my own gang and that's exactly what I did.

Liliana—And you thought this would give you standing in the community? Some safety?

Gracia—It wasn't even so much as safety, because um . . . I'd say because I was a really good fighter and because I had older brothers, of course a younger brother too, but because of who my dad was. He showed us a lot of . . . how can I say . . . ? He showed us a lot of love, but not love to where . . . gentle love, it was tough love. So through that tough love, he showed us how to fight and how to defend ourselves. And because he was in and out of prison, he taught us where you could hurt someone or hit someone in the neck and they'd drop instantly but you won't kill them. So that alone, I already thought I was the number one fighter, I had nothing to worry about. But when I say "safety," I knew that because I wanted to be in a gang, I knew I was gonna have to face my enemies. So in order for me to stand up to my enemies and be brave against them, and not get my butt kicked, I had to have a group of protection, someone who was going to fight with me, fight for me, someone who's going to be there, as we'd say, "through thick and thin," from the beginning to the end, all the way. So, I did need some kind of protection, some kind of safety, to help me go through with whatever I wanted to go through, and that was having my own gang.

Parenting approaches come in many styles, shapes, and colors; for some, they come only in red or blue. Many parents have had to counsel their children after someone bullied them at school, and unfortunately many parents would advise their offspring to fight fire with fire. Depending on who is telling the story, this approach could be either foolhardy or courageous. For Gracia, there were no other options: When someone pushes you around, you take matters into your own hands, so you'd better be prepared to expertly inflict sufficient pain to make them not just regret it, but fear you enough to leave you alone, and thus respect you.

Liliana—And how did you go about starting it?

Gracia—Well, how I went about starting it was, I already had a group of friends, and of course we were only eleven years old. We went to school one day and people already were claiming red and we were already considering ourselves, back what we'd call Norteñas so, what happened was, I was in the back and there was someone in front of mine, she was a best friend of mine, and I told her, "Hey, I want to start my own gang, you know, I'm tired of hanging out with these other gang members and I want to do my own thing, I want to be my own leader," and she said . . . and I asked her if she wanted to join me and she told me, "Well, I don't want you to be my leader," and I said, "Well, I don't want YOU to be MY leader, I'm asking you to join me!" So, we were both at the point where we didn't want to be each other's leader, we didn't want to be told what to do, so we said, "Okay, we'll both be leaders of this gang," and that's what we did and we had two other best friends and they didn't want to be part of a gang, they wanted to be leaders too. We kind of fought for a little while and we said, "We can't all be leaders," and of course we're still young but we wanted to be leaders. So we all fought among each other to see who was the toughest and who was baddest. Whoever got beat up wasn't going to be a leader and whoever stood up was going to be a leader. And it ended up being that it was the four of us that were leaders, from the beginning. It didn't quite work out so we kept on fighting and fighting and to see who would be the actual leaders and it ended up being me and my friend, one of my friends. So we were the leaders and then that's when we started recruiting the gang members, from school. It all started from school and then outside of school and then within the neighborhood.

Striking me as inane is the idea that friends fight physically to determine an official hierarchy within the friendship group. The concept of being jumped, where one receives a summary beating from friends and soon-to-be ersatz family (discussed repeatedly in these women's stories), presents logical challenges to those of us outside the gang lifestyle. This notion of ersatz family is discussed in more detail under Olga's story.

Gracia—As years passed, about a year went by and we ran into some older people. When I say older, I mean people . . . I was only eleven, twelve years old and they were already eighteen and over. And so, we started recruiting them. They started coming . . . even from fifteen, sixteen or seventeen, all the way up. I think the oldest was probably twenty-one. She was twenty-one. We had joined up with another gang which was a boy gang. So we had the girl gang and then we had the boy gang. The boy gang, the leader was my boyfriend, which is my husband now. So we had these two gangs together and we always got together and basically had our meetings and told each other what we were going to, what our plans were, how we were going to stay safe out there while we were wearing our red *paños*, and who was going to cover what point to what point of the neighborhood. Who was going to be like the . . . how do you say it? The person that was going to keep point, like if the enemies came around, they'd do the whistle [mocks a whistle], make sure they run . . . either if they had a car, they used a car, if they had a bike, they used a bike, to let everyone in the neighborhood know that there are enemies in the neighborhood and we have to kind of get together and take care of business. So I was one of those people who said who was going to be here at this time and who was going to keep watch at the store and stuff like that . . . I was a shot-caller 'cause I was the leader.

Liliana—And how would you go about recruiting? You said you started recruiting in middle school, high school, and then you went to the older kids. . . .

Gracia—First things first, they couldn't be a sissy. When I say "sissy," they couldn't be somebody who just wants to hang out, they had to be ready and willing to fight if we told them to.

Liliana—Did you approach them or did they come to you?

Gracia—Most people came to us and we let them hang out for a while and saw if they had what it took. Because we had a reputation by that time, we had huge reputation, not only because we had the guy members, the gang members that we all kind of, not looked up to, but wanted to be included with them as well, because they were the guys. So I guess you could say we kind of looked up to them a little bit, but we still wanted to do our own thing and be our own bosses. And so . . . they would come around or we'd see someone tough at school or around the neighborhood and we'd go up to them and "Hey, where are you from? What's up? What do you claim?" And then we'd make friends with them and before you know it, they're either hanging out with us or we kind of watch them and see who they are, what they're about and see if they could hang with us. In other words, could they back us up and are they worth us backing them up? Are they going to be with us from the beginning through the end? And how we'd pinpoint that, is making them go do things. Like, if we told them, "We don't like that girl over there and I want you to go beat her up," so we could see how good they fight. Or we'd tell them, "We need you to go put this person in check, go put them in check," or we'd say, "We want you to . . ." or in other words, if someone was mad-dogging us or acting stupid, we'd tell them to put them in check and let them know who they're messing with and they better stop and they better correct themselves before they get messed up, beat up or hurt.

Liliana—Like a warning?

Gracia—A warning. If they were brave enough to do that, then we'd see they were brave enough to stand getting jumped in. And our major themes were, "You gotta be where we tell you to be and you've gotta do what we tell you to do, and if you can't do those two things, we don't want you to have any part of us, we don't want you to even come around us." We didn't want no cry babies, nobody who cried or I would say, because I wasn't an emotional type person, sometimes I could be, but when it came to the gang part, I was really tough, so I said, "No emotional stuff here, no crying, no sissy here, no complaining, no nothing." But at the same time, it was weird, because a lot of the girls would come because they didn't have nobody at home. You know, they didn't have those people, like older brothers or older sisters to hang out with, to share problems with. As you know, recruiting people, and becoming this gang, we realized a lot of the girls came with a lot of problems. There was some that came where they'd been molested by their dad or uncle, even a grandpa. There were some that came in and there was no food at home and there's nothing to do and they were bored. A lot of them came because they were bored. I remember a lot of girls 'cause they would say they were bored, there was nothing to do, and mom and dad were always fighting and they were tired of being at home so they'd come and hang out with us and we'd hang out at school and we would just . . . the majority of the time I think we were probably partying. A lot of it had to do with partying.

Gracia's story of forming her own gang places her squarely in the role of protagonist. No surprises here, as storytelling serves not only a self-referential but also a self-creating purpose. What is noteworthy in this segment is her age at the time, the decisions she had to make, the leadership abilities she demonstrated precociously, the steely determination to shun weakness in others, and, paradoxically, her keen observation that girls' attraction to her gang arose from their dismal home situations, especially their victimization at the hands of relatives. Is it really any wonder that being jumped in or inflicting pain on others as a way to demonstrate loyalty seems acceptable to such young girls? The strongest legacy of gangs is how violence is routinized, expected, and accepted in the eyes of these girls (Miller, 1998). For someone like Olga, this violence was inhabited through her parents' fights and her siblings' gang involvement.

OLGA

Olga's story of how she got involved in gangs resonates with so many others: the lack of a firm family structure. Although both parents were present and worked hard, their own lifestyles made at least some of their 10 children feel irrelevant and unappreciated to the point that they sought relevance and appreciation in the gangs. The special bond that persons sometimes feel between them and others that go beyond biological relations or marriage has been referred to as "fictive kin" (Schneider, 1980). Here, I argue that, more than fictive kin, the gang functions as ersatz kin for many youth, insofar as it actually replaces the family in economic, emotional, and moral terms. This definition may be in keeping with more recent accounts that define kinship in terms of relatively flexible solidarity that endures over time and circumstance (Schneider, 1984). But it differs in that the young person may not have bases for making a "real" versus "fictive" comparison: Because the family as conventionally conceived is missing, the gang provides them with their first and only family. As an example of this notion of ersatz family, I offer Olga's dependence on the gang for what one's birth family typically provides: food, lodging, school attendance, and emotional and financial support. Another peculiarity of Olga's story touches on issues of racism and discrimination felt by immigrants that also contribute to their choosing the gang lifestyle. Olga and I spoke both in Spanish and English, the latter here indicated by the use of *italics*.

Olga—My older brother [started] to get involved, to find friends outside, in the streets. Between them, they started a gang, here in San José, because there were lots of obstacles. I don't know if they were obstacles, but a lot of people discriminated against Mexicans. At that time, he together with some friends started to hang out and then my other sister started to hang out. They started cultivating what is a gang, to jump in more people. They started to . . . like sow ill will among other Hispanics, right? And then one has to be like family. Because in our house, we didn't know what it's like to be a family. That was lost when we were little. By the time we were grown, to understand what is going on in our home and see how *dysfunctional* we were, and we wanted a family where we could belong and there was somebody there for us at any time we needed them. *So*, inside a gang, that was what my brother and my sister cultivated with their friends. A safe place. *There was safety*. There was a place where you felt good.

Liliana—Did it have a name, a color, or how was it?

Olga—When we started, like the majority were Norteño, here in Northern California, Farmeros is how they are known. My brother and my sister and some of their friends, they started to wear blue. Because that's how they'd heard about it in Los Angeles, about colors, about *varrios*, that's why they started to wear blue. And where they got their name, I still am not sure, but they were "Shadows," "VSL." At that time, there also were like three more gangs that were Sureños, but they were more Veterans. They had years in and out of jails. To all this, my siblings decided not to hang out with them and decided to start their own gang. And that's how it happened and that's how they were known: VSL, Varrio Sombras Locos [Shadows Neighborhood Crazies]. And there were fights every day. Even where we lived, I was about nine or ten and I still remember how about fifty kids came to my house looking for my brother, looking for my brother-in-law.

Liliana—To beat him up?

Olga—To beat him up; my brother-in-law and my dad and his friends were, "Get away from here!" All of that. Like there was a fear and we had to belong to something, because if we didn't, we'd have had a hard time, because people knew us. There were people who knew my brothers and my sisters. And you had to be careful. If they knew we were siblings of somebody at school, they'd just say, "Are you *so-and-so*'s sister?" And we'd say, "Yes," and right from that we'd get it bad. They'd hit us, they'd try to hit us, if we didn't run, okay? But, if . . . it's like I saw myself at a point where I had to make a decision. And even my siblings didn't like the decision, because they had been involved for years in that. I, around the age of twelve, I started hanging out at school with people who were not Sureños, they were Norteños. But they were my friends and I knew the difference, but they were my friends. I didn't consider myself to be like them, but I knew where I came from, I knew where my siblings came from. But when they started seeing that, the signals that I was leaning to the other side, they started to forbid me from having different friendships and not hang out with the same girls with whom I used to hang out. Then at thirteen, my sister started inviting me to go out with her and she was already involved at that point.

Liliana—And how old was she?

Olga—She was like seventeen years old. She'd been hanging out for three years, since fourteen. She had my nephew at sixteen, so I always helped her out with him. She started inviting me to go out, to go to the *varrio*, to smoke, drugs, everything.

Liliana—Were you jumped in?

Olga—No, because my brother started the *varrio*, my sister was loyal, faithful to the *varrio, so it was more like a family thing.*

Liliana—And the others, were they jumped in?

Olga—The others *were jumped. Three people jumped, four people jumped them. Sometimes it was up to eight people jumping a person.* It all depended, and usually they'd do that when they were crazy, *and I mean,* all drugged.

Liliana—And the women, were they jumped in too?

Olga— . . . too. *And I remember* that I, at fourteen, used to say, *"Why don't you guys jump me?"* I wanted that *they would jump me* because *in a way I didn't feel part of the varrio* because *I would say, "Well, everybody's got jumped and not me!" I would say, "I'm not part of the varrio!"* But, *you know like my sisters would say, "You don't need to be jumped, you're in the varrio, I know you're down, everybody knows you're down, you don't need to be jumped."* And within me, *I always had like, "Well, you know, I probably got . . . no, I don't feel like I am . . . I'm down and,* and wherever I go, *you know,"* I would wear blue in school, I would get kicked out, every day they would jump me because the majority were all Norteños, and even so, *with* my attitude here in school, in *eighth grade, ninth grade, tenth grade,* I was seeing that *some guys,* mostly guys, *they started asking me questions regarding the varrio. And they started forming their own varrio, a Sureño varrio.*

Liliana—Your classmates?

Olga— . . . of my class, *and I guess because they did . . .* they saw how . . . *like I was down. I wasn't afraid, I wasn't ashamed and I wasn't gonna wear something or say I'm not because you know . . .* they would come *and they would ask me where I was from, and I wouldn't back down even if they was five of them. You know, and I would tell them. And sometimes it was to the point where they did, they did jump me,* but *I never backed down, so* people started seeing that in school *and they started asking me, telling me, "Well you know, how do you get jumped in,* and this and that," and between them, they started forming *varrios.*

Liliana—But you were very young when you got in, you were twelve years old?

Olga—I was twelve years old, I was twelve years old . . . I was really, since I was like the youngest one, I was like the baby, so I was protected all the time. . . . They would look out for me. Even if there was a fight, they would try to protect me, you know? "Go with Giggles! Go over there, go with Olga, go watch 'Little Giggles.' " I always got that like, "They care for me, 'cause they're looking out for me." So I got that. . . . So they were always taking care of me. You know, looking after me. So, that made me belong. "Okay, I finally found my place."

To say that all stories are unique could amount to a platitude; to say that Olga's is unique requires qualification. Lacking in family structure and support, feeling alienated, and now finding a home in the gang provided a situational trifecta for Olga to join a gang. With such a prologue, her story of inhabiting the gang was foretold.

MARISA

In comparison and contrast to Olga, Marisa's experiences around the gang were remarkable in that she was enlisted at a young age as a drug distributor. Her "good girl" image provided the appropriate cover at school and with law enforcement. Yet, she shared a common story with other gang-involved Latinas: alienation due to a felt lack of belonging, inattentive parents, and unconditional—if only in word and not in deed—acceptance and protection by her fellow gang members. Marisa's relationships with her brother and the people in his gang fulfilled many of her needs despite the fact that some of these were illegal activities. Although she never got jumped, had gang tattoos, or claimed, Marisa was not only impacted but deeply involved in the gang, in terms of her participation in her brother's drug-running enterprise (Fagan, 1993).

Marisa—My parents were married when my brother, Matthew, who was born before me, was three, and I was born three years later. My father, he used drugs most of the time, the first ten years of my life. And that was never really that bad, 'cause I didn't . . . I was too young to understand what was going on, but my brothers took a lot of it, um, and my oldest brother ended up leaving and having his own family, having four kids by the time he was twenty years old, and that was his escape.

My brother Matthew joined gangs, started to sell drugs, stuff like that. After my parents got divorced, it was pretty much just me and Matthew. My brother was selling drugs, my mother was a single mother, working as hard as she could and um, and um, I noticed something was different 'cause he would come home with nice clothes, with nice shoes, and he wanted to take me to Burger King and stuff like that, but he was six years older than me, so I couldn't really understand. When I was ten, my father got pretty much sober and he came back into our lives. By that time, I wasn't doing drugs, but I had already known what was going on as far as the drug scene was, with people coming to the house, calling my brother, going outside, things like that. So, by that age, I was running drugs for him, but the agreement always was I would go to school and bring home good grades. That was the agreement. So I did that off and on for about five years. And then I started to do drugs myself.

Liliana—How old were you?

Marisa—About fifteen.

Liliana—When you say "running drugs," what does that mean?

Marisa—Basically, he sent me to school with a bag, with my backpack, and inside it was like a little lunch box full of whatever. . . .

Liliana—Pot?

Marisa—Crystal meth. I was to go to this . . . he told me who . . . it wasn't like any strangers, it was all people he knew in the area. So after school, I was to go to their house, go inside, give them the lunch box. They would take the lunch box into a room, put the money in there, and then I would come home. That's how I did it, pretty much, until I turned fifteen. Then I learned how to drive and he bought me a car, then I was driving him around pretty much everywhere he went. I never really got into the gang per se. There've been times when I had seen my brother kill people and people shooting at us and things like that. Nothing a girl should see, especially a young girl. It never really scared me, you know? Never really bothered me. I kind of liked it! You know? Everybody . . . it was like an excitement. I felt like I finally belonged.

Liliana—What? So why didn't you feel like you belonged before? What do you think . . . because your dad was not in the picture?

Marisa—Well, no, 'cause when I turned ten, he came back in the picture. He made sure he cleaned up before he came back. I guess being a chubby girl, kids . . . you know? Kids can be mean, yeah, and they were, they were mean. And my brother's friends, like his homegirls, they were always nice to me, taught me how to put on make-up and do stuff with my hair and things like that. I finally felt like I fit in. With my mother working all the time and my oldest brother having his own family, it was just me and my brother. Me and Matthew. He always made me feel special, you know? I was his baby sister, and he taught me everything I know. He taught me how to shoot guns, how to make drugs, sell drugs, things like that, and I liked it. I think what I liked most, what I was most attracted to, was the money.

Liliana—So when you ran the drugs, you started when you were twelve?

Marisa—Ten.

Liliana—So you did it until about fifteen. You were just running them, so you had money to spend?

Marisa—Yeah, he always gave me money. At ten years old, you don't know what to do with money like that.

Liliana—What DID you do?

Marisa—I saved a lot, I saved a lot of it. And one day my mom found the money and, um, I didn't know what to tell her, so I just let her have it. It was better for her to have it 'cause she was always struggling. Me? I didn't have anything really to spend it on, you know? By the time I hit the teenage years, I was more into the buying . . . going shopping, buying pot, smoking weed, drinking . . . things like that. And then I started to do meth. My brother wasn't too happy with that 'cause he never GAVE me drugs, but he allowed me to sell them. And um. . . .

Liliana—So, you, even though you were kind of in it, I mean, you didn't get jumped . . . did you have a gang name?

Marisa—I asked. Yeah, they called me "Mousy" 'cause when I was little I had buck teeth and really squeaky voice and big ears, it was horrible! [Laughs.] But I asked [to be jumped] one time and my brother told me "No!"

Liliana—That you wouldn't be jumped? So you don't have any tattoos?

Marisa—No, I've never even been affiliated. . . .

Not even affiliated, but to law enforcement it matters little that Marisa got good grades. A judge might take that into consideration, as well as her age at the time the crime was committed. Yet, the strength in Marisa's storytelling comes from the idea that gang membership is irrelevant for her and her business-minded brother. Although, on the one hand, the risk factors may predict affiliation, and, on the other hand, drug-dealing enterprises avail themselves of many a worker (Fagan, 1993), these factors alone could never predict a story like Marisa's.

DISCUSSION

As some of these stories make clear, the lack of basic necessities can certainly bring disadvantaged girls and women, especially Latinas, to enter a life of crime. The risk factors mentioned in the first few lines of this chapter allude to predictors for gang entry for youth in general, although samples of females, and especially Latinas, have been quite small to serve any predictive role. Miller's (2006) work does focus on females, although Latinas are again a small percentage. To supplement the extant literature on Latinas in gangs, let the voices of Lupe, Eréndira, Florencia, Margie, Olga, and Marisa function less as samples and more like a network of stories whose similarities provide refrains to keep in mind when we seek to understand what life is like for a young woman who inhabits a gang. Because many of these young women reside in communities that dictate constraining gender roles (Horowitz, 1983), they struggle with issues of race and class (Moore, 1991), and as they confront their marginalization from society due to such issues (Campbell, 1995), these girls desperately lack the economic and emotional resources that would facilitate their inhabiting a different story—one of life outside the gang, despite their being impacted by it.

5

Family Violence

Florencia, Olga, Angela, Gracia, Margie, and Lucha

Violence is such a pervasive phenomenon in the life of gang-impacted and gang-involved women that it bears stressing that it is also little understood (Hunt & Joe-Laidler, 2006). Fights between the parents or other adults living in the home, psychological abuse in the form of threats or taunts, and sexual abuse of girls by someone acquainted with them are all precursors to or co-occurring phenomena with a life in a gang. One may be tempted to assume that girls' membership in gangs is a relatively new phenomenon or that girls' violence has been on the rise in recent years. As gendered notions of violence are of paramount importance, Luke (2008) succinctly argues that

> focusing attention on whether girls' violence is increasing has the potential to detract from the reality that violence, whether or not it is increasing, is a part of girls' lives. More attention needs to be directed to delinking the connections between masculinity and violence and to understanding the meanings that girls and others attach to their use of violence. (p. 47)

Witnessing violence very early and regularly, as well as being the target of violence in the home does little to prevent girls from becoming violent. The stories of Florencia, Olga, Angela, Gracia, Margie, and Lucha illustrate the magnitude of the situation, how they cope, and how they make sense of it in order to transcend the gang.

FLORENCIA

The theme of violence pervaded this woman's story, specifically violence in her family of origin and generally violence in the gang. The latter account is discussed in Chapter 8, "In la Vida Loca." In the vividness of her own words, here are Florencia's recollections of a childhood marked by a variety of violent encounters and chronic situations.

Florencia—My father was an alcoholic, was always very abusive toward my mother. Physically very abusive, hurt her many times in front of my brother and my sister. My mother put herself through school, became a nurse, was very hard-working, tried to provide for us. Even though my father was also hard-working, my mother was the one that financially took care of the family. My brother and my sister are much older than I am. One is thirteen years older and the other is eleven years older, so I kinda came later on.

At that point, my brother was into heroin and was into gangs himself. It was outside San Antonio, a small town called Hondo. My brother, just seeing the violence at home, he wanted out. He left the house and got into drugs, and got into . . . left at fourteen or fifteen, gangs, carrying a gun already. My sister left too, she went a different route than my brother and me. She got into school and she went into the Marines, like the day after she turned eighteen. So it got really kind of lonely growing up, because at this point my brother was gone too, and it was just me. One of the things I remember, my father being an alcoholic and my mother, she was a real hard-working nurse. But on the weekends she would also go out with my dad. So I got dragged around, and I'd go in the bars and fall asleep in the chairs.

But the abuse got really bad. I seen him break beer cans and bottles on her face. I seen where my brother almost shot my dad, but the gun got jammed. He was going to shoot him for hitting my mom. So I saw all of this at a very young age. Also my father would come home and my mother would lock the door, put things in front of the door so he wouldn't come in. Sometimes we would wake up with a shotgun to our heads, because he was really violent and would taunt and laugh at us, "Let's see who I'm going to shoot first." I still remember how big those bullets were—it was a hunting rifle. So he'd load the rifle and put the gun to our heads. Just taunting. There was a day, I remember that . . . because I was so scared, I'd be really scared and didn't know if I was going to live or die. I remember grabbing the gun and slamming it against my forehead, and I'm seven years old. "Just kill me because I don't want to live through this anymore, this is torture!" And shortly after that, my sister came back from the Marines on break and convinced my mother to leave with her. So we kind of snuck away from my dad, basically just two bags of clothes, and moved to California with her. We lived in California for two years with my sister, and then my dad found us and he came to live with us.

In that time, a lot happened, because when my dad came back, the drinking and the party scene came back in. My father brought a lot of men home and there was a lot of molestation that happened in our family, even with my father's side of the family. I remember growing up with a lot of anger, a lot of hate, just seeing a lot of the violence taking place. For me, I can't speak for anybody else, but for me I think that being a young little girl and always feeling timid, always feeling afraid, always feeling like um, basically like anybody could do whatever they wanted to me. I wanted to get to a place where I felt like I had power and I wanted to dominate instead of being always the one dominated and on the bottom, always the one afraid. I wanted someone else to feel the fear that I felt. And at that point, where we were living, there were a lot of gangs in the neighborhood, stayed there until I was nine. It was in Oceanside. Got some exposure but at that time I was still young, but it was more the abuse that was taking place at home that, I guess you could say, had me. It wasn't the streets or gangs or anything like that.

I was molested for a lot of years and nobody ever knew, nobody ever knew the things that happened.

We moved back to Texas and stayed there. It was kind of like a back and forth between my dad. When we moved back to Texas, my mother went back with my father. The next year it was living . . . it was worse. It got to the point where my dad stopped hitting my mom because I remember one time he came home and hit her really hard in the face and she jumped up and went outside and there was an ax because they had been chopping wood. So she grabbed the ax and started chasing him around. I think at that point he realized he couldn't lay hands on her because she was starting to fight back, but there had been years already. So, they, she finally divorced him. She got given the house and the car, you know, these things. But we never stayed at our house. We'd go stay with her friend who worked the graveyard shift at the hospital, because my mom was a nurse and so was her friend. She had three sons, fourteen, sixteen, and seventeen. So I'm nine and I'm staying with them. The youngest one was fourteen, and I was nine years old, about to turn ten. They became I guess you could say like my family. At that point, so he and I had a lot in common, because both our fathers beat our mothers. Both our fathers never supported us or showed us any kind of love or acceptance. Both of our mothers, even though we both viewed them as good mothers, they provided, they worked hard for us, they both used to like to go out on the weekends, go out drink, party, you know. My mother never did drugs, but she did like to go out and drink, dance, have a good time as she saw it. All of this came later on because of all the years of being in this very violent, jealous relationship, she never lived her own life, so at this point, I'm going to live my own life now. Just saw a lot. It just got to a point where, I think just the violence and being afraid of death just went away.

The last time I really feared death was when my dad one time had a big machete and he was putting it through the door; we lived upstairs. This is before we had come back to Texas. And I remember just thinking, "I'm just going to jump out this window, because he's gonna come in here and he's gonna kill us, slaughter us," and I was so afraid. I don't know, that day something just changed in my life, I was no longer afraid of anything. I was not afraid of anybody, I don't care if they were a man or a woman, how old they were, how big they were, I was going to take care of me, and that's all I had, was me. And so, I at that point, even though my mom got a divorce, and all that happened, they went back together again.

When you're seven years old and a rifle is stuck to your head two or three times a week and you think you're going to die, you lose all fear of death. It's almost like death is your friend, death would do you a favor, when you grow up with that. I never thought I would live to be twenty-five years old, if I'd live to be twenty-five.

Sexual abuse at an early age, coupled with the extreme psychological abuse from her birth family, moved Florencia within range of gang involvement. Finding kindred spirits in other youth whose experiences of violent families she shared and unwilling to continue being the victim of "torture" any longer, she authored a story of fearlessness. As François de la Rochefoucauld (1678/2009) wrote, "Neither the sun nor death can be looked at steadily": the possibility of death in Florencia's life turned to fearlessness toward death, which led her to look away from her birth family and facilitated her entry and success in the gang. Her story also gives credence to Cooper, Anaf, and Bowden's (2006) claim that terms such as "domestic violence" are inadequate to capture women's experiences of violence by their kin. Instead, they argue—as Florencia herself suggested—that the term "torture" would be more helpful in addressing the issue from the perspective of human rights. The quotidian nature of this violence, violence between parents and fueled by alcohol, also characterizes Olga's earliest recollections. Olga's use of English is here shown in *italics*.

OLGA

Olga—What I remember, really I don't remember much from when I was young, I just look at the pictures, but since seven years of age, I begin to remember more: Lots of fights, lots of drinking, lots of partying . . . well, like a life really from party to party.

When [my father] came home, he was tired, wanted to relax, friends would come and they would drink outside. Then that was the environment we saw. My mother, when she was home, did cook, but used to go out again, with her girlfriends. Really, there wasn't that much attention. The attention stopped and they separated, they divorced, but they still lived together. It was an environment very . . . how do you say it? Like, nobody was happy then, *it was a real weird place to be. . . .*

Liliana—Not stable?

Olga—Not at all stable. At times, we were between a rock and a hard place: to choose my Ma, to choose Papa, since we all lived in the same house. So, it came to a point where in reality I believe my older siblings, we all decided on different types and styles of life. [. . .] In my house there was nothing stable. My mother was never here, and when she was there was just screaming, fighting. My father really during that time had been . . . he was happy with his vice, the alcohol. Really, there was nothing he cared about.

Liliana—Was there violence, did he hit her?

Olga—There was more violence between my father and mother when they were drunk—when they were intoxicated was when there was violence. And even separated, divorced, living in the same house, it was something so unstable, and at that time we had our other littler brothers and sisters. We wanted to help them up to a point, but we better wanted to wash our hands of anything to do with family and get out of that place and make our own lives. When one is young, one does not think in the consequences. One only thinks, only wants to *numb your pain* and search for something. You don't even know what, but *you want to look for something else.*

Liliana—But you knew that . . . what you had was . . . you didn't want it, it didn't fulfill you. . . .

Olga—No, it didn't fulfill me and it was more despair and an inability that *there's nothing I could do to help the situation* because. . . .

Liliana—Your parents' situation?

Olga—Uh huh, *so pretty much,* between all that, I decided I better look outside.

By "outside," Olga meant the Sureño gang her brother and sister had formed. Although for some youth, escaping a violent and emotionally unfulfilling home might be a pretext for joining a gang, for Olga, joining truly became her strategy for survival. At one point, however, she considered returning home:

Olga—And home wasn't getting any better. At that point, my dad had already moved out with my other sister. He was living with my sister. My mom was living with her boyfriend and my little brothers and sisters. And then her fighting with her boyfriend, you know, it's like the same, nothing had changed from 1974, 19 . . . you know 88, it was still the same. Nothing had changed there with my mom.

Relating the relationship she had with her gang-involved sister, Olga discussed how the sister reacted to the family violence:

Olga—She was a very prideful, prideful, prideful woman. You know, I think out of all of us, she was the most prideful of all. You know and felt she had to be that way, because she felt she had more hurt than anybody else, that she had the right to whatever she was doing.

Liliana—What do you think made her think that way?

Olga—I'm thinking maybe because she was really close at one point with my dad, and I think it really tore her when my mom started dating other people and we were all living around the same house and my dad wouldn't really say anything. If she would be like my dad's voice and start yelling and screaming, fighting, punching, physically, with my mother. So, she endured a lot of that, a lot of like abuse, you know that my mom would tell her a lot of ugly things. Um, so she kinda pretty much was the one that would put up with all the mess. But she didn't stay quiet. A lot of us stayed quiet and wouldn't say anything. But she would be the one that would voice everything, you know, she couldn't quiet her down. So, a lot of anger and a lot of hate toward my mother, my father, for him being quiet, for not speaking up. . . .

Olga's sister might, of course, tell a different story of violence in their birth family, but the experience of emotional strife among their parents nevertheless weaves a common thread in the stories of several women, such as Angela. Because Angela switched between English and Spanish during the interview, I indicate her use of English in *italics*.

ANGELA

Angela—. . . my father, before he had the heart attack, my father was very cold, he was very alcoholic. My mother and my father used to hit each other; it was horrible. It was a horrible thing. Then my mother was a very bitter person. She was not happy.

Once I was by myself at home, I don't know what happened, the neighbor came and reported that I was alone in the house and well . . . I was alone for a long time because they worked a lot, but for me that was normal.

I think I felt very alone. I felt I had no one and I believe that, when I was the victim, *it was more depressing for me.* When I was not the victim,

I *felt that I was more included, more accepted, that I had more support, more friends . . .*

I grew up with them hitting each other all the time. In my memories of my childhood, I have a good, pretty memory: it was my birthday and I had a very pretty red dress and . . . the rest was when they used to hit each other and I would scream. . . .

My mother was very aggressive and my Pa wanted her not to scream too loudly, so they would hit each other in front of me. Once my father got up and she threw the clothes iron at him and he grabbed a wine glass and threw it at her head and I was seven, eight years old, I was little, so that, *if you ask me about my childhood, it's all I can remember. I remember the violence.* There was an emptiness between them too. I don't believe they were happy and they didn't realize there was a girl between them who was left asking, "What is happening here?"

Liliana—What were the fights about? Do you remember?

Angela—My mother had resentment with my grandfather when she was little and was not happy. She was very bitter. In Mexico, there used to be abductions, so they abducted her for real. They threw her in a car, they raped her, got her pregnant and they left her. She lived a very harsh moment. And my father, his ex-wife left him for another man and left him with their four children. When they got together, maybe that was the reason [. . .] very hurt, very bitter. They used to go to church, and my mother would take my father's hand off her shoulder because she didn't want him to touch her. I was about seven years old. Then we'd come home and suddenly they would start throwing things and hurting each other, and I between them screaming for help, because I didn't want to see them fight. *It was really painful.*

My father, his father abandoned him when he was young and his mother was a single parent and it was very hard for her too. I believe they both grew up with a very hard emotional problem and I can tell you I am not, but I went with my counselor last week and I recognized I had a problem. It comes from my childhood and just now I'm getting it out. But at times, it *has lot to do with your childhood, what you grow up with, what you see, what you are exposed to, and sometimes if you're not guided the right direction, you make the wrong choices.*

Angela justifies her parents' outbursts and long-standing animosity toward each other by telling a story of their own sufferings: abduction and rape for her mother, abandonment at an early age for her father. Caught in the midst of their physical and verbal fights, Angela found loneliness, exacerbated by her being an only child. But even for women who had siblings, the violence experienced beyond the home, through

Gangs of Family, also drew them toward gang involvement, as Gracia described.

GRACIA

Gracia—I can remember as far back as when I was four years old when I saw gang violence, gang activities, and gang fights, and it involved my parents. So that's when I first witnessed it, and it had guns involved and a couple of gang names being yelled at, my brother and I were fairly young, peeking through the fences, the cracks in a wooden fence, and so that's when I first experienced it and something very violent.

So by the time I was eleven years old, I had a brother, at the time he was twelve. He was heavily involved in gangs. That was the red and blue, he was involved in one of the biggest Norteño gangs in San José. And he would come home beat up, full of blood, bruises and chain marks on his body, whip marks on his body and you know, really hurt. I remember I was the one that would help him, clean up the blood, or I would help him gather his self together and my mom would be in her room crying and hurt that that happened to her son, but she wasn't really an affectionate woman, she wasn't really loving, into showing this by physical, emotional, or mental ways. We basically had to learn it on our own, and some of us didn't learn it. So I was the one to help my brother with things like that. My mom was there of course, but again, she wasn't too much involved in it because she'd say it was his fault, he shouldn't be doing it, she did try to keep him home, she wouldn't let him leave, she'd try to get him to change his colors, even though she was involved as well, hers wasn't more of the red and blue. Hers was more of the low rider Cholo, Chola style. She did try to encourage us to not be in gangs, but again, that's all we knew, so we thought it was the thing to do, we thought that was going to be our lifestyle as well.

Parental advice against gang involvement alone was not sufficient to keep Gracia and her brother from the lifestyle. Her parents did not succeed perhaps due to their own involvement in gangs. In the Gangs of Family, violence may not necessarily be directed at the youngsters; sometimes exposure to the violence can either normalize it, as it did for Margie, or repel them from the gangs, as it did to Lucha.

MARGIE

Margie—I don't like to talk about my parents because they were never there. My dad, he was in and out of prison. My mom, she was always partying. So I took care of me and my sisters. I'm the oldest of eight, two boys and I took care of all of them 'cause they were always fighting.

LUCHA

Lucha— My dad passed away when I was five. My mother is in and out of prison. She is in gangs, *Nuestra Familia*. That's Mafioso shit. I was raised like that, but I made a choice to leave . . . when I was twelve, because she remarried, she had my . . . she had another baby and she was so caught up into her new family, it's like I wasn't even there, or my older brothers. Being that she was in that gang and what not, she did a lot of things just to get herself into that prison.

So I made the choice that I didn't want that life. I had seen too many things. When I seen my cousin's tongue get cut out by the gangs for saying something he should not have, I decided that was not for me, that just scared the shit out of me.

DISCUSSION

To say violence exists in gangs may seem redundant, for situations of domestic violence are documented to lead adolescents and women to join gangs (Miller, 2006). The aforementioned study that identified "family problems as precipitating circumstances" for joining gangs found that 52% of gang-involved girls had been sexually assaulted, and among these, 66% of those who assaulted the victims were a family member or someone acquainted with their families. Regarding drug abuse, 58% and 56% of the girls in that study reported seeing one or more family members use drugs and alcohol, respectively, in the home on a regular basis. As to witnessing adults engaged in physical violence, 56% of the girls surveyed had experiences with it. Having incarcerated family members accounted for 73% of the respondents. So a young woman might join a gang to escape a violent home life, only to find herself the victim of more brutal violence at the hands of rival gang members and of her homies, especially while being jumped-in (Molidor, 1996). More recently, others (Archer & Grascia, 2006; Hunt & Joe-Laidler, 2006) have called attention to situations of violence in the lives of girls who join gangs. Their pervasive victimization not only forces them to join a gang in order to avoid a violent family life, but also continues as they join the gang.

In a study of Australian women involved in motorcycle ("bikie") gangs, Cooper, Anaf, and Bowden (2006) critique the inadequacy of describing as "domestic" or "intimate" the victimization of such women at the hands of their sexual partners. In asserting that a "major contribution of feminist social action and understandings around sexual violence has been to create new words by which women describe their experiences" (p. 316), these authors propose using the term "torture" to describe the treatment that women endure in and by the gangs. In many cases, so ruthless is the violence that it functions as a silencing force for the victimized women, as in Margie's case. These are post hoc stories of violence, many of which remain untold until after the women have managed to escape the gang and the violence associated with it. So long as the violence is not labeled, addressed, or acknowledged, it might as well not exist, so powerful and oppressive is the silence associated with abuse. But as Florencia, Olga, Angela, Gracia, and, to some extent, Lucha and Margie demonstrate, telling their story implies acknowledging a shamefully brutal past not entirely of their own doing; seeking refuge in a gang, which provided them the illusion of safety; and eventually finding a way to transcend not just the gang but the violence that prompted their involvement in the first place.

6

Tattoos and Identity

Gracia, Florencia, Eréndira, Teresea, Marisa, and Chakira

Gang members embody the warrior mentality—indeed, the warrior reality—by decorating themselves with the well-known accoutrements of their feuding lives: colors, tattoos, bandanas, features such as shaved heads (to keep their hair from being pulled during fistfights), military-issue metal buckled belts (the better to use as weapons during a fight), specific brands and styles of clothing (typically those worn by blue collar workers), and certain ways of wearing such clothing, such as "sagging." The gang lifestyle demands complete submission of mind, body, and soul, and one way to signify one's bodily submission, of course, is through a ritual jumping in; another is through tattoos, which often accompany the jumping in. For example, a new gang member's tattoo might be one dot in the crease of the hand between the thumb and the index finger and three in the other hand, or "XIV" to signify claiming Norte, because "N" is the 14th letter in the alphabet. Upon being jumped in, a Sureña would obtain tattoos depicting "13," "X3," or "XIII" as well as one dot in one hand and three on the other because Sureño gangs are loosely connected to the prison gang Mexican Mafia, and M is the 13th letter in the alphabet. In some cases, tattoos are earned after performing a drive-by shooting or some other gang-related event. Police officers use gang-related tattoos as a way to identify or "validate" gang members because tattoos may signify membership, completing specific—often illegal and criminal—tasks, or remembering dead fellow gang members. As several women interviewed for this book discussed the role of tattoos in their gang experience, they punctuated tattoos differently in their stories. In exploring the relationship between tattooing/piercing and self-esteem among non-Latina at-risk adolescent females, Carroll and Anderson (2002) document that "the greater the number of [tattoos], the more negative feelings toward the body" (p. 635). In this chapter, I highlight the experience of Gracia regarding the role of tattoos in her life story, while Florencia, Eréndira, Teresa, Marissa, and Chakira provide counterpoints.

GRACIA

"Gangs of Family" is a term used by professionals who dedicate themselves to gang prevention and intervention (Poumele, 2007) to describe experience of the gang: When one or more members of one's family, such as Gracia's, is so heavily involved in gangs that the experience is normalized, it is the logical thing to become involved yourself, like going into your family's business. Having a family member in a gang is also one of the top three reasons girls join gangs, with the other two being living in a neighborhood where there is gang presence and experiencing violence in the home, often directed at them in the form of sexual abuse (Miller, 2000). As part of "Gangs of Family," Gracia's experience within the gang was prefigured in her life. In discussing the normality of the Gangs of Family, Gracia brought up the ubiquity of tattoos this way:

Gracia—And my brother continued on in gangs and that's when I realized I wanted to be like my brother, I want to be tough like him, I wanted to be bad, I wanted people to be scared of me, I wanted to fight, I wanted to be a tough girl, that's what I wanted my reputation to be, that's who I wanted to be known as. And I realized that, going to school, I tried to be tough, I tried to be like my brother, people knew of my brother and they knew of my family, and they would see when my dad or my mom would pick me up and they'd go, "Oh, that's your mom? Wow! Look at all those tattoos she's got! Dang! your dad has a big tattoo on his head," 'Cause they were just . . . my dad was just sleeved down [animated, brushes arms with hands from shoulder to wrist], tattoos on his head, on his face, my mom has some on her body too, so I was like "Yeah!" and I would feed into that, was like "Wow!, I'm a tough person, look at my mom and dad, look at my brother, I can really call some shots here, I can really be a well-known person." So that's when I really started liking it even more. And then I got involved in gangs.

To distinguish from getting a tattoo as fad, getting a gang tattoo seemed like a logical step among the several that Gracia took for granted in her descent to inhabit the gang lifestyle. The more enlightening question here is not "Why would she get a tattoo?" but rather, "Why not?"

Liliana—And you had tattoos. . . .

Gracia—I had tattoos all over my body. I had one on my neck, my chest, my arms, my hands—gang-related stuff. And so the more I tried to get out, the more I kept getting pulled back. The more I tried to seek some kind, something different, some kind of positive, the more I kept getting rejected, the more I kept getting turned down, the more I kept getting put down, the more I kept getting labeled and judged. And so, it was really discouraging for me, really discouraging. Because not only did I have to fight my gang, the gang lifestyle, fight trying to get out of it, the homeboys, the homegirls, or the neighborhood. The lifestyle itself, not only did I have to fight that, but I had to fight the world, I had to fight society. I had to fight the community, the people. So here I was in the middle, trying to live a good life, and had nowhere to go. No positive role models, no one to go to, no resources, no services, nothing.

Liliana—And then the markings on your face . . . what were some of the tattoos that you had . . . that were visible?

Gracia—The main ones were on my hands, 'cause these [motions to forearms] I could hide. The ones on my neck I couldn't hide unless I wore turtlenecks.

Liliana—What did they say?

Gracia—It said "Trust no man," and so it was a big old huge tattoo, which people saw me as a Hispanic with tattoos on her neck, "she must be some kind of something," it ain't good if they see me with a tattoo on my neck. And then with my hands, tattoos on my hands were visible.

Liliana—What did you have?

Gracia—I had fourteen here [points to right hand between finger and thumb], I had a rose here, I had "San José" here, "XIV," and then I had a couple—"Norte," "East San José"—on my arm. Then I had a couple of tattoos on my legs. A lot of them were gang related, and roses were my gang symbol, red roses. And so, I had "Junior" here that had a "one-four," so that's where all my tattoos were.

Although gang tattoos carry a powerful currency among gang members by demonstrating one's commitment to the gang, outside the gang, the currency stigmatizes the bearer.

Gracia—Everywhere I went, people looked down at me. They did that throughout all my years, even when I was a teenager, wearing my Ben Davis pants and my little low-rider tank tops that had low-rider designs on them and stuff. I remember all the way back when I was twelve years old and some older lady looked at me and said, "Oh! That is pure trash!" And I, I was so mad. . . .

Liliana—Was she white?

Gracia—Yeah and I was always raised as to respect your elders, be respectful to them, no matter what. And when I seen that lady, I said, "Forget this crap! This woman gets no respect from me!" So I cussed her out and started throwing my gang signs at her [rocks head and neck around in circles], and I said, "You think I'm pure trash! This ain't pure trash!" and I started doing my signs, pulling my fingers, telling her where I was from. Then I even threatened her, and told her me and my buddy were going to hit her up and we were going to take her off [laughs]. That was my very first time experiencing somebody putting me down and belittling me.

Liliana—But you didn't want to, you defended yourself.

Gracia—I defended myself out of anger, and it was out of anger, which was the only way I knew how to threaten her and send my gang signs, or say what my gang was or say what my preferences were, how I wanted to scare her, which was saying rude, cruel, mean things to her.

Liliana—If you don't feel comfortable with the expletives, that's fine, but, what would you say? Could you remember or not use those words, of course it's been a few years back, what were the . . . if you had a transcript of what you would say?

Gracia—Well, I don't curse now, so. . . .

Liliana—That's what I was referring to. . . .

Gracia—I know I probably said, "Puro Norte, it's all about that one-four, East Side" [rocks neck, head side to side]. I would say, ah, ah, "Where you from? Where you live?," and I'd just say, "I'm gonna hit you up, and I'm gonna make sure I go in your house and take everything that belongs to you and I'm gonna rip you dry and . . ." just stuff like that [scrunches up nose].

Liliana—Is that "trash talk" or . . . ?

Gracia—Yeah . . . just basically trying to you know scare her. Let her know how mad she made me, and I said a couple of F-words "and F you!" and "You ain't about S-H-I-T" [giggles]. Yeah, and then I, I think I remember seeing a lot of nice jewelry on her and so I told her, "You better get going before I take your jewelry."

Liliana—What did she do?

Gracia—She started looking at me ah . . . in a really mean, ugly way and then said, "See exactly, just what I said, 'Pure trash!'" [laughs]. So, yeah, and that made me even more so mad, 'cause I think of it that I just proved to her right there and then, not that I was trash, but the choices that I chose by saying the things that I said, were very poorly, but I didn't care, that was the only way I knew how to defend myself.

The concept of "Mean World Syndrome" purports that people who view many hours of television are more likely than others to believe that they could be the target of crime (Gerbner, Gross, Morgan, & Signorielli, 1986). Gangs, of course, consider each other and the police as the enemy, rather than average people, regardless of their viewing habits, unless they (we!) get in their way or provide a convenient source of funds. Gracia's story here is unusual for those reasons, but also because it highlights the deep chasm that exists between the life of an "average person" and the life of a gang member. Her tattoos signified her leadership role, but these held little currency with outsiders to the gang.

In a Canadian study about attitudes toward women with tattoos, Hawkes, Senn, and Thorn (2004) found that both men and women without tattoos held negative views of women with visible tattoos. (See the discussion at the end of this chapter for a brief review of the literature to date on women and non-gang-related tattoos.) Although men and women with tattoos felt that women with tattoos were more powerful, some held negative views of the tattooed women. The authors believe that this may indicate "the tension that exists between the perception of the assertiveness of the statement made by marking one's body and the transgression of the stereotypical feminine role that ensues when a tattoo is visible" (Hawkes et al., 2004). Nonetheless, Gracia felt obligated to defend not only her image vis-à-vis the woman in her story but, more poignantly, her image vis-à-vis the gang. The white woman's put-down of Gracia, prompted by the sight of her gang tattoos, elicited a barrage of insults that did not cohere with the woman's social world: Could she have cared at all that Gracia's gang tattoos were about claiming either Norte or Sur? That she came from the East Side? Could the gang hand-signs that Gracia threw have been intelligible to her? Would the woman have known anything about "Puro Norte"? Thus, Gracia's range of responses was quite limited outside the world of gangs, and because her physical signifiers seemed to command little attention or respect from the woman, she used whatever her verbal arsenal contained to frighten her. In this case, however, her verbal arsenal backfired, for the woman used it to confirm her assessment of Gracia. Outside of the gang story, tattoos not only lack the interpretive force they have in the gang but exact a heavy toll on a person's identity development efforts. Gracia found this out when, as she tried to leave the gang, her tattoos impeded her getting a job.

Liliana—So you transition, you're trying to concentrate and are being rejected. . . .

Gracia—Well, I kept on getting rejected because I had no experience of course, and because of my tattoos. When I first started going, I didn't see a big problem because of my tattoos because that was a part of me, but I was being rejected because of my tattoos, and. . . .

Liliana—But nobody said that to you?

Gracia—No, they would just say I wasn't qualified for the position . . . um . . . most of the time because I wasn't qualified for the position or they weren't hiring anymore.

Liliana—And you'd look in the paper?

Gracia—I'd look in the paper. I don't think I EVER went on the internet, so most of the time, I'd look in the paper, but would go through temporary jobs. And of course I was only seventeen at the time. Then when I turned eighteen, I started looking for temporary jobs. And so, they'd say, "Yeah, we've got a job, come out here!" I think it was through "Mad Power" or some other program, I don't remember. I remember going through it and they said, "Yeah, we're hiring!" and 'cause on the phone I can be a really talented person [laughs] with a lot of potential, but when I met them in person they said, "Oh, um we're, we've filled the position this morning, I'm sorry." And I knew, 'cause everything sounded really good, it was like a for sure thing when I was on the phone, but when I got there, "Oh, no!"

I remember I got this other job, as a receptionist. I started getting really smart, covering my tattoos, I'd wear gloves and I looked foolish 'cause even in summertime I had a turtleneck on, and I'd wear these gloves trying to make myself look really nice and so, if I didn't I'd put a Band-Aid on, I'd make sure I'd walk in like this [puts hands under armpits] or put my hands in my pockets. I got hired on to, for this one job and I stood there for a couple, I don't even remember if it was a month or a little bit longer, but, so I was wearing turtlenecks and I was there in the summertime and was so sick and tired of wearing turtlenecks. I was really, really hot. And I thought, even my mother told me, "You look so foolish wearing those turtlenecks in summertime." And I told her I had to hide my tattoos; I had to hide my tattoos.

So one day I got brave; I did not wear a turtleneck. I wore like a half-long sleeve shirt up to here [points to middle of forearm], so all my tattoos that were visible were showing. The next day, it wasn't even the next day, I think it was, I don't, a couple of days, um, maybe it was the next day? It was either the next day or a couple of days; my boss calls me in my office and tells me that, calls me into her office and tells me that the assignment has ended and they longer needed me anymore, that I'm being laid off. But when I first originally started that job, I was told that there was definitely growth for potential [sic] in their company and I could go a long ways as long as I'm excellent in my performances, my job performances. So I said, "Okay, cool!" 'Cause it had a lot to do with customer service. So I was really happy about that, because I was all for making the money, you know, and getting raises and had a job and was excited about it, and they let me go. They let me go . . . I remember everyone told me that my work was great and that I was really good at what I did, so 'cause I didn't see no reason, I talked to other co-workers. And there was a supervisor that said, she's the one that gave me the idea to think that they fired me because of my tattoos.

Liliana—She stood up for you.

Gracia—Yeah! She told me that they fired me because of my tattoos, or laid me off because of my tattoos. And so, that's where I decided that, "Man, I'm not going to get nowhere with these tattoos!" You know, "I already ruined part of my life and now that I'm trying to get my life going straight, I can't even do that right!" So that's when I came in play with the "Clean Slate Tattoo Removal Program."

Liliana—Well, before we get to that, let's focus on the tattoos themselves. How you . . . how old were you when you first got one, which was the first one you got, [and] why you chose that one. I want to hear the history of the tattoos and then the history of how they ended as well.

Gracia—The first one I got was when I was twelve. When I first started my gang, I got "Norte" and then ESSJ, for "East Side San José," 'cause I was born and raised on the East Side of San José and that's where our gang was. That's the first one that I got, to represent that I was a Norteña and that I lived on the East Side, that's what I claimed. Then I started getting the ones on my hand, this said [points to right hand] fourteen. . . .

Liliana— . . . and fourteen means what?

Gracia—Fourteen means "Norte," that's the number for being a red rag. Then I got "San José" for claiming San José; then I got "XIV" because that's the number fourteen and that's our gang symbol and well, "14," "XIV," "San Jo," and "El Norte" that all represented my gang.

Liliana—You had a red rose?

Gracia—It wasn't red, it was a rose. It never got colored in. But the one on my leg did get colored in red. So then I also had my son's name here that said "Junior" that had the red rose symbol here [points to chest].

Liliana—You could keep those?

Gracia—But I chose to have them removed as well, for the fact that they came up and you could see them. So any type of t-shirt that I wore that had any kind of, I didn't wear really low, low blouses, but it was still part of who I was when I was younger and I just wanted to change everything. And I wanted to change everything and get them all removed, because I had to answer to my children for why I got them and I didn't want to give them that kind of example, that kind of role model. "It's okay to get tattoos 'cause mommy has them." I didn't want that, I don't want them to get them for any kind of reason; I don't care if it's a butterfly. When they turn eighteen, then that's their decision, but I wanted to be a good role model to them so that's why I chose to remove them. Some people who live a similar lifestyle as me, chose to keep their tattoos to show part of who they were and who they are now, and they say, "Why should I remove something that is part of me, that's who I am? People don't like it? Oh, well. . . ." But to me, I don't need to have that kind of personality or that kind of attitude. I know who I was, I know the kind of life that I lived, and I know who I want to be now. Just because I wanted to remove my tattoos doesn't mean I wanted to remove my history or my past. It just meant that I was making a huge change, a big change, and that was part of it. I haven't forgotten who I was or where I came from, I continuously share it, but it's just something that I wanted to do for me. And now that I did it, I felt pretty, I felt really nice. I really like that I don't have all kinds of tattoos. Even when I run into people that I knew from back when, "Oh, where are all your tattoos? What happened?" I get great responses from it. Okay, I like it. I like that people recognize it and they see the changes that I've made, 'cause not only are they hearing it but they've seen it. And I know some people say, "You don't got to prove nothing to nobody!" Yeah, I believe that, but I have a lot to prove to my children. And that's what part of me said, "Okay, removing them is proving a lot to my children, regardless what people say or people think. That's what I chose to do, it's my life, my decision, that's what I chose."

Liliana—So now that you don't have them, you feel pretty, and you, it shows . . . their absence, shows that you've turned a new leaf, that you've made a decision to make a difference in your life. And you're a role model to your children, et cetera. What did they mean to you when you had them?

Gracia—[rocks head side to side] I looked like a hard-core Chola, I was tough, they represent who I was, part of who I was, what I lived for, and what I was down for. If people looked at me, I wanted them to be scared, I wanted them to know what neighborhood I was from, I wanted them to know what I claimed, what I banged, what I was down for, who I was down for. That's what I wanted to show.

Liliana—Without them having to ask? They would just take a look at you and they would know "I mean business"?

Gracia—Yeah.

Liliana—Or to join you, if they were not the enemy. I mean what function they served? They function to warn people to leave you alone, or to jump you, to challenge you? They had this sort of dual function as far as . . . ?

Gracia—Oh, yeah. That's how it was. It basically said it all. Whether who I was from . . . where I was from, what I was down with, and . . . and the kind of people that were drawn to me. Either they were going to be my enemies, or the cops or people that were scared of me because of them. And that's what . . . that's the kind of reputation that my tattoos put out there. And for the fact that, if the enemy was just walking by me or sitting by me, if I wasn't wearing the color red, they'd know, because they'd seen my tattoos. We would fight. That's it. There's probably not even words. There's, we'd start fighting. And people don't realize that. That's how big of an expression tattoos give out there to people. And so, with my tattoos, as I was trying to make the positive changes, I was still being judged, I was still being labeled as either a gang member or a loser, or trash.

The tattoos represented an identity that, as Gracia tried to leave the gang, she came to feel no longer told her story accurately. She was trying to disassociate herself from the gang lifestyle story, which posed challenges not only for her identity development but also for her quitting the gang and for trying to stay clean and out of trouble. Through her church, she met a woman who worked for the City of San José and who knew about and referred her to the tattoo removal program.

Liliana—Were those some of the stepping stones to the new Gracia? So how does that go? She introduces you to the new program; you and your husband start going. . . .

Gracia—The tattoos start getting removed. . . .

Liliana—How long did it take?

Gracia—Mine two . . . I don't know . . . couple of years, I think a couple of years.

Liliana— . . . and then you also had counseling through the program, right? What is the program?

Gracia—The Tattoo Removal Program, basically you had to go, I can't remember if it's Wednesday or Thursday night meetings where they came in and gave us the tools and resources that we needed to stay out of gangs and to hang out with good, positive people, and to kind of make wise decisions and to think before we act out and to learn stories about people who, you know, were in gangs. Police officers would come in and share their stories, about how people have lost their lives, how gang members have taken other people's lives, and how they're in prison. Just kind of sharing a whole bunch of stuff about what we can do to kind of keep going forward and not fall back, and came along with the resources and tools and what agencies we can go to get help, who we can talk to and why it was very important that we were deciding to remove our tattoos, why it was very important to not be in gangs, and uh, what it meant to us, what it meant to us to have people like them on our lives.

Liliana—So, they're presenting you with choices, right? And then you have now a better sense of what choices, I mean through this program. It was, you go through so many meetings, right? You get a certificate afterwards?

Gracia—Yeah, we got a certificate. We went through a ceremony. My husband and I actually got recognized and we were on TV and we didn't even know that, because it was a husband and wife team. And so, they really were impressed by us, for the fact that we came in as these two . . . even when we started with Juan, we gave him a hard time. He was the one who ran the program for Clean Slate, and we gave him a hard time and I was always . . . my husband is like a tough, quiet guy and I'm like a tough, big-mouth person. So I always had something to say to him. Because he was able to stick it out and deal with my . . . you know . . . crap! He just kept pushing us and kept pushing us and kept pushing us, it was so weird because I was like, "Isn't he tired of us? Isn't he tired of me?" Because my husband would tell me, "Be quiet already! You're always picking on him!" [laughs]. I was like, "He's too bossy and he's too mean, he's not going to tell me what to do!" That's how I was. But because I wanted it so much, I learned to um, humble myself, be quiet, not always speak out when not necessary, and to learn to hold things in, whether I liked it or not. You know, there's an appropriate time and place to say things and doesn't . . . if it's not something that I can change, then just leave it alone. If it was something part of my life, then do in an appropriate way and in a positive way to get, make the situation better. So he kind of helped me uh . . . humble myself and not be such a big mouth.

Gracia's disinhabiting the gang lifestyle and the corresponding identity was at first impeded by her tattoos, yet as she found the resources to get them removed, she could reconstruct her identity into that of someone who could renounce the lifestyle in its entirety, tattoos included, and thus articulate a different story. Transcending the gang for Gracia required her to be, like the tattoo removal program's name, a "clean slate." By contrast, Florencia also left the gang lifestyle but chose to keep her tattoos, although she acknowledged the role they play in challenging her identifying storytelling.

FLORENCIA

Florencia—I have a lot of tattoos, everywhere from my forehead down to my feet, and I started at nine years old, got my first tattoo. My friend did a heart on my ankle. It was . . . that was one of my best friends, he's dead now. He shot himself in the head in front of his mom . . . he started slamming . . . shooting up cocaine and heroin. We just said, "Half my heart, half his love." I loved him like a brother, and he loved me and he took care of me. So, he kind of showed me things and how to take care of myself, because I was really alone.

I had all these tattoos before I was fifteen years old. That's a lot of tattoos for a young girl to have. I have "XIV" here, "1-4" here, "Nor Cal" on my [points to body part], "Norteña" here. [Points to another body part] This says "In Memory of 'Rose,'" this is my friend who died. This is the name of the boyfriend that I was with the four years. This is "China y Gata de San Jose," that was my crime partner. This is a cover-up. On my legs, I have four tattoos, my neighborhood, things like that.

Liliana—Did you ever think about getting them removed?

Florencia—I have thought about getting them removed. I'm kind of scared about getting these [points to neck] removed, but I've seen other people's and they look kind of ugly. I want to start with these [points to wrists]. I've been out of that lifestyle for thirteen years.

The Clean Slate Tattoo Removal Program is considered to be the flagship in the San José Mayor's Gang Prevention Task Force for its effectiveness in helping men and women quit and stay out of the gang lifestyle. Because Florencia already had left the gang, the possibility of free tattoo removal, even if she wanted it, might not be available to her. Given her position in her church as the pastor's wife, she chooses not to remove them, for she uses the tattoos as a way to relate to young gang members in order to help them quit the gang lifestyle.

Florencia—When I share my testimony, I always say, this is what I used to be. My tattoos I've had for so many years. I was interviewed by the paper and I said they're like battle scars that remind me who I used to be and make me never want to be that person again. Sometimes I feel like I get judged a lot, when I go places. I don't blame them because I am marked pretty deeply and I look scary sometimes. I've gone to a lot of meetings where they know I'm a pastor's wife and I've felt they look at me and I wonder what chances these kids have, if they know I'm a productive member of society. I'm a married woman, I'm a mother; if I still get that [response to my tattoos], what about some of the kids? When you're involved in this work, it follows you in a good or bad way. I've gone to stores and the security starts following me around. I tell them, "I'm not going to steal anything," and they get like "I understand you feel like you have to follow me," and I'll pull out a church flyer with my husband's picture, and they go, "Oh, but. . . ." No, I understand, really don't judge a book by its cover, but in my case the cover really stands out, so they'll say they're sorry. My son and my daughter at school: when they get a new teacher, I go and explain to them, my husband has a lot of tattoos. When they see us they expect our kids to act a certain way. One time this one teacher goes, "I'm so glad you came to talk to me, because I just couldn't piece the puzzle. I'd see you and your husband all full of tattoos but your kids are so dressed nice and so cordial and so polite, it just doesn't match. I'm so glad you told me." It's good, but sometimes I'll see someone of another race covered in tattoos and it's just a fad [makes quote marks with fingers]. They get all these tribal tattoos, and it's like "Ooo, it's cool." As a Latina, I walk into the same store and I get looked at as a thug, a gang member, like "she's going to steal!" It's sad, but it's true. I've seen it at different schools. I've seen a girl walk with a tube top with all colorful [tattoos], and I walk in and they go, "Ugh!"

This is who I was, what I used to be, but some people who are close-minded think, "Well, this is who you still are." But it's what I use when I get questioned about my tattoos; it's part of my testimony. "This is what I used to be, why can't you be somebody else?" I do have a desire to remove them. I get scared about this one [points to neck], because it's so big and it's going to take a lot to remove. The darker you are, the more it takes. I rather stay with this than have a big old smudge. . . .

Liliana—What about covering them up?

Florencia—I wouldn't do a cover because of my beliefs as a Christian, the tattooing, so would not do anymore. Part of now my morals, my principles as a Christian: I don't smoke, I don't drink, I don't cuss, I don't believe in tattooing. I am a new person, I am a new creation. I cannot dip into any old ways. I cannot afford it because that would open doors that I can't . . . some people say "I smoke and I go to church." Well, I can't, because then I'm gonna wanna smoke something else. I am an extreme person. "Why don't you drink a glass of wine with dinner?" I can't have a glass, because then I'm going to want a forty, and after the forty, I'm going to want a twelve-pack, then I'm going to drink a whole keg, then I'm going to want vodka or tequila. So I stay away from it completely. My husband was a heroin addict for 22 years; he smoked two packs a day. My home: there's no smoking, there's no drinking, even the things that I allow my kids to watch on TV. We're not extreme; we celebrate birthdays and things like that. I don't allow my kids to watch TV. I don't like it, I don't like the music, I don't like what they represent. I try to teach them that this is what I believe, but they're gonna have to make choices in life. I tell my son who's seventeen, "I'm not with you at school all day, I don't know what goes on. I can't tell if you're telling the truth or if you're lying. I'm going to keep pressing on you to be truthful, to be open with me, and you're going to be a man and I can't tell you what to do when you're a man." One time he wanted to get a tattoo and I said no. "Well, you have them, why can't I?" I knew this question was going to come. "You're right, I do have them. I'm stuck with them, it's part of who I used to be, I'm not proud of them, I don't want any more." Because we're a Christian home, I explained what the Bible says about tattoos, and I told them about the consequences.

Florencia's identity as a gang member required performing memory work on her body to chronicle her relationships with men and with other women in the gang. In transcending the gang lifestyle, her identity work has faced a paradox: Although when we met she told a story about no longer being a gang member, she had the tattoos to remind her. Even as she voices a new story of her as a new person, people who are not acquainted with her see the tattoos as evidence of her involvement and may reject or challenge her story of change. If she chose to remove them, not only would she still be differently scarred, but she would lack something to point to as living proof that the gang lifestyle can be abandoned. She has chosen to keep them, although she suffers from having them and cannot cover them up due to her beliefs. Tattoos give her credence in her ministry and testimony to herself of the excesses of her past, warnings to stay away completely from drugs and alcohol. Yet there are other ways of leaving the gang and confronting the marks on one's body that cannot silence the story of gang involvement, as another example of gang tattoos and transcendence comes from Eréndira.

ERÉNDIRA

Eréndira had several tattoos, although she was in the process of getting the visible gang ones on her hand covered up with tattoos with non-gang-related themes, specifically, her "dots" (one on one hand and three on the other hand, signifying "13," her Sureña claim, because the 13th letter in the alphabet is M, which refers to the Mexican Mafia, the prison gang loosely affiliated with Sureños). Because Eréndira and I switched between English and Spanish when we spoke, I signify her use of English with *italics*.

Eréndira—Actually, right before I went in, I got my first tattoo. It was a "13" on my hand; those were the ones I just got covered [points to the rose].

Liliana—Did you know you were going to jail when you got it? I mean, did you get it because you knew you were going to jail? So they'd know?

Eréndira—I got it because I said, "If I'm going to be Sureña, I want everybody to know." I want them to know that *I'm down* and I'm going to do it. I got a one here [points to right wrist] and a three here [points to left wrist]. Where else does it show most, if not on the hands?

The subject of tattoos came up again during the videotaped interview, when she answered a question about whether she would tell her son about her gang experiences.

Liliana—When he grows up, how do you think you'll tell him about it?

Eréndira—I'm going to tell him, I prefer he knows about me, because I have tattoos, one day he'll see them and he'll say, "Oh, mom, this and that, I didn't know." So I want him to know, but I also want him to know that it's not all *bright colors and happy rainbows.* I want him to know what happened to me, so that he may learn from my mistakes. That he learns that *it's not a game.*

Either way, he's going to find out in school, from his friends, do you understand me? I prefer to be the first one to inculcate good things in him, so that one day he won't say, "Oh, well, my mom never told me; if it were bad, she would have told me not to do it," do you understand me?

Although Eréndira's gang-related tattoos are no longer visible, the coverings function as a palimpsest. She knows she cannot hide her story from her son and is determined to be proactive about sharing that information with him, as a warning to stay away from gangs, yet she knows what lies beneath the dainty and ladylike rose tattoo on her hand: a symbol of her past.

MARGIE

As a contrast of someone still in a gang, Margie is unable to articulate a coherent story about her tattoos. Margie and I met at a drop-in center for homeless youth; she was one of the few active gang members I interviewed. She agreed to my taping the interview, although because she said she was wanted by the law in another county for an offense she would not disclose, I had to turn the video camera lens away from her face. Although I was conscious of the fact that one of the methods that police officers use to identify or "validate" gang members is through their tattoos, I asked her if she had any tattoos, whether they were gang-related, and, if so, what they signify.

Margie—I have gang tattoos and at times they're a problem, like if the cops see them. The first one I got was my dots. My 'hood leader did it. Every time you get a tattoo you have to get cleared by the 'hood leader, you just can't do it.

Liliana—So, what did you have to do in order to earn your dots?

Margie—I can't tell you. It's not that I don't want to, it's that I can't.

I did not press any further, although I wanted to see them and hear the story about each one of them. Tattoos tell a person's story, but this story cannot be told to just anyone, anywhere, as Mendoza-Denton (2008) painfully found out when she was summarily dismissed as she tried to coax a gang member to explain the nature of his tattoos. The coherence of a story about a person's tattoos depends on an apt interlocutor; its coordination, on a specific setting. Speaking with Margie, I was neither apt nor in the right setting. Margie gave similar answers to other questions; her current involvement in the gang functioned as a silencing force to such an extent that she was unable to articulate a coherent story of her present or future. Although I believed it was important to learn about her tattoo story, I relented because I wanted to not "reify or replicate the abuse by becoming voyeuristically involved and pushing for more detail about the problem story than the person freely and comfortably gives" (Freedman & Combs, 1996, p. 92).

Another woman I spoke with at the same drop-in center was neither a gang member nor had tattoos, but her mother was a gang member and had them. Teresa's mother used the tattoos as a cautionary tale to steer her daughter away from the crazy life.

TERESA

Teresa, like Gracia, belonged to the "Gangs of Family" and yet somehow claimed that she managed to transcend the gang without ever being part of it herself.

Teresa—My mom's crazy. She has tattoos, the ones she got a long time ago are fading, like her four dots, you can't even see them. She's okay with me having tattoos, because I have two, but they're not gang tattoos. I have Virgo symbol on my arm and I have a marijuana leaf on my shoulder. My mom is okay with it, because she says, "M'ija, as long as they're not gang related or guys' names, I'm okay." I was just looking at her and said, "Yeah,'cause that's where you fucked up." 'Cause she has like two guys' names on her. That's my mom. But she graduated out of high school. My mom did go to college. She didn't drop out. She told me, "If you drop out of high school, I'm going to kick your ass, because I made it and I was gang banging. So there's no excuse for you."

Gang-related tattoos are often done by the gang members themselves, using ink drawn from a broken ballpoint pen and any object sharp enough to break the skin and allow the ink to penetrate, whereas tattoo parlors cost money and, although the laws vary from state to state, generally require proof of adult age and reserve the right to deny service to anyone under the influence. Still, making a living as a tattoo artist or as owner of a tattoo shop is a viable option for someone with an enterprising mind. Marisa had been involved in gangs, acting as a drug runner for her brother, and had been out of the gang for some time when we spoke. She did not have any gang tattoos herself, but the subject came up when we were discussing her education and her future beyond college.

MARISA

Liliana—So, how . . . do you have an idea what you want to study?

Marisa—I think maybe business. I have a cousin that does tattoos, so maybe get my degree in business and open a tattoo shop. I don't know yet. Business is definitely something I'm looking for . . . maybe [I'll study] Communication, I like to talk.

Some girls who are peripherally involved in gangs recognize not just the stigma but the danger of having gang-related tattoos. Fifteen-year-old Chakira discussed how having tattoos affected her brother who claimed Sur. The interview was in Spanish and is translated below. *Italics* denote when she spoke English.

CHAKIRA

Chakira — To each one, if they're in a gang, they have a name, a nickname, and the police find that out quickly. If you have a Cholo tattoo, the police have it written down and it's faster to find you. *That's how easy they can get you because of the tattoo.* They caught my brother because here [points to her forearm] he had our last name tattooed and that's how they grabbed him.

Liliana—He gave himself away . . . but there are a lot of people with tattoos. . . .

Chakira — But I say that if they do something bad and the police catches them, they write down what tattoos you have, things like that, related to *gangs.* There are different tattoos. There are dots: Sureños have three dots, Norteños have four dots. Norteños have stars; the stars mean Norteños. Sureños have letters written of them. The S, W, Westside, Eastside, Southside, Northside, *you know,* things like that.

Even at the age of 15, Chakira was well versed in tattoo taxonomy: Gangs of Family exerted a strong pull on her, for, at the time we spoke, her Sureño brother was in jail for a gang-related attack. She was painfully aware of the risks as well as the consequences: Tattoos signal trouble.

DISCUSSION

Although several recent studies about women and tattoos vary in their focus, and although few if any touch on women in gangs, there has been no comprehensive study to date of tattoos among women in gangs. The extant literature includes a visual history of Western women and tattoos, including Victorian ladies, American suffragettes, and breast cancer survivors, all tattooed in the service of self-expression (Mifflin, 1997), and the history of women in circus sideshows (Osterud, 2009). Although both depict tattoos as body art, neither includes women in gangs. A recent history of counterculture women is also a tribute to tattoos, indeed, to their tattooed bodies as works of art (Webb, 2007). Attitudes toward tattooed women have been explored in the last decade (Braunberger, 2000; Carroll & Anderson, 2002; Hawkes, Senn, & Thorn, 2004). Some focus on career-oriented women with tattoos (Armstrong, 1991), address the process of body modification (Atkinson & Young, 2001), explore the tension between conformity and resistance through negotiation (Atkinson, 2002), and consider reasons for getting tattoos, such as a need for closure (Doherty, 1998). Thus, the subject of tattoos among women in gangs generally, and gang-impacted Latinas and tattoos specifically, remains largely unexplored.

Despite this lack, not only have tattoos gone from the societal margins to the mainstream, but the practice has "been granted a degree of academic legitimacy through recent scholarship" (Kosut, 2006). Although Kosut's focus is on the relationship between tattoos and deviance, this deviance is mostly psychological, not criminal. On the connection between tattoos and crime, DeMello (2000) points out that most tattooists will not tattoo a person's face because these tattoos "are traditionally the mark of a convict. Even without that explicit connection, facial tattoos are extremely stigmatizing in a nontattooed world" (DeMello, 2000, p. 197). She argues that there is such a thing as a tattoo community, glossing over the Chicano style of tattooing without delving more deeply on Chicano/Latino gang tattoos and their corresponding community-building possibilities, but concludes by inviting further study on this and other subjects. Bazan, Harris, and Lorentzen (2002) interviewed both male and female teenagers involved in Salvadoran gangs and addressed the intersection of religion as a driving force to exit and a tattoo removal program in San Francisco.

From this brief review of the literature, I conclude that not all tattoos and tattoo bearers are created equal. Tattoos sported by gang members have not received sufficient academic attention perhaps precisely because this population is doubly marginalized by their gang membership and their body inscriptions. In the case of Latinas, I believe this marginalization triples, regardless of the increased popularity of non-gang-related tattoos in the mainstream, gender notwithstanding.

Although tattoos are common among gang-involved and even gang-impacted Latinas, not all such girls and women have them or choose to remove or cover them after leaving the gang. Tattoos signify experience with La Vida Loca, the gang lifestyle that even some of the women who have transcended the gang view with nostalgia. Girls who are peripherally involved in gangs understand the nomenclature of tattoos and recognize that tattoos are indelible marks on their bodies, their records, and, indeed, their lives. Some of the Sureño tattoos even say "Por Vida"—For Life. While someone is in a gang, tattoos serve as bodily encryptions of her or his toughness, loyalty, relationships, losses, achievements, and risks. The bearers expect others to read them as warnings, visual complements, and, in some cases, supplements to a story lived but seldom allowed to be told to outsiders. Once outside the gang, tattoos can function as oppressive reminders with deep resonance to a renounced lifestyle, sometimes negating the privileged story of transcendence. Removing them may facilitate some women's ability to get and keep a job, which is crucial in staying away from their gang peers. By keeping the tattoos intact, other women use the tattoos as cautionary tales, as evidence and credibility, and as testimony to help some youth leave the gang and prevent others from joining. As the women negotiate their identity vis-à-vis the gang, the significance of tattoos is transformed; they are able to restory their experiences by transforming their self-identity because of and despite the tattoos.

7

Of Colors and Names, or "What Are Colors Good for, Anyway?"

Teresa, Daniela, Elisa, Chakira, Eréndira, Gracia, Marisa, and Florencia

Colors, according to some of the women interviewed, have not always been the primary means to identify or claim a gang. As these women tell it, in the beginning, there were only *varrios*. To this day, many of the street gangs in San José claim loyalty to a specific *varrio* (as gangs tend to spell the word for neighborhood in Spanish, *barrio*) in addition to a given color. This chapter focuses on the significance of colors and related names that women insert into their stories—specifically, what the color stands for before, during, and after gang involvement; what claiming a color invokes for gang members; and the names given to those who claim a color themselves and the names given to them by those who claim another color. The purpose is to draw similarities and differences among colors, names, and insults, as well as to address the process of self-identification used by some of these gang-impacted and gang-involved women.

Poumele (2007) states—and several women who have transcended gangs echo—a story of genesis not only for colors but for gangs in Northern California. In the beginning, so goes the story, the State of California prison industrial complex grouped the inmates into work groups depending on where they came from. Prisoners from the north got a red bandana to wipe the sweat off their brows, and those from the south got a blue bandana. The northerners were mostly second-generation Mexican Americans from the rural areas, calling themselves "Farmeros," whereas the southerners were mostly immigrants who spoke little or no English. The northerners formed the Nuestra Familia prison gang, and the southerners formed the Mexican Mafia. The color affiliations were thus inadvertently created by the same government that now works assiduously to eliminate their deleterious effects.

This account coincides with what Mendoza-Denton (2008) writes about the confluence of the Nuestra Familia gangs, the Chicano Rights Movement, and the prisoner self-help movement. Due to increasing incarceration rates for Mexicans and Mexican Americans in California, prison authorities chose, unthinkingly, to segregate inmates by their region of provenance in California (North/South, rural/urban), which solidified the territorial and ideological chasm between the existing Mexican Mafia prison gang (formed in 1958 and now a symbolic inspiration to Sureños) and the emerging Nuestra Familia (formed in 1967 and the forebears of the Norteños). Nuestra Familia, according to Mendoza-Denton, has always had a social activist strain, in that they attempt to educate prison members in a style of liberation through resistance similar to that of Malcom X and Mumia Abu Jamal. In 2010 in San José, Norteños outnumbered Sureños four to one, in both membership as well as crimes (Rodriguez & Rosengren, personal communication, July 1, 2008).

But what relationship is there, if any, between prison gangs and street gangs? In Chapter 9, "Time Served!," some of the women speak about the perceived prestige that men who have been incarcerated acquire once they return to their street gangs and how those high up in the hierarchy often call the shots from prison through an intricate system of communication. This project does not have the breadth and depth to include such discussions, which pertain mostly to men. Yet gang colors and their attendant meanings provide a powerful identifying mechanism that gang-impacted women use to construct notions of self and other.

The women who spoke about colors had strong feelings about them regardless of their status in, out, or around the gang. They are Teresa, Daniela, Elisa, Chakira, Eréndira, Gracia, Marisa, and Florencia. The discussion will focus on colors and names according to the gang-impacted, for whom colors and related names represent the inescapability of identifying with one or the other (Teresa), an insult that must be avenged (Daniela), the impossibility of claiming neutrality when wearing a gang color (Elisa), or being related to a hard-core gang member (Chakira).

TERESA

Teresa seemed quite willing to express her knowledge about gang history and legend. Her story is unusual in that her extensive knowledge coincides with both lore and documented research, yet she seems sufficiently critical of color-inspired violence that she speaks about the challenges she faces in sidestepping the entire color-coding system.

Teresa—. . . and California was the birthplace of the colors. Like there's a debate saying that Blacks started the colors. What actually happened, it happened in the Pen, and it happened to be both races at the same time. Black people say "Mexicans started the colors." No, it's just the fact that each one started at the same time.

In discussing her own views, Teresa first talked about gang colors almost as though they were an aesthetic choice:

Teresa—I was kind of discouraged from the gangs, not really. . . . My mom, she really didn't want me to be in a gang, but she taught me about them. It's funny now because she's trying to be better with her life and she's in Modesto, you know she doesn't put up with it anymore. But it's so funny, because when I was young, she'd be in the kitchen looking at the "Scrap" walking down the street, "Fucking Scrap!" I'm like, "Fuck!" Sometimes I don't care, I've got into fights, not into gang fights, but I've got into fights. I've always been my own person, done my own thing, I've always been about what benefits me and the people around me. I think it's fucking retarded to jump someone because of a fucking color. Dude, I'm wearing blue right now, I have to, for my work. I honestly don't like the color blue, and that's just because, like different shades. I don't like pink, I don't like yellow, I don't like orange, unless it's with black, I don't like certain, I love green, green is one of my favorite colors. But there's certain shades of green I don't like, just like there's certain shades of blue I don't like, like I don't like this color, it's too dark. I just have to wear it. I like that color blue [points to my jacket] because it's more like an ocean color. And it's funny too because I like the color red, I like it, I wear a lot of red, I think it's just a beautiful color, I like to wear a lot of it. So, I get people telling me "Norte, Norte!" "Bitch, I don't claim!" People don't really fuck with me because I don't give them an opportunity. You have to get hellah opportunity. I've got people saying "What? You're a Norteña?" because I do wear a lot of red, I have a lot of red clothes, but I don't bang. Like what some little girl told me the other day, "So, you bang?" and I was like "Is it fucking like . . . racial profiling? Just because I'm Mexican and I'm wearing red, I automatically have to gang bang? Are you serious? That's racial profiling on your own race! What is your problem?"

The verbal somersaults Teresa performed about gang-related colors work in the interest of a story of self outside the gangs. Prominent elements of this story include the challenges she faces for liking to wear a gang-associated color, such as red, and having to wear blue for work, a color that normally would provoke a fight, although she does not "bang" Norte. Because her mother cautioned her—apparently successfully—to avoid the gang lifestyle, her mother's rants against blue-wearing Sureños served to strengthen the force of Teresa's story of self as individual. Although she asserted that she sees beyond color, she used a derogatory term for Sureños in critiquing her mother's hatred of them: "Scrap."

In discussing colors, Daniela expanded on the usage of this denigrating term, her attitude about it, and the term used by Sureños to disparage Norteños.

DANIELA

Although Daniela knew I would ask her about gangs, neither she nor I had brought up the topic directly. She eased into it by talking about whether she has ever been sent to the principal's office.

Daniela—I've been sent there, well not from classes, like from teachers, but I've been sent there for fighting. . . .

Liliana—What was the fight about?

Daniela—You know . . . like . . . gangs? They called me a name I didn't like and I just started fighting and I got sent to the principal.

Liliana—And they called you a name?

Daniela—Uh huh.

Daniela described her injuries and the injuries of her opponent and shared that they both were suspended for 5 days. I was curious as to why she did not explain what the word was or the name she was called, so I asked her.

Liliana—You remember what the name was that she called you?

Daniela—Yeah, 'cause it's not a name that she just says, but that a lot of people say it.

Liliana—What was that name?

Daniela—You know like the gangs are Norteños and Sureños? Norteños calls Sureños "Scraps," and Sureños call Norteños "Busters."

Liliana—You didn't like to be called the name. . . .

Daniela—The name that she called me, I kick it with . . . well I kick it only with Sureños. I don't talk to Norteños. If I were to pick a color, I'd pick the Sureños. Yeah, I kick it with them and she called me a "Scrap" . . . and I got mad.

Liliana—So she's Norteña?

Daniela—So she called me a "Scrap" and I got mad and like yeah, we started fighting.

Although 14-year-old Daniela was born in the United States, her association with Sureños makes her a "Scrap," which she deemed insulting enough to engage in a violent response. She was careful not to specify whether she is in a gang, but that she "kicks it with them." I was intrigued by her equating color with gang and with her use of the conditional tense when saying, "If I were to pick a color, I'd pick Sureños." So I asked:

Liliana—So, you said that if you were to pick a color, you'd pick Sureños; what is it about it that you find . . . that you'd want to be a Sureña?

Daniela—I don't know . . . first, I don't like the color red. I've even like kicked it with Norteños. . . . I remember like since I was small, before I knew about all of this, gang stuff, I didn't like the color.

Liliana—So, when you see somebody in red, I wear red, or somebody who doesn't know about the color, what does that bring up for you?

Daniela—If it's like young people wearing red around here, well they know they shouldn't be wearing red around here, but like older people, I wouldn't care.

By "around here," Daniela refers to the community center she attended, which is considered a Sureño hang out. Although as neutrals, the staff members at community centers take decisive steps to prohibit attendees from donning garments of one color or another, it is common knowledge that many of these centers are frequented by one gang or the other. To come to a center wearing the wrong color provokes a fight, so all centers state clearly their strict policies prohibiting certain types of clothing, colors, styles, hats, and, of course, bandanas. Daniela's story begins to illustrate the process by which young people not just join gangs but join a particular gang or side, especially because she volunteers the fact that she had "kicked it with" Norteños at one point.

Now that Daniela's friends "back up" blue, she considers any insult to them the same as an insult to herself, thus the compulsion to fight when she was called a "Scrap." More interestingly, what is the process by which young people determine each other's membership in gangs?

Liliana—If they're wearing your color, the color you'd pick, do you try to figure out if they're wearing it because that was what they had in the closet or if it's a choice that they made . . . does that happen sometimes?

Daniela—I guess that happens sometimes, but I guess if they're wearing like the color that I'd prefer, I wouldn't do anything. . . .

Liliana—Do you see them and you think that you could kick it with them or . . . what other ways do you have of knowing who they are? Who your friends are? Who you can kick it with?

Daniela—I don't know like, maybe they talk to me. Around this neighborhood, I know almost everybody.

Liliana—So, the lines are pretty much. . . . Is there anybody who kicks it with both? Who kicks it with neither? How would you know?

Daniela—I don't know.

Liliana—Is there a choice? Are there people who don't . . . ?

Daniela—Yeah, there's people who like, they prefer not to do gang things. It's their choice, I mean.

Here Daniela seems to imply that membership in one gang or the other is determined by one's fashion choices; in other words, it is just about liking one color or another. Fashion in the gang, of course, runs the gamut from colors to specific ways of wearing clothing, the length of one's hair (shaved heads for men, the longer the better for women), to make-up (Mendoza-Denton, 2008). Just as none of us can get dressed and be neutral about issues such as gender and social class, so the gang-impacted woman cannot take the choice of colors lightly, as Elisa painfully discovered.

ELISA

Gang impact does not always lead to gang involvement. One woman's defining moment for entry into a gang might become another woman's galvanizing event away from and even against the gang. Elisa was a young woman who facilitated a youth group at a community center whose programs focused on providing alternatives to the gang lifestyle.

We were discussing the subject of choosing sides when the subject of colors came up.

Elisa—No matter what, even if you're not involved. Like me, I decided to come to this center, and it's like . . . just by coming to this center, I decided to come to the Sureño side, and I wasn't a Sureño. You know what I mean?

Liliana—Would you say that you are Sureña now?

Elisa—No. But when I was a youth, I was portrayed as being . . . if not a Sureña, a "paisa" . . . which . . . it doesn't matter . . . [hesitates, then continues] is like a Mexican. And even if you're "nothing" and you . . . say I want to bring a red sweater, like for example there was this instance, I live like two blocks away, so I would come walking, and one time I said, "Well, I'm going to wear a red shirt, with a red sweater." And I just thought, "Well, I'm going to look cute, I'm going to come." So I came walking two blocks away and I played, everyone was cool. When I walked out the Center, they were waiting for me and they were telling me, "If you don't take that off, you're not passing by." So I told them, "Well, I'm not going to take off my shirt, I'm not going to take off my sweater, so, I'm 'nothing,' just let me go by, I'm not a Norteña, I'm not a Sureña, I'm just a soccer player." But they just wouldn't let me go. There was like five girls there and I can tell you this because I'm in school, I was so good, so like it happened to me, imagine all these girls that are coming here, that are hanging with the Sureños, you know what I mean? And it was like, they wouldn't let me go and I was there for like forty minutes [gets teary eyed, voice breaks]. They were determined to not let me go unless I took off my shirt. So that's how deep it is, that you, even if a person like goes to school, and is involved in all these things, in some way is involved in it. So like every time after that, this kid came and saved me and took me home, it's like, I never wore red again, in this community. Not blue, nor red, none of those two. So that's how deep it is. That you can't even wear a certain color because even if you're not, it's like they were telling me, if you're coming to the center, you're not allowed to wear red. Like you can walk . . . in some ways, all the people that live in this community, are in some way related, or affected by it, impacted. . . .

Liliana—It is interesting because it could be just a fashion choice, but your choices of color are not free. In some ways, what you can wear out in the streets if it's a blue street, they refer to Sureño, Norteña.

Elisa—Yeah, like this Center is Sureño, you can walk around the center wearing blue. But if you walk two blocks that way, and someone sees you with a blue shirt, they would still go up to you and ask you why you're wearing that color. So the colors are not, it's not your choice, it's not like you just can wear them.

Liliana—So, if you want to be left alone. . . .

Elisa—Yeah, if you don't want to mess with them, you just don't wear them.

The word Elisa used to characterize herself as neutral is "nothing." Yet by wearing a garment, the color of which was already prefigured in gang nomenclature, she became a target. She claimed neither side in this rivalry, to no avail. Her seemingly innocent wardrobe choice carried symbolic implications that she could not disavow. The harassment she endured would have been sufficient encouragement for her to identify with the Norteños in order to seek revenge against her aggressors, yet she had her own story: The membership in her school's soccer team inscribed her into a community in which she was able to avoid becoming enmeshed into the Norte–Sur dichotomy and thus transcended the gang.

Some of the other girls from the community centers recognized that colors are a poor excuse for fights. Colors can become indistinguishable from neighborhoods or *varrios*, and in this way a young woman on any one given street has little choice but to support the color sported by her neighbors. On this topic, Chakira gave an eloquent critique of gang colors, from the perspective of a 14-year-old sister of a "validated" and incarcerated Sureño. Chakira's and my use of English is here indicated with *italics*.

CHAKIRA

Liliana—So, when you were a little kid, when you first noticed that there was something called "gangs"? What is your most . . . earliest memory of gangs?

Chakira—Seven years, when my brother started doing the same. My big brother, he rooted for the blue. He started doing that. I knew them and there were some whom I spoke to, since I was seven.

Liliana—When you say he rooted for the blue, what does that mean, that he cheered for the blue? The blue are the Sureños, right?

Chakira—Sureños. A color . . . that they root for their *varrio*, for their own *varrio*. They hate the Norteños even though. . . . I don't know why they fight for a color, when, if at the end they all end up dead! What are colors good for anyway?

Liliana—What do you think is attractive to him, or to all the other people?

Chakira —Well, for example, my brother, I think the friends just told him, "Get in here, it's a *varrio*, it's a color, we have to fight, it's because . . . how do you say . . . of our Raza that we have to do this." There are some who get into it just because. Others not, they care about their *varrio*, they care about the color. There are some who just get in, just like that.

Liliana—Are they all Latinos?

Chakira —Yes, there are a lot of Latinos into that.

Liliana—I mean the reds. . . .

Chakira —Norteños are almost all gringos, but not the Sureños. Sureños are black . . . everything [. . .] Sureños are all about fights, look after their *varrio*. Like here, it's like a *varrio* too [circles her hand with her index finger, referring to the community center]. It's part of the Sureños too. They have to look after here and fight if they see a Norteño, who is wearing red or looks like he roots for the red, well, they fight against them to defend their . . . their *varrio*.

Color and *varrio* conflate in this story of difference between Sur and Norte, where race and ethnicity matter, yet country of origin matters even more. In saying that most Norteños are "gringos," Chakira uses this term, which is typically reserved for whites, to refer to U.S.-born Mexicans or Latinos. (A derogatory term for second- or third-generation Mexican Americans is "Pocho," yet she didn't use it to refer to Norteños.)

Liliana—And you, for example, at school. What effect does it have on your school, the presence of gangs? In your classes?

Chakira —Well, there are mostly Sureños. I don't really speak to the Norteños. Not because of the color, but, just because, well I've lived more with Sureños; I also speak with Norteños, but not as much as with Sureños.

Liliana—Are you considered a Sureña?

Chakira —They don't consider me nothing. I'm nothing.

Liliana—So, if they ask you, how do they ask them if they're in a gang?

Chakira —"Do you back it up? Do you bang?"

Liliana—"Do you bank?" What is that?

Chakira —BANG. Yes, if they asked me, well, obviously I would say no, but if I must root for some color, if they asked me "Why are you using that color?" then, well, although I'm nothing, I like the blue. Well, yes, that's all. Although there are people who consider me . . . well, because of my brother, but that doesn't mean anything, because I am nothing.

As the 14-year-old little sister of a validated Sureño, Chakira is in a bind: She assures me she is nothing, yet if she must claim allegiance to any side, it would have to be the blue. The "Gangs of Family" ties exert such a strong pull on that presumed affiliation that, wherever she goes, she's assumed to claim Sur, to back up the blue. Yet she also seems to conceptualize the gang as a multifaceted entity: The Center is a gang of sorts, as are the dancing groups her big brother has shifted toward. They have names, enemies whom they harass, territory to defend, and places to perform the actions—such as dancing or fighting—germane to the group.

So far, these explanations about the significance and function of color give the perspective of the gang-impacted young women. How does color figure in the story of the gang-involved woman? In their stories of transcendence, colors take on a different meaning. The women in the following section all left the gang and decry the brutality of color-inspired assumptions (Eréndira), regret having invested so much of their lives on something now so unrewarding (Gracia), feel disdain for the color-clad youth of today (Marisa), or interrogate the avowed neutrality of someone wearing a given color (Florencia).

ERÉNDIRA

In talking about the rivalry between Norte and Sur, Eréndira told a story about color and names. In it, she illustrated the dire consequences of making assumptions based on clothing color. For those dressed inappropriately for a given *varrio*, these assumptions could have lethal consequences. Switching back and forth between English and Spanish was a frequent occurrence while Eréndira and I spoke. *Italics* show English usage here.

Eréndira—If it's about neighborhoods, Sureños just try not to be at the same place. Whether they want to or not, they always try to avoid problems. They call it *buster hunting* or *scrap hunting.* . . .

Liliana—If someone dresses in a neutral way, do they leave them alone?

Eréndira—Sometimes just for wearing something red or blue, they get jumped or hit. It's not anymore "Where you from?" Now it's about "*You can't wear this, you can't wear that.*" It's just stupidity, something *so silly that you can't even wear blue, you can't even wear red, 'cause you're already something.* You can't wear red or *if you feel like wearing blue,* because then, if you wear both, like you balance it out. If you're wearing one, *you're that.* If you're on the street with pants down to here [points to her hips], shoes, all Cholo, then it's obvious what they're going to think, but if you have a tie, what are they going to think? [. . .] Once, they were jumping a boy who only had something red and he was saying, "I don't bang! I don't bang!" but they kept hitting him. I told them, "He's saying that he doesn't bang, leave him alone!"

Beyond not being able to walk down the street in other neighborhoods alone, not to mention being interrogated about one's origins or loyalties, lies the issue of identifying fellow pedestrians as "one of us" or an "other." This is the process of elimination, discrimination, or incrimination that gang-impacted youth must engage in, unable to simply stroll down the street, ever-conscious of the decision to wear a particular color, the need to find someone so as to not walk alone, or the obligation felt to acknowledge—or, worse, defend—a particular neighborhood.

GRACIA

After discussing the significance of protecting neighborhood prior to color allegiance, Gracia described her own ritual for displaying her color loyalties and her current beliefs about wearing red or blue.

Gracia—You know, it wasn't really over colors, at that time, it was territory, it was more like neighborhoods and them crossing into each other's territories that they would fight over. It was more over territory than neighborhood, the streets they lived on, that's what they would claim, so it wasn't so much of colors.

Liliana—During your talk you mentioned that you had this ritual, I don't know if you used those words. You mentioned that when you left the house you always had four paños that you would sort of decorate yourself with. . . .

Gracia—I started on with that when I was twelve years old because that's how my brother was. He had a red *paño* over his forehead, he had one thrown over his shoulder, one in his back pocket and one wrapped around his fist.

Liliana—His right fist?

Gracia—And it was his . . . I think it was his right fist because he's left-handed. His right fist he wasn't going to use, but his left one he had to make his knuckles visible, to hurt. Because if he hadn't . . . if he would hit, it was something he did, he didn't put them on both hands because he had to make sure he kept one of them because if he was going to hit someone, that it was going to hurt because of his knuckles. And that's what he used to do. And for a while I just carried a *paño* in my back pocket or something. Then I got into a car accident that gave me a huge scar, a gash right on my forehead, so what happened was I started wearing one on my forehead to cover my scar and then it turned into one in my back pocket, because I used to wear Ben Davis pants really baggy, so I would hang one all the way down. And I would wrap one on my fist just like my brother. Most of the time it wasn't wrapped around my fist because I had a really little hand and it was like really big on my hand and sometimes it looked funny, but if I wore sweaters or jackets, then I'd have it over my hand to kind of keep my hands warm. So, it was, the majority of the time it was all four of them, but I mainly had one on my forehead.

Liliana—And you went to school like that?

Gracia—No, you can't go to school like that. So, at school I wouldn't wear them like that, but as soon as I walked out of school, I took them out of my backpack or my back pocket and I'd wear them like that and that's how we left school.

Liliana—And your homegirls . . . ?

Gracia—All of them had theirs too. All of them had theirs hanging out from their back pocket. My Samoan friend always had hers on her fist. She was the one that always wrapped hers on her fist. She had really big hands. She would wear hers, I think I still have a picture of her; she would wear hers on her forehead. But we always had red on, always had red or burgundy on. And you'd never see us wear blue. Even it took me a lot of years before I could wear blue.

Liliana—Do you wear blue now?

Gracia—Yes, I won't wear it . . . and . . . forgive me but I still will not wear a solid blue t-shirt. And it's not because I'm gang related, it's because I never wore it that I just don't. I mean I wear blue jeans. I still won't wear a blue rubber band wrapped around my hair, like some girls wear a blue rubber band. I always have black or white, but I won't wear a blue one. So people tell me "You're still involved in that" and I say, "No, I just don't own anything blue and it's not appealing to me." But I won't wear all solid red either. And the reason I won't wear all solid red is because if someone sees me wearing all solid red, they will quickly be . . . be quick to judge me as a gang member. Because I'm Hispanic, I have long hair, and because I look like somebody who possibly has a history of being gang related. If I'm wearing red, that's probably the first thing they're going to think [shrugs her shoulders].

Mindful that color carries heavy connotations as she left the gang, Gracia appropriates this usage to describe the event that endangered her children and that led her to question her loyalty to a color:

Gracia—Dying for the color red was not worth anything, anything for no one, and that's when I said, "Am I willing to lose one of my kids over this color? Red is not going to get me food on my table, food in my stomach, my children's stomach, clothes on their backs, diapers." Red wasn't going to pay my rent, you know, the color red wasn't going to get me a job and get me, you know, living the right life, and I kept thinking about, "All because I want to gang bang and claim the color red. Look at me now, look at the situation I'm in now." And so, that's where I really made up my mind. "Was it really worth it? Was being in gangs really worth it?" I wasn't, you know, getting any younger, I was getting older, I had two children, is this the kind of life I really wanted to live?

Although Gracia has transcended the gang, the signifiers of being gang-affiliated remain deeply ensconced in her habits, patterns, and practices. Simple wardrobe choices do not come without consequences for any gang-impacted Latina: They do not choose their clothing and accessories idly. Gracia began the process of giving up the gang life-style when she realized the irrationality of entrusting her future and of endangering her own children due to her loyalty to a color.

MARISA

For others, leaving the gang means leaving the entire lifestyle behind, including the previously meaningful events and objects, through a

reconfiguration of meaning, a devaluing of standards, and a restorying of plot lines. As Marisa explained, transcending the gang implies
believing that loyalty to color is absurd.

Liliana—Do you ever wear colors?

Marisa—Not anymore! I'm too old for it. The way they've got all
these youngsters coming up, they don't know any better. They don't
have anyone teaching them, telling them to go to school the way I did,
and things like that. So, the game is all messed and I don't got. . . . I
don't have time for it. And I don't want my daughter to see any of that.

Liliana—So, you see them and it doesn't make you proud, it
doesn't make you angry, when you see red, or blue?

Marisa—They kind of make me laugh [laughs] because they're
foolish! They really are. I just want to kick them in the ass and tell
them to go home, you know, go to school, do something, you know,
brush your hair! I don't really care. Half the time, I don't really notice it.

The gang, in Marisa's story, is now virtually nonexistent. Colors
have no emotional pull for her; on the contrary, she feels ridicule and
scorn for those caught up now in the tendrils of the gang. Protecting
her daughter from its influence has becomes her priority, as it is for
Florencia, who wants to protect her son from seduction by the gang
habits.

FLORENCIA

The children of former gang members exist in a category by themselves. Were it not for their parents' departure from the gang, they
could be statistically and culturally expected to join a gang. As it is,
the former gang-involved mother must strive to keep her children away
from inhabiting the lifestyle (more on this is discussed in Chapter 10
"Mother'hood"). Florencia's efforts include supervising her 16-year-old
son's wardrobe to ensure that he avoids inadvertently claiming one side
or the other and also to not be a target at school or in the streets.

Florencia—I don't let him wear red or blue. He had a Stanford sweatshirt
on and he wanted to wear it, he had already ironed it. I told him, "You're
not wearing that!" and he goes, "Why?" I told him, "You know why." He got
mad. I don't want him wearing red because some of the kids in school will
think, "Oh, he's a Norteño now," and they'll mess with him. The other day

his friend came over, his friend is not in gangs but all his cousins are Sureños, so he's like, "Mom! It's hard because you get caught in the middle." At home, I don't have a problem with whatever he's wearing, but for school, I have to be careful because they'll think he's a Norteño or Sureño and he gets hit up. So he feels punked. "I'm getting punked and I'm going to do something about it, defend myself." So he feels like man, I need to do something. He goes, "I don't have nobody, Mom, I don't have nobody to back me up." I tell him, "You shouldn't be thinking like that," but that's the way he's thinking because he thinks he needs to defend himself. That's the mentality. Middle school is the most dangerous place right now.

Because Sureños prefer blue articles of clothing such as sweatshirts and baseball caps with an "S" on them, like those worn by fans of the San Jose Sharks hockey team, and Norteños favor red articles of clothing with an "N" on them, such as the University Nebraska logo, the Stanford shirt would have been neutral or rather ambivalent, in that it blended the two: a red "S." Regardless, Florencia was taking no chances in keeping her son insulated from the gang. The boy invoked a common justification for gang involvement: To ensure protection from my enemies, I must find the enemies of my enemies and join them. Florencia rejected this claim and encouraged him to author a different story, one in which "protection" from being harassed or "being punked" are not priorities, and the enormous pull of colors is interrupted by avoiding wearing either blue or red. There is much more to Florencia's views on color (presented in Chapter 8, "In la Vida Loca") that elucidates her own former convictions about and defense of the color red, the craziness of engaging in that belief system, and the lengths to which she risked her life for it.

DISCUSSION

It may be the case that two or more *varrios* in San José that "back up" the same color will fight among themselves. For the purposes of this project, however, the data do not suffice to substantiate such a claim, so the examples here focus on the aggression between Norteñas who favor red and Sureñas who favor blue. In the blue-red coding system of most California Latino gangs, some articles of clothing are neutral, such as blue jeans. The hues that Sureñas favor to indicate their claim runs more toward the printer's cyan, aquamarine, and teal, and not exclusively or necessarily navy blue. Norteñas don red or burgundy, and therefore make a more pronounced statement as to their affiliation.

Law enforcement statistics in San José, California indicate that there are four Norteño gang members per one Sureño gang member, making the red almost unnecessary. Because of the ubiquity of blue clothing, Sureños can either blend in unnoticed, or they need to make an effort to signify their gang involvement through specific articles of clothing or the way they wear those items. In some gang-impacted schools in San José, security personnel prohibit students from bringing red or blue notebooks, backpacks, and pens to school, and from wearing red or blue sweatshirts, hair ties or hairbands, nail polish, and even the miniature rubber bands on braces or other orthodontic appliances.

Certainly wearing colors out of school provokes fights, as does calling someone a name; if the girl who is the object of the verbal attack is wearing red or blue, the name-calling implies that if she is "down," she must either "back it up" by fighting or "get punked" by disassociating herself with the color, and thus with the gang. Besag (2006) points out that, among girls, name-calling is one of the most common categories of insult. The power of name-calling can be underestimated until we are the subject of such an act: "As with other terms of abuse, the potency of name calling lies in the manner in which the name is spoken and received" (Besag, 2006, p. 124). If a recently arrived Mexican, regardless of whether she "backs up" or "claims" blue, is addressed by a Norteña as "Scrap," is it reasonable to suppose that she possesses the cultural resources to interpret this as an insult? Names are necessary to establish our uniqueness and our identity, as well as to signify belonging in a myriad of groups. Whether they are avowed or ascribed, names must be agreeable to the one being labeled.

A (nick)name one gives oneself can be used by others to single one out, but it seldom is chosen by the perpetrators of name-calling unless in mocking. Conversely, a derogatory name that others have given the members of a group can be appropriated by that group in order to disarm the insult, as in the use of the word "niggah" by some Blacks to signify their brotherhood, and of the word "queer" by some homosexuals, in an appropriation that has political ends. However, using a derogatory name for a person who appears to be in the same category as the person issuing the insult can also be a "mode of transferring the repressed, unacceptable aspects of our personality onto vulnerable others who display the same or similar characteristics" (Besag, 2006, p. 124). Furthermore, as the insult is uttered, the person becomes stigmatized, often permanently. Insulting name-calling might appear to come out of nowhere, but in fact it comes from our cultural and interpretive resources, our social realities, and the conversations we have in everyday life to segment or categorize the foreign, unknown, or unsettling characters we encounter. Insults target difference, and even if no difference existed before, it certainly becomes established by way of the name-calling; hence the significative import of Mexican Americans' disdain for Mexicans, for in the eyes of whites, they are all just brown. As Mendoza-Denton (2008) points out, in fights, gangs draw "on the racist discursive practices of their respective countries of orientation" (p. 61). For Norteñas, this always means the United States, whereas for Sureñas this means México, regardless of their actual country of birth.

The previous storytelling summary has alerted us to the significance of colors among gang-impacted women, the allegiances that these colors represent, the subtle yet meaningful distinction between "claiming" and "backing up" red or blue, and the risks confronted by all women, but especially by those who are "nothing" yet dare to wear a gang-related color in a gang-impacted neighborhood. Some women, like Teresa, find that the identifying force conveyed by color positions them in a situation where they are seen as "guilty by association." Others, like Daniela, assume that when insults are lobbed their way because of "kicking it with" those who back up one color, they must fight to defend their and their friends' color. On the topic of neutrality, even those who see themselves as neutral, like Elisa, must forgo wearing either red or blue, one color or another, because others in their *varrio* will assume that their wardrobe choice reflects a statement of allegiance and reject their claim of being "nothing." Garot (2007) pointedly mentions "how various aspects of identity, such as kinship or participation in sports or music activities, for instance, may conflict with or complement gang affiliations" (p. 76). And still others who avoid "claiming," like Chakira, whose relatives are gang-involved—or "validated," as the San José Police Department describes them—face a stigma that can either help or harm them, depending on the situation. The statement by this young woman about colors bears repeating: "I don't know why they fight for a color, when, if at the end they all end up dead! What are colors good for anyway?" This illustrates the significant parameters that colors afford to women in their stories about gang impact and involvement. Just as colors are used to determine selfhood in relation to the neighborhood, so the bearing of one color versus another indicates a friend-or-foe dichotomy. For the gang-involved woman, colors prefigure who belongs and who doesn't. Based on that simple yet effective identifying process, gang-impacted women find the opportunity to insult, disparage, harass, or, even worse, attack the other.

For the gang-involved women, color plays a different role in their story of transcendence. Some of these women regret the brutality of fights provoked by color. Even more egregious are assumptions made about someone wearing a color who claims neutrality, as shown by Eréndira's story of the boy presumed to be Norteño by her Sureño homies, the boy who screamed "I don't bang!" ineffectively, for they continued "jumping" him. This event prompted her to question the benefits of claiming colors specifically and of gang involvement in general. Regret for spending so much time and energy on color loyalty, with little return for herself or her children, was also expressed by Gracia. In her story of transcendence, she recognized that imbuing color with meaning and the accompanying acts to demonstrate loyalty might have a currency in the gang; outside the gang lifestyle, this currency is worthless. To get a job, feed her children, and pay the rent, she must un-inscribe loyalty to the color red from her story. Such is her story of transcendence that, although the former associations she made about gang-identifiable colors still dictate her wardrobe choices, she keeps those meanings in mind as she works to avoid both red and blue. The same un-inscribing characterizes Marisa's story of disdain both for colors and for the youth still preoccupied with them. As a woman who lived far too fast in a gang but denounced the lifestyle, she hopes to help these youth see the absurdity of proclaiming loyalty to a color. Grappling with the reverberations of color meaning as it challenges her own son's experience of gangs, Florencia copes by eliminating all color references from her son's wardrobe, even the seemingly neutral or ambivalent ones. To help him transcend the gang without having direct experience of it, she guides her son's storying by rejecting and re-inscribing the meaning of phrases such as "being punked" and needing "back up."

For the women who transcend gangs, colors lose their meaningful force, and through a process of restorying the color, one's role in that semiotic cosmology changes, as do the range of responses that are now made possible given the reconfigured story.

8

In La Vida Loca, "You Get Up to Get High"

Eréndira, Angela, Lupe, Olga, Marisa, Florencia, and Margie

Life in a gang is rife with drugs, crimes, fights against rival gangs, homelessness, weapons, truancy, sex, and untimely death, hence the moniker of "The Crazy Life" or, among Latinas, "La Vida Loca." Whether they are gang-impacted or gang-involved, women are exposed to risks associated with this lifestyle in various degrees of immersion. Although "La Vida Loca" often refers to being high on drugs, here it is used to encompass all of the above risky activities. The Crazy Life is signified by a tattoo consisting of three dots in a triangle on a person's hand, although not all the women whose stories of gang involvement included some or all of these activities had this tattoo. The life and the tattoo are independent; one can live the Crazy Life without having a tattoo as testimony to the fact. Being in a gang most often implies participation in some or most of these conditions, however, as is evident by the stories of Eréndira, Angela, Lupe, Olga, Marisa, Florencia, and Margie.

ERÉNDIRA

Eréndira started using drugs when she was 11 years old, and soon after she was jumped and joined a gang of Sureñas. Her drug use and her gang involvement were a puzzle to her teachers, many of whom counseled her by pointing out that she had the potential to make a difference in her life. She consistently got good grades, but her fights with other girls, mostly Norteñas, not only prevented her from staying in school and graduating but also landed her in various correctional facilities. We spoke in English and Spanish during the interview, and I use *italics* here to show when English was spoken.

121

Eréndira—So by the time I was sixteen, I didn't feel sixteen, I felt nineteen. Not like I was working and everything, but like I already enjoyed all that. When I was young, I'd go to dances, I *partying, drinking, drugs.* They'd let me in because sometimes when you dress up, you look older. You don't have to be eighteen, some dances, like the Monaco, there's no alcohol or nothing, you don't have to be eighteen, or Quinceañeras. Many places, I'd go with them, I'd go to Sunnyvale, or Santa Cruz, I lived what would have been my summer, my vacation, my *Spring Break,* like in three years, I lived it all. So by the time I was sixteen, oh my! It was the last time I came out of jail and okay, "*That's it!*" I did everything I had to do, *I partied all I had to party* and I felt like *all right,* already. *Tired, tired of it.* I wanted something else already. "If I start working, I can earn my own money, I can buy this and that." It was when I started working, because I've always fended for myself. I told my mom, "I'm going to get a job to be able to support myself, that is, for my expenses. I want to go to the store, or this and that, I want to have my own money." Then she said, "It's fine, so you can become independent, *financially.*" So, when I got my job, I started to see it wasn't the same. "Do you want to go to the dance?" I knew how it was going to be like at the dance. "Let's go do something!" I was "Ah, it's boring; I've been there so many times." "Let's go do this." I was "*Ah, I've been there, done that.*" I was living it at my age. The clubs at eighteen, twenty-one, to drink at twenty-one, no more, because I started so young. I had lived all that at twelve or fourteen. Then they'd tell me, "You're still too young." I'd say, "Well, you have no idea how fast I've lived my life." I even said, "*Okay, I'm ready to have kids.*" I felt something mentally, that I was ready for whatever came my way. I was always like, "*Okay, what's next? what's next?*" Like that, accelerated. And now that I've done that, *now what?* And I've always been like that.

This acceleration of childhood is rampant for gang-impacted and gang-involved girls because almost all these women were exposed to some of these situations before the age of 16. Dealing prematurely with preoccupations that some adults never come to experience at all is normative for Latina girls in gangs.

ANGELA

Beginning somewhat innocently, for protection, Angela's experiences of violence soon led her to become the instigator of harassment of others.

Angela—So, I started, like, looking for such friendships because I wanted protection. Then I started to feel like I didn't want to let my guard down, because before, I left it down and they hit me, they actually hit me. Then, it was a short time when I started hanging out with these girls and they'd tell me, "Go tell something to that girl," and I'd run and do it. I wanted to blend in.

Liliana—Like what?

Angela—"Look at that girl, she's looking at us!" You're in sixth grade. You do childish things. "Go tell her something." So long as they accepted me in their group, and not be the one to be mistreated, I wanted to make a good impression. And twelve years, my gosh! So, I started to be known myself as the bully.

Liliana— . . . to bother the others. . . .

Angela—Exactly! Always be the one they would tell, "Go do this!" I'd go. I'd get into fights. I'd started to be in that environment, I think, about a full year.

What I did was be a front. "Oh, yeah?" [makes threatening face]. I'd get angry, or I'd say things verbally to other girls. Like if I was standing up for myself. . . . I never got to the degree of doing what they did to me. Never that violent.

At that time, there is a lot of peer pressure going on. There came a moment when I started to wear Dickies. That is, my father said, "What are you wearing?" He didn't know. I started to hide them in my backpack and hang out with them. My father's clothes! And he said, "What is happening?" Only once I left wearing his clothes, the others I hid them when I left with my friends.

They were Cholas . . . that is . . . since they were the younger ones, they were protected by the older Cholas, the sisters. They also lived in the real *barrio*, where they killed people. In those days, it was ugly.

I started to get involved a lot with Cholos who used to hit each other. You were in that environment because you wanted to be in the protected environment. Up until one time they started to use drugs. At twelve, you are afraid. Between them, they always did drugs. But I wanted to be like them, I wanted to be protected. I did not want to be left out anymore.

It's the whole pressure. That is, I didn't go as far drastically, because I remember that in those days they talked a lot about "she stabbed someone" and "she stabbed someone"—in that case, one of my friends, I think it was in seventh grade. [. . .] There was something that . . . one of my friends stabbed another girl.

Then I said . . . that's when I started to get fearful. I was twelve, and to see all that, it's very ugly, very ugly.

Then there was . . . I remember that once a friend of the family, the parents used to go to church with my mom. The girls were outside and I was in the house of one of the girls and on a block . . . they used to call him "Hershey" . . . they killed him, some in the military. They came and shot the guy in the very door of the Royal Liquor, so it was called in Vista. And they killed this one . . . we ended up seeing. . . .

Liliana— . . . and why? Because he was from another gang?

Angela—The ones from Vista . . . the ones from the military, maybe they were not in an official gang, but they had their little group, and the Cholos had their little group. And just because the two groups didn't get along, it was a pretext to come and look for a fight, simply because you were in a clique or in a gang it was reason enough to gun you down and to kill you.

Liliana—And what happened to the military guys?

Angela—I never found out. I was very young. But the guy died. It was very sad, a very Christian family and for that to happen to them . . . it was very hard.

Angela's exposure to violence foments a story of violence perpetrated on others for self-preservation. Through this, the untold story, the unspeakable reveals itself: that gang-on-gang violence is not the only violence that inner-city youth experience. Police and, in this case, the military perpetrate violence on others, feeling perhaps justified because of the low currency that youth of color hold in society. In effect, a series of miniature Zoot Suit riots may occur more often than reported by the media in neighborhoods where there is gang presence, and for the people who live there, it is the greatest story never told. The idea that the gang lifestyle affects most everyone around it is confirmed by Lupe's story. Lupe spoke intermittently in Spanish and that is distinguished below in *italics*.

LUPE

Lupe—Things begin to happen in your life because it's affecting . . . it's impacting others. The gang lifestyle, because it's destructive, it impacts your whole entire *familia*. Because you're not doing well in school and your parents see you changing . . . everything from your friends to how you look, to how you talk, to how you treat them. So, you are starting to deal with the repercussions of the lifestyle. And the more you get isolated from the *familia*, if they're no longer accepting you, the more you get drawn into the streets, the more you get drawn into the gang. So you start really losing the ties and you start, "I don't care, this [the gang] is my family anyways." You run away, you leave home.

Liliana—You don't care . . . if they flunk you at school. . . .

Lupe—You don't care if you drop out. You don't care, you're hanging with the homies. And with the drugs, the addiction part and the gangs. Addiction alone does that, so with the gangs, it's a marriage. It's a double whammy. Because when you're addicted, the drugs are your family. That's where you put your value, your time, your everything, your efforts into that. It's no longer communicating and . . . it's about me . . . it's a very selfish lifestyle . . . you get up to get high.

That night that I went out, on New Year's Eve, my father begged me not to go. "M'ija, no, *don't go, there's nothing good.* It's New Year's, stay home." I was like, "No, Dad I wanna go, I wanna go," and I'd bug and bug and bug, until finally "*Okay, but you come home early!*" "*Well, what is 'early'? At four o'clock in the morning?*" My parents went through so much, I'd come home . . . pfff . . . shoes in my hand, staggering, tore up, wasted, I don't even know how, sometimes I'd drive like that, I'd look out, "Did my car make it?" I don't even remember driving. My parents went through so much, and my father would try so hard to . . . to make me realize . . . *hitting me and slapping* . . . nothing was able to change me. . . .

Liliana—That it pulled you closer, you said earlier . . . it pulled you closer to your. . . .

Lupe—Actually, yeah, because of the shame, and the guilt, so I know, "I'm letting them down," so I know people who accepted me, that I could please. Being approved by them. It's just a vicious cycle.

La Vida Loca for Lupe emanated from her addictions insofar as she was mostly involved in the consumption of drugs and alcohol, partying, and sex. Her experience of the gangs, because of the time of her involvement, kept her from the more violent aspects of it: fights, weapons, crimes, and drug dealing. And yet, on that fateful night (discussed at length in Chapter 12, "Betrayal"), she met violence in full force. In contrast, it was drug dealing rather than drug taking that was the initial focus of Marisa's gang experience. She purposely kept a low profile in order to protect her brother's business interests, but soon her experiences ran the gamut of the gang lifestyle.

MARISA

Marisa—I've always been attracted to the bald head, tattoos, . . . tattooed men, things like that. I got myself into a lot of as far as relationships go with men, and I allowed myself to be hurt and be put into really dangerous situations.

Liliana—Can you tell me a story about something like that?

Marisa—Just like getting drunk around five, six guys and letting everyone take advantage of me, things like that. Nothing that any girl should put themselves through . . . anybody, not even a man, should allow themselves to be disrespected like that, and I did. And I was okay with it. There was times when I would feel okay with that, and I wonder if it was because I felt I was missing something. You know? You ever feel like that? Like something's not there?

Liliana—You felt you had to do that so they would like you or. . . .

Marisa—Sometimes, sometimes I'd do it for that. . . .

Liliana—Acceptance?

Marisa—Yeah, 'cause I always had money and I always had drugs, why not take them . . . you know? I kind of felt like they were taking them, so why not give them all of it, know what I mean? It was just a really, really crazy time period, it was only about five years ago.

The age was fifteen, sixteen; my brother bought me a new car and it turned into instead of me carrying them in my backpack, I'd just drive him around and drop him off. That's how it was, but I was still bringing in good grades.

Liliana—And he couldn't drive?

Marisa—No, he still can't drive, to this day, he just never learned. But um, I . . . and that was always the deal; that I had to bring him good grades or else I wouldn't be able to hang out with them, be around them or anything like that. And um, then, I, my drug use started to get really bad. It got to the point where my father told me that I needed help. So I did it. I got help out in Santa Cruz. I was out there for like about . . . God . . . about eight months?

Liliana—What's there? A treatment center?

Marisa—Uh, hum. The Camp. The Camp, and I also went to a treatment center called Rescue House for adolescents in Watsonville. I graduated high school from them, and then when I came back home, I did good for a little while. And then I ran into this homeboy of mine. That was it: I was back out there selling drugs. And then I ended up homeless . . . I never had to . . . ssssell my body, you know? But eh, ah, I just, you know? I was losing a lot of respect for myself, fast. My self-esteem got really, really low and I was unhappy, I was out in the streets, not knowing . . . you know, it's sad going from having a lot of money all the time to having a little bit of money but not knowing where your next meal or your next shower is going to come from, things like that. And it's nothing . . . nobody should ever have to go through that, especially after seeing how hard my grandparents, my parents, my uncles struggled just to put food on the table, and I allowed myself to get to that low point, you know?

Liliana— . . . and you wouldn't go back to your parents' house?

Marisa—I would go back when it was convenient for me, but with my father being clean and sober, he didn't want me at his house if I was getting loaded. And by that time, my mother had washed her hands of me.

Liliana— . . . and your brother?

Marisa—I would stay with him when I could, but he, himself, he was getting loaded too. So, since he wasn't giving me drugs, I didn't want to be around him, 'cause nobody ever wants to come down . . . and uh, it was just . . . things got really, really hard, you know? And um, with the grace of God, I found out that I was pregnant, and I had to, I had to let that lifestyle go. I had to, you know? Like, my perception of gangs, we were always just the moneymakers. You know? My brother was never really violent as far as going to the street and fighting with rival gang members. It was all just about bringing money for everybody else.

The business of dealing drugs took precedence as Marisa stayed away from the related violence; regardless, she did not escape some of the other risks encountered by women in the gang lifestyle.

Marisa—I was . . . well, there would be times when I'd be driving down the street and there'd be a cop behind me and I'd be like, "God! Just let me get through this and I promise I won't be, you know, I won't do it anymore!" I did a lot of that. I'd be . . . then the cop would turn the other way and I'd be right back to what I was doing, you know. And um, that was me: "Just get me through this!" That was the kind of praying I did when I was using drugs. "God, just get me through this!"

Liliana—So, let's say, when you, you never really encountered many fights, like with rival gangs, you never really got . . . so that wasn't . . . why do you think that happened?

Marisa—My brother always wanted to keep me safe. There were times when we were run up by, but if we had to fight, he always made sure to get me out of there. Because if they were to get busted and I was there, I was under the age. If they were to get busted and I was there, my mother would have had his ass, know what I mean? My mom never really knew what was going on. She knew we spent a lot of time together, she didn't know what was going on. She knew I was using drugs, but she knew he wasn't giving them to me. Never, ever. When I started doing drugs, he told me, "I don't care if you get high, but don't ask me for it." So, she knew I was doing drugs, all she knew was that we were together.

My brother is a really respectful man, he's always been. He knows not to put me, not only being a woman but his little sister, in trouble like that. He did teach me how to shoot guns, but that was only because somebody would have come to the house looking for him, or if he wasn't there and I felt threatened, I knew what to do. That was . . . it never really came to that point. I threatened somebody one time, but um, he left. He knew . . . he didn't think I was really going to pull out a gun on him and when I did, he was like, "All right, I just, I just . . . tell him I came by!" But we never really, we were always about making money.

Brothers and sisters involved in gangs increase a girl's chances that she will be involved herself (Miller, 2006). Marisa's brother focused on the business and ensured her protection, yet she still managed to get into the lifestyle on her own. He acquainted her with fights, drugs, and guns to such an extent that, despite his efforts to protect her and the deal they had (described in Chapter 4, "Inhabiting the Gang"), Marisa easily transitioned into the drug-dealing, sex, and homelessness part of La Vida Loca. Siblings and other relatives play this paradoxical role by encouraging girls to get into a gang or to perform gang-related activities, on the one hand, and by commanding the girls not to take drugs or protecting them from attack by rival gangs, on the other.

OLGA

La Vida Loca implied both drugs and fights with rival gangs for Olga. It offered her companionship but also exposed her to activities inappropriate for her age. Olga's usage of English during the interview is shown in *italics*.

Olga—I was really, since I was like the youngest one, I was like the baby, so I was protected all the time.

Liliana—Like a pet?

Olga—Yeah, by everybody. They would look out for me. Even if there was a fight, they would try to protect me, you know? "Go with Giggles! Go over there, go with Olga, go watch Olga." *I always got that, like, "They care for me, 'cause they're looking out for me." So I got that.*

Liliana—Did you have a gang name?

Olga—Yeah, Giggles . . . Little Giggles. So they were always taking care of me. *You know, looking after me. So that made me belong. "Okay, I finally found my place in the varrio."*

Liliana—When you say the varrio, what are you referring to?

Olga—The *varrio* was the place where we hung out. In reality, in those days from 33rd Street in a *golf course*, they'd get together at night, since there was nobody, so that's where we'd get together in the *varrio*. From there, the police, the Norteños, there were a lot of problems there, so we had to find another place. *So,* we found the Tropicana. The famous Tropicana, on Story and King. And we'd all get together there. It was a club, there was a bar. *So,* those who wanted to dance, drink, or anything, it was open, because it was open to young people and the bar to the adults. But it was like a parking lot, so we would just hang out outside. At that time there wasn't that much *loitering,* but I think that it was more for fear that people would talk and say something and something would happen to them. *So,* no, really nobody messed with us. Nobody intervened with us. And we would get together just to be kicking back, and when I say kicking back, it was just standing against the wall, talking, drinking, smoking, sometimes fighting. . . .

Liliana—Smoking marijuana?

Olga—Yes, and sometimes there were police officers who were inside guarding the safety of the bars, but one always had to be careful, because everyone knew what they were doing. And so the *varrio* was there, we went there for many years. Many fights, many fights. . . .

Varrio Sombras Locos was the only Sureño varrio for years . . . in all of San José. *Everybody knew VSL like the only one.* And after that, they started coming out, *around '89, no, not really, like '89, '90, '91,* others started here and there. *Like little Sureños, like you know,* kids who *you know had heard and they were, they wanted to be strong.* And now they are *one of the most strongest.* Now *VSL* does no longer exist. *Many of the older guys—the "Veteranos"—they OD'd. A lot of them got addicted to heroin, a lot of them overdosed; a few are doing life in prison.*

Liliana—For . . . ?

Olga—Murder, homicide, *three strikes, so you know. And it's sad.* [. . .] *You know, wherever you're at,* you have to be ready to fight. Because by that time, *there was nothing but Norteños, there was a lot of Norteños, you know, and you had to be ready. You had to be ready and you had to be down and you had to,* be what it may, *you know,* here, *even if you would get in a fight with one of your own homeboys or homegirls, you know, you need to squash it because we were too little with a whole . . . a bunch of enemies, so we couldn't . . .* we couldn't *afford to fight each other 'cause we had to protect each other because there were so many of the . . . so many enemies. So the requirement were pretty much be loyal to the gang, be loyal to the color, be loyal to VSL, who we are—you know, "Thirteen"—different ways that we were known.* At the same time, *it was like if your homeboys would get locked up, if our homegirls would get locked up, we couldn't say nothing, you know what had really happened, you know, they had to do their time, whether they did the crime or not. . . .*

Liliana—When the police spoke with you, you didn't . . . ?

Olga—Like when things would happen, here in the *Varrio La Tropicana, like let's say a shooting would happen, or a fight would break out and the cops would pull us over and ask us,* "Okay, *what happened here?" "We were just kicking back, we were just kicking back."* But even knowing that *all of us were fighting and in that fight, we would never talk. "Don't talk, the Code of Silence,* don't say anything." *You know, "Whatever they had, whatever they get, they have to figure it out on their own." If they get locked up. . . .*

Liliana—And why is that? Because if you speak perhaps the enemy will come and avenge? Take revenge?

Olga—Yeah, the *Code of Silence* was more to protect the *varrio. Like we couldn't . . . we had to let everybody know who we were.* And we had to be recognized that *we were in town* and that we weren't going to be quiet or let others take advantage. But *you know,* it was also more revenge. *Like, "Don't say anything and we'll get them back. Forget the law, the law ain't gonna help us. You know, we'll take the law into our own hands." That was our mentality.*

Liliana—It's like a paradox, no? Like you're caught between a rock and a hard place, right?

*Olga—*Yeah.

Liliana—That you wanted to establish a reputation but you couldn't do it in the face of the law.

*Olga—*It was more like . . . *undercover,* more like *undercover* because *I'm sure the cops at that time didn't know what was going on. The rates of violence* that were taking place *and they all wanted to know what was happening. And especially the guys getting locked up, the girls starting to get locked up* and that's how they got started in *Juvenile, the Ranch, the YAs, they started spreading out who we were,* and that's how one starts to get built up, *build up like a reputation in the system. So that's pretty much what took place, so it was our responsibility to hold up our reputation.* But when I saw that *our reputation wasn't that good, meaning* what I spoke about earlier, *the responsibility of the parents, PCP all the time, you know, fighting each other . . . then the heroin* and what not. *I remember a few times* that I broke their syringes of *two or three of my homeboys. They got all mad at me and they were chasing me and I didn't see myself . . . that's not how it was when I first started out. And I just seen how* their loyalty changed *to a drug.*

So yeah, at *sixteen, yeah seventeen, I was just tired of that, seeing the same, and I had already lost my education.* I had lost. . . .

Liliana—Because you never went to school?

Olga—Because I never graduated from *middle school. I dropped out like in the beginning of my sophomore year. I only had five credits for my freshman, or ten credits. . . .*

Liliana—Because you never went to school?

Olga—No, I would . . . I had *homegirls* who were *older* in age and were *thirty at that time and they would go and they would say that they were my* aunts *and they would take me out of school, or I else they would . . . I went like . . . maybe to four or five different high schools and my mom never knew. Even from middle school, my mom never knew.* And *supposedly your parents are the only ones allowed to enroll you and dis-enroll you but there was my homegirls that were helping me do all of this. And just because I didn't want to be there no more, or I was having too much trouble there, you know, I would go to a different school.*

The vicissitudes of *varrio* life that Olga encountered were many and varied. Already dropped out of school, always on the defense against a more numerous enemy, and unwilling to rely on the police, hoping instead to settle affronts to their *varrio* on their own, VSL was both a home and a hell to live in. The Code of Silence that Olga refers to also plays a significant role in the victimization of women in gangs, for their subjugation festers in stories untold. Olga recognized these aberrations when she had a fight with her sister (discussed in Chapter 12, "Betrayal") that made her question her place in the *varrio*. She was still trying to find a place she could call home, and she hoped it would be with a homeboy called "Güero."

Olga—What happened there with [Güero] is that he was going to come out for an OT, like a pass, a weekend pass, and he was staying in uh, somewhere in . . . gosh! In Stockton, around that area, Tracy. And he had come, ah he was supposed to call me, never called me and I thought "That's kind of weird," 'cause he always used to call me. And it was when they celebrate ah . . . [makes circles with hand], I don't know, they celebrate something in the mission, every May, and ah, and ah, there was a shooting and there was something and it was a Sunday and

I got a call from the home where he was staying at, the Ranch where he was staying at, and one of the guys asked, you know, "Is this Giggles?" I'm all "Yeeeesss!" and he's all, "Hey, this is ah So-and-so and I'm calling from where Güero's at. . . ." And I'm like, "Okay, where's he at?" He's all, "He went home, didn't he call you?" I said, "No, I didn't hear, I didn't know he had gone home." He said, "Well, I just called to tell you that he's dead." And I'm like, "WHAT? He's dead?" I couldn't believe it. I'm like, "Who's this? Stop, stop joking around! Who's this?" He's all "I'm not joking around. If you want, you can talk to a counselor, but they just gave us the news that he got shot this day, you know, and he died on the way to the hospital." And that like totally broke my heart, 'cause I felt this is the only person that had been communicating and giving me any kind of support uh, and when I found out that he was dead, and then uh, the next day I asked my mom if she could take me to San Francisco, 'cause I knew where his mom lived and uh, and I went, and uh, she dropped me off and I never. . . .

Liliana—Did you tell her why you were going?

Olga—Yeah, I had told her that they had killed my friend, if she could please take me 'cause I wanted to see him. So the next day she gave me a ride and she dropped me off right there at his mom's house, and he had two sisters and a little brother, one older sister and one little brother and one little sister, and his mom was a single mother as well. She had got together with his dad that was from El Salvador, but he used to beat her a lot, so they, she left him. And uh, so they grew up without a dad as well. And I was talking to her and she was just sharing her heart, crying, remembering him. And I had never met her before; she just asked me to stay there with her and I did. I ended up staying with her. I stayed there for a month. We were there for the burial, for the wake, for everything. And I found myself living in this little room, taking care of his little brother and his little sister 'cause she would lock them in their room and close the door, while she was partying and doing whatever in the other rooms. So I was staying in the room with them.

Liliana—So the situation was similar to your home situation?

Olga—Yeah. So I found myself back in square one. And I think at this point I was like, I was just lost. I was just lost [begins crying]*, I was sixteen and felt like it was the end of the world, you know. That I didn't belong nowhere and all the people that were close to me had let me down somehow, or were taken away from me. I had a lot of anger, hurt, pain, a lot of things. And then one day finally I just decided, I told her, "You know what? I'm going to go back to San José, but I don't wanna lose contact with you guys, you know, with Esperanza, Mauricio, don't want to lose contact with you guys." 'Cause I had grown close to them. I felt I had grown close to them. So she was like, "Fine, you could go back, you know, that's cool."*

So, I was in and out of my house, running away, staying here, staying there. If I had nowhere to stay, I'd stay at the airport, the San José airport, until they would kick us out.

Liliana—At the terminals?

Olga—Yeah, the terminals. And then we had to take off walking, go by Zanker, go by Roswells, where the houses were, so we just kept on walking, until day came and then, "Let's go to homeboy's house, let's go to homegirl's house." You know, that's pretty much how I grew up. And then when. . . .

Liliana—So where did you get money, how did you get food?

Olga—Homeboys . . . used to deal. I never dealt, you know, but like people who I was with, they would, that's what they would do. They would ask, "Have you ate? Do you need this? Let's go to the store. Let's go look at this." Stuff like that. Stealing. We'd go stealing if it was clothes that we needed, so we'd go to the mall and steal. Stuff like that. 'Cause, I mean, even that, I wasn't much to really want things, 'cause my need was greater than materialistic, the way I seen it. It was greater than that and none of that filled me. I just never wanted to be alone, 'cause I felt I was alone all my life. You know, so I rather be with people, I'd know I wasn't alone, even though I sometimes felt so alone in the midst of twenty people and I still felt alone. But I could not explain that then, now I can, now I can. Had no clue then, 'cause I was in the midst of it.

The relational connectedness that Olga missed at home and was hoping to find in the *varrio* eluded her there as well. During her time in the gang, she saw La Vida Loca as normal, a welcome respite to the rancor at home, and assumed it was what homies did for each other when they needed help. But with the death of her one-time boyfriend, she realized the help she needed could not be found in the *varrio*. Other parts of her story of detachment from the gang can be found in Chapter 12, "Betrayal," and Chapter 15, "Transcending Gangs."

La Vida Loca also implies life in the fast lane, however unwittingly it is begun by the gang-impacted or gang-involved girl. In cases like Margie's, the gang lifestyle was the only one she knew, and the choice was obvious.

MARGIE

Margie was barely an adult when we spoke, yet she had had to take care of her siblings and her own child from a very early age; that she had to do so through illegal means did not give her any apparent cause for concern.

Margie—That's nothing new to me, because I grew up around that. I grew up sitting at a coffee table playing with guns and drugs. So it was nothing new to me. My whole family was gang related, the people I was selling to was gang related.

I was dealing crack, marijuana. I was bringing in $8,000 a day, in my pocket. I started through my dad. He was a drug lord where I'm from. So, one day I said, I need some money and he said, "You know, you can make your own money." I was like, "What? All right!" So I did it.

There were gang fights, a lot of them. [. . .] I fought mostly with Sureños, against other guys. In my clique, it was all girls, but there was another circle of guys around us.

I ended up in group homes and now I'm emancipated. So, I don't have an income, besides the drugs.

I used to do meth, but I've not done it since 2005. I'm happy, I quit drinking, I quit smoking. I don't have a place, but I stay with friends. They're not clean. What everybody else does, does not affect me at all whatsoever. Like you could be smoking crack in front of me, and I'd be sitting there talking to you. They know I don't do that. Everybody that I hang out with, they know what I do and what I don't do.

To me, it's not a lifestyle; it's the way I live. A lifestyle is what you . . . the way you choose to live. The way I live I was born into it, it's my background, it's my family. Okay, if I was raised by black people, that's the way I'd live. Me being Mexican that's my lifestyle, 'cause I would choose to.

The only woman I interviewed who was still an active gang member at the time we spoke, Margie went from being reserved and secretive about her gang involvement to being quite expansive. As already mentioned, Margie was barely an adult at the time of the interview. She became a parent to her siblings and then to her own child when she was a child herself. She was visited by the worries of an adult who has the responsibility of caring for small children, and she responded as expediently and efficiently as she knew how—namely, by engaging in the highest income-earning activity available to someone of her age and social position. In the eyes of women like Margie, the gang gives them a way to surmount the abject poverty they would otherwise face (Campbell, 1995). The force that Gangs of Family exerted on Margie to engage in the lifestyle was inescapable. Although there are many non-gang-affiliated people in other walks of life who make a living—modest or handsome—by selling drugs, in Margie's environment, the gang provided not just protection but also a convenient market for her product. This seemingly inseparable connection between gangs and drugs also played a large part in Florencia's story of La Vida Loca.

FLORENCIA

Florencia—Like, we did a lot of things together. We called it "dirt," we did a lot of "dirt" together. But it was not considered a big deal. We would do little things, like do a beer run, we didn't do heavy drugs, it was just drinking. I never liked smoking pot or things like that, some of my friends did. I always wanted more, like it was never enough. We started like that, there's gotta be more. As time went on, we got stronger and stronger and I wanted to do more things than just having a party, [which] wasn't enough. Like one time, this is the influence I had over them, I told them, "We're going to steal a car and drive over to Texas." So all night long we're looking for a car to steal and all these girls are willing to steal a car and just take off driving it. We had no money, we had no nothing; they were just following me. Another time we stole a truck and took like eight people to Modesto because I felt like it. It was like there were risks and whatever.

My influence started going over to the guys. I started getting into drugs myself and just a little bit, started messing with drugs.

I got really addicted to PCP. Most people take two hits of what they call a *leño* ("log") and they're zombied out. They're gone. My level was so high, my tolerance, I could smoke a whole *leño* to myself. . . . I got really into PCP. You smoke with parsley, it's an elephant tranquilizer. You make into liquid form and then dip cigarettes into it. You just touch it and it gets into your pores. It's in the streets.

But it just got really violent, got really into. At this time, everybody knows, don't mess with us, we're in the neighborhood, and I start. . . . One guy, I remember growing up in school and he was a skater, he wasn't into neighborhood or nothing. My mom and dad separated again, this time for sure. He goes to live with my sister and she's alone in the apartment. By this time, I got my friends, I'm established, I'm partying. By established I mean I have a group of kids I run around with. I'm involved with things, she's not home on the weekends, so everybody comes over to my house now. My house kind of becomes party house. At first, we got close to the time she'd come home, sometimes she wouldn't even come home. One time this kid had come over and I'm like, "What are you doing?" I didn't know he had eight older brothers in this other neighborhood, so we started hanging out with them. We would eventually some of us, probably end up in that neighborhood, it's kind of like you graduate. It's all one neighborhood but you kind of graduate levels. Through him what happened was . . . they had more access to guns, to everything, and they've been there for many years, so they were very well known.

I started hanging around with him. Slowly some of the guys that used to hang around with me, now they looked weak to me. First the girls, now the guys look weak. I need to establish myself more, "What can I do to get higher?" I promoted. That's what I was looking for. He hooked up with me and his mom kicked him out because he started getting into trouble and started wanting to be part of his brothers . . . and she didn't want . . . they had a different mom and she didn't want him to be part of that. So when he got kicked out, he came to live with me and my mom. He became kind of like my first friend was like, he was my brother. Whenever everybody saws us they saw us as we were brother and sister. He's about a year older than me. So we became really tight and we started running around. At this time, this other group was into snorting and smoking crank. I wasn't into that.

As time goes, I get involved with him and we meet a guy from another neighborhood and they run with much more higher ranks than just street gangs. . . . Prison gangs, they run way more than we do. So we hook up with him, and I was really street smart, I pick up things really fast and I watch everything. He liked that about me, so we start kind of wheeling and dealing with him and we get all kinds of dope.

So now I'm selling drugs, selling, making money. That's a whole other realm. There is this unwritten rule in the neighborhood that "You don't get high off your own supply" because you mess up. At first I was okay, because I had a connection where I could get a lot of crank. It's a form of crystal, I think it's worse, but it's still in the family. But this other neighborhood, I got involved with another man and I stayed with that man for about four years. I was sixteen and he was thirty-four, much older, got involved with him. He didn't like the hardness about me. I would run with his homeboys. I would smoke with them. I would smoke them out. I could drink as much as they did and still hold my own. He was like a strong guy, tattooed, and he didn't like to look like punked by his old lady, because here I am, holding my own, taking care of my own, had my own place. So they'd, say, "Man! What's wrong with your old lady?" He didn't like that. "No, m'hija, don't do this, don't do that."

I had a connection to get PCP, which they all liked in that neighborhood. Then I got another connection for crank, I could get a little of everything for everybody. The violence just grew. Now I'm carrying a gun, I'm not going to carry a knife. I've done a few robberies; I've done a couple of car jackings. I wasn't afraid to put a gun to someone's head, I stuck a gun in somebody's mouth, pistol whipped, I did a lot of things and not caring, I don't even care. I was involved with Norteños, gangbanging Norte. Some Sureños tried to break into my house, to steal the dope, cut my electricity, tried to rob my house. I had guns throughout the whole house, just crazy like that, got into a lot of fights.

It got to the point where I would smoke PCP and do crank all night. A lot of times I was really high all the time and didn't even care. Got to the point, at first it wasn't a big deal. I got to that point because I was sedated, medicating myself. I got to the point where I'd be asleep and I'd have really bad dreams, nightmares about all the bad stuff that happened to me, stuff I'd forgotten. I would get really bad dreams at night and I didn't want to sleep because I didn't want to remember, so I'd do drugs. My house became the party house. I would never sleep. I slept maybe two hours every week because I didn't want to sleep. Going to sleep was like the worst because I'd go back and remember all the stuff that happened and I didn't want to remember that person. I hated the things that happened to me, so I didn't want to be that person. I didn't want to remember. So I did drugs. Nobody knew. What made it worse was that I could really drink and do drugs a lot. I had such a high tolerance that made me look like "Man! She's really crazy, she could put away this much, she could get high. . . ." I could hold my own. So I could go anywhere with anybody because they didn't have to take care of me. If anything, I had to take care of other people.

I think for me, it just got really bad. The drugs and this guy that I was with four years, was like the only boyfriend that I had, and I really loved him. He basically told me, "You stop getting high or I'm going to leave!" We were living together. They called us Bonnie and Clyde because we did a lot of stuff together. We had a high-speed chase with the cops. They got us but they ended up letting us go, because what they were chasing me down for they didn't have evidence enough. He would take care of me. I would do crazy things and then he'd go hide in Santa Clara until they stopped looking for me. I was more crazy than he was. He was at a point in his life where he wanted to mellow out. He didn't want to get married, just live low-key. He didn't want to live crazy and I wanted to live crazy. "C'mon man, let's go, let's rob a bank, let's do crazy stuff, let's live on top, let's be feared." He was like, "No, I don't want to go back to prison, I want to. . . ."

I really cared about him in my own way, he did take care of me, but he came through with his word and he left me. That was like a really hard time for me because I was like, "I don't need anybody," but when he was gone, that feeling alone, like I used to feel before; oh! it was an ugly feeling. I got worse into drugs, got really crazy.

I've lost like some really good friends. People you love and you lose them out there. I never thought about dying like that. I was scared I'd do something like that to somebody, just the way I lived, fearless.

Because I went from someone who could handle business, take care of things . . . we would be up days straight, weigh dope, bagging it, selling it, counting guns, the whole thing. It went from that to me getting so into dope and nobody knew why, like, "What's wrong with you? Come on, get it together!" I would . . . one time I got loaded, I got really high, and I started having flashbacks about when I was abused as a little girl. I literally went back to that place and I ran outside and I was hiding underneath this dumpster. One of the homeboys went out and asked me, "What's wrong with you?" I started telling them what was happening to me and they thought I was talking about my dad. My dad lived a block away from my house. My homeboy pulled out a 45 and started to walk over to his house. He was going to shoot him because he thought I was talking about my dad doing this stuff, but I was just flashing back and they got on me. "You're slipping, you gotta stop doing so much dope, 'cause you're tripping, you're going out there!" They didn't know it wasn't just a trip that I went on being loaded. They didn't know that everything was coming back that had happened to me.

That's the hate, the rage that had built inside me that it lets me never want to be weak like that again. I started getting, I wasn't getting high anymore so I started shooting up, I started slamming, using the needle. I tried heroin but I didn't like it. So I started shooting up crank and cocaine, just to be high all the time. And I started losing everything, little by little. I started doing what they call "shisty moves." I'd sell you some dope, and I'd cut it up and wouldn't give you the real deal. See, my name was good before; I'd give you good dope and give you your money's worth, you could leave your dope at my pad and when you came back you were going to find it there, every bit of it. You could leave money with me, you could trust me. But now I'm starting to get as they say "shisty," shady, because now I am so out there in my own self. By this time I'm really bad in the dope. I'm still out there gangbanging, I'm still holding my own, thinking I am. Little by little. . . .

I got to the point where I had no shoes, walking on the streets. I still had my house and I could live here with this guy, but the drugs take you to a place that's ugly. I'm blessed to have made it out of there. Because the places I went to mentally, I shouldn't be in my right mind today. The drugs . . . think of all the things you've done, the people you've hurt, everything starts coming back at you.

You're just going to do something crazy and whatever, you don't care. [. . .] I started getting to the point that I didn't care. There's a lot that I can't . . . so much about that lifestyle.

The refrains in such a long and detailed story are the drugs, the crimes, the violence, and the men. For someone with such loyalty, Florencia's place in the gang nevertheless remained defined by the status of the men she was with. Her story, too, exemplifies La Vida Loca, a lifestyle driven by a fearless and fatalistic, drug-instigated, hard-core attitude.

DISCUSSION

Not all women who abuse drugs are in gangs, but most Latina female gang members abuse and sometimes deal drugs, if only on a small scale (Moore, 1994). Miller (2000) discusses the participation of girls and young women in gangs and the implications of such behavior. The "Choloization" of these women implies their participating in crimes and violent encounters, engaging in sex, sometimes unprotected and with multiple partners, and using drugs and alcohol. In contrast to average populations and to gang-impacted women, women who are gang-involved are more likely to engage in sex, crime, drug use, and violence (Fagan, 1990; Palmer & Tilley, 1995).

What is it about Florencia's story in particular that emphasizes La Vida Loca? Cepeda and Valdez (2003) explored how gang-impacted women's "connection to the gang differentially exposes them to situations often resulting in serious social and health consequences" (p. 92). They developed a typology of three categories of female gang involvement: "girlfriends," "hoodrats," and "relatives." Whereas women in the first and last categories were those whose involvement was limited by their position, by the men in the gang, or by both, the "hoodrats" were the most "down"—that is, active, loyal, and/or committed to the gang's illegal activities. Through interviews, Cepeda and Valdez concluded that women in all three categories were "prone to some degree of substance use, crime, and high-risk sexual behavior," and that "hoodrats were clearly the most at risk due to the nature of their involvement in gang activities" (p. 102). Although she most likely would identify as a "girlfriend" and not as a "hoodrat," Florencia emphasized she was "down" and obviously encountered many of the risks identified above.

For the women whose stories make up this book, La Vida Loca includes activities such as an accelerated childhood through partying, intimidation meted to others and violence witnessed, life-endangering addictions, sexual promiscuity, homelessness, the death of a loved one, car-jackings, and drug dealing. As Lupe poignantly remarked, "You get up to get high." All these women recognize that there is such a thing as "the lifestyle," activities unique to the gang environment that, whether sought or not, place them at a disadvantage. Although at the time of their involvement this lifestyle was necessary in and of itself, as a refuge from solitude or attack, as an emotionally or financially rewarding place to belong, or as rebellion, in retrospect they all realize the huge price it exacted from their lives. And although their stories may at times make the women sound nostalgic for such exploits, like Florencia, all of them, except Margie, have transcended living crazy. They have transcended the drug and alcohol addictions, the fights, the weapons, the homelessness, the indiscriminate sex or sexual exploitation, and the crimes that typify La Vida Loca.

9

Time Served!

Eréndira, Lucha, Gracia, and Margie

Living La Vida Loca implies that, at some point, the woman who lives it will be apprehended by police, which might lead to conviction and incarceration. Jail, prison, Juvenile Hall, and The Ranch denote various contexts for the loss of liberty due to a gang member's criminal activity. But these also are linguistic as well as correctional terms that carry different connotations depending on her experiences while in custody and how the gang-involved Latina stories these events on the outside. Not all the women I spoke to went to or spoke about jail. Here are the voices of those who talked about serving jail time: Eréndira, Gracia, and Margie. Although Lucha was not gang-involved, she was nonetheless impacted, and her time served animated her story of life beside the gang, so her voice is also included here. For all of them, time served in custody influenced their move away from a criminal lifestyle, if not the gang itself.

ERÉNDIRA

How does a child feel when she goes to jail for the first time? I posed this question to Eréndira. For ease of reading, *italics* indicate the usage of English by Eréndira.

Liliana—. . . and your experience in jail was at thirteen, the first time? How was it?

Eréndira—The first time I was only in for four days. They arrest you, they take you, they take your picture, *they check you, they strip you down* from your clothes, they give you their clothes, of *Juvenile Hall*, they give you your first call. They take you inside, and then they ask you, "*Are you gang*

141

related, yes or no?" So they know, so they don't put you in with a Norteña. Then they know what you are, they put you with a Sureña. If not, they put you in by yourself, if there are no others. If you tell them you're nothing, they put you up with whoever is available. A typical day is to sit down, eat, brush your teeth, do what you have to do. Depending on whatever level you are, they can let you do different things. Eat, come out again, shower. They bring it to your room and you eat there. *Breakfast, lunch, dinner.*

Liliana—Does the room have bars?

Eréndira—The room has a door, with a button, which they *unlock; if not, you can't move it,* it's locked. So, when they press the button, it's when it can be opened. The windows are like *foot and a half by half*, they're up high. The beds are like *big old concrete* and on top a sofa. Before they had bunks, but now it's a room, a *lump of blocks* there and a *lump of blocks* there, *that's your bed.* Many girls fell down. I once almost fell from the top, you're used to sleeping on a bed and then in a turn . . . they even had the bathrooms outside, but many used to fight in there. Now the *sink* and the bathroom is in your room. The shower is for one person. Before there used to be five showering at a time. Now you shower alone, but it has a little thing that covers from here [signals to her face] until here [signals to her knees]. From the shower you have to come out . . . they give you *lotion* and *shampoo,* and many that are in *Level A,* that is the *good one,* they can give you *good kind of lotion, conditioner, shampoo, they let you shave,* if not, you're all hairy, however you can manage.

. . . when you arrive, you're like *under their rules,* whatever you've done. It's obvious if you've killed somebody, they won't let you go out with the others. You have more if you're in for like *misdemeanor or felonies,* something that says, "This one stole a car," something not for life, all are in the same.

Liliana—What were you in for the first time?

Eréndira—The first time, I had a knife at school. I was just about to turn thirteen. I remember that I took it out, to brag, "*Look what I have,*" and somebody must have seen me, because they called the *cops* and when the *cops* arrived, they made a *search* on me and they asked me if I had something and I told them "No," and then they found it on me and they called me inside and called my *probation officer,* and she said, "No more! Lock her up!" because she was tired of my running away from home, cutting my *house arrest* [bracelet], I never went to school. So that's when they locked me up. I was never told for how long, and they locked me up.

Liliana—And when did you go back to Juvenile Hall?

Eréndira—The second time was for two months, for leaving home. Since I already had *probation,* any little thing, "Done, *you're going to*

Juvenile Hall!" You hung out with people that also had *probation,* and you couldn't . . . your officer recommended how much time, and that's how long they gave you. Unless it was something exaggerated, they'd reduce it or increase it. It was easy for me; I didn't like being home, but being with my friends, *away from home, going to school, but just one or two hours a day. I liked it,* but it bored me afterwards, *"Is that it? I'm bored."*

Here she was referring to boredom with school, but running away from home landed Eréndira in a secured residential facility, where the regimented schedule became more oppressive and limiting for frequent offenders. Kempf-Leonard and Johansson (2007) have noted that, although boys and girls run away from home in roughly the same numbers, girls are more likely to be arrested for it. For girls, leaving the home significantly affects the transition into crime from mere delinquency (Chesney-Lind, 1997). This raises questions about the wisdom of confining young girls in such a way for relatively minor offenses. Again, Kempf-Leonard and Johansson (2007) observe that, "[j]uvenile justice officials must have ways to respond to runaway youths that are effective" and that "the main problem is lack of alternatives and understanding about how best to respond to runaways" (p. 324).

Taking a cue from Eréndira's assertion that it was easy for her and loath to presume that jail is necessarily an unpalatable experience for all, I wonder if her recidivism might be driven by something positive Eréndira received from being in jail. This reward, unbeknownst to others, could be so strong that it keeps her coming back. In their study of the construction of a moral self, Green, South, and Smith (2006) found that for some of their respondents, prison was "safe, offering a place to relax, reflect, and even rebuild self-esteem," whereas "others claimed to have acquired a heroin addiction" while incarcerated (p. 318). It seems perverse to ask, yet the story of time served acquires texture from such a question.

Liliana—What did you like about it?

Eréndira—I was looking for something new. But when I came out of jail, I fell into The Ranch. There it was *much better, the food was better,* it had no *locks,* and you could come and go. The showers, *you could lock your showers.* When I was, the first time, *you could take your own pluckers,* your *own toothbrush,* your *own shampoo* and *conditioner, like* things, your comb. Then, afterward, like supposedly many [girls] had no money, or their families didn't send them to have their own, they took it away. It's like a privilege to have; now you have to use theirs. One thing I didn't like about The Ranch was that you only had one call, five minutes to your mom, per week, to your parents, per week. One call!

The one thing she was running away from on the outside was what she missed the most at The Ranch: contact with her family. In Chapter 15, "Transcending Gangs," Eréndira recounts how, on turning 15 years old while incarcerated, she was allowed a half-hour phone call to her mother as a birthday present, and after this conversation she recognized the many dangers that gang-banging brought, including incarceration. In this way, she recognized she enjoyed certain privileges in The Ranch that allowed her to keep a semblance of dignity and that this face-saving would motivate her to stay out (Chesney-Lind, 2001; Goodkind, 2005). Therefore she used the story of time served to punctuate the beginning of the process of leaving the gang.

LUCHA

Time served in jail can be useful in the process of a young woman storying herself out of a gang, as we have just seen. For Lucha, who was not gang-involved but living La Vida Loca nonetheless, confinement apparently accomplished one aspect of its intended purpose—reformation, albeit by prompting Lucha to vow not to return.

Liliana—So, you've been in Juvenile Hall?

Lucha— All last summer I was in jail, my first time ever in my whole entire life.

Liliana—So you never went to Juvenile Hall?

Lucha— I've never been in Juvenile.

Liliana—And you got caught as an adult? And what was that like?

Lucha— It sucked!

Liliana—Did you get jumped? Does that happen?

Lucha— Yeah, if you're punked, you get jumped. It's like they didn't even know it was my first time, you know what I mean? See, I adapt to situations, learn fast. I grew up everywhere. I jump from place to place. I've been in Texas, I've been in Utah, I've been in Turlock, Fresno, Modesto, Gracie, Bernales, Patterson, Monterey, San José. In three years I've been in San José, I've lived in the North Side, East Side, South Side. I mean, I adapt to situations. If I see it and if I don't know it, I will kick back for a moment, I will look around my surroundings, "Okay that's how they're rolling," and I'll jump right into it. So, I don't look like an oddball. It's the same thing in jail. I don't want to look like I'm fresh to the game, because they're going to try to pick and poke at you.

Liliana—Did they ask?

Lucha— Yeah, I told them, "What, is it your business?" As soon as I walked in, I flipped my wristbands around. "Why is my information any of your business? Why are you asking about my case? You're not a jailhouse lawyer. I'm doing my time just as you're doing your time. What do I do that concerns you?" One girl got mad, "We just want to know what you did!" I told her, why, "What the fuck is it your business? What did YOU do?" She said, "Oh, I did this and this and that." So I said, "So one of these snitchy motherfuckers can easily go to trial and go against you, stupid idiots, and make something you say . . . somebody can go to trial against you and make your case that much worse!" So I stick to my own. I was the youngster and I just hustled in there. I stuck to the older Mexicanas and I just trade for trade, like commissary. 'Cause nobody sent me money, nobody really knew I was in there.

So, the whole summer of last year, I stayed in there, almost four months. Nobody sent me money; nobody knew I was there, so I just did what I knew and that is to hustle. You know those little bars of soap? I shaved them down with a card, put them in empty conditioner bottles, filled them with hot water, and shook them and that became body wash. Because the soaps would slip so fast and they're so little, those cheap generic hotel soaps. I shaved them down because they'll absorb water so, you know what I mean? So I shook for like twenty minutes and then I'd sell the body wash for whatever I needed: trade for trade, know what I mean? Because nobody was going to sit there for like fifty soaps just shaving them down, so I did.

Hustle is not just about dealing drugs, like "I'm dealing drugs." To me everything is a hustle. You know what I mean? You just do what you do, you have something of a little bit and you turn it over to make it a lot.

People who are ascribed a negative label use narratives that deflect fault or that position them as well intended in order to demonstrate that they know and respect societal norms (Green, South, & Smith, 2006). In this way, they assume a sense of self that rejects and contradicts the ascribed negative label. Although she was convicted of a felony, Lucha distanced herself from the other women in jail, paying homage to her ancestors by staying with the Mexicanas, keeping to herself and thus out of trouble. Moreover, she used the expression "to hustle" to justify how her habit of making the best out of a bad situation served her as a survival strategy while she was in jail. And hustle she must to stay out, too.

Lucha— I'd need my driver's license . . . I'm in the process. I've got a few tickets I need to take care of. I got my car, it's got tags; I just don't have that license. The only thing stopping me right now, I'd go back to county jail for restitution.

Liliana—And what is that?

Lucha— The money that I owe the county. I owe $4,600 on one case and I owe $270 on my other. And then I just accumulated hellah traffic tickets. I've got about $4,000 in traffic tickets.

Liliana—So, you owe the county money, you haven't committed a crime. Fine money? So. . . .

Lucha— No, I committed a felony. I'm a convicted felon. They arrested me on 21 counts, felonies. I walked out with one. It was just a bunch of bullshit. So, yeah, I'm a convicted . . . that's another thing holding me back. People look at you and "Damn! You're a good candidate for this. . . ."

Liliana—For scholarship? For jobs?

Lucha— Anything! "Soooorry . . . your baaackground. . . ." I'm just, "No problem, I expected it." And that's why a lot of people coming out of prison, and everything else just like that, especially the Mexicans, there's no chance, they're set up to fail. The system is setting you up to fail. How in the hell do you expect me, fresh out of county jail, to walk out, and one week pay $170 fine from a restitution?

It's just set up to fail. The longer they have us in there, the more money they get. Why do you think that in prison they're opening up the gyms? They're triple stacked bunks. They're not just double, they're triple. The more they have us in there, the more money they get. And that's why they profit. We could owe them up the ass, but they'll still get my money.

I already went in front of the judge, I'm doing community service. He says I pay $1,500 back, he'd wipe away everything [laughs]. It's funny, I went for a loan. I had the *feria* to put up, 'cause it was a secure loan. That was my ticket. The company ended up being fraud. They took my money. So, a lot of bad luck has been hitting my way lately, but I laugh at it. I just know there's something else coming.

Liliana—So they took $1,500?

Lucha— No, they took $500. They were going to give me a $3,000 loan and I got took for $500. It was like this big old scam. You live and you learn. To me, I know God will punish them. Well, God does not punish, but I know they'll end up getting caught and going to jail. I know I have that money, it's there, I know when they get caught I'll get my money back, but who knows when.

It was my first time in trouble. I was lucky. I've been out ten months; June 1st will be one year. I've not been back for nothing; I always pissed out at my PO clean. I know I'm not going back.

Liliana—So you're clean?

Lucha— Oh, yeah! It only took this Mexican once to learn I do not like jail! Serious! I hated it! I hated it with a PAAASSION! A white man told me what to do and I had to listen. Oh, I couldn't stand it, I could NOT stand it! Especially those little punk white girls, the CO's, "Get down the bunks now!" "Bitch, if I see you in the streets, I will destroy you. You're not . . . nothing! You're just hiding behind the badge," and if you hit them, my God, you're going to prison. So I stuck it out though.

They wanted to give me five years, but the judge is Mexicano. He goes, "You guys are trying to ruin her life. Time served! Pow!" [slams fist against table]. That was it. I just looked and sat there and thought, "What the fuck did you just say? Time served!?" I was out because I had no violent crimes, I had no past crimes or anything. The majority of the people who were going up in front of him was Mexicanos. Half, no, more than half that courtroom, 75 percent of that courtroom was Mexicans. . . .

It's just . . . hard being Mexican American and it's hard being Mexican from Mexico. The thing is if you're determined . . . that's what Mexicans don't have, determination.

Lucha's time served story helps to position herself as in control, but that control only goes so far in the face of so many obstacles. She acknowledges the bit of good luck that sharing the judge's ethnicity played in her getting off relatively easily, yet it is the same ethnicity that she claims keeps her and people like her down. Even being the victim of fraud for trying to pay her debt does not deter her because she knows eventually the defrauder will get his comeuppance and she her lost money. There is a rudimentary Marxist critique in her description of the prison industrial complex, as well as the racist undertones that she claims machinate to keep Mexicans down, but at the same time, Mexicans themselves lack what she has in abundance: determination. For Lucha, time was well served to get her out; the hustle to stay out, however, is ongoing.

GRACIA

Twenty years old and with the only income to support her two children—5 and 3 years old at the time—coming from the sale of drugs, Gracia and her husband got caught selling to a "narc." As Moore and Hagedorn (2006) observe, "drug offenses are among the most common offenses committed by female gang members" (p. 197). When Gracia and her husband went to prison, their children ended up in the care of a cousin.

Liliana—For how long were you in?

Gracia—We just did a little over a year. Before that, he was always in and out of jail, in and out of Juvenile Hall, in the Boys' Ranch. He spent the majority, a lot of his time in and out, in and out. That was the first time I ever went and that was in . . . it was, it was hard, it was really hard because I had liked that lifestyle but because I was re . . . a person, had to be responsible and I had to do things differently, I didn't know where else to go, who to go to, or how to do it or why I was even thinking about doing things differently, but I just knew things had to change. I just knew I didn't want my child to live the life that I had lived. Although I thought that it was fun, it was cool, it was a hard life. It was a hard life trying to keep up with my reputation and keep up with all these people and fighting all the time, always having to watch my back, not being able to be safe here or safe there, having to either carry a knife with me to school, and I, you know, it just, I was like, I kept thinking like, "Is this the life that I want to live? Is this who I really want to be?"

From this brief reminiscing, Gracia hints that the heavy toll put on her by inhabiting the gang, the prospect of leaving, and the seemingly insurmountable obstacles in doing so had occurred to her even before she went to jail. The incarceration also gave her time to reflect and to gain advice. In Chapter 10, "Mother'hood," she elaborates on how her loyalties turned toward her children, leading her to exit the gang. Here, her storytelling focus is on how she managed her time.

Liliana—And then what happened in jail?

Gracia—Um, it was a whole different world in there. Actually, I take that back. It was only a whole different world because now they were adults that I was dealing with and no more kids. I mean, I dealt with adults when I was in gangs and stuff, but there they were hard-core criminals, and so they didn't take crap from nobody, you know. You had to, um, you couldn't cry, you had to be tough, you know, so the toughness, that stuck with me, so I didn't have to worry about being tough. It was the fact that I was away from my kids, away from my family, away from all the people that I loved, and had no kind of communication or connection with them at all. Ah, I was locked in a room with a whole bunch of women and, in a cell, couldn't get out when I wanted to, and I had to do what the CO's in there told me what to do. No privacy, the food was disgusting; there was a lot of fights going on. I was in there with murderers, so it was just different.

Liliana—So, you were not at the top any more, you couldn't be a leader. . . .

Gracia—No, not in there. I mean, I hooked up with people that were from San José, and that most of them were Norteñas and were from San José, so that's the crowd that I hung out with. Although I didn't want to be in it no more, but in the prisons that wasn't more so . . . for the women! Men are different; it is all about the gangs in there, for the men. You have to pick a side! If not, you're a loner, and there is a strong possibility that something is going to happen to you, if you don't pick a side to be on. And, so for me in there, it wasn't more so, "Oh, I'm a Norteña and there's a Sureña; let's get down with her, let's fight." 'Cause a lot of the people were trying NOT to fight and just trying to do their time and get out. The majority of the fighting there was done . . . was either because of the TV, fighting over the TV, or people were fighting because somebody was looking at somebody's girlfriend. Or somebody took somebody else's phone time, laundry time. Or somebody took somebody's food, or somebody looked at somebody wrong, but it wasn't because of gangs. So, the majority of it wasn't because of gangs. I mean, there was some stuff going on in there like that; it was more so out in the streets.

And when I was in there, I had to grow up, grow up really fast, and there is some wise women in there. There really was, although they were criminals, there was some really wise women and I learned a lot of wise stuff. And, and that's where uh, I started seeing some people who, or meeting women who ah, would encourage me to do good and not to go back there and "that was no kind of life" for me and that, if I kept doing what I was doing, I was going to be getting the same old results, that things weren't going to change unless I changed it. And so that's where . . . [laughs] . . . and it's funny because I guess I would say that's where some positive role models came in for me, because. . . .

Liliana—Some of these old timers?

Gracia—Some of these old timers, some of them who were lifers, some of them who lived the lifestyle for many years and kept going in and out of there, and they told me, you know, some positive ways to deal with life and how to do it. I remember some woman telling me, "You just need to stay away from all that completely." She said, "If you stay in the environment, if you stay in the atmosphere, that's what you're gonna get. If you remove yourself from it, things are gonna change."

Liliana—And how credible were they? I mean, because they . . . to you, you, they're positive role models and they are because they've done something worse than what you have. . . .

Gracia—One killed her husband, it was domestic violence, and he was beating her all the time, so she killed him. Some were either for robbery or auto theft, drugs and stuff like that, so yeah. . . .

Liliana—And yet, you know, you were willing to believe them? Their statements made sense to you somehow?

Gracia—Of course they made sense, because obviously I wasn't getting it when I was outside, and being in there not only had they already lived the life, but they had enough time to think about how to do things differently. So, although they weren't really, um, I didn't really hold them accountable for what they were saying, but I took it in as new information, some new stuff to know about. All I had was listening to them, so eventually I got something out of it. I was hanging out in the same atmosphere and the same environment, so eventually you're going to get the same results.

Liliana—. . . You mentioned there was some preacher. . . .

Gracia—He was there at the prison, he was the chaplain, yeah. And so I would go to church, I had to go to church, too, 'cause either you were out there with all the girls fighting with each other or dealing drugs in there, or just up to gossip. So I chose to do things differently in there as well. And I was, fortunately . . . I hung with the San José people but some of them were, again, they were in there for a crime but they weren't horrible people. They were people that you couldn't take seriously 'cause they were in prison. They, some of them, like I said, were wise, had some good things to say and so they invited me to church with them, there on the weekends, and I'd go with them. That's when I got involved in getting to know God and hearing things differently, you know, about how life can be . . . easier and, um, in a much healthier way by going to church and reading your Bible and praying and stuff.

The time Gracia served in prison, the unexpected yet poignant advice from her fellow inmates, and the initial encounters with religion, in addition to her prior misgivings about the lifestyle and her longing for her children while being separated, coalesced into the story that allowed her to transcend her life of the gang.

MARGIE

The story of time served by newly emancipated Margie is ongoing, as this discussion shows:

Margie—I got locked up; I've been twelve times total in Juvenile Hall. Fighting, drugs, stolen cars, robberies, assaults, different gang stuff.

Right now the reason I don't have a legit job is because I'm wanted in [another] county and have detectives from [another town] looking for me. I want to turn myself in, because I think it would be better that way, but at the moment, that's not in my plan, to turn myself in yet. I'm not worried about what the sentence would be. I've been in institutions too long. Juvenile is like day care compared to prison. I still don't like it. I don't want to be locked up, but I know I'm going to have to be sometime, before I get cleared.

Being a fugitive of the law places an immense burden on the storytelling process of self-identifying. In acknowledging her past offenses, Margie casually mentions she has served time in the past. But how to story the debt she still owes for the undisclosed crime for which she is being sought? Her sense-making process must include some admission not just of the misdeed, but also of the overarching societal norm that requires payment in the form of incarceration. This move also attests to the moral fiber in her character (MacIntyre, 1981) by submitting that the time she will serve, although unpleasant, will help to clear up her record, which, like Lucha, might keep her from getting a job if she is a convicted felon.

Other aspects of Margie's story dealing with the subject of correctional institutions are discussed further in Chapter 10, "Mother'hood." In brief, her son's father was in prison, and she actively corresponded with and sent him pictures of their son but disagreed with her stepfather's decision (as her son's guardian) to take the boy to meet the incarcerated father. She declared a prison was no place for a child. I did not ask nor did she volunteer whether her son visited her during any of the many times she was incarcerated. Perhaps she wanted the boy to come but he was not brought, so through parts of this story—namely, prison not being "a place for children"—she reconciled that discrepancy; or maybe the boy came but it embarrassed her that he saw her there and she didn't want him to see his father in like circumstances. At any rate, if and when she decides she is ready to turn herself in to clear her name, her time served story will continue to emerge.

DISCUSSION

While it is said that men in gangs typically find that their reputations on the streets ("street creds") are enhanced by going to prison, these women did not seem to find this to be the case. On the contrary, for most of these women—Eréndira, Lucha, and Gracia—all proclaim themselves to be reformed, in the sense that they found the experience unpleasant (even Eréndira did after a while) and that their sentences functioned to further repel them from engaging in the activities that caused their incarceration in the first place. Both Lucha and Gracia acknowledged seeking and finding support from older Latinas in jail, and this topic could be further explored. In describing their experiences of confinement in the past—or, like Margie, in an unknown future—they go to great lengths to establish their sense of self as repentant, knowledgeable and respectful of the law, and resigned to accept their sentences. Although there were some benefits found, they would rather not repeat the experience of incarceration. Overall, these stories play a significant role in narrating their way out of the gang and away from the actions that led them to serving time.

10

Mother'hood

Eréndira, Olga, Margie, Marisa, and Florencia

The image of the teenage mother, especially a young woman of color and, even more poignantly, a gang-involved one at that invokes little sympathy in some segments of society, for she and her offspring are assumed to perpetuate the poverty, dysfunctionality, and criminal patterns that Gangs of Family cultivate. On one end of the storytelling spectrum lie outsiders' assumptions about such a girl: that her condition was brought about by her sexual precocity, that she exploits the social services system by having children just so she can earn more welfare money, and that she supports the various fathers of her illegitimate children and buys them drugs and alcohol with this plentiful handout. At the other end of the storytelling spectrum lies the stories of Margie, Gracia, Florencia, Marisa, Eréndira, and Olga: women whose harsh lives are now on a different path—one that, if supported, can lead them on to a brighter future.

What better way for someone who has heavily tread the path of gangs to journey away from it toward clean living than by literally embodying the agent of the change itself: a pure and innocent child deserving of one's attention, care, support, and advice. These gang-involved women aspire—some explicitly, like Margie, Gracia, and Olga, some implicitly, like Eréndira and Marisa—to be better mothers to their offspring than their own mothers were to them.

Indulging in creative punctuation and alternative spelling, I am offering the term "mother'hood" to signify the storying process that gang-involved women perform relating to their pregnancies, childbirth, and childrearing. Similar to the religious conversion discussed in Chapter 13, "The Narrative of Redemption," mother'hood sometimes appears as a pivotal plot twist in stories about leaving the gang. Invariably, in these stories, women present themselves as treasuring their children above all, which supports the notion that many women in gangs hold traditional beliefs about gender roles and their own parenting responsibilities (Campbell, 1987). All the gang-involved women I spoke to had children, some even while still active in the gang. Some, like Margie, the 18-year-old mother of a 6-year-old son, was still active in the gang, although her son was cared for by her stepfather. Gracia became a mother at 15 and Florencia at 14 while still very much involved, and they did not leave the gang until after their teens. Both temporarily lost custody of their children—Gracia while in prison and Florencia due to her drug addiction. In contrast, Eréndira and Marisa became pregnant and had their children in their late teens as both traversed the path of mother'hood toward inter(in)dependence. Finally, Olga's mother'hood story was rife with challenges and contradictions, which she managed to overcome.

Their stories are not unusual, for as Moore and Hagedorn (2006) have observed, "Regardless of the cultural context, there is one constant in the later life of most female gang members: most have children" (p. 201). But being a mother while in the 'hood is neither a fail-safe way to disinhabit nor a practical way to continue inhabiting the gang. Although mother'hood presented challenges to these women's level of involvement, it was the presence of a child or losing a child to "the system" (Child Protective Services), the child(ren)'s potential endangerment, or the realization that a child's future and well-being required that the mothers adopt certain attitudes toward her or him that empowered these women to shift the focus of their stories toward responsibility and away from "the 'hood."

MARGIE

Studies of gang-involved mothers (Hunt, Joe-Laidler, & MacKenzie, 2005) indicate that the age of first pregnancy can be as low as 11 while the age at birthing as low as 13. Among Latinas, the same study identified 35% as having had at least one abortion. Margie's story is an example in both respects.

Margie—I got pregnant when I was eleven and had my son when I was twelve. Right after that, I started smoking crystal meth.

My son is now with my stepfather. He used to be an alcoholic, but he now works and takes care of my sisters, my brothers. He's a single parent doing it all on his own. Of six kids, only two are his own. He has a legit job, not sure what he does now.

My son's father is in prison right now. I'll send him pictures every year. My stepdad will take him to prison to see him; I honestly don't think he should be going to visit his dad in prison, which is why I never take him to see him.

[My son] already knows about gangs, but my uncles hang out with him a lot. I don't want my son involved in gangs; he's not too much in that environment. He goes to school . . . I don't want him to gang bang. I don't want him to be a drug dealer. I don't want him to go through what I had to. He's born into it, the gang life. I rather he didn't get into it, but if he does, I'll be there for him. He already knows a lot. But I can't stop him and I'm not going to try to stop him. If he wants to be a Northerner, more power to you.

From this brief excerpt, Margie's story of mother'hood emanates from a dialectical tension between hope and destiny. Because her son is being cared for by someone who is clean, sober, and employed legitimately, she hopes he will stay away from the gang. Nonetheless, she acknowledges the extraordinary pull of the Gangs of Family legacy. Although she wants to spare him the trouble she has seen as a drug dealer and gang-banger, she sees it as her duty to support his choice and even pride if he claims North. She discussed her future as a mother this way:

Margie—I know I'm going to have more kids. How I am going to raise them depends on what stage I'm in my life. I actually just recently had an abortion. It sucked, but I can't have it right now. It's just not the right time. I mean, I never believed in them before, but then I threw upon the situation so . . . I did what I had to do.

Here she identifies a tension between who she is and what she is going through in the particular storytelling moment. This logic of meaning and action (Pearce & Cronen, 1980) guides her choice to have an abortion in the specific context: A person like her in a situation like this would make this choice regardless of whether one "believed in them before." In the context of not having a job, being on the lam, and dealing drugs for income—although she claims to be clean—having an abortion becomes an obligatory ("I did what I had to do") move. She seems detached, matter of fact, not cynical, but also not remorseful. Might this decision impact her future ability—heretofore untold, unimagined, and unforeseen—to transcend the gang? Does mother'hood function to further ensnare or release? Studies about the correlation between teenage motherhood and problematic outcomes show that what determines a negative outcome is not age but poverty (Hunt, Joe-Laidler, &

MacKenzie, 2005). For gang-involved women like Gracia, Florencia, and Eréndira, mother'hood is a harbinger of their descent into gang obscurity, yet it also could serve them to restory their lives beyond the gang.

GRACIA

Although Gracia had her daughter at 15 and her son at 17, she continued the gang habits until her early 20s. The "glass ceiling" that keeps professional women from achieving top leadership positions manifested for Gracia in the fact that mother'hood dictated the extent—or lack of—her gang activities. In forming her own gang (see Chapter 4, "Inhabiting the Gang"), she saw herself as in control of her own destiny, but the birth of her first child began to erode her influence. Like many teen mothers, Gracia was forced to leave school to care for her infant; unlike many mothers, regardless of age, her reluctance to forfeit her leadership position in the gang endangered her baby's life.

Gracia—I didn't resent having the baby but I was really emotional because a lot of my freedom was taken away. Wasn't able to do a lot of the stuff anymore. . . .

Liliana—And that was a contradiction for you then, right? Because you're trying to be better, for her, but don't know how to snap out of it. . . .

Gracia—We didn't know how! We didn't know . . . there was no other positive role models in our life. My husband's mom and dad, he was an alcoholic, he was, you know, selling dope too, and his mom was a dope user and my mom was drinking at that time. My dad was in and out of prison, he was a dope addict too, and they lived the gang lifestyle. My dad was this big old huge, hard-core Norteño, and so was my brother. Everybody I knew was getting high and everybody was into gangs. I didn't even know any other way. I knew there was another way, but there was like no positive role models in school, trying to work with us or encourage us. . . . There was—you know what?—I take that back. There was the Community School that I went to, but I only went there for a little while because I was pregnant. At that time I was eight months, and they told me I had to leave because I was so big, it was a safety risk for me being there. So I had to leave and I was supposed to go to some Foothill School or something like that, but I said, "Forget school! I'm done with school. I'm going to be a mom now. What's school going to get me?" That's the kind of attitude that I had, so I completely dropped out. I didn't want to have anything to do with school because I felt that at that time our life was already ruined, I was going to have a baby and nobody is going to want somebody with a baby that you know, and so. . . .

I noticed that I had to spend a lot of time at home with my baby while my boyfriend was still out there kicking it with all the homeboys, homegirls, and partying; of course all the homegirls are still there, and I couldn't be there no more. I could, but it wasn't so much being able to be there the whole time, because I couldn't be running around the streets with my baby. And so, a lot of the homegirls wouldn't come around to visit me. They wouldn't come over and hang out with me. They would still be at the party house, it wasn't like, I was there when they needed me, but when I needed them to hang out with me, keep me company and stuff, they weren't really so much around. So I wasn't able to go to the same neighborhood or go to those same houses because I had my baby. A couple of times I'd do it, but every time I'd take my baby with me, there was either a fight or they were leaving somewhere and I couldn't take my baby along because there was either going to be guns or some kind of weapon like that in a vehicle or the people were going to be carrying it. Of course if there was going to be a gang fight I couldn't take my baby, so I couldn't go.

And so I just started noticing that I had a whole different role. I had to be, I couldn't be who I was anymore. Not only because I had a baby, but because when I really needed them, they weren't there for me. Like if I needed money to buy my baby milk, they didn't give me any money, they couldn't help me. They didn't have it or . . . but they were still young too. But they still had money to buy beer and buy drugs though.

And then, well, my husband would go to Juvenile Hall, and I didn't live with my mom at that time because she had kicked me out because I became pregnant, so I was basically on my own. I lived with my husband's or . . . boyfriend's parents at that time. So I had to provide for my baby. When my baby needed milk, needed diapers, needed clothes, or if I needed a babysitter to do something, my homegirls or homeboys weren't there!

But . . . we got into fights, there was nobody to help me, you know, protect my baby. And I started thinking a lot about, "Was it worth me losing my child over the color red? Over gangs, was it worth it?" And again, when I started weighing things out, I'd do all this for them, but what are they doing for me and my child? So, I couldn't think of me anymore. I brought a life into this world, and she's the one I had to think about. She's the one I had to put first.

There appears to be no equivalent expression among gang members to describe how Gracia's "fair-weather friends" excluded, disappointed, and ignored her during her pregnancy and after the birth of her children, although this is a common phenomenon (Becerra & de Anda, 1984; Hunt, Joe-Laidler, & MacKenzie, 2005). Thus, I offer the term "mother'hood" as also encompassing this alienation from one's peers, among other patterns that the gang-involved Latina mother experiences. Although some might find that having a child provides them an exit from the gang—albeit increasing other challenges in terms of accessing future educational and career opportunities—this option eluded Gracia undoubtedly because she sought to sustain her leadership role, which she had fought so hard to earn and maintain. In gangs, leaders fight their way to the top; if and when the time comes, they must also fight their way out. In Gracia's story, this process appears protracted. Gracia's standing in the gang was diminished by the birth of her children, yet the children also gave her a different perspective to challenge the assumptions she made about having "back up." Mother'hood also presented a practical challenge for Florencia, not so much in terms of her leadership, but in terms of reconciling her hard-core image with the desire to do right by her children.

FLORENCIA

Pregnancy and mother'hood among gang-impacted girls often occur through sexual relations with older males (Hunt, Joe-Laidler, & MacKenzie, 2005) because the social standing of a girl is directly influenced by the reputation of her sexual partner generally (Joe-Laidler & Hunt, 2001) and by the father of her child(ren) specifically (Cepeda & Valdez, 2003). Florencia's story fully corroborates these research claims.

Florencia—I started getting into drugs, and I got one of my friends, another girl, she was a really good friend of mine. . . . She introduced me to this guy who had just got out of prison, and he was twenty-five and I was thirteen. So that . . . I ended up being with him, he was my boyfriend, and everybody knew he was my boyfriend. That was like a big "theeng" when you're a young girl like that, being with an older guy like that, all tattooed down, done prison time, he was from the neighborhood; that was like a big deal for a girl. You were looked at with more respect.

Then I got pregnant. I had my first baby when I was fourteen, and she was born with spina bifida and hydrocephalus. He went back to prison and stayed in prison.

Getting pregnant changed something inside me. I wanted to love my baby and be a mom to her and take care of her. And I thought that was going to change everything, but it actually got worse. I stayed clean my whole pregnancy.

I didn't do a whole lot of drugs before I got pregnant, but after I had my baby, I got really badly into drugs.

But I'd take care of her, in my own way. I lived in Santa Clara at the time, and I would take the 22 bus to Stanford Hospital. I'd get off there and had to walk the last few blocks to Stanford. When she was born, they wanted to take her away from me. They said, "No, you can't have her! She's going to have to go into a home, she'll be taken care of." But I fought for her, I said, "No! I want to keep her! You can't take her away from me!" I was like, "There's no WAY you're taking her away from me!" I fought and fought and they had to release her to me. She had a big hole in her back and I would bandage it every day. I took the best care that I knew how, as a kid having a kid. But I loved her so much. I lived with my mom and my dad. They didn't know I was pregnant until I was about eight and a half months. My sister came in the room and I was changing. "Oh, my God!" and then she knew I was pregnant.

It was really scary because this man was really like my first experience really loving someone—well, what I thought was love. That other situation [her being molested since the age of seven] I guess I just blocked out of my mind, the things that happened. It was a decision that I made. Thinking this is love, this man, loving me and I love him. Like I knew I was pregnant but I was in denial because I was scared. He's back in prison and I'm thirteen years old, I don't know anything about having babies. Then I wore big clothes, I looked like a homeboy, I wore Pendletons, Ben Davis, big T-shirts, so you couldn't tell, and I was really small. It looked like I had gained a little bit of weight. So I went to the hospital. My mom, because she's a nurse, she's like, "You haven't had any prenatal care; you don't know what's going on!" I knew immediately that I was going to have a baby born with . . . I knew inside my heart because during the ultrasound, the girl's eyes just got really big. She had a huge hole and her head was the size of two babies' heads. She had a lot of fluid in her brain.

With that happening and having her, a new love took place inside my heart. I never cared for anyone like that; I never thought I could care about anybody so much. I loved her so much. My daughter went through a lot of surgery. (Read more about her daughter's health condition and treatment in Chapter 11, "Loyalty and Respect.")

Unfortunately, the love I had for my daughter didn't keep me from growing into this other lifestyle. The gangs, I got violent, into drugs, into PCP. . . . The first time I started smoking it, I was buying it from a girl who had four kids, and she was living in an apartment and she had just had a baby. She was using it and selling it. To buy it, I would just go out and hustle money. You lose all morals and principles, if you ever had any in the first place. But in my own ways, I had my own morals, my own things I'd never do.

My daughter was disabled and she received a disability check but I would not touch it. I promised I would never use her money. And I would not get high with another girl who had kids, I'd go outside. That was at the beginning. For years, I never did that. Toward the end, I got really sloppy because I'm a hard-core drug addict and didn't care about anything. In the beginning I had my own mindset, "Okay, don't do drugs around the baby, don't use her money, don't touch . . . keep the household clean." Just like thinking, "You're going to do all right and she's going to be okay."

By this time, I'm like sixteen, now I'm . . . I have my place . . . my daughter is with me this whole time, she couldn't talk. She didn't need a wheelchair until much later. I've had her with me through all this.

When I was pregnant with my son, I was "No, I'm not touching drugs, no way, no how." That was the only time I completely stopped, stayed clean. I started going to school. A teacher told me I scored really high on my SATs. She told me, "You're really above average; you should be in Advanced." I, "What?" Every time, I'd go so far, and every time fall back. One time I had to write a paper and the last question was "What is your biggest fear?" I wrote, "Who I am: that is my biggest fear." I remember writing her and telling her I was getting really scared because I knew I was going to have my baby and once I had the baby, no one knew what was going to hold me back. Sure enough, three months after having him, I went back to the drugs, to the neighborhood, back to everything. I've had a lot of ups and down at that time.

Florencia entered the "paradox of deviance" (Moore & Devitt, 1989) in knowing that she needed to stop her drug use and found the strength to do it, only to return to the lifestyle once her overt motivation (pregnancy) was gone. Although it is not apparent from this extensive description, Florencia's roller-coaster of good intentions while pregnant and failing to maintain the same discipline after the birth is consistent with findings, albeit scant (Hunt, Joe-Laidler, & MacKenzie, 2005), about the risk behaviors of gang-involved pregnant women. The ones who have children may narrate their way out: In order to story a new identity for themselves as "good mothers," they must not only stop partying, drinking, and doping, but they also must refrain from banging and concentrate on their children and their futures. What is to keep those without children from continuing inhabiting the gang? What slowed Florencia's runaway train was having her children taken away, being rejected by her homies, an overdose, and a momentous experience with religion. Her current story now inscribes mother'hood both because of and in spite of the gang.

Florencia—I also want to have a well-balanced home, and they hate being Christians, hate the very thing that helped me and my husband. There's things I let them watch, things I let them do. I let my son go to the movies for the first time and I was, "Where's he at?" He was at the movies; his friend's mom picked him up. He went, "Thanks for letting me go." For a while he was lying to me about his homework. I want them to talk to me, I don't ever want them to feel they cannot talk to me. My son comes to me a lot. My daughter goes to my husband. Even if I'm bugging him and he'll come later: "I'm so glad you are who you are, sometimes you're strict . . . ," but I don't want to be extreme.

Now, for my children, their education is really important. My son, he's a smart kid, but he started having a lot of trouble with his math, he was getting Fs, and I was so concerned: "I can't let this be, I have to help him." At first he didn't understand, "Why are you in my business? Why do you have to know everything?" because I got him a tutor. The other day he comes in my room and says, "Mom, I'm so glad that you love me and that you care. I get mad at you but I'm grateful." He's making up a lot of work.

I look at that, and those are the words. Every birthday my kids have, especially the two older because of what I went through, I look at them and they love me no matter what. My daughter, though she is disabled, not where she can tell me "I remember who you used to be," but I know she knows. When I speak at different places, they'll record it and give me the copy. She tells me, "Momma, I want to listen." She'll be crying and crying, because I speak about the person I used to be. In her ways, she'll find a way to tell me "I love you" and she'll hug me.

Florencia took a fortuitous route out of the gang after a protracted experience with La Vida Loca, hard-core gang-banging, and severe drug addiction. A religious transformation (described in Chapter 13, "The Narrative of Redemption") helped her give voice to this transcendent story of mother'hood. Storytelling parameters now focus on giving her children discipline, supervision, support, care, love, and concern. In this story, Florencia knows that, despite her children's protestations, they know whence she came and where she wants to lead them: to transcend the gang.

ERÉNDIRA

At the age of 19, Eréndira struggled with finishing school and raising her son in the dialectical tension because of and in spite of her gang involvement. The child in Eréndira's mother'hood story signifies an opportunity to disinhabit of the gang. Because she stopped doing drugs and started to disinhabit the gang at 16, her pregnancy served as prologue for a mother'hood story on her way to transcending and inhabiting inter(in)dependence. Recall that my research consultations with Eréndira's were in English and Spanish. To indicate when English was spoken by either one of us, I use *italics* in the transcript.

> *Eréndira*—And now I am . . . I talk with my girlfriends, but they have children, we talk and go out and it's no longer about "Hey, what about *dope* and 'Goofy' [a homeboy's name]." Now it's, "No, my son got sick and wow! He's gotten sick of this and that . . . I remember when he did this and that." It's no longer about gangs, it's more about stories of young mothers. . . . It's like, "How is your son's life" or "How goes it with his father?" No longer "We went to this and we were doing that, we went to this *party*." You understand? The talk changes.

The talk changes as well as the walk, for she now tells a different story with her words and deeds. While she talked to me, she nursed her 8-month-old son. In contrast to Gracia, Eréndira's former homegirls become co-authors of this story as they shift from inhabiting the gang to inhabiting mother'hood. Like Florencia, Eréndira is determined to articulate a cautionary tale to ensure her son knows about gangs as a way to keep him out. When I asked how she had changed, she storied a new reality as a mother:

> *Eréndira*—Before, just how you were dressed, they'd know. They wouldn't care, and right there they would start a fight. But now, I go places and what can they say to me? What is the reason? Do you know what I mean? They see I've changed, I don't dress like before, I have my son, I don't do my make-up. I'm not giving them any motive now; they don't have to say anything to me. It's like, not invisible, but *I guess like, yeah whatever*. . . . When you change, if you really want to change, you make your life a lot easier.

To punctuate this sentiment, during the car ride back to her home after the interview, a few blocks away from her house, Eréndira noticed a teenage girl, her advanced pregnancy accentuated by the burgundy-colored sweatshirt she was wearing, as she walked past a park known to be a Norteño hangout. Eréndira said in an accusatory tone, "Look at that girl! She's putting not just herself but the life of her baby in danger wearing those colors!"

Many single mothers find that the fathers are not involved in child-rearing, either financially or emotionally. Eréndira's mother'hood story accounts for this lack of "back up" from her son's father and for the fact that sustained contact with him keeps her ensnared in a Sureña identity that actually contradicts her efforts to live beyond the gang.

Eréndira—That's how his father was [points to baby], "I'm nothing, but if something happened, I'm gonna back up Norte." And that is why we had many problems about that. He'd say one thing which would offend me and I'd hang up or didn't say anything. He'd say, "I'm sorry." Then he'd say it again and I'd get angry and I'd say, "You know what? Whatever, it's over, I am going to work, because you don't know how to respect me. After all, I'm not into that, but keep your mouth shut, you don't have to go around insulting every time we fight." Even though you say you're not, you always have to choose a side.

Another distinctive element in Eréndira's mother'hood story is that, in contrast to Gracia, Eréndira neither lived with the father of her son nor had much contact with him. Despite her assertions that she was no longer "down" and that the father of her child was "nothing," the two felt obliged to back up different colors, which created problems for them. This complicated Eréndira's process of storying her way out of the gang because she was offended when her son's father would "dis" Sureños and felt compelled to respond in kind. As a result, she decided to no longer be in contact with him. Yet for Florencia, a hard-core Norteña who married a Sureño, this juxtaposition of former selves actually gave higher credence to the couple's ministry work to keep kids out of gangs.

MARISA

Pregnancy was a direct trope for Marisa to exit from the gang (see Chapter 14, "Disinhabiting the Gang," where we learn that her brother urged her to get help when she told him about the pregnancy). Moreover, mother'hood included not just cleaning up during pregnancy but staying clean and shifting storytelling focus toward empowerment and transcendence.

Marisa—. . . by the time I was pregnant, I knew pretty much that [my brother] was going to tell me it wasn't up to him to take care of me anymore. It was up to my husband. And while he was in prison, I took care of myself, and when he came home I told him that I . . . you know . . . "Either you're with me or you're not, and my bus, is you know, ready to go!"

Liliana—. . . and how did you meet him?

Marisa—At the bus stop, to be honest . . . I gave him my phone number, he called me. We hooked up one day, I had dope, he had some dope, we partied, and then, after that, that's about the time when I stopped going home, started hanging out, you know, on the streets. After that we were just together. He was a . . . to be honest, we weren't together that long before I got pregnant. And yeah, I got pregnant, we were together for a few months and he went back to prison and, um, I had a beautiful baby girl.

Liliana—And did you go see him?

Marisa—No, I refused. I refused to take my child in there. I know that, as a child, I went in there one time with my mother to see my dad, and it's no place for a child. It's up to him to stay out and see his kid, 'cause I'm not gonna . . . you know. I'll send him pictures, sure, but it's different. It's one thing to see them in pictures and it's another to hold them in your arms. So, it's up to him. Sounds kind of . . . shitty, but sometimes a woman has to put her foot down and that's where I draw the line.

Liliana—So kind of like your brother drawing the line: you get the grades. . . .

Marisa—Yeah, kinda. . . .

Liliana—But in this case, you're not asking him to do something . . . illegal. . . .

Marisa—. . . illegal . . . yeah [laughs]. I'm just asking him to be a father. . . .

Through his jail term, Marisa managed to stay in touch with the father of her daughter, and she hoped her refusal to bring their daughter to visit him would motivate him to get out of jail and stay out of trouble. Her mother'hood story encompasses not just caring for herself and her daughter, but also for her partner, as she urges him to become interested in the same academic pursuits that have helped her transcend the gang.

Marisa—I already got him started reading the text [used in a class she took]. He likes . . . and you know . . . it's very interesting . . . there was a lot that I thought that I knew, and didn't know. So, and he'll come to me and he'll be like, "Oh, I didn't know that!" You know . . . if I'm going to be educated, then I would like for my spouse to be educated, so that we can . . . if I'm talking something, we have . . . we can be able to talk about and understand each other, you know, just . . . you know. . . . We're gonna . . . you know, life is what you make it, and I plan to make it really good. I was forced to grow up really fast and I'm still young, so might as well slow down and do what I can.

In contrast to Eréndira, Marisa's mother'hood story includes the presence and active involvement of the child's father, her own supportive father, as well as her own academic preparedness—all this despite her involvement in La Vida Loca from the ages of 10 to 15.

Marisa—I definitely could have gone back to drugs after I had my daughter, but um, by the time I had my daughter, my father was working for the County, with the drug court and Prop. 36. He had, he has a lot of pull with the County; he basically told me that if I started using, he'd take her from me, and without her, I don't know where I'd be. She's what keeps me going every single day. . . . I don't want it to have to come to that, you know? I don't want to have to be wondering who she's with.

What Marisa refers to as "Prop. 36" is California's Substance Abuse and Crime Prevention Act of 2000. This state law allows first- and second-time nonviolent, simple drug-possession offenders to receive substance abuse treatment instead of incarceration. Marisa's story reinforces the notion that having a child can improve the life of a gang-involved woman (Moore & Hagedorn, 1999), for the child provides a way to restory her identity into a new, less risky, and more honorable role of caregiver, which also implies taking care of herself by staying clean, getting on with her education, and pursuing healthier relationships (Miller, 2000). Yet the child or children do not function magically to steer women away from La Vida Loca, although the pregnancy could amount to a life-changing event (Lesser, Anderson, & Koniak-Griffin, 1998; Lesser & Koniak-Griffin, 2000). In Olga's case, children and single parenthood brought tremendous despair and a deepening of her addiction, although she had already stopped claiming years before.

OLGA

Mother'hood sometimes presents a challenge in the process of disinhabiting the gang; for Olga, the birth of three daughters in 4 years, from the time she was 18 until 22, frequent breakups and reconciliations with her husband, and her own addiction kept her in the habits of the gang, if not in the gang itself, as she attempted to right her ship. Olga's use of English is shown here in *italics*.

Olga—And he stopped going to school and . . . but I still continued and I got pregnant with my first daughter. I was eighteen already. And then when I gave birth to her, me and him were, we were already like having a lot of problems 'cause he started hanging around again and he started doing the things they do in the varrio, you know, which is everything he wasn't supposed to be doing. So, I was like, I resigned myself and I said, *"I have my daughter." To me it felt like a joy I had never felt before, when I had my daughter, and I actually had somebody to look after . . . it was mine and nobody could take this away. To me it felt like, "Wow! You know, I never had this, I never felt this," and it felt good, so whatever he did, I didn't care no more, whether he came to sleep or not, I just didn't care.*

You know, 'cause yes, I was eighteen, and yes, I had my baby, but thereinafter I got pregnant again with my second daughter, like two months after. So then I had her and I was still going to school at nights. I would go once a week, every Tuesday night, and the teacher which was both of our teacher's, [sic] he would tell me, "Why don't you leave him? You know, you deserve better. Man, why do you put up with all the stuff he's putting you through?" And he would just encourage me, "You stay in school, you do this, you could do it, you're strong young woman, you know, you're a strong mother. I could see that you have a lot of love for your daughters." You know, so I started feeling like, my confidence and self-esteem started getting like built up 'cause I felt like I was keeping a job, you know, already for years. I was going to school, for my high school diploma, not just my GED. I was raising up my two daughters, you know, even if I was bringing them you know, wherever, you know. I felt I was doing good like I never felt before in my life, you know, so I felt really confident, that I could do this.

Liliana—So you had a structure now?

Olga—Yeah, I had a structure that I had to create. Though it was difficult in the beginning, I felt like the more, the more, the sense of warmth, of love that I needed I found it with my daughters, you know, and the security was my job, the education, and how I was actually building one now, um, so I kind of started feeling like, "Okay, I could do this, whether he's here or not, I don't need him!" You know, that's kind of like my attitude! And um, that's how it was for years, until '94, when I had my other daughter and I was gonna graduate, because I had already been going to school for four years. And we had a big blowout you know, and he didn't let me go to my graduation. By that time he was already using drugs and he was really bad already, and I decided to just leave him after four years that we had been together, living together.

Liliana—And you had three daughters now?

Olga—We had three daughters now. And my youngest was two months. I decided to leave him and I went to my mom's and I was there for a couple of months, then I went back home, back with him. That's how it was like, I would leave him for a month, three weeks, go back home, he would come looking for me, very unstable, you know. . . .

Liliana—So that stability that you were looking for, that you were working for, it just, it seemed to . . . escape you . . . out of reach?

Olga—Yeah! Because, again, the gang life creeped in you know, through him, you know, to rob, to take away what I had built, what I felt I had built and I was losing that. I was losing that so I started getting very angry, started like abusive in the sense that I would yell at my daughters. They were young, two, three years old, and my baby, you know, she was one. I couldn't stand it, you know, not even looking at them. I had no more peace, I had no more . . . like all this stuff . . .

I would think, "The *varrio* once again came and took away, *you know,* took away from me *you know, the most dear I have.*" *I thought I had it for a while and then I was so confident. . . . I had hope that I was gonna keep it and again, it stripped me, when that started happening.*

Like Eréndira, Olga stopped claiming before she became pregnant; unlike Eréndira, Olga continued a quarrelsome involvement with the father of her children. Because of her husband's gang involvement, she encountered (but managed to surmount) tremendous obstacles in achieving an education and keeping her job. Although she also saw childbearing as a blessing, one that gave her a new purpose in life, the instability of her relationship with her husband initiated a lived story of depression, despondency, and addiction. The "good mother" story she was hoping to tell required her husband as a co-author, and when she tired of his inability to support her, she relinquished the "good mother" story altogether. Olga's experiences are further detailed in Chapter 13, "The Narrative of Redemption," for her story infuses the themes of mother'hood and disinhabiting the gang with a vivid description of how her newfound faith provided her the positioning to transcend the gang.

DISCUSSION

In summary, mother'hood entails pregnancy and childbirth within the gang habits. It forebodes alienation from one's peers and a decreased ability to participate in the activities of the gang, such as running around in the streets, committing crimes, engaging in fights, and consuming alcohol and drugs. Mother'hood functions to rewrite one's identity from gang member to mother and to help a young mother engage in relational practices that support this newly authored self. The lack or paucity of knowledge about what form such relationships may take and how to engage in them complicates this process for the teenage-mother storyteller.

There is yet another feature of mother'hood: the struggle both within herself and against the discursive forces that the young mother must face in order to become something for which she has no exemplars. In the *barrios*—here I explicitly mean neighborhoods, but also imply "*varrios*" or gangs—there is wide acceptance of the idea that a gang-involved woman who becomes pregnant can leave the gang and go on to clean living to provide for her child. Mother'hood earns respect, and it gives the storyteller wider storytelling latitude. But how can she tell a story that for her is unlived, unimaginable, and unavailable? She must avail herself of useful odds and ends, bits of linguistic resources from old stories and from stories heard from others but not yet lived, to construct a story of mother'hood.

The mother'hood story helps young women transcend the gang and inhabit inter(in)dependence because it entails a restructuring of their own identity vis-à-vis the gang. It includes a challenging and sometimes alienating yet helpful maturing process, in which they acknowledge the consequences of their choices; a reevaluation of relationships (with the father, their families, and their friends); and a struggle to avail themselves to resources to facilitate their turnaround. As they transform their identity through mother'hood, they become poised to transcend the gang.

11

Loyalty and Respect

Florencia, Gracia, Eréndira, Angela, Margie, and Lupe

Given their criminal experiences, a gang might be an odd place to find some code of ethics on loyalty and respect, yet these two values make up a large part of gang-involved women's storytelling. Gangs clearly are not alone in demanding loyalty from their members. For example, military groups are incapable of performing their functions when any one of their members questions orders. In the voices of Florencia, Gracia, Eréndira, Angela, Margie, and Lupe, loyalty and respect assume various forms and serve different functions.

FLORENCIA

Gangs provide not just the fictive kin (Schneider, 1980) but what I call the "ersatz kin" who give youth much-needed support in confronting life's vicissitudes. I use the term "ersatz kin" to signify people who replace the absent family of origin as those whom youth depend on for support and turn to in times of crisis, filling a void never or seldom occupied before (see Chapter 4, "Inhabiting the Gang," for more details). Although for many children, nuclear and extended family members provide company as well as emotional and financial support in times of crisis, Florencia found that her fellow gang members seemed to provide this kind of support.

Florencia—I know a lot of people think gangs are no good, and they're not, but when you're in a gang, you kind of look at it as all you have. If these kids get reached and worked with the right way, they're good kids. They're just really looking for something, because in my little group, the gang that

I was in, I remember when my daughter would have surgery, they would all go. We'd sleep in the lobby of Stanford Hospital, a bunch of gang members, lying asleep in the lobby. My daughter is in these nine-, ten-hour surgeries, and they would all be there with me, until she'd come out of the surgery. It was like, my family members; besides, my mom, my sister, and my dad at that time, they didn't care to come. . . . They were there, it was like loyalty, "I'm there for you and you're going to be there for me."

In addition to characterizing this ersatz kin support as "loyalty," Florencia extends the definition of loyalty to include the "secrecy" or "protection of identity" that loyal gang members are expected to provide, as the following excerpt demonstrates:

Florencia—Loyalty is so important because, once you lose that loyalty, you're no good no more. Like being a snitch in the neighborhood is like the worst. Like we had this girl that they told us snitched out, and I was selling dope out of my house and I had a couple of guys living with me that sold dope for me and there was people that weren't allowed to buy dope at my house. These guys weren't allowed to sell dope to those people, because it would come back to me. One of those guys sold dope to her, so I had her on her knees in my house, with a gun to her head. We took her in the other room and beat her, almost killed her. The other guy I was telling you about was choking her; she was foaming, her eyes were rolling, she was turning purple, to put a scare on her. Because they said she had already snitched. To come buy dope for us, it was like she was setting us up. It was her first warning. Had she come again, we probably would have done something worse. Then we let her go, and we told her never to come buy dope from us again. Then she kind of disappeared for a little while, but that was just word. But once there's word that you're a snitch, or a "leva," or you're no good, that's it. A "leva" is . . . you're on the "leva," you're on a no-good status with me. Once you get there, you have to work your way up, you gotta do something drastic to regain our trust, something that's going to really, really make people change their minds that you're really loyal. And then they have to let you do it, because if you can't do it, you still can't come back.

Despite the brutality of this attack, Florencia's story points to some ethical standards about the treatment of others. More pointedly, as she describes below, if the identity of the "other" deserved it, they would receive special dispensation from Florencia based on aspects of her own identity as a victim of abuse when she was a little girl. Thus, her honor code also included some self-imposed limits, such as not using her children's money to buy drugs (as we saw in Chapter 10,

"Mother'hood") and protecting or avoiding hurting the weak and innocent, as we see below.

Florencia—Me personally, I never got into. I could never steal from
people. That's one thing my mom taught me: "Don't steal! That's ugly." But
I got into, like I would steal a car; I never mugged people, I guess it just
bothered me. I never messed with anybody that wasn't the same lifestyle as
me, 'cause I felt like those were the people that were weak, they were weaker
than we were, it wasn't a fair fight. It's weak to walk up to someone and rob
them, like they don't have a chance. If you're going to do something, do it
with someone at your level. I never liked messing with someone who was
elderly or disabled. It was never my thing. I guess because I was a little girl
and I remember this man hurting me and I couldn't fight back, was an unfair
fight. So that stuck with me and I never wanted anybody to feel like I felt as
a child . . . basically, taken over by somebody else, so I never wanted anybody
to feel that. I wanted people like him and others that hurt me to feel what
I felt, but I never wanted nobody weak. They're innocent, they're weak. As
long as I had control of whoever I was with, we never did anything like that.
It wasn't okay. You were going to be no good with me if you did that because
it wasn't right for you to hurt somebody.

Although she expected—demanded, in some cases—loyalty, Florencia also recognized that it could not be proffered blindly, and she
protected her vulnerability by following her brother's advice to be self-
reliant and always keep the upper hand, much like the fictional character
Don Vito Corleone (Puzo, 1969), with his penchant for banking favors
and then asking the debtors to pay in kind when he needed them to.

Florencia—It just got really bad. It got to the point where the guys they
would see my level of commitment, my level of loyalty. So now they're asking
me to get gigs. I was like, "Yeah! I'll do it, I don't care!" I wasn't going to be
anybody's "mule." I would tell them, "Do whatever you want! I'm not going
to do that." The only thing I ever did do, I helped out two homeboys that
just got out of prison; I let them stay at my house for a little bit, until they
got on their feet. My brother taught me, "Never borrow money and never let
them do you any favors, because then you owe them. Never let them get you
out of a bind. Work your way out, because you're going to owe and you're
going to owe with your life." So that stuck with me. So if they'd say, "Hey, let
me give you this *feria* 'cause the homeboy stayed with you," and I'd say, "No,
keep it for yourself, I'm all right." I didn't want to take any money because
then they'd come back and "Hey, remember I did that for you? Remember I
gave you that money?"

Being a "mule" means doing somebody's work for them. Hosting the two homeboys and then not taking money for it was not being a mule in Florencia's eyes. Rather, this action meant she followed her brother's advice by doing someone a favor so that then they would owe her. As a complement to loyalty, the concept of respect did not just apply to Florencia and her homies but extended to her family members, as shown in this vivid description of how Florencia exacted retribution for an attack on her mother:

Florencia—One time my mom, she was at a bar and got jumped by like eight women. My mom said something to them and they said something back and then just jumped her. So my mom went to the hospital and I found out and went back to the bar, looking for them, but it was already closed. So my homeboys said, "Let's just shoot up the whole bar!" and I said, "No, I want them to suffer like they made my mom suffer." So the next weekend, I went back and there were three of them that came out and I beat one of them really bad with a bat in front of my mom. I beat her really bad until she was moving no more. They had to pull me off her, I was beating her with a bat, and it didn't matter. I walked away laughing from that; it got that bad, the violence. I was probably high then.

Drug-induced violence is a short explanation for such behavior; the larger frame on which this incident gains meaning includes primarily the desensitization to violence experienced while witnessing similar behavior and experiencing similar treatment as a child. Additionally, what gives coherence to such brutality is the notion that she must retaliate for the disrespect shown to her mother in the most violent, personal, and humiliating way and feel no regret at that time.

GRACIA

A loyal following is what a leader must rely on to make her gang status meaningful and keep it that way. In conflating loyalty with respect, Gracia required her homegirls to be loyal to her, and they enacted this loyalty in showing respect toward her relationship with her main sex partner, who was the father of her children. As this situation devolved, it figured prominently when she storied her diminishing leadership role in the gang, her disillusionment with it, and eventually her leaving (see Chapter 10, "Mother'hood"; Chapter 12, "Betrayal"; Chapter 14, "Disinhabiting the Gang").

Gracia—And after I had my first child, uh, remember I talked about loyalty and my homegirls didn't do this and didn't do that and they were trying to be with my boyfriend, and I noticed that, um, when I wasn't around most of the time, a lot of the homeboys would tell me, "Oh, so and so, was flirting with 'Loverboy'; they disappeared for a while" and I'm like, "Oh, no! What's going on?" So it was like, loyalty just started slipping. Everything was real good, almost perfect from the very beginning, and as years went on, I realized that there was nobody loyal . . . and the ones that were loyal . . . already gotten out, got out and moved on. They already had their kids, or their child, they were with their boyfriends and settled down and they didn't get out of the gangs, but they didn't hang out with us so much either because they had their own family. The ones who didn't, started becoming unfaithful and disloyal and backstabbers. So not only was my fighting going on with gang fights now, but it was going on with fighting with my boyfriend, fighting with the girls, and fighting with other people.

Liliana—With your own homeboys and homegirls?

Gracia—Yeah.

Liliana—I'm intrigued by that, in contrast to the idea of loyalty. For example, loyalty to the gang, when we started talking about why you formed your own gang, well, you said, first of all, there's no sissies. And then of course, you'd case them out, you'd look at them and see if they'd be a good element to invite. . . .

Gracia—Definitely loyalty . . . that was a big part of it. . . .

Liliana—How would they demonstrate their loyalty? And again, I'm interested in loyalty to the gang, and loyalty, or lack of loyalty to a couple, you know. . . .

Gracia—Loyalty would definitely be, "Don't disrespect us in any kind of way."

Liliana—And what would that mean?

Gracia—That would mean like, how you carry yourself out there, don't make us look bad. Loyalty would mean, if I tell you something, you keep it as a secret. Loyalty would mean if we do something and we get in trouble, if the cops come, you better not tell on us, you better not be a snitch. Loyalty means one of us gets locked up and goes to Juvenile Hall or whatever, that you'd still be there for us and make sure that our family members are okay; take care of the younger brothers or sisters, or even older brothers or sisters. Loyalty is "Be there when I need you." If I'm going to get into a fight you better be there to back me up, you better not run and back down. Loyalty means if I ask you to do something, you have to do it, no matter what. If you can't do it, then you ain't with us. Loyalty, it could mean, even in some gangs, "Okay you have to do a beer run, go steal me a pack of cigarettes, I want some candy, go steal me some candy. If I tell you to do it, go do it." Loyalty could mean, "Don't disrespect others' family members. Don't talk about my mom, or if you come to my house, keep it under the hush-hush, don't let parents know or people know our business. Don't go sharing our stuff, what we do, or what crimes we commit"—that kind of loyalty. "You keep everything a secret, to be there when I need you." And loyalty definitely means, "Don't you ever be with my boyfriend, or else I'm going to, . . ." you know, somebody would say, "I'm going to kill you!" Or "I'm going to cut your hair off or I'm going to slice your face," or . . . loyalty is "You never try to be with my guy, no matter what, don't look at him wrong, don't flirt with him, don't disrespect us in any kind of way." So loyalty could be a lot of ways.

Liliana—So, this friend of yours who said your boyfriend tried to be with her and she declined. . . . What happened to the other one, the one that said she declined?

Gracia—She became my best friend. She was my very best friend from the beginning, and still to this day, she's one of my best friends. So yeah, she's always been my best friend. There's about four of us out of the group who are really, really close. For a while, we were recruiting, but then we stopped. It became a problem having more girls in a gang. When I say that, it's because they weren't loyal. We couldn't trust them, they were backstabbers. Like talking about us, whatever we shared with them they'd share with other people, they're telling people our business; they're messing with all the guys, sleeping around with them. We didn't like that kind of stuff. That was disloyalty to us, so we kicked them out and ended up staying with the loyal ones, with the righteous ones.

Liliana—And how many were they?

Gracia—There was about twenty-one. When we first started, there was little over thirty, and I can't quite remember but there was a lot of us. But in the end there was about twenty-one, until some started having babies, some got locked up, some went to YA and some just never came back; they got out and never came back.

Liliana—And when you say they were the righteous ones, what made them so?

Gracia—Like if I gave them $200 to put in their pocket, they'd be right there staying with it in their pocket, they wouldn't do nothing with it until I told them otherwise. Or like if I told them, "Hey, I'm going to fight this big old huge girl, I need you to back me up, no matter what. If she's starts beating me up, at least throw her off of me so I can get another chance to get on her, do something like that" [giggles]. Um, be righteous and loyal means having my back no matter what. Don't disrespect me in any kind of way as far as trying to be better than me, talking about me, trying to make me look bad or something like that. If somebody said something bad about me, they were real quick to back me up, to defend me, whether I was there or not. Somebody that was not going to burn me and be with my boyfriend or somebody that wasn't going to steal from me or take something that belonged to me and someone that was going to be jealous or greedy. A lot of why the gangs are breaking up too is because of jealousy. A LOT of huge jealousy.

Liliana—Jealousy over position? Jealousy over boys or . . . ?

Gracia—Position, the boys, trying to be prettier, trying to be better, to dress better, trying to look like the number one. . . .

Liliana—So there is a hierarchy then, there's a pecking order that some are the established leaders, if you will, and some are challenging that position, but those advances are not . . . are not accepted . . . ?

Gracia—They're not accepted and we'd kick them out. After a while we didn't have a problem with girls, other than them getting drunk and fighting with each other for some stupid reason. Other than that, we all pretty much got along. We . . . there were times that we'd run away and stuck together with each other for a while. May not have been all of us, maybe not all of us together, but there was a good group, maybe eight of us, who were always together no matter what. The parents let us sleep at their houses, we'd go to school together, we'd get drunk together. When we'd fight together, we'd fight with others, we'd even be with our boyfriends together, we'd go out together, everything, everything together. Most of my time was spent with my friends than with my parents. Most my time was with them than at home. And when I did go home, I hated it. Even though it was . . . my mom provided a good home for me, I still didn't want to be there. I still wasn't getting . . . I guess I could say I didn't want to be told what to do no matter what. And I wasn't going to let my parents tell me what to do when I could go over here and tell these people what to do. And even if I wasn't telling them what to do, it was still an equal thing, to where we were able to hang out and kick it, do whatever we wanted, nobody was going to tell us what to do. We wanted to have fun, and that's what that was all about: having fun, being without boyfriends, having fun, beating up people if they deserved it, being tough, and defending ourselves and defending our neighborhood. And that's what it became; just being who we wanted to be and nobody was going to stop us.

Gracia's gang was challenged by dwindling loyalty as the ranks swelled, for as more girls joined, the less Gracia could take their commitment for granted. She made a strategic choice to reduce their numbers to a select few—to downsize—in order to maintain the high quality of loyalty. This way, the righteousness in Gracia's story about gang loyalty signifies trustworthiness as a superior character trait, even among people involved in breaking the law. Coupled with the need for respect is the inadequacy of the home environment to provide a sense of belonging and, with it, loyalty and respect. In other words, Gracia lacked the lived experiences to tell a "typical teenager" story about nagging parents who nonetheless give offspring a moral compass with which to navigate the rough waters of public middle school.

ERÉNDIRA

Gang-involved women perform loyalty in a variety of ways. In Eréndira's case, she specified that both Norteños and Sureños manifested in like fashion: by showing colors, by claiming or backing up, by upholding the Gangs of Family tradition, and by demanding that others express a claim one way or another. Noticeably, Eréndira recognized that, just because another girl may claim Sur like she did, this did not mean that they could settle their differences in a nonviolent way. In this segment of the transcript, *italics* show when English was spoken.

Eréndira—. . . sometimes you have problems among yourselves, but that would be like supposedly she thinks you are with her boyfriend or things like that. It's not longer that "You are Norteña, you are Sureña"; it's different. These are the typical fights between them. There are times that "Oh, I can't stand her, even though she is Sureña." That is typical, and you're going to see that among Norteños as well. That is why I tell you, many things are the same. How a gang works, how are the youngsters, it's the same; just *background-wise* is different.

Liliana—So, what about those who don't belong to either side? That are nothing? Is that how one speaks about someone who's neither Norteño or Sureño? Or is there no one who does not belong?

Eréndira—There will always be some that prefer one side or another, even though they say they're not in the gang, they are. Some say, *I'm not Sureña, but I back up Sur, I back it up.* If something were to happen, I'll choose that. . . . Sometimes it's because of family, "Oh, my family was Norteña, I have to be . . . since my cousins are Sureños, then I have to be. . . ."

I'm curious to see how she conceptualizes loyalty while just taking a stroll down the street. What kind of respect does Eréndira and many youngsters like her expect when they walk down the street in the course of their gang-impacted or gang-involved days?

Liliana—. . . and, let's say you'd get dressed in a certain way, when you walked alone in the streets. . . .

Eréndira—I was NEVER [emphatically] alone! *If you're smart*, you know that being alone is like having a *big old target sign*: "I'm here: get me!" That is why *like* I never walked alone. If I knew I had to walk alone, I'd cover myself, or something. Not because *I wasn't down or anything*. You know that if you're alone, that is, I tried to avoid a confrontation because I had to tell them where I was from, or what I was, do you understand me?

Liliana—That's what I want to know! How does this encounter happen? You're walking alone or with company, then . . . ?

Eréndira—One or the other: they look at you or you look at them. One or the other: you're up to it, or many start talking, "Oh, *where you from*? What do you know? *You're a Scrap, you're a Buster*, or *what's up*?" And right there and then, a fight. Then the neighbors look and say, "*I'm gonna call the cops*," and then everyone takes off running. It's not so big where you say, "Wow!" but sometimes they have knives or guns and a confrontation like that could cause, well . . . like an ex-boyfriend of mine is in jail for twenty years because a Norteño confronted him and in the end, he killed him with a gun.

Her textured story of profound similarities among gangs, despite the professed differences, gains depth in her explanation that covering herself up while walking alone was not "ranking out"—a sign of disrespect by her not backing up the color—but merely a precaution against assault. As Garot (2007) has argued, demanding to know " 'where you from,' [though] intended to resolve any ambiguity, actually becomes merely another resource to be worked in the contingent, variable effort in which young people everywhere engage in molding the self" (p. 51). In showing that gang identity is a "doing," Garot urges researchers to conceptualize identity as a "sensual response to a moment's vicissitudes" (p. 50), rather than as some static character trait, and argues that, through this interaction ritual of reconnaissance or "hitting up," a youngster's gang identity is made relevant because it is a "constitutive feature of a local [gang] ecology" (p. 53). Eréndira thus explained that covering herself did not mean she was not loyal to the gang, but that, being alone, it made sense at the time to avoid exposing herself to attack by rival gangs.

Despite sworn allegiances to the gang, girls will feud among them-selves, often vying for the favors of a male in a leadership position, and just because someone claims Sur this does not automatically make her a friend of another Sureña. The experience of being disrespected by her own homegirls was also visited on Eréndira. Yet through this, she came to scrutinize her own loyalty vis-à-vis the gang, specifically in the aftermath of a confrontation with another Sureña while she was in the park alone primarily because a presumed homegirl failed to back her up (see Chapter 12, "Betrayal"). To add insult to injury, although her homeboys initially postured themselves to condemn the other girl's untoward act against Eréndira, they soon lifted the ban against talking to the girl who had assaulted her, admitting that they did so because she was a "hoodrat" who provided sex to them. This incident of misplaced loyalty and undeserved disrespect served as punctuation in her story about disillusionment and departure from the gang lifestyle; the fact that her homeboys would prize this other girl's sex more than Eréndira's company seemed unconscionable and inconsistent with the way gangs typically classify women (Cepeda & Valdez, 2003).

ANGELA

A girl does not have to actually be gang-involved to consider respect and loyalty important to her sense of self. Gang-impacted "wannabes" may prove their worth by showing respect for their target homegirls and by loyally following orders to exact revenge when others disrespect them. Angela's peripheral gang involvement was characterized by this role of "enforcer of respect," for she had experienced its counterpart as the victim of such affronts (see Chapter 8, "In la Vida Loca"). As a bilingual speaker, Angela's use of English is shown in *italics*.

Liliana—And what were the topics that would come up when the others would tell you, "Go say this to her"? Was it about the fights?

Angela—Looks, it's all. Looks. Someone is looking at you the wrong way. Supposedly, that someone gossiped about you. That is, one is eleven, twelve. When I got to high school, I decided to distance myself from that group, thank God. But, they were ridiculous things, about a look, about that she is from another place; any excuse to starting a fight.

Liliana—And that was . . . say the fight, when it was resolved, was it to say, "Don't mess with me! You now know who's boss around here." What was accomplished with the fight?

Angela—Acceptance.

Liliana—No, but I mean, the group, let's say. What did they accomplish with . . . ?

Angela—They were leaders, they were the ones who controlled.

Liliana—Now, I'm going to tell you, you said it was an act. I'm going to ask you, I don't know if you feel comfortable doing this, but I'm going to ask you to give me a look like I'm one of the girls. . . . I'm a victim, I am the one you want to . . . or one of the looks they'd give you that required me to go and tell them, "Don't look at me like that!" or whatever. . . .

Here I was attempting to flesh out Angela's idea that gang behavior is as much posturing as any other adolescent behavior: For example, cheerleaders, smart kids, band members, Emos, and jocks all feel an obligation to be "someone," in that they have specific roles with scenes, dialogues, scripts, costumes, gestures, and spots to perform and fulfill as expected. But because Angela is no longer an actor of that role, it is difficult for her to embody her inner bully; it just is no longer there, deeply felt, or ready to emerge unprovoked, especially by someone not considered a foe.

Angela—It's been so long! It's difficult for me, but I could tell you that with a look directly in your eyes, it was already a defensive look. And later, the fact that I made *eye contact* and you were looking at them like saying, *"I'm not scared of you."*

Liliana—Like challenging. . . .

Angela—Exactly. There was then the usage of a term like *"mad-dogging,"* and *"mad-dogging"* was when they look at you from head to toe, and that was a challenge. And it's something very ugly, what immaturity! But so long as they accept you. Sometimes they wouldn't look at you, but someone else would tell you they were looking at you, just to *push* you to do that. And they'd all get together and it would be like a challenge, to see who's better than whom. And it's hard because in that stage is where it starts. There you have the decision to say, "I'm going to continue with this or I'm going to stop." Because it starts, *literally* at a very early age, eleven, or perhaps younger depending on where you live.

Liliana—At that age, one is very vulnerable, right? One wants to know who is one's friend, who's with me.

Angela—Very vulnerable! *You want to fit in.*

Liliana—So, okay, "mad-dogging" would be one motive, one reason . . . what are others?

Angela—*Talking* [makes quote marks with fingers]. . . . The biggest, you won't believe, is *"mad-dogging."* They'd look at you and they'd give you this look [turns to her right, looks me up and down with disdainful look on her face—in effect, engaged in the performing of "mad-dogging"], and that was a pretext to go look for a fight. Fights that, in my friend's situation, she was, uhf! . . . twelve . . . ah . . . she went and knived [sic] another girl . . . she almost killed her . . . who was much older than she. The other one was in ninth grade, and my friend was I believe in seventh grade. *So.* . . .

Liliana—And what happened to your friend? Did they catch her?

Angela—She ran away. I remember she ran away, she moved away from the area. I didn't have any news about her until just recently that she came back to her mom and family, a housewife. And the other girl was in the hospital, almost died from the *wounds.* But she survived.

Liliana—She survived? And nobody came to try to avenge her afterwards . . . from that . . . ?

Angela—It was not an act of gangs. We were very young still, we were not involved. This was not a case of rival gangs, but rival friends. The other girl was not in the gang. In those days, they used a lot of "Clubs de Quebradita." I don't know if you remember that? It was a mix between Cholos and people who liked Mexican music. Clubs would compete in dancing with others. You could say it was a type of gang . . . simply was that *"we were talking smack."*

Liliana—And what does that mean?

Angela—*In general you were just talking shit, excuse my language,* excuse this, but *that's just the verbiage people used to use, and that was, for some people that was just an excuse for not liking someone else, thinking they're better than you and some type of negativity growing between two people. Um, again, I think it was just the whole mesh of blending and looking for ways to prove yourself to other people.*

Liliana—Oh, so, it wasn't just the content of the stories, of the things they'd say to each other, but that they said something, right?

Angela—And the value that you could create in confronting the problem . . . the value you'd derive . . . and proving to the others that *you were tough.*

Liliana—. . . that you wouldn't let them talk about you like that. . . .

Angela—Uh huh.

Liliana—And of the . . . that is, you were the front, and they'd use you as. . . .

Angela—. . . in many cases, and I'd do it. I'd be the first to want to do it, because I did not want to be rejected, because I came from an environment where I was, *I was a goody-goody and I didn't want to be the goody-goody anymore 'cause it didn't bring me any benefit or acceptance and I wanted to be accepted. I was never fully in that group.*

Liliana—That is, they never jumped you, they never took you to do any. . . .

Angela—Something in me, did not allow me. . . . They'd hang out. They were so little, they were so young, that some decided to continue and *they got jumped in . . . the whole nine yards . . .* and the others decided not to do it. But it was the "Vista Cholas Locas" . . . that's who they hung out with.

She makes a distinction between those who continued a more active involvement and those, like her, who chose not to. I theorize that "wannabes" pay their dues by defending the honor of this junior-varsity "para-gang," the precursor to the real thing, by doing their storytelling bidding for them. The gangs establish their sense of grandeur and power by counting on aspirants to make their name known, to demand respect, and to instill fear in others. These uninitiated ones earn membership—among other ways, as we previously learned from Gracia—in stories lived through ferociously responding to face threats victoriously. Facework, the actions to establish a positive account of oneself vis-à-vis negative accounts from others, is an ongoing pursuit (Goffman, 1967), so one of the functions of this constant phenomenon of demanding deference might be to establish and maintain the gang as a relevant storytelling topic in girls' lives.

Although Angela's acts of toughness were not intended to elicit an identification of gang membership, as Garot's (2007) consultants did when they "hit up," by attempting to regulate the nonverbal behavior of others, Angela nonetheless tried to uphold the reputation of the para-gang and its boundaries, as well as to punish those who would ignore the hierarchy. Ultimately, by bullying others into nonverbal deference, she might be "showing . . . she is down for the hood" and hoping to earn points toward membership from among the leaders (p. 56). Yet something in Angela kept her from descending deeper into gang involvement, and that "something" is further discussed in Chapter 15, "Transcending Gangs."

MARGIE

Is there a difference between how a "wannabe" like Angela and a girl from Gangs of Family like Margie construct stories of loyalty and respect? Obviously, not all youth in Gangs of Family will choose the same color, even if they do claim. For Margie, loyalty and respect as the overarching claim to a color is signified by what it meant to be a Northerner. This subject came up as we discussed her son's hypothetical decision to claim North (see Chapter 10, "Mother'hood").

Liliana—What if he wants to be a Sureño?

Margie—No! [emphatically] He can't do that! But it gets crazy, all your soul is in it, you'd disown your kids just because they do that. I've disowned plenty of my family because of that. Well, not actually, just a few of my cousins, like three of them, because they decided to be Southerners. Who knows why, because they were raised by Northerners. So, now nobody talks to them. None of my family talks to them, but they're not out to get them because they are family. I've gone to their house before, one of their houses, brought hellah people to their house, torn the house down pretty much, she didn't want to come out of the bathroom, so we had to tear the wall down, get her to come out.

Liliana—Do you know why they did it?

Margie—I don't know why they claim South, I don't talk to them, whatsoever.

At this juncture, Margie's story invokes a paradox through talking about what happened to her cousins who became Southerners. Although she said nobody in her family went after them, she followed by telling about one such pursuit. Yet Margie declined to speculate as to what might have made her cousins betray the colors of the family, and she failed to explain why she and her homies wanted her cousin to come out so badly that they tore down the walls of the bathroom in their efforts.

Liliana—I wonder how respect is shown, what happens when you don't show it, how do you show that you do? What are the moments when you can say "that's respectful"? What does it mean?

Margie—As long as they show you respect, there's no problem. Respect depends on the situation you're in. Out here, they [Sureños] fear us, even though we're outnumbered by them, they don't know that, we're just more organized than they are. Most of the time, if you're just walking down the street, if they put their head down normally, that's that. If they don't put their head normally, then you have to decide what you want to do after that. I've never got nobody to not put their head down.

I continue asking her about street encounters and whether people who don't know each other and nonetheless greet could be interpreted as disrespectful.

Margie—There's nothing wrong with greeting people, but not everybody is the same. There's a lot of Northerners that are disrespectful and a lot of Northerners that are very respectful to everybody. Some just like to be stupid and be out there, hellah loud and make us look stupid.

Her story of Northerners being outnumbered by Southerners contradicts official law enforcement figures (Rodriguez & Rosengren, personal communication, July 1, 2008), but who am I to challenge her lived experience? Here, too, I wonder about its utility and argue that portraying her group as the capable underdog resonates with the story of The Alamo. The exhibits in the monument and museum in San Antonio, Texas, while polysemic, like many other stories, privilege a story that represents the "Texians" as noble and courageous, willing to stand up for their principles even in the face of danger and peril (Rossmann, 2004). Where sense would have dictated that they capitulate to the Mexican army led by Santa Anna, their love for freedom (so goes the story) transformed natural survival instinct into a duty to stay and die to defend what they thought was their land. Is there any more or less honor for Margie in being the dominant gang in the community? If everyone wears the same colors, then one gets complacent and less vigilant. Yet to be outnumbered and still succeed in earning the respect of the enemy implies that her group is "more organized," smarter, more valiant and courageous, and thus more deserving of respect.

Margie hypothesizes about the encounter of greeting rival gang members on the street, invoking a rule for constituting her understanding the meaning of actions and words, and a rule that helps her regulate her decision for how to go on. If they don't show respect by putting their heads down (respect equals deference), then she must decide what to do (challenge them, jump them, run away, leave them alone, keep walking). Yet, by acknowledging that she has never had to make that choice, she implies that their show of respect is a result of her actions and not a corresponding choice that others make (Pearce & Cronen, 1980). Recall that Margie was active in the gang when we spoke; there was no subsequent story of betrayal that followed her story of loyalty and respect, as it did for Florencia, Gracia, Eréndira, and Lupe. Curiously, she and Gracia both use English to designate not just their own claim—"North" versus "Norteños"—but also the others' claim—"Southerners" versus "Sureños." I offer as an explanation for this peculiarity that how Margie and Gracia linguistically align themselves with hemispheric localism (Mendoza-Denton, 2008) functions as a variant of storying loyalty and respect.

LUPE

Distance from the gang also enables meaning to continue emerging, as Lupe's loyalty and respect story, 25 years in the making, demonstrates. Her story of loyalty and respect takes a quick turn toward betrayal, as seen in Chapter 12.

Lupe—. . . the respect . . . they talk a lot about respect . . . it is a very distorted respect . . . even the pride is a very distorted pride, and the love is very distorted because if you cross the line and if you don't follow through with whatever that "code" is, of belief—'cause they have a code of ethics, they have a belief system and they have rules, and this structure, the gang is structured—you cross that and there are consequences. That's not always talked about and it's not clear, in stone, you don't see it. . . .

Liliana—You don't sign a form. . . .

Lupe—. . . you don't sign a form: "These are the steps and this is what happens."

Gang violence, the gang lifestyle, there is nothing positive about it . . . the whole lifestyle is very disturbed. It's good for a little while; it's fun. I can't tell you that I didn't have fun, that I didn't make some friends, I learned some things that I still carry with me, but not in a positive way. . . .

Liliana—Such as . . . ?

Lupe—Loyalty . . . respect . . . that I learned how to treat people respectfully, and yet, if they disrespect you, disrespect them. Those things: commitment, being committed to something, being willing to die for something. I just wasn't ready to be killed by my own! If somebody would have hit me from the opposite gang, I would have accepted it, but it was from my own people. That . . . that wasn't okay! 'Cause I felt they could kick me, push me, but whatever! I'll go with, but . . . don't hurt me. . . .

Liliana—So let's go back, if you don't mind, to talk about those moments where you were asked . . . you were talking about respect, loyalty, commitment . . . how would that be . . . when you were involved? How would that be presented? Would they tell you, "You need to be loyal to us"? Maybe they wouldn't use those words, how would that be communicated?

Lupe—Well, like the loyalty part, it was like, "Okay, you belong to this clique." So, because you belong to this group, you have certain ethics, you have certain rules, obligations. Like, if there's people they don't like, you don't associate with them, you don't cross the line, you don't talk about the gang, you don't talk about the members, you don't talk about your business, things that. . . .

Liliana—When you say business . . . ?

Lupe—Drug business, maybe incidents that happened, things that you saw, things that, where people got maybe . . . that happened in the gang, there is a lot of things that happen, people get extorted, people get intimidated, people that are getting killed. At this time, the guys wouldn't let girls in a lot of the business, 'cause that was guys' stuff. At this time us girls, we didn't know a lot of that. But the girls where we played a part in relation to the gang members, we were looked as like property, "You belong to us, you're ours" [makes sweeping motion with arm as pulling something toward herself]. They are very controlling who you talk to, other guys they haven't approved of, where you go, things like that.

So, that was the loyalty part, so you learn to be loyal, learn to stick with each other, you don't go outside with the other gang to discuss the business, you're loyal to if the leader says something, if he makes the decision, and that's the decision for everybody, everybody has to follow. "We're going to be at this place tonight, everybody has to be there!" Everybody is there. "We're going to have a *junta* over here!" Everybody had to be there and you don't question, you don't argue with the facts, with the leadership, because they have a chain of command. We really didn't have, the girls weren't structured like that. We just fell under the guys. . . .

Contrasting Lupe and Gracia's stories of loyalty and respect, the latter speaks about being liberated by the gang experiences (Chesney-Lind, 1993; Harris, 1988; Mendoza-Denton, 2008; Miranda, 2003), whereas the former speaks about being subordinate to the males. Specifically, instead of setting up the rules and expecting them to be followed, as Gracia did, Lupe performed loyalty to the gang by having to obey rules set by others, namely, men. And even when she was so disrespected by her own homies during the fateful New Year's Eve attack on her life, she refused to reciprocate with disloyalty by not speaking to the police about it (see Chapter 12, "Betrayal"). What might have kept her so steadfast in her convictions not to expose those in her own gang? The answer lies in the transcendent story she tells in Chapter 13, "The Narrative of Redemption," and in Chapter 14, "Disinhabiting the Gang": that being in a community of faith gave her a new script with which to structure a new meaning of loyalty and respect.

Liliana—So . . . you said that was one of the good things you learned: to give people respect, and if they disrespect you . . . but respect to a gang member is different from respect to you as a counselor . . . so can you contrast that for me?

Lupe—Yeah, because the respect you give to a leader of a gang, you give allegiance, the authority figure, this person is the person we listen to, he gives us commands. It's like the general, gives out orders. And you're like a soldier and you're just, "About-face! March!" whatever . . . directions. . . .

Liliana—Like a Marine.

Lupe—Yeah, but a lot of it is intimidation. It's more of a fear, the respect you give is more like a fear, because you don't want to cross the line and be disrespectful; and the respect you get now as a helper, as a provider, as a counselor, is not an intimidating respect—"You look at me and I'll slap you!"—it's more like, "Okay, there is some credibility here in what you're talking about." Gang members, if you respect them, they respect you. They live by that rule. They know what respect means. But it's how you treat them.

Sometimes we'll pass out flyers, information, inviting them to something, an event, and how you approach them. Me, as a female, I'd rather approach females. Sometimes, if I see a group of gang members hanging out . . . I saw some at the store one day, they were all in their colors and buying beer and I had some material and I said, "Now it's a good opportunity, we're in the check line right now," and so I went up to them and said, "Excuse me, can I give you something?" And one of the guys was like [makes face of disgust], "What's that?" He wasn't very respectful. I said, "My name is so and so, I'm from Victory Outreach and we're going to be having this event, and just wanted to invite you guys. When I was younger I used to gang-bang and I was a victim of gang violence . . ." and I just shared with them real quick because you gotta get in there real fast, "I've been there, done that." One guy was like, "Psh! I don't want that!" One of the other guys said, "What? I'll take it, because I know someone who goes to your church," and he put the other homeboys in check, "Hey man, don't be disrespectful! My aunt goes to that church!" They will put themselves in check. So, it's all how you go about them, approach them, and how you talk to them. Even if I'm talking to girls and guys are in the room, I won't be so blunt about fronting them off about their beliefs, I'll just lose them. So, that presentation will be done with all girls, after I build trust with them, because the last thing I want is for them to go out and tell their homeboys, "This counselor, what she's telling us?" Because what they can do is say, "Don't be talking to her anymore!" So it's a really fine line, so it's building a rapport with them. "This is confidential, what we talk about, it's between us, just to give you some insight, something that will save your life." Sometimes it gets really difficult.

Among the gang's many characteristics, instilling loyalty and respect among their members could be seen as an advantage. In her new role as a drug rehab counselor, Lupe's past experiences gave her a special status from which to expect respect from others. More importantly, her work with Victory Outreach benefits from her having been active in a gang, by giving her credibility and earning her respect from those she hopes to help transcend the gang.

DISCUSSION

Gangs impose silence on their members due to the sometimes illegal nature of their patterns of action. People often treat traumatizing events as if they never happened, denying their occurrence as a way to avoid speaking about the unspeakable and thus render it nonexistent. If a story—about beating someone in a rival gang, a convenience-store theft of beer, drug dealing, or even homicide—cannot be told, did it really happen?

The main difference between stories told by a gang-impacted girl and a non-gang-impacted girl rests on the idea that, for the gang-impacted girl, others are seen as "enemies" and they "deserve" to be recipients of one's violent acts of "defense" against behavior perceived as "disrespectful." The sensitivities developed at such an early age toward perceived personal slights stand in stark contrast to sensitivities developed (or not) to others' humanity. From these stories, it seems as though only those who recognize "us" as humans by respecting us enjoy being recognized by "us" correspondingly. Obviously, there is much more that can be explored about gangs, loyalty and respect. Here are a few topics ripe for explanation from the communication perspective: How are loyalty and respect co-constructed or performed in communication? Whose notions of loyalty have greater prevalence? How are loyalty and respect different inside a gang than outside the gang?

Transcending a gang implies rejecting the demands for silence that loyalty requires, being able to acknowledge these activities as wrong and immoral, and aligning oneself with the prevailing notions of moral society. Transcending a gang means being able to tell a story, however unpalatable, incriminating, or face-threatening it may be, that both accepts and rejects previously held notions of loyalty and respect and thus constructs a new identity.

12

Betrayal

Lupe, Florencia, Gracia, Eréndira, Olga, and Chakira

Following the argument that their families of origin were either not there for them or dysfunctional, some of the women enter the gang to look for the missing human connections in their lives. As ersatz kin, the gang provides them with an instant family (which they lacked or disliked before), the *varrio* gives them a home, and the "homies" serve as their siblings or peer relatives. The expression "to back it up" means to stand up for the gang, to defend its name, to put in work to support it by "ratpacking" or assaulting rival gang members, and to keep the business of the gang secret: in short, to story tell and story live in the service of the gang. The gang's longevity depends on the loyalties and selflessness of its members, many of whom believe they are in it for life—"Por Vida," hence the storytelling force of the tattoos. Yet at some point, the gang also disappoints or turns its back on them when an event—or a series of events—that defies the gang member's expectations becomes a catalyst for detachment from the gang. This section discusses the experiences of various women for whom betrayal prologues the story of transcending the gang. The women in this section are Lupe, Florencia, Gracia, Eréndira, and Olga. Additionally, I offer the story by Chakira to illustrate how betrayal functions as a cautionary tale for a girl to stay out of the gang.

LUPE

Lupe—So, after being involved in this gang for a couple of years, I believe probably at the age of fourteen through seventeen, I had a real awakening on a New Year's Eve . . . when I was at a party there in the neighborhood; it was no longer in the neighborhood I was raised in, this time we had moved to another area in San José . . . it was up on the hill, same area, South San José, and we're partying, everybody is drinking, having a good time . . . and . . . I was talking to this guy and he was from LA as well, he was from another *varrio*, I didn't know that he, that there was problems. I had no idea that the guys, my homeboys, didn't like him, so I had no inclination that was issues . . . so I was talking to him and then all I remember is that they came around me, what we could call "ratpacked" him, jumped him, and started to beat him up. I got hit . . . I got hit really hard . . . in . . . in my right . . . chest, so, I lost consciousness and I remember when I came clear of what was going on, regained consciousness, I was in the ambulance and I had been . . . I just remember that in the bathroom before I passed on, I was like holding myself and I could feel the gushing coming out like a warm sensation, but I really didn't know that I had been stabbed. So when I was in the ambulance, all connected to all of the equipment, I was just wondering "What happened?" . . . and the guy that was stabbed along with me, he was also on the other side of the gurney, and he said, "We got stabbed." He had been stabbed twelve times; I had been stabbed once in my right lung, it had punctured my lung. And that was kind of like a turning point in my life, when I realized that . . . I mean, being in emergency and ICU and wondering, "What happened?" and my parents were at my bedside, but they didn't know, they had no idea. I mean, they knew we were involved but they didn't know how serious this gang lifestyle was. . . . So. . . .

Liliana—Would you have died?

Lupe—If they would have hit me close enough to my heart, yeah, they punctured my right lung, and so I had a collapsed lung, so if they had got close to my heart, it would have killed me, definitely. And, I think that's what made me realize that, "Wait a minute, this wasn't supposed to happen, this is not what I signed up for"—not that I signed up but "this is not what I gave pretty much my loyalty to this family," and I think what hurt the most was that, after being in the hospital, being approached by certain individuals that . . . began to intimidate me, which comes along with the gang behavior is that, "You're not supposed to snitch, 'la rata' you can't be 'la rata,' you can't tell on your fellow homies," . . . which to tell you the truth, I don't even know to this day who stabbed me, I was so intoxicated, I used to smoke PCP at the time, I don't know if you're familiar with it, it's an animal tranquilizer? I smoked PCP that night, I was drinking beer, I was gone pretty much, I was there probably having a good time, but clearly I wasn't all there, so I don't even know who stabbed me, but when people started to approach me in the hospital and when people started to call me and started to put fear, intimidation, "You better not snitch" . . . and all of that . . . or "We'll take you out," that's when reality hit and I thought "Well . . . ?"

Liliana—. . . these are your homeboys . . . ?

Lupe—Yeah, these are my family! These are my homies. I'm practically dead and that's all they care about, if I'm going to snitch on them . . . and not realizing that, on the other hand, I was also being pressured by police, questioned by police and they believed that I knew who had stabbed me, 'cause there was several other stabbings that had happened right there within the same neighborhood and I said, "What? I don't know!" and for years, they tell me I had to deal with homicide detectives and was recorded and I had nothing to hide. . . .

Liliana—Was somebody killed that night . . . the one they jumped?

Lupe—No, he lived . . . he lived and another gentleman who was walking in, he was stabbed on his way in, but that really was when all hell broke loose, 'cause I was so angry I didn't want anything to do with these people . . . and I cut ties with them and my brothers and . . . since we were tight, we were blood . . . but my brothers also severed that relationship with the gang, so they came after us and they began to retaliate against my family, so we had to form a gang to protect ourselves from that gang . . . so for two years we lived in retaliation. They at one point, they came and broke my brother's windows; he had a really nice '54 Chevy. They broke his windows and my father heard the commotion and he walked out and they were doing a drive-by and they shot him twice, my father . . . and thank God he lived! He lived with a bullet until the day he died. It was lodged in his body and he took it for us. . . . I mean he was an innocent bystander, he had nothing to do with any of this, but the gang didn't care, they don't discriminate . . . they don't care if it's a child, they don't care if it's a mother, if they're going to go after you, they're going to go after you and whoever you love, whoever is around you. So, that's what happened for the next two years. I began to 'cause I would . . . you would think that after I got stabbed that my life would get better . . . that I would start to make some changes, and I think that really deep, deep down inside I really was like trying to find myself, I enrolled in college [. . .] it was my last year of high school, which it was difficult 'cause I was a senior, so I missed a lot of school, I was in the hospital, I had to do summer school and catch up on credits. I graduated, and then I began to try to find myself, kind of like in a journey to improve my life.

Although this attack on Lupe and the subsequent betrayal by her fellow gang members did not immediately end her gang involvement, in retrospect she stories this moment as a pivotal event in the process of disengagement from the gang lifestyle. The loyalty that she expected from her homies was not matched by their lack of concern for her well-being. In her eyes, the disappointment she felt was exacerbated by the scrutiny she endured from the police as a possible witness or informant for the ensuing acts of violence. The betrayal through the attack merely served Lupe in her efforts to distance herself from the gang she had joined, but, as she described it, her siblings and she formed a new gang to protect themselves from their old homies. Eventually, as described in Chapter 14, "Disinhabiting the Gang," when the gang became more trouble than it was worth for Lupe, she began to story herself out of it.

Similarly, Florencia experienced a period in her life marked by lack of reciprocity in loyalty when she began to see the gang in a different light.

FLORENCIA

The Crazy Life—La Vida Loca—makes up the bulk of Florencia's story, which is discussed at length under the chapter of that title (Chapter 8). Here, the focus is on the downfall from that life, which, ironically, proved pivotal in the process of transcending the gang. The dénouement of her gang involvement and the betrayal she felt as she hit rock bottom with no one to catch her were harnessed into a new plot line for her story of transcending the gang.

Florencia—We were at a party, I was so high, and I walked away and I fell asleep by a phone booth. They were like, "Get up, what's wrong with you? You're like really bad." I just lost it. I would just lose it and I didn't want anything to do with him anymore, and one day I just lost it. We're bagging dope and I got so tired, I started crying, I was sitting there, thinking, "Man, my life's all messed up, my kids got taken away, I got notin', I'm no good with my people no more, how did I get to this place?"

I had one loyal homeboy who was like by brother. To this day, we still keep in touch. I remember grabbing a bunch of rocks of the dope, and swallowing them with gasoline, I just wanted to die. "You know what? I don't care! I just want to die!" Then I started going into seizures. He dragged me three flights of stairs and my brother, my homeboy, they wanted to drop me off at his house and I'd just OD'ing right there. I was just tripping out, going through it. They called my mom, and she came to pick me up and take me to the hospital. I was so mentally out there. The cops were looking for me, so when my mom called 911, for the ambulance, the cops came and they took me. She wanted me to go to the hospital 'cause she knew I was OD'ing. The cops came and they took me to the mental . . . out ward . . . at Valley Med.

The neighborhood, gangs, as long as you're good for them, they're good for you. But when you're not good for them, you're just like an old shoe; they throw out. I ended up, there was nobody there to help, and I helped out a lot of homeboys, I did a lot for a lot of them. I put myself out for them in the sense, like family. "You need something? I'm going to help you. You need . . . ? Don't worry, I'm gonna take care of it. I got your back," for nothing to come back to me. I remember I made a phone call, I called my homeboy, "Hey man, I'm right here, I'm at this place." He goes, "Yeah, I know," and he hung up on me! I was like, "Man, I threw my life in front of yours like so many times, yet this is what I get back!" [voice breaks, looks upset].

Florencia's story of betrayal evidences the rise and fall of her power and leadership in the gang. Although she had enjoyed a particularly prestigious position in the gang through her own status as a fighter, an effective and a discrete drug dealer, and a dependable and loyal friend, her drug use began undermining these leadership qualities and thus decreasing the respect that she commanded in the gang. Florencia's drug use (described in Chapter 8, "In La Vida Loca") functioned as a form of self-medication to cope with memories of sexual abuse that she endured as a young child. As she became more and more encumbered by drugs, she became a liability rather than an asset, putting the gang's business in peril, for she could have fumbled a drug deal, been caught by the police, or called unwanted attention to the gang. Florencia's story seems to point to an unspoken rule that, even for a gang member, drug use should be kept within control, if only to protect the gang's interests. Outside the gang, friends might engage in an intervention to help the person in need. But in the gang, alienation of the one who is "no good" works to remove the imperiling element from their midst, for what good is a gang member without her homies to "have her back"?

As captured in Chapter 8, even when Florencia had a child, it didn't stop her from continuing to rise through the ranks in the gang's hierarchy: She resisted the "mommy track." For other women, mother'hood signified the beginning of the end of their gang affiliation, both in their words and in the eyes of their fellow gang members, as Gracia points out in her story of betrayal.

GRACIA

Gracia—Well, it all came about when I was fifteen and I had my first child. . . . So I started noticing that I wasn't included in much of their stuff. I started thinking like, and they, I started realizing they were trying to tell me what to do and when I could come and when I could do this and that. And I'm like, "Hey, I'm the leader; you don't get to tell me what to do." And so that's where it started. I started thinking, "Okay, I'm limited to what I can do." I started, I thought, "No, I'm going to do what I want to do and nothing is going to stop me!" So I played a hard-head, I was being hard-headed. So I started taking my baby places with me. I started taking her to hang out with me at the liquor store. I started taking her with me to my friends' houses where we kicked it and stuff like that, and I noticed that, if we fought, if we got into a fight, I was the only one who was going to be able to protect my baby. Nobody thought, "Oh, Gracia's baby, protect her," anything like that. I had to do that. Not only did I have to protect myself from getting beat up, I also had to protect my baby and I was putting my baby in danger. And so, there was a one incident where we were at the liquor store. There was a huge gang fight. There were a lot of us in the fight. I had to push my baby into the liquor store [. . .] and when that happened, I remember fighting and at the same time still trying to keep an eye on her and I remember seeing some guys walk into the liquor store. And these were the type of guys that, you know, are always whistling at girls, perverts being pigs. First thing I thought about was, "My baby is in there," you know, and I started yelling for the girls, or even the guys, even my boyfriend, I was like, "Go get my baby, somebody help me," 'cause I'm still fighting at this time, and I even see some girls run away like they were just running away from the fight and nobody thought about my baby. Nobody thought about getting my baby and protecting my baby. At this time I'm fighting with a couple of girls, even guys, I even fought with the guys. The girls fought with the guys, the guys even fought with the girls. We didn't care, we just want anybody, and I kept thinking . . . I remember seeing a couple of my friends run away and thinking, "Nobody thought about my baby." So at that point I was like, "That is it!" That was it. I was furious, I was mad and the first thing I thought about was loyalty. You know, my daughter was a part of me and my friends couldn't even think about helping me to protect my baby. Then I started thinking like, it was my mom who told me, she said, "You're so stupid! Who's going to want to protect your baby before themselves? They're going to protect themselves before they protect you or anybody else." I was like, "No, they've been with me through thick and thin, they've got my back, they're there for me!" And she'd tell me, "You're so stupid! Nobody is there for you! Who does most of the fighting?" She started pointing out all these things, and I did most of the fighting. I did most of the crime work because I guess I don't know if I was the bravest one to do it or the stupidest one, but I started analyzing these things, like who did what and what my role was. I was just like, "Man! What do I do now?"

And when I had my child, that is when I saw that I needed to be the one to make something different. And it didn't really take place until I had my second one, where I encountered a drive-by shooting. We'd encountered a couple of those, but my kids were never involved in it but that one time.

Liliana—I think this is the event you referred to in your talk. . . .

Gracia—Yeah, it was a drive-by, and the guys did it on bikes so they were really close. We were all hanging out in a front yard of my friend. . . .

Liliana—. . . where was the older child?

Gracia—The older one was in the front room and my son was in the bedroom, in his crib. During that time, the only thing I could think of was getting to my children.

Liliana—Where were you?

Gracia—Outside, and so the only thing I could think of . . . before the guys drove up on the bikes, we knew already because someone had already saw them coming, and we already knew that they were, you know, our enemies. And so, we knew they were coming but we didn't know what to expect. So, a lot of the guys had already walked up to the front to approach them.

Liliana—Instead of hiding? They wouldn't hide?

Gracia—'Cause we didn't see the guns. We didn't know. So they were going to approach them like, "Hey, what are you doing in our neighborhood?" They were going to beat them up. And so one of them had already pulled it out right before, 'cause we had a fence, and so right before he pulled out his gun he was coming here and then the guys were already walking out toward the street, so they pulled out the gun, so some ran that way and some ran into our house and some ran the other way. So they just started shooting wherever and, um, all I remember was ducking for cover and, um, seeing my boyfriend duck for cover too. He was yelling my name and first thing, the only thing I could think of was, "My kids. My baby is in that room, in that front room." So I made my way to the front room and all I could, and she was on the couch and was just thinking, "Oh, she's going to get it, they're going to get her, the bullets are going to get her" [cries]. And that is when I made up my mind, when I got to her, I just kept hoping that, that she was fine, that nothing happened to her, and it was really hard for me because I had to go to her and then I had to run to my son. And my boyfriend was outside running to get revenge. And here I was going to go help my babies. And here I'm thinking, "I'm not going to go out there to see if any of the homeboys or homegirls are okay!" You know, all I could think about was my kids! None of them came in to see if my kids were okay. You know, they all checked on each other or went to get revenge, but nobody was in there with me checking on my kids [sniffles]. And so, that's where I made up my mind, I was done. I was done. [. . .] From that day on, that's when I started deciding that I wanted to live life differently and that I didn't want to be in gangs no more. Of course I had to fight my way out of gangs, I couldn't just get out.

The hardships of starting a gang, being its leader, and calling the shots did not compare to the travails and tribulations brought on Gracia as she entered mother'hood. She tried to continue living La Vida Loca but learned that it was a poor milieu in which to bring up a child, not only for the dangers it posed to the child, but for the fact that, despite their claims of loyalty and support, the gang members only looked after themselves. This was a lesson that Eréndira also found out, in a series of events echoing the experiences of Gracia.

ERÉNDIRA

On the topic of leaving the gang, the main reasons that this 18-year-old cited were that the homies were not really there for her like they said they would be. When I asked her specifically what she meant by that, she explained that, while she was incarcerated, two of her friends had an affair with her then-boyfriend, and she felt betrayed. Another instance she mentioned as a catalyst for her to begin severing her relations with the gang was that of being raped by members of another gang. She told only the men in the gang about it, expecting they would avenge her. When they failed to do so, she realized they did not "have her back." She said that, although she always felt very independent, not needing anyone's help for anything, these instances left her feeling that the gang life was not for her.

After one incarceration, the terms of her probation required her to have a job, so she worked at the mall. This gave her another excuse to start distancing herself from the gang. Nine months later, she got pregnant. Although she worked until she was 8 months pregnant, the birth of her son provided an additional excuse to be left alone by the gang members for not spending time and doing things with them. Even while pregnant, she would tell them she could not go to parties if there would be alcohol because she would not be able to drink.

Her younger sister also has played a vital role in her attempts and evident success to leave the gang lifestyle behind. One time when her sister visited Eréndira while she was incarcerated, she asked whether Eréndira would be coming home with them and told her that she did not want to sleep alone in their shared bedroom. As Eréndira told me this in the car on the way to the interview, she became visibly upset and her eyes filled with tears. Yet the theme of betrayal by the gang members also resonates in her story. Like other gang-impacted and gang-involved girls and women who either claimed or backed up Sur, Eréndira spoke mostly Spanish. In the transcript, her and my use of English phrases is denoted in *italics*.

Liliana—So, when you got out, the last time you told me there were certain incidents that made you think, "This is not what I expected, they don't got my back," that you thought they would defend you but they didn't, your own peers, your homies, and that they . . . did they leave you alone once you had a baby?

Eréndira—I also felt like I distanced myself. Once they jumped me in a park and one girl who supposedly was Sureña did not get involved. And they were all saying about her, "*No, she's no good*; she better not be coming around and this and that." But three months later, they were all talking to her. I said, "You know what? If that's how it is, it's okay. Stay with her, I don't care." I resented it, and that's when I said, "Okay, supposedly *they got my back*, but if somebody . . . *they messed up*. If it had been me, I bet you they wouldn't have done the same." And only because *she was like, she slept* . . . that is, she slept with all; she got with all of them. That's why they talked to her. In any case, I said, "That doesn't matter, look for another, whatever," and they said to me, "No, we just want her for that." I said, "I don't care, you're telling me that supposedly you don't like her because *she's no good*, and you have her here. Where is the respect toward me?" And they were, "No! What do you think? How are we going to respect her if she's a . . . [mumbles and rolls eyes] *hoodrat*?" And she was Sureña, but since she got with all of them, and that's all they wanted her for, so then I said to them, "It's okay. I say do whatever you want." Then I was getting out and said, "*All right*, what do I care?" That's when I saw it and said that supposedly *they got your back, but* it's not always like that.

It is relevant here that, although these women realized that their fellow gang members left them behind, literally and figuratively, this did not lead them directly to taking steps to disinhabit the gang. In Eréndira's case, stories about her new job and her younger sister's longing for her paralleled the story of betrayal and the story of loyalty and respect.

For Olga, it was family violence that brought her into the gang, but also family betrayal that triggered the process of disinhabiting, yet the lack of direction regarding viable options kept her adrift for a number of years, as discussed in Chapter 14, "Disinhabiting the Gang."

OLGA

Olga spoke mostly Spanish, like all the Sureñas I spoke with for this project, but code-switched for the gang-relevant words in English. She eventually switched to English, and this is indicated in *italics* in the transcript. In the following segment, she discusses the aftermath of her gang-involved brother being stabbed in a gang-related event.

Olga—. . . And well, my siblings, because after what happened with my brother, he stopped hanging out with them, because what he told me was that "I was willing to die for the *varrio*; I was willing to show my face, but when I looked and saw all of them running, it made me realize where my *homies* stood and they let me down." So, even he started to begin reconsidering and saying, "*Wow*! I'm going to die! Why? For a color?"

Liliana—So they didn't try to take revenge?

Olga—Well, yes, they tried, and I knew there were different fights, more violence. One even lasted many years, and my brother, well, he recovered and got out and formed his own gang now outside the *varrio*. But all the others in the *varrio* recognized my brother. He was gutsy. *They would say,* "*He's down, but it's cool* that he got out, *it was his time, he did what he had to do* in the *varrio*, *he started the varrio, he made us strong, now we're here, we have to carry on.* . . ." So, it was like something very *false*, false. . . .

Liliana—Like they honored when he was . . . ?

Olga—Yeah, between them there was like a *false doctrine*, one could say. And they did not capture reality. One could see and say, "That was false! What kind of family is going to leave someone there to be beaten and killed?"

In Olga's case, some of her own family members were also her homies. So, as she composes her story of gang involvement followed by gang transcendence, betrayal by her own family compounded the betrayal by those in the gang.

Olga—. . . *So* they were always taking care of me. *You know, looking after me. So that made me belong.* "Okay, I finally found my place." *But until I started seeing everything and then how my sister started getting more addicted into drugs and to the point where I was babysitting* . . . *not my nephews, but I was babysitting her and the rest of the girls, you know, the rest of the homegirls.* They used to get all crazy *and guys tried to take advantage of them. You know, stuff like that. I got tired of it. I remember I was sixteen and we were in a party and everybody was drinking, everybody was smoking and everybody was dancing. We were at a homeboy's apartment and uh, and then ah, my* brother-in-law, *the father of her kids, got really crazy on PCP and started going off 'cause he was jealous, he thought my sister was burning him with another homeboy. They started fighting, his brother was there, his two brothers were there and they tried to break up the fight. So it was this big old thing, even between everybody* inside the gang. *You know, and I seen* [sic] *that and I remember I was just crying 'cause I was telling my sister* "Let's go!" *and she threw me and she goes, you know, she started telling me off, that I thought I was too good and so, I'm like, "WHAT? You know. . . . What is going on here?" And I just looked at everybody and I felt really ashamed. I think of a lot of things she had said, and I felt really hurt. And I remember I just left that day and my* brother-in-law's *brother came and said, "You know, she's just messed up. Don't listen to her what she said"* [gets teary-eyed]. *And I remember just thinking in my head I'm like, "You know what? I'm never gonna come back. That's it, you know, this is not my family. I thought it was my family, but it's not and this is MY OWN SISTER!" And then he was just like, "Oh, no. . . ." He tried to talk to me, he tried to talk to me. And I that point, you know, it was like 3 o'clock in the morning and he walked me all the way to my house and then he left. And since that point, I never went back. And I was going to be almost seventeen. And for a year, for a year or two years I never talked to my sister. I never talked to my sister. For a while, I tried to go back to school. I enlisted myself in Job Corps, 'cause they take you there from sixteen to twenty-four. So I went to Job Corps to . . . um . . . and I was there for like three months. I was there and I figured, "Oh, I will just get my GED" and, um, throughout the time I was there, we had some other homeboys in San Francisco. I used to be with one of the guys there and he would always, even when I left the varrio and stuff, but he was always in and out of jail, of ranches, group homes, and foster homes, and all this other stuff in the system. He would always tell me, "You should just move over to San Francisco! You know, my mom says she'll take you, we could be there and stuff," so like a fantasy at sixteen years old. I had nowhere, nothing, like I felt like I didn't belong nowhere no more 'cause I had left the varrio and everything.*

As a member of Gangs of Family, Olga's involvement began early in her life, but, although categorically unlikely, she also disinhabited the gang at an early age. She still longed for a connection, for a relatedness that neither her family of origin nor her ersatz family in the gang—members of which overlapped—could provide. For her, leaving the *varrio* equated to leaving her family, and in leaving her old self behind, she found herself still looking for a home.

By contrast, Chakira is another member of Gangs of Family, yet so far she is not gang-involved. Her gang involvement may be staved off by the force of the story she tells of her brother being betrayed by his gang.

CHAKIRA

Chakira — My brother, he was shot three, four months ago. He was at a party. It was an ambush. An ambush. There came a group of Sureños and they shot them. My brother was one of them, who did it. My brother was lucky not to have died, because there was one who died of the same thing later. Just for a color [. . .] shot him. And just now they cannot take out the bullet and he's still in danger. He came out, then they arrested him; my mother has suffered a lot because of him. She loves him very much, she gives him advice, but he still has that kid mentality, that he still . . . like . . . he doesn't learn still. He wants to continue with the same steps. His friends, he thought that his friends would support him, like his family, right? And he just figured out that it's not like that, because not one of his friends has visited him in jail. None. Letters, phone calls, nothing. And my mother, we who are his true family, we have supported him and now he understands that his friends . . . there are no true friends in this world.

The uniqueness of this story hinges on her brother's immaturity and disregard for danger, on loyalties misplaced on fair-weather friends in contrast to the blessings of ever-lasting family bonds, and, at the end, on Chakira's own understanding of the difference.

Chakira — My brother, the one in jail, says he's an example, that I shouldn't follow his footsteps. That he wants to see us happy, that I get ahead, that I become something important in life.

Liliana—But he doesn't see himself changed.

Chakira — Yes, I think now he is.

Liliana—It hit him hard?

Chakira — Because now he knows, because before he had friends, but not anymore. The light bulb went on that no one is going to be there for him. There may be a few, but the ones he thought were his best friends have not gone to visit him. He has a friend that to him, he's like a brother — and nothing; he has not shown up once to see him in jail, to find out about him. He knows, and it makes him sad because he now knows how it is.

Chakira's story condemns the gang for abandoning her brother in his time of need and highlights the importance of one's own family. Incarceration might not have decreased his loyalties toward the gang were it not for the fact that his "homies" have forgotten about him, which she surmises he knows. Her gang impact is obvious: She lives in a Sureño neighborhood, her friends at school are Sureños, and her brother was in a gang. These factors alone almost guarantee that she will become actively involved in a gang. Yet, through this story of the betrayal of her brother and his advice to her to avoid the pull of Gangs of Family, she transcends the gang vicariously as she recognizes that the fictive kin that the gang provides is just that: a fiction.

DISCUSSION

The theme of betrayal seems prevalent in stories about leaving gangs. From these stories, it seems clear that for women betrayal from their fellow gang members plays a large part in storying themselves out of a gang. A betrayal story, especially when the event that was considered to be betraying was public and thus difficult to challenge, allows these women to adopt a superior moral position in the obviously unequal exchange between the gang and any one of its members. Gang members might not want to engage in debating, refuting, or confirming a story by a fellow member that paints them in negative terms or in terms different from those they would choose for themselves: not having everyone's back, for example. The danger of this portrayal might be that others would see the gang as not worthy of respect or would consider leaving the gang. It might be better to have one less gang member than to retain someone who feels cheated and whose loyalty wanes. For these reasons, the betrayal story also gives these women the upper hand in disinhabiting the gang and moving toward transcendence. If their story of betrayal goes unchallenged by their fellow gang members, their exit seems plausible. Perhaps coincidentally, most of the experiences of betrayal presented here are storied by women who transcended the gang by joining a Christian religious organization, where their fellow church-goers may have found it natural to sympathize (given the biblical story of Peter's betrayal of Jesus, for example). This is discussed further under the theme of religion in Chapter 13, "The Narrative of Redemption."

Certainly, time elapses between the actual event that comes to be considered as a betrayal, one's realization of it, and one's actual departure from the gang, as it did for Lupe and Gracia. Additionally, simultaneous events function as co-stories that provide texture and nuance to the primary story, as they did for Eréndira. For Chakira, the story of betrayal is buttressed by the cautionary tale her brother tells from his jail cell: don't end up like me, even if I still have not figured out how to stay away from the gang.

Giving birth may be a necessary but not a sufficient condition for a woman to be able to leave the gang (Varriale, 2008), but it provides a punctuating device for a story of betrayal: Although the gang members pledge loyalty to each other, when it comes to infants, the mother is the only one responsible for looking after the child. Florencia, Gracia, and Eréndira expected to be able to continue their involvement with little change after they became mothers, but they found that the pledge of "I got your back" did not apply or extend to their infant children. In the cases where mother'hood becomes the privileged plot element in restorying a woman's position vis-à-vis the gang, it presents a different set of challenges for getting back to or staying in school, getting and keeping a job, and sustaining a relationship with the child's father. The stories of Florencia, Gracia, and Eréndira demonstrate these challenges. Although in Chapter 4, "Inhabiting the Gang," Olga punctuates the attack on her brother as the decisive event for her gang involvement, in her reconstructive logic (Pearce, 1994), she incorporates it into her story of transcendence using *post hoc ergo propter hoc* reasoning. That is precisely what transcendence is about: to reconstruct events in a story previously accounted for under a different frame to serve different purposes.

13

The Narrative of Redemption

Eréndira, Marisa, Angela, Gracia, Florencia, Lupe, and Olga

Skepticism was my response when I first heard about former gang members turning to God and religion as a way to disinhabit the gang and, moreover, to help others get out. I thought it too expedient, and perhaps a bit hypocritical, that someone who had broken the law, intimidated people, and abused drugs would avow a radically different identity and expect others to agree with him or her in their ascriptions. I grappled with this idea: you can take the homeboy or homegirl out of the gang, but can you take the gang out of the homegirl? It turns out, after listening to the stories by Eréndira, Marisa, Angela, Gracia, Florencia, Lupe, and Olga, that one does not have to take the gang out of the homegirl because the Narrative of Redemption, preceded by Betrayal, makes transcending the gang possible for them. Below I cite their words to this effect. I begin with Eréndira and Marisa's slight references to God and his role in their transformation; continue with Angela's account of the impact of church-going on her parents; augment my argument by tracing Gracia's story trajectory out of prison and into a new lifestyle; revel in the compelling words of repentance by Florencia; and end with Olga's extended narration of the vagaries of her life beyond the gang and how faith helped her transcend the gang lifestyle.

ERÉNDIRA

Of all the women I spoke to who were gang-involved and for whom religion or spirituality had been instrumental in their leaving, staying away, or staying out of the gang lifestyle, Eréndira was the youngest and had most recently left the gang. In the car on the way to the interview, Eréndira shared with me a flyer distributed by her church about a program they administer to reduce gang violence. Pictured was a green-eyed white man wearing a bandana on his head, half of which was painted red and half painted blue. When she shared this image, she mentioned that the program stressed that the bullets did "not care which color you claim" and that every homeboy's and every homegirl's "blood is all red, no matter what you claim." Later on, we were discussing whether she would tell her son eventually about her gang involvement (profiled in Chapter 6, "Tattoos and Identity").

Eréndira—That is why I say, "Thank God that I calmed down, had my son, had the joy of being a mother and this is simply a blessing!"

Poignantly, Eréndira sees God as the intervening agent in giving her a child—a reality that forced her, literally and figuratively, "to get religion" with respect to abandoning her damaging patterns of action and focusing on her own well-being.

MARISA

Having a child was also a blessing for Marisa as she recognizes that, were it not for her daughter, she might still be in the gang habitus.

Marisa—And now, I wake up every morning and I thank God every day for that little girl, 'cause without her, I would . . . I'd probably be doing the same thing. You know, life wouldn't be this good right now. You know, I thank God for her every day, because he's the one that put her in my life. He's the one! Of course it takes a man and a woman to reproduce, but he gave her, he put her in my life for a reason. By me getting pregnant, that was God's way of telling me, "Marisa, it's time for you to clean up!" and I thank God for, you know, just my life, just everything that I have, you know. A place to lay my head, 'cause there were times when I wouldn't know where I'd sleep, so I would stay up all night partying 'cause I didn't have anywhere to go. I thank God for a man that loves me because there have been times when I've been with men who didn't give a . . . any, didn't care anything about me, you know. Life's really good.

Both Eréndira and Marisa are not just invoking God's name in vain, as a euphemism, or as matter of idle talk: Rather, they both believe firmly in the existence of a higher power that intervened in their lives and gave them a second chance to turn their lives around by giving them a child.

ANGELA

Religion in Angela's family was one of the elements that worked in favor of her journey away from the gangs. She was not actively involved but for a while worked as a front to intimidate others, just as she herself had been intimidated in her previous middle school (see Chapter 11, "Loyalty and Respect"). As one of the several coinciding features (see Chapter 14, "Disinhabiting the Gang"), a religious conversion by her father figures significantly in her story of redemption.

Angela—It was the change, because when my father, before he had the heart attack, my father was very cold, he was very alcoholic. My mother and father used to hit each other: it was horrible. It was a horrible thing. Then my mother was a very bitter person. She wasn't very happy. And that happened, when my father had that heart attack, there was a very big change in him. He became very Christian. He gave himself up to God.
       . . . and the drastic change within them had a great impact on me. Because I started going to church with them, and to start going to that group, I felt much more supported by my dad and mom. To be honest, before that, I didn't feel it. Eleven, twelve, thirteen years old, there was nothing. This started around fourteen, fifteen, but before that there was absolutely nothing. It was . . . once I was at home alone and, I don't remember what happened, a neighbor came and reported that I was staying home alone and . . . I used to be alone a long time because they worked a lot, but for me, that was normal.

Her father's heart attack serves as a punctuation mark in Angela's story of staying away from the gangs, followed by her parents' own restorying toward a more harmonious family lifestyle.

GRACIA

Elaborate details about Gracia's situation, how it transpired, what prompted it, and the innumerable benefits that resulted serve to enrich her redemption story. To contextualize, she had started attending religious services while incarcerated and continued this practice after her release. She met a woman at her new church who introduced her to the Clean Slate Tattoo Removal Program (see Chapter 6, "Tattoos and Identity").

Gracia—. . . so when I got out, that's what I started doing. That's what my husband and I started doing. We started praying, we started reading the Bible, we started going to church. We started getting to know people at church and hanging out. We just kind of, we really departed ourselves from that gang lifestyle completely and involved ourselves in the church activities, with church people and um, you know, like I said, church activities, church functions. Started thinking differently and just prayer itself was what really helped us go forward in life and leave our past in the past and move on and do new things and make big changes and just, that when we started growing, that's where we started being a whole new people [laughs]. You know people will say, "How can you be a whole new person?" It's just, my choices were new. So my choices were . . . different. I had these positive people in my life to kind of guide me, to direct me, to give me the tools and resources that I needed. Stuff that I knew about but didn't take it seriously.

Liliana—Would you have been able to access those choices before?

Gracia—Probably not, no. . . . So when I started going to church, the people there, they didn't give up on me. They didn't give up on me. They didn't label me and my husband as "losers" or "gang members" or "trash" or "people that would rob us," or "people that were going to get a shock 'cause they're gang members and they're near us." They didn't do any of that! They accepted us, they welcomed us, they were willing and ready to help us, they'd be there for us and show us another way; they didn't give up on us. They kept on pushing and pushing and pushing and pushing to get involved in our life and to be there for us. You know, versus before that, we had nobody. Nobody wanted to take the time to help us or give us food, even to take the time to get to know us. There was nobody there, nobody who wanted to be in the same room with us!

And I see that today, with some adults and youth who are involved in gangs. I see sheriffs calling them "losers" and "trash," cussing them out and saying, "People like you are no good!" and that really makes me upset and that's why I share my story, because if I didn't have those people who were in church, to help me and to show me the way and to encourage me and . . . and to empower me and be there with me to do it, I'd prob . . . [fights back tears], I don't know where I'd be right now. And, and it's God. Honestly, I believe it's God who changed me, who helped me make those steps, helped me be a better parent . . . helped me be a better role model for my family members and the youth out there today.

My story, my testimony, I share it because I know there's children and even young adults out there that want a way out but don't know how to get out.

Choices, albeit limited, figure prominently in Gracia's story. Therefore, transcending the gang lifestyle was not due exclusively to one element or the other but a combination of story lines that included narrating her redemption. This was only possible because she found a community of support, unconditional acceptance, and respect in the church, as well as multiple resources for living clean in the tattoo removal program.

FLORENCIA

A most dramatic change came gradually for Florencia, over a period of time that included numerous attempted interventions, a drug overdose and hospitalization, various periods of drug rehab, losing her children, and, eventually, a breakthrough. Her story best exemplifies the narrative of redemption.

Florencia—After I got out of the hospital, my kids and my mom had come back from Texas, there was a drama show at church Victory Outreach called *The Duke of Earl*. My mother had tickets from this guy from church who told his life story: he was a drug addict and a gang member and that he lost everything and went to the Victory Outreach Christian Recovery. So my mom got lit up and went, "Omigosh! This is my daughter's story, except you're a guy! This is my daughter's story!" She got a bunch of tickets and she came home saying, "We're going to this theeng." Even though I went through all this, I'm still getting high. I hooked up with this other guy that I knew and we're still getting loaded, still partying, still getting high. I'm still kind of not all together up here. So, I go see this drama and I'm sitting and I'm like, "Oh, my God! That's my whole life up there!" You see killings, you see gangs, you see the want for love, for family, you know. You see everything and I'm going, "Oh, my God, how do they know?" Then they did an altar call: "If anybody wants to give their life to Jesus . . . ?" I ran up there! It was like something was pulling me up there. I still remember the lady's name, it was Carina. She was standing up there at the front and she had her arms out like this and she just hugged me and prayed for me. I was just . . . tripping out, I never felt somebody loved me, really loved me that didn't even know me. I never felt like kindness, like somebody touched me without wanting something else. They didn't want anything. I could just come as I was. They didn't care what my background was, they didn't care who I was or who I knew. They didn't care what respect I had or didn't have. They just accepted me, welcomed me.

Respect: a concept that had eluded Florencia in her birth family due to violence, and in the gang, where she had worked so hard to earn it. But as her drug use increased, the level of respect she could command among her homies began to wane (see Chapter 12, "Betrayal"). Florencia's narrative of redemption relies on incremental changes of grammar like this one, where the meaning of an utterance depends on its usage (Wittgenstein, 1953/2001). Like Gracia, Florencia found that this type of respect did not have to be earned by blows but by active surrender.

Florencia—After that, they told me that they had a women's home and just packed my stuff and went. I still remember it was at [gives address, starts crying]. My life has never been the same. God forgave me for all the evil that I done, all the people I hurt. I hurt so many people in that life. Lives I almost took, the people whose lives I devastated, the violent acts I committed, my children, my children, God restored my children to me. I graduated the Victory Outreach Home, I went to a second phase. I got my kids back eighteen months later. I got married; I married the director of the Men's Recovery Home [wipes tears], who directed a home of thirty-nine men. I got involved in my church, I got involved in going to schools talking to kids, doing everything I could to prevent kids from the lifestyle of gangs and drugs, and I live for that now. I live to preach the gospel of Jesus Christ, I live to give back to the community what I took. It's been thirteen years, but still, I want to give back. I live to see young people live a life, not to die. I've lost many friends, many of my good friends I grew up with are in prison. They're doing life, thirty years to life, fifteen to life.

When I went to *The Duke of Earl*, it wasn't the first time I heard of Victory Outreach. When I was fourteen, I was already very addicted to PCP. I got into some trouble with the law and was committed to out-patient programs. I went to a program and I was the youngest one there. Everybody was sharing there about their experiences. I remember a lady, I'll never forget her. She wrote me a quick letter with a highlighter. She said, "Hi, my name is so and so, I smoked PCP for ten years," and this is the first time ever somebody told me about Jesus or anything "church." She said, "I gave my life over to Jesus and he changed everything." [Mocks a response:] "Jesus. Who's this? I don't know anything about this?" I grew up very . . . ignorant about it. She wrote her number down and I got home and . . . I knew about Jesus, son of God, but that was about it. I ended up calling her and talking to her, cussing . . . I didn't know who I was talking to. She was really cool with me and she invited me to something called "The Love Circle." She asked, "You have to do a twelve-step program, right?" I go, "Yeah." She goes, "Well, there's a Christian twelve-step. . . ." I thought it was somebody called Christian who did a twelve-step;

I didn't know anything about that, right? [Laughs.] "If you go to this, they'll sign your paper off and you'll get it done faster." I thought, yeah, "I'll get off probation faster." That's where I met Lupe [see her story below]. I never went to church, but I went through their twelve-step. It's like AA, but focused on Christianity. I had turned fifteen, and remember Lupe came to the house with these people from church. There was a bunch of people over at my house, partying, and I was in the bathroom, getting high by myself. She knocks on the door, comes into the bathroom, and takes me with my clothes wet out of the washing machine throws them in a suitcase and takes me to the Women's Home. I was there for two weeks. So it wasn't the first time, but they were so consistent. They'd leave flyers on my door with a little note: "We're praying for you, we're thinking of you, God loves you, you're not forgotten . . ."— little things like that. I didn't respond right away, but the fact that I knew that they cared about me. . . . "Why do these people care about me? I don't know them. I haven't done anything for them?" And everywhere I go, there's Victory Outreach, passing flyers, doing something, some drama, or some kind of something. I'd stay away, but I think there was just consistency.

Not too long ago, I went to a church service in Stockton, and a woman came up to me and hugged me and it was the young girl who we almost beat to death and had a gun to her head (see Chapter 11, "Loyalty and Respect"). I asked her for forgiveness. She's now a Christian and she's saved in Victory Outreach Church. For thirteen years, this girl was on my mind, because I almost took her life. I was able to ask her for forgiveness and thank her for her courage now. I just am blessed today.

In the ersatz family provided by church, Florencia found respect, unconditional love, and a way to transcend the gang.

LUPE

The end of gang involvement for Lupe did not immediately lead to the end of her involvement in the gang lifestyle. In Chapter 14, "Disinhabiting the Gang," we will read about how, as a drug counselor, she was challenged by a young client for having PCP-induced glossy eyes while talking to the girl and her mother about the symptoms of PCP usage. This irony prompted a different story line: that of redemption.

Lupe—I was so ashamed . . . and I started to . . . that's when I started to cry out to God, "What is going on with my life? I'm trying to do this, I'm trying to do that, nothing seems to work, I can't quit using this drug," and so I began like a spiritual search within myself. I was also attending junior college at the time so; again, I'm in school, trying to get ahead in life. I remember I was walking around the campus and I just felt a really strong call. It wasn't an audible voice calling like "Lupe!" It was like a . . . this inner voice that was speaking to me about my life. Everything started to flash before me: "Look at what you're doing, look at where you're headed, the missing link, the most important thing that you don't have is me." I started to look around and up and said "Are you talking to me?" I felt like I was making this connection and so I said, "Okay, if you're calling me, if you want my life, hey! I surrender, 'cause I'm so tired, I'm so sick of this, I don't want to live. I'm not going anywhere in life and yet I feel like I have it together and I have nothing." The only thing I knew was go to church [laughs], and so I went to a church that night and they had a call, what they call an altar call. It was interesting because a man that was preaching that night was a hard-core Southern preacher. . . .

So I went to a Christian church but when the guy, the minister . . . ah . . . I thought that the way he presented it, the way he did the altar call, he said, "If you're sick and tired of living the way you're living," he goes, "I want to call out people who are not ashamed . . . people who have guts to come to this altar . . . you won't even just walk, you will run down here," and I . . . "He's ask . . . he's calling me!" So I kind of, I ran down there, and that was it! I just, "Here I am, I can't do this anymore . . . I'm so tired," and that's when I had a transformation and my life began to change spiritually and I feel that was the missing piece in my life: that I really needed to find myself, to start to find my purpose, who am I and what was I created for and what is my destiny? And it changed everything, it changed my work ethic.

In Chapter 11, "Loyalty and Respect," we read how Lupe uses her past gang involvement to gain credibility and respect among current gang members to help guide them away from the gang. Here she gives an example of the crucial role that faith can sometimes play in helping others narrate their redemption. The emphasis here is not only on being saved but also on being excused from the gang, so to say, due to divine intervention.

Lupe—It's God's will that I come clean. One of my clients . . . wanted to give up the lifestyle, but was afraid to be seen as a ranker, or a dropout, to deal with his homies and their disrespect. He said he was thinking about calling Victory, because, he said, "They're probably the only ones that can help me." I listened for a while and said, "I think I know who you're talking about, he's a friend of mine." I called Ricardo and got him on the phone talking to the client. I hope they got together. You gotta get right in there, when they open a window, because it may never open again for a long time.

As for Florencia, the notion of respect within the gang held a different currency, one without which Lupe's client felt unable to function. "Banging for God" was how one of Garot's (2007) consultants replied when asked about gang affiliation. In that account, "Buck" reported, "So if you say anything having to do with God, they gonna bow down, like 'all right, all right'" (p. 70). Similarly, Lupe's client no longer banged but still needed a male example to help him try out this new meaning of respect, hence the need to connect him with Ricardo, a former member of the Nuestra Familia prison gang and now a minister in Victory Outreach.

Liliana—What would happen if someone said, "It's God's will that I live the lifestyle? . . . that I be a gang-banger"?

Lupe—Many gang members have a reverence for God. They connect with that, because many have a Catholic background. I ask them, "What is your concept of God? Who do you think God is?" Many identify God as a "vengeful, all-powerful being." I tell them that God is loving and kind.

What's interesting is that even though the gang members are so violent and antisocial and all that, they still have a little reverence for God and faith. Some of these guys obviously did, because when we, when I started going to the church and give my life over, my brothers actually came along and joined me. The gang, they confronted us and said, "We understand you're going to church now and we call like a truce. The violence, it will stop. We will stop going after you, but if we see you on the streets and if you go back out there, it's on." So they respected the fact that we had made a change of life and so that was when peace came.

But they really did respect the fact that we changed our lives. That's also scriptural because there's a scripture that says that if you find peace with God, that he will make your enemies your footstool. So you find peace with him, you find peace with men. It's like a principle. We had no idea that they were just going to leave us alone. But I swear that's how the violence ended.

Liliana—So this was your experience . . . what have you seen in the last twenty-five years that you have done that, you've been involved? You mentioned there was a code and rules . . . would that be one of the rules, in the rule book of gangs? Once somebody changes and finds God? I don't know if everybody who gets out necessarily . . . finds God . . . ?

Lupe—. . . not everybody accepts that . . . what I've seen from the years that yes, because there's countless people that I know that have surrendered their lives over, people like Ricardo, who have dropped out of prison gangs, that's really like, "You get out and we kill you!" They're still alive today! They might get threats, people might intimidate them. But there is some, I believe, some fear of God, some reverence in people's lives that take a step back and they say, "What. They're doing a good thing now, let's just leave them alone." But I do believe that they do respect that. Some people, some of the gang members don't believe. Nah! They're not going to care, but see, that's where the faith comes in. You have to believe that it's all going to work out. And you have to take a risk, because if you don't take a risk, I mean you're going to give your life anyway. Eventually you're going to die for the cause, you might as well take a risk getting out and living, 'cause if they kill you at least where you're gonna be going . . . you have eternal life. But if you go down that road with them, something happens to you, which . . . it's gonna happen. . . .

Lupe's story seems like a modification of Blaise Pascal's wager on the benefits of believing in the existence of a higher being (Jordan, 2007; Rescher, 1985). In summary, gang-bangers benefit from believing that God exists because if they leave the gang and there is a God, he will protect them from their former homies, they will be accepted by society, and, when they die, they will go to heaven. But if they don't believe and there is a God, there is no salvation for them, whereas if they believe and there is no God, they will have at least gained a clean lifestyle. Additionally, the special dispensation granted by gang members to those who have found a spiritual route out of the gang is respect within a different context, and this allows them to sidestep the ascribed identity of being a "ranker" or "dropout" of the gang. They manage to incorporate themselves into a different set of events and circumstances, such as attending church and living clean, that are perfectly acceptable in mainstream society.

OLGA

Olga's was a case apart: Although she had left the gang, held a job, got married, and had three children, her husband's continued involvement in the *varrio* lifestyle and their marital strife brought deep despair to her. As she stories how this dismal part of her life evolved, she prominently highlights the role that faith played not just in the reconciliation with her husband but also in ending their respective addictions and in turning their lives around. During the research consultation, Olga and I switched between English and Spanish. In the following transcript, our use of English is denoted in *italics*.

*Olga—And with my husband . . . I wasn't married when Patricio . . .
"Pato" . . . we were together in the varrio, but he got locked up, went to CYA.
Got out that same year they killed Güero, I kind of like started looking for him
again. So I did go to King and Story, where the varrio was, with some girls from
work. I wasn't alone. I went over there looking for him and I kind of started asking
some of the guys that I knew, you know, that wouldn't look at me bad, or that I
knew I kind of left in good standing, in the sense that they wouldn't look at me
different. And one of the oldies, he told me, "Yeah, homie's out! I'll tell him. I'll tell
him you're looking for him." And I gave him my number and so, he did. He gave
him my number and he called me and we started talking again. 'Cause when he
left CYA, it's like I was still out here, I was doing my thing, and he was there, he
was doing his thing, being locked up. So I did, I still had a void, I still felt empty.
So, to me at that point, I felt like, "Okay, I have a job. Okay, I stopped going to
Job Corps now, so what else can I do to fill this void that I have?" And I thought,
"Maybe I need to get married?" So that thought just kept coming into my mind,
and I never even thought of the marriage my mom and dad had. I just thought,
"Well, I'm not going to be like her. I'm not going to be like that. I'm going to
have a better marriage. You know, I'm going to be well." So, yeah, we started
talking you know, and he wasn't supposed to be here 'cause they deported him after
YA. . . . They had deported him but he came back, and he was calling me, I was
talking to him and then . . . I went to live with him . . . he had four brothers and
a younger sister and his mom and dad, or his stepdad. It was a dysfunctional family
there too! Everywhere I went, it's like there was no examples of parents, or like a
good home, I had no idea. . . .*

Liliana—. . . How marriage worked . . . ?

*Olga—Yeah, I had no idea, I was seventeen. I moved in with him and we
were there, I was still working, he wasn't working. He was pretty much little by
little starting to go back into the varrio. But for me it's like, "Oh, well, I'm here,
I'm living with him," you know. We weren't married, his mom and his dad were
okay with it, his brothers were okay with it, and that was cool. And I would tell
him, "We gonna get married?" [laughs]. And even the word to him it was like,
"You're living here, why we need to get married?"*

*So it was like that, back and forth, back and forth, until like the summer of
'89 . . . yeah, of '90, the summer of '90. This girl called looking for him and he
answered the phone and she asked, "Is so and so there?" and he answered, "Yes,
this is me." So this girl told him, "You know you're not supposed to be here, right?"
and he didn't know what to say, so he said, "Well, I came back 'cause I want to
get married." So that was his excuse that he came back. So she asked, "Oh, you
are? So who's your fiancée?" And then he put me on the phone and she asked me
some questions about him and then I told her, "Yeah, we're gonna get married,"*

and she's like, "Well, I need both you guys to come in to the parole office and fill out some paperwork and I have to talk to you guys." So we did, we went the next Monday, that was a Friday she called. Went on Monday and he [a man at the parole office] *started telling him, "You know. You shouldn't be here. I should actually call right now Immigration and tell them you're here, except I'm not going to do that." He's all, "Let's do this right, if you're going to get married, you know, you're a citizen"; I was a citizen at that point,* I had become a *citizen. He's all, "So, I guess she's a citizen, if you're gonna marry her, so I'm sure she's gonna fix your papers." And I said, "Yeah, I guess! You know, I don't know, I guess I am!" And he's all, "Okay." Then he started asking me if I'd gone to school, so I told him, "No, I dropped out" and this and that. So he enlisted me and him in like adult school in Santa Clara, in Wilson High. And he's all, "This will be one of the requirements of parole. You can't hang out with your old friends, you know, you can't do drugs, you can't drink, you know, you need to get a job, you need to go to school. . . ." So all these requirements you know,* that he gave us. *And we were doing good you know, for a while. We got married in September. I had . . . my mom and my dad wouldn't sign for me 'cause I was underage, so my brother, the older one, signed for me. And by that point I was like, "I really don't want to get married no more!" But I felt like I had to 'cause* I had already told the *parole* that *I was gonna get married, so* I saw myself *in a situation like, "Man! I have to do it because I said, or else they're gonna deport him!" So, we did get married in downtown. No ceremony, no nothing, it was just in a lunch break 'cause I used to work right there on Park Avenue. At that point I was a receptionist for an answering service. So I just took a break and my boss and two other girls from my work went with me, he met me there and yeah, we said the vows and yeah, he went home and I went back to work and so it was no big thing. . . .*

And after that, we started going, we were still going to school. But then like he started hanging around with his friends again at the varrio, people were looking for him in the sense of "C'mon, let's go kick it!" You know, they would come looking for him and I was angry! I was like you know, "What are you doing? You're not supposed to be doing this! That was one of your conditions; you need to stay out of trouble."

In Chapter 10, "Mother'hood," we learned about Olga's efforts to maintain her family together, to stay in school, to keep her job, and to raise her daughters. This was a challenging process that was exacerbated by the fact that her husband deeply inhabited the gang and left her questioning the benefits of their relationship.

Olga—And it was like that for a while. And then in '95, I finally did decide to leave him and I did. I left him. He got worst [sic]. We were still married. In summer my sister was helping me with the divorce papers, um, and I had my own place by that time, six months. Um, then I got a call from Valley Medical, from the Psych Unit, you know, for my husband, if I could go and sign some papers, because they found him and he was going crazy. I don't know what drugs he was taking. So I had to take time off from work and go, see what was going on. He was crying, he was *so violent and the doctors were telling me, "Well, you know, he's under the influence, we don't know of what, he's under the influence. He had overdosed, but he came out of it and he's really violent and he's in a rage and he's just crying out for your name. That's why we called you." And I went in there and as soon as he seen me, he started apologizing, saying, "I'm sorry, I'm sorry, this and that, I miss you, I miss my daughters, I can't take this no more!" He's all, "I was wrong, I'm not going to do this again, I'm going to leave the varrio, I'm going to stay away, you know, we're going to be a family." And this is all, in my mind,* "He's just still under the influence of drugs!"

He had never said anything like that, because he was really angry, he was controlling, you know, he was always like . . . belittling me, *you know, abusing me in the sense, that we would physically fight. So when he's telling me this, in my mind I was like, "This is the drugs!" You know, "He's just saying this because of the drugs." And then he told me, "You know what? I've been bumping into a friend, he's been telling me about God. I want to go to church, I want to go to church." And that's all he would tell me, and before to go to church, I had never in my life, maybe once when I was seven, my father took us once to the Catholic church, but never in my life had I gone to church, except just that one time. And I'm like, "Church. I don't need church! What do I need church for?" And he's all like, "No, c'mon, he told me how he was and how he and his wife had already separated and God put them back together, he could do that to us!" He was speaking all this nonsense, then I thought. And then I'm all, "Well, okay, when you get better . . . get better, you come looking for me and then we'll go to church."*

And they released him, they kept him there for twenty-four hours, they released him the next day and he went back home . . . and he called me, he's all, "Well, are we going to church or what?" And I said, *"No, I'm not going to go to church!" "Well, you told me!" I was like, "Well, I told you a lot of things, I didn't mean it! I don't want to go back with you." He's like "Why?" "You still ask me why.* Look at all the problems we have been having, *I'm not going back with you." Yet I have a big void in my heart* [makes sleeping circular motion with right hand] *once again, I had a big old void. At that time, I was already twenty-two . . . and I had my three daughters still . . . and ah . . . I kind of little by little started being irresponsible. Going out to clubs with friends from work, having my younger sisters come over to sleep in my apartment to watch over my daughters, and I started meeting other people that were totally not from the varrio, totally lifestyle, working people, that had a weekend lifestyle, if you could call it, you know. Drinking, which I never really drank before. I probably . . . in the varrio, I probably smoked weed one time, tried acid one time, you know, try coke one time, it was a one-time thing and I didn't like it. I didn't like one cooler, beer, you know, none of that. And yet, twenty-two years old I kind of started slipping into beer, into you know, liquor and started feeling more ugly inside, like, "What's happening to me?" and I felt a bigger void than I felt before when I was younger. And yet I had my three daughters, and my apartment, I had my job. But now I'm getting written up in my job for being late, for being irresponsible, you know, for not following through on things. So I'm like starting to lose it. . . .*

And my friend, one of my friends from work, she started telling me, she's all, "Are you okay?" I'm all, "No, I don't feel okay, you know, I have everything but I don't feel okay. I feel like something's missing!" And then I just started getting a lot of suicidal thoughts at that point. A lot of suicidal thoughts, thinking of all my life, from young to teenager to everything, and [starts crying] *I just started saying, "Well, I really don't want to live, my daughters are better off without me!" And I remember one time um, I just told my sister if she could come pick up my daughters. She couldn't, so I called their dad's mom and she said she'd watch them so I dropped them off there. He wasn't home but I still dropped off my girls there. And I went back to my apartment and I remember just thinking like, "Man! I feel so bad, so lonely, I don't even know why, I don't even know why."*

And then I remember I had a bunch of vicodin that I got through a dentist, so I just said, "Well, I'm gonna swallow all these and see what happens" [cries and laughs at the same time]. *And I took the bottle and swallowed a bunch of them and then I just went to sleep. And I was asleep, I remember I was asleep in the living room and I remember I heard a lot of knocking and knocking at the door and I was asleep, I couldn't get up, I was just asleep and forget about everything. And then um, it was my babies' dad, well, my daughters' dad. And he broke my window and he was slapping me to wake up, and to wake up and he threw me in the bathtub and he splashed all this water on me and he's all, "What are you doing? What are you doing?" So I told him, "What are you doing here?" and he said, "What are YOU doing?" He started slapping me, and telling me, "What are you doing? I already told you, let's work things out. I'm going through it, you're going through it; we need help!" Then he tried looking for the church where this friend that had told him to go to church and we couldn't find the church and that was a Friday night. . . .*

He couldn't find the place! So I guess they had moved or whatever, and then we were driving, we were dropping off his mom to Al-Anon, 'cause she used to go to Al-Anon, and we were at a light and we had just dropped her off. And at that light, there was a poster, a flyer in the light, and then we both look and it said, "Victory Outreach." He said, "Get out and get it!" 'Cause that was the church that his friend he was talking about used to go to. So I got the flyer, got the address, and we were right around the corner from it, and he's all, "Let's go! It's Friday, they have services tonight!" So we did, we showed up at the church and it was maybe almost over, because when we walked in, it was full and it was a tent and it was outside. The guy who was talking up there, he was giving his testimony. He was saying that his name was so-and-so and he used to be in La Eme, he used to be in a prison gang and that's how he was. He started talking how he . . . his upbringing, he started talking . . . and I started seeing myself in everything he's saying. And then he just said, "You know, all my life, I was just looking for, to belong to something and I thought I had a cause that I would die for, but when I got out of prison, I knew I had to do things different. Somebody gave me a flyer and told me that Jesus loved me. And I didn't know up to that point in my life . . ." and he was an older man! ". . . I didn't know what love was to that point, and when they invited me to church, I felt like a peace I never felt. I felt loved, that people were looking at me not from the outside but through the eyes of Jesus, and since then I never looked back." And I remember when he said that "I was hard, I was, you know, I was hopeless, I was hurt, it was so many things going on in my life," that I was, it . . . that caught me, when he said "I found that place where there was peace," and that's what I've been looking for all my life, peace, you know.

And then the music started and stuff, and then right after when church was over, I just wanted to get out of that place, 'cause I felt good, but I just didn't want to be there either. His friend looked at us and he came running and he hugged him and he's all, "Oh, you're here!" And . . . 'cause he had met him through a job that he had done painting. They both were painters. And um, and he remembered him and he's all, "Oh, come! Let me introduce you to my wife!" And I'm all looking at him like . . . and we were barely getting back together, we had left each other, you know, I was already filing for papers. He's all, "Let me introduce you to my wife," and she started talking to us, "Oh, it's good to see you guys! God could do miracles!" Just pretty much just preaching to us. And we just looked at each other and we left that place, then we just said, "Let's try this. Let's try this, let's see what happens, you know, what do we have to lose? We've lost everything already, you know." And then, then, he's all, "Well, okay," but he told me, "But you need to move back in with me," to his mom's and I was like very hesitant about that because I really liked my own place! You know and I didn't want to lose my own place, my daughters had their own room, you know and I had privacy. So I really didn't want to go back. . . .

I ended up moving back and we went back to church, and you know everything ministered to us. That was a turning point for him and for me. That's where I found peace, that's where I found love, that's where I found God. For himself too, he felt delivered from drugs, delivered from those generational curses; the violence, the life that he lived himself. Um, and that pretty much I felt was a point of reference in our life that changed everything and everything was never the same. Ah, all my past I came to understand that, you know, God didn't make it happen, you know. I made wrong choices as a young person; I didn't have to end up like that.

Although she incorporates the dysfunctionality of her family and her loneliness into her story of "Inhabiting the Gang" (see Chapter 4), Olga also recognizes that she could have made different choices. In her story of redemption, Olga's logical force (Pearce, 1989) shifts from contextual—for a person in a situation or context like hers, inhabiting a gang would seem appropriate—to implicative, by alluding to the fact that there were consequences and implications to her actions that she did not consider, but now she owns up to them. This restorying move works to provide Olga with a new purpose in life, that of imbuing the youth to whom she ministers with a newfound meaning of respect that implies being looked after and having a home away from—or instead of—home.

Olga—And now I know it was through God's grace, and even then, that was taking me out of all of these bad situations. When we had . . . and when we had fights, I was kidnapped at points, yet, I was let go. Other girls were beat up with jacks, everyone came out really bad and I was the one that wasn't, you know. So now I look at all those things and say, "God has always been and have his hand upon me." Why? Now, I say it's to make it . . . to be an intervention to help them many kids that come . . . they don't have to go through everything that I went through. That sense of belonging, to belong to something, *you know, it's just false, it's false. And a lot of them come from dysfunctional families. That's what we give them here.*

If you see, we have games, hockey things, there's handball. We make this a place where they could come. . . . Hang out, where they don't have to go look at a varrio, they don't have to be jumped in to somewhere, they could come to a safe place, you know, where there ain't gonna be no trouble, nobody is gonna judge you, call you out, you know, and you know, you're just accepted. We love you and we care for you. A lot of these kids to this day, they'll say, "Yeah, you know, I like going there." They're probably not all, you know, committed to God, *you know, we don't expect them to, but we show them the love of Christ and that's the best thing that gets revealed to them, you know that they're able to say, "You know what? I don't have to be like everybody else. I don't have to be like that, like my, you know, my friend from middle school who's starting to hang around with the wrong crowd." 'Cause that's when they make a lot of the choices, in middle school. So, we have about sixty youth, you know, that come. And we pick them up all over the city. You know, we have vans, us, our cars, we'll call them, "Okay, are you going to come to church?" They say yeah, so we'll pick them up and then we just take them all, by nine-thirty we say, "Okay, lights off!" Start taking everybody home.*

The lights in Olga's life have been turned on and stay on to light her path out of the gang and into transcendence through the Narrative of Redemption.

DISCUSSION

Here I must return to explain the shift in my views from skeptic to believer in a religious conversion as a "valid" story line for transcending gangs by citing some literature that aided me in my own "conversion." In arguing that the academic study of religion is both renewed and also engaged in "critical paradigmatic reflection," Smilde and May (2010) identify certain "discursive fields" as areas "in which discourses function not as cultural templates that individuals enact, but as contexts within which individuals make intelligible their actions" (p. 3). They refer to these discursive fields as emerging in the publication of articles about religion in top sociology journals in the last 30 years, but I am more concerned with the use of that term to analyze how gang-involved Latinas move toward religion and how it helps them transcend the gang. Although religious beliefs may seem like an individualistic accomplishment, they arise from conversations with others: Our beliefs may create our identities (avowals), but these must be corroborated, challenged, or substituted (ascribed) by others with whom we interact. To return to Lupe's oblique reference to Pascal's wager, I argue that, because religion makes a direct connection between divine-inspired action and positive consequences, it is also possible to counter that "positive consequences of religious practice are entirely compatible with its being a fictitious illusion" (Smilde & May, 2010, p. 6).

This tome is far too short to engage in the debate over the academic study of religion. Suffice it to say that I am not arguing that just because religion "worked" for these women in their process of disinhabiting the gang, religion will work for everybody seeking a way out of a gang. I must now turn for help in making this argument to Bellah (1970), who provided the antecedent for Smilde and May (2006). Bellah offers the notion of "symbolic realism" as a candidate to grapple with the appropriate place of religion in our culture (p. 92). Symbolic realism emerges from the interactionist model and from action theory, where "reality is seen to reside not just in the object but in the subject and particularly in the relation between subject and object" (Bellah, 1970, p. 93). The position of symbolic realism is that the nonobjective symbols used to express the values, hopes, and dreams of subjects also help manage and organize interaction, but, most important, these symbols constitute reality:

> If we define religion as that symbol system which serves to evoke what Herbert Richardson calls the "felt-whole," that is the totality which includes subject and object and provides the context in which

life and action finally have meaning, then I am prepared to claim that, as Durkheim said of society, religion is a reality *sui generis*. To put it bluntly, religion is true. (Bellah, 1970, p. 93)

Rather than arguing against the canons of objectivity and neutrality, Bellah recognizes that these are not ends in themselves but "methodological strictures"—dare I say "methodological scriptures"?—which bind us to conduct our studies of people as whole entities, including the religious aspects of their lives. He claims that taking this approach is not tantamount to playing dress-up as theologian, but that it helps us to strive toward a new integration between science and religion through symbolic realism that would allow theologians and secular intellectuals to "speak the same language" (Bellah, 1970, p. 93). More relevant to my own "conversion," and whether I believe my research consultants' stories are "true," is his statement that "no expression of man's attempt to grasp the meaning and unity of his existence, not even a myth of a primitive Australian, is without meaning and value to me" (Bellah, 1970, p. 96).

Let us now consider research on whether religion benefits gang-involved youth. Just as gangs provide social networks for those who are enduring multiple marginalities (Vigil, 1988), so religious groups are known to provide safe and nurturing alternatives. Despite the benefits to at-risk urban youth by being involved in religious organizations, females are oppressed by the traditional gender roles these groups promote (Armitage & Dugan, 2006). Some researchers, while not claiming that only religious groups benefit gang-involved youth, readily acknowledge that "churches are rather famous for their success with gang members" (Bazan, Harris, & Lorentzen, 2002, p. 379). Others document vividly moving stories of Chicago youth who "followed Christ" out of the gangs and of the reconciliation among previous enemies that was facilitated by their newly found faith (McLean, 1991). Reflecting on gun crime and gang culture from a theological perspective yields a four-part model and action plans (Beckford, 2004) that help navigate analyses by steering clear of vilifying gang members and oversimplifying the motives for gun crimes. Considering the use of religion as a stress-coping mechanism among low-income urban adolescents (not necessarily gang-involved), Carleton, Esparza, Thaxter, and Grant (2008) found that for those with low levels of stress, ease and frequency of access to religious resources helped prevent depressive symptoms. However, for those with high levels of stress, the mere act of seeking resources with which to ease the stress provided social support, not necessarily the nature of the resources themselves.

What is it, then, about beliefs about God and religion that Eréndira, Marisa, Angela, Gracia, Florencia, Lupe, and Olga found as a way to disinhabit and transcend gangs? For Lupe, it is the idea that she surrendered to the will of God and "it's no longer about you." According to Wittgenstein (1953/2001), when we follow a rule, we do so by corroborating our actions with expectations set forth in a certain "form of life" where we interact. Inhabiting the gang, like following any other set of rules, is a social activity. Therefore, to invoke a religious conversion is following a rule for a particular form of life that is intelligible to and respected by most members of society, even the most hard-core gang members. As a form of life, the gang provides a set of rules, some of which are harmful to a person's life but others of which may be conducive to social transformation (Brotherton & Barrios 2004). The church, by contrast, does not require people to commit crimes or to harm others or themselves. There is unconditional acceptance, no physical harm required for being embraced by this group, and society generally accepts this change of heart as genuine. Although the women profiled here do not specifically refer to Betrayal in their Narrative of Redemption, the enthymeme is that God and the members of their church would not betray them as the members of their gang did.

Although it may seem out of place to include such a lengthy discussion about religion and the role of God in a book aimed at professionals in lay and religious community service agencies working with gangs, as well as at law enforcement officers, policymakers, and academics interested in the subject, my reasons for doing so arise from social construction and grounded theory, for my purpose is not to proselytize but to inform and educate. Ultimately, I hope that, by learning about what religion provides for these women, I can provide some resources for those who are developing equivalent lay programs to help young Latinas specifically and youth in general, regardless of their religious persuasion or lack thereof, to transcend the gang.

Part III

APPLICATIONS FOR PRACTICE AND THEORY

14

Disinhabiting the Gang

Eréndira, Florencia, Gracia, Olga, Lupe, and Marisa

It bears repeating that one of the driving forces of this book is to iden-tify ways of leaving the gang and to provide practitioners with some humble suggestions for helping gang-involved youth generally, and Lati-nas specifically, disinhabit and transcend the gang. What better place to start than by listening to stories of those who have transcended their previous gang habits? Just as there are risk factors identified as predictors of entry into a gang, so the voices of these women evoke a series of events as significant in their disinhabiting the gang. As long as they remained focused on the locality of their wretchedness, the women encountered many challenges as they found themselves with no interpretive resources to author a different story, write a different chapter to the course their lives had taken, or visualize alternate end-ings. For all of these women, disinhabiting was not a single, one-time event; rather, it was a matter of gradually restorying themselves into a different inhabitance. Although some of the women may speak about a single defining event that signified their separation from the gang, in their overall story, this event figures as one of several in a series that, retrospectively viewed, seemed like a momentous change. Whether they identified that event or moment as pivotal in their disinhabiting the gang at the time of its occurrence is irrelevant, what matters is that they utilize it as a marker in the evolution of their story of transcending the gang. Of the previously discussed theme chapters, betrayal and the narrative of redemption figured prominently as a prologue in their disinhabiting stories, as did pregnancy, childbirth, and mother'hood. Other events or pivotal moments used to punctuate the disinhabiting story include injuries sustained by them or a loved one, attending religious services regularly, and getting clean and sober. Herewith are the stories of how

Eréndira, Florencia, Gracia, Olga, Lupe, and Marisa left not just the gang but the crippling habits of the gang behind.

ERÉNDIRA

Eréndira's story of disinhabiting the gang begins after she had been incarcerated for several months at "The Ranch," one of the juvenile rehabilitation facilities in Santa Clara County, which is where she was when she turned 15. This process for Eréndira formed around her not wanting to repeat the incarceration experience. Once she got out, her homies accepted her lack of enthusiasm for banging and agreed with her desire to stay out trouble, and thus out of jail. She switched between English and Spanish during our consultation, so I indicate when we spoke English with *italics*.

Eréndira—I even remember that for my birthday, I turned fifteen there. There it was, I never had what you'd say, "Oh, my Quinceañera!" Nothing! *I was locked up at The Ranch.* Supposedly, my gift from the supervisor was a half-hour call. No, it was *like, the best gift ever.* I remember that I called my mom and there we were crying *like for half an hour*, but Ay! There are so many things that . . . but you learn, all of that, you learn to value the things you have. Like there are some friends that, youngsters that haven't been what you've been through. I thank God I have my mom who always tried to help me. There are some who say, "No, my mom's also taking drugs," and I could never imagine my mom like that. That's why I said, "*Oh my God, you know*, other people have mothers worse than I do," and just because my mother scolded me, I'd get out of the house, but I didn't see that it was for my own good. I myself matured a lot because I saw the experiences of other people. I said, "*Dang!* I am taking . . . I'm exaggerating my life, *like* 'Oh, yeah, like my life was all in pieces.'" I myself was making it like that, rushing it. I told myself, "No wonder my mother said that!" Then I started seeing my mom in a different light.

Her mother's support served Eréndira's purposes immensely as she began to restory her life. Although their relationship had troubles before, she later came to understand her mother with a wisdom found during her incarceration, and this proved invaluable in helping her begin the process of disinhabiting the gang.

Eréndira—It was when I started to mature, and from that point, I said, "Well, you know what? *I'm not going to go back.*" And when I got out, but when I got out, I was still running with the gangs, so I still talked with them, still hung out with them. But it was not the same anymore. It wasn't like, "Let's go to *rock and roll*, let's go here." They'd pick me up at my house, I'd go with them, but at night time I didn't leave the house anymore. It was like, I still hung out with them, but we weren't about doing crimes. It was more getting together and *partying*. I didn't want to any more, and they saw that already, because I told them, "I did the time that I had to do; I suffered what I had to suffer inside, and enough." They themselves would say, "Well, okay, you better stay outside, it's better for us. . . ." For them, it's better that one is outside [jail] than inside. What do they want you all locked up for? Then they'd say, "Okay, *you know*, stay outside, do this, do that." After that, I got a job and got together with the father of my son. He didn't want me to hang out with them.

Severing the ties with her Sureño homies did not happen immediately once she returned home from jail. Instead, she took time to transition into new habits: school, work, a new look, a new boyfriend, and eventually motherhood, which brought with it different storytelling possibilities.

Eréndira—. . . And afterwards, I started hanging out with him, began to work. One or the other, I started school at eight in the morning, got out at three, to work at four, and got off at ten. That is, you understand? I had no *chance* to go out. On the weekends, my boyfriend wanted to go out with me, well, my ex-boyfriend, the father of my boy. Then I had no time. That's how it was, *slowly slowly*, I started kind of getting out, I was like. . . .

In "Mother'hood," Eréndira disapproves of a girl we saw who, although heavily pregnant, wears burgundy gang colors. Given that the first time I met Eréndira she was wearing a very feminine teal-colored shirt and teal-sequined ballet flats (a variant of the Sureño blue), I wondered whether she would have noticed—and if she would have been as incensed—if the pregnant woman had been wearing blue to signify a Sureña claim. Eréndira indicated she no longer claimed Sur, as she had come out of detention and had begun what I call the "disclaiming" process of leaving the gang 2 years ago. When I asked indirectly about the inconsistency, she assured me that despite the presence of blue in her attire, it was more the style of clothes than their color that identified the wearer as a "banger." In her case, disinhabiting the gang entailed enacting and performing different habits although still identifying herself as backing up Sur. One can take the girl out of the gang, but can one take the gang colors out of the girl's wardrobe? Transcendence does not mean a discrete, abrupt, final, and total disassociation from the gang; it is not a radical disinhabiting of it. Transcendence means operating within the allowances of past, present, and future stories in order to envision, welcome, rehearse, and eventually inhabit new, more complex, and sometimes contradictory storytelling realities.

FLORENCIA

In Chapter 12, "Betrayal," Florencia's story coalesced around various events that began to foreground her disillusionment with the gang life-style, and as she told her story, she punctuated this series of events as precursors to disinhabiting the gang. She detailed how despair about her diminished standing within the gang—a "shot-caller" turned "no-good"—combined with concomitant disdain, disrespect, and dismissal by some of her homies led her to consume large quantities of drugs, bringing about a near-fatal overdose. This story seems unique in that it pivots on a single, memorable event when she was 19 years old that allowed her to begin inhabiting the meaningful process to transcend the gang.

The impact of religion on the process of transcending the gang for Florencia is discussed at length in Chapter 13, "The Narrative of Redemption." There she details how, in previous years, she had been the recipient of efforts by members of the same church to bring her into the fold. She credits their success in helping her get out of the gang to their commitment, their refusal to take no for an answer, and their unorthodox tactics. To exemplify this, here is an excerpt that bears repeating:

> *Florencia*—I had turned fifteen and remember Lupe came to the house with these people from church. There was a bunch of people over at my house, partying, and I was in the bathroom, getting high by myself. She knocks on the door, comes into the bathroom, and takes me with my clothes wet out of the washing machine, throws them in a suitcase and takes me to the Women's Home. I was there for two weeks. So, it wasn't the first time, but they were so consistent.

Despite the fact that she indirectly recognizes the numerous attempts made to help her disinhabit the gang, by both herself and others, in Florencia's story of disinhabiting the gang, this single event functions to punctuate a radical restorying of her identity and introduces the possibility of using different linguistic resources, an altogether fecund meaning-making system to engender a new, purposeful, empowering, and transcendent story.

OLGA

Like Florencia, Olga's story of leaving the gang follows from her betrayal story. In retrospect, she stories the betrayals she experienced as stepping stones in her exit from the gang, although they occurred much earlier and did not lead directly and immediately to disinhabiting. The series of punctuating markers begins with the dismal relationship between her parents; subsequent events include a fight with one of her gang-involved sisters, the shooting death of her gang-involved boyfriend, and the stabbing suffered by her own gang-involved brother. These moments punctuated the beginning of her "going to the *varrio*," for at the time she seemed to lack an alternate way of connecting these events in order to identify, and therefore to inhabit, a new story. Her process was protracted, involving marriage, children, separation, and drug overdoses for both Olga and her husband, and culminated at the open doors of a church and with the storytelling possibilities afforded to her there. These latter recurring and disempowering challenges are discussed in further detail in Chapter 15, "Transcending Gangs." As previously mentioned, the transcript shows in *italics* when Olga used English.

Olga—So, for me, that's how I got, that's how I got out of the varrio, because I realized that it wasn't what I first had experienced, you know. And I felt like really disappointed at that point, with the varrio and then, well, [with my sister,] too, "Güero," dying, and where were the homeboys? They all ran. Meantime, this [stabbing] happens to my brother and I said, "This is just a cycle!" Something inside me just snapped. "It's just a cycle, it's false, everybody is killing each other; nobody cares about nobody. Everybody is just in it for their own." Whether it's a sense of family, a sense of love, or belonging, whatever it is, everybody is just in it for their own. When it comes down to it, nobody is around. And I realized that, at the age of seventeen.

And well, my siblings, because after what happened with my brother, he stopped hanging out with them, because what he told me was that "I was willing to die for the *varrio*; I was willing to stick my neck out, but when I looked and saw all of them running, it made me realize where my *homies* stood and they let me down." So, even he started to begin reconsidering and saying, "*Wow*! I'm going to die! Why? For a color?"

Liliana—So they didn't try to take revenge?

Olga—Well, yes, they tried, and I knew there were different fights, more violence. One even lasted many years, and my brother, well, he recovered and got out and formed his own gang now outside the *varrio*. But all the others in the *varrio* recognized my brother. He was gutsy. *They would say,* *"He's down, but it's cool* that he got out, *it was his time, he did what he had to do* in the *varrio, he started the varrio, he made us strong, now we're here, we have to carry on. . . ."* So, it was like something very *false,* false. . . . Between them there was like a *false doctrine* one could say. And they did not capture reality. One could see and say, "That was false!" What kind of family is going to leave someone there to be beaten and killed?

Liliana—So, when you say you don't want to kick it with them anymore, they didn't jump you out, they left you alone . . . ?

Olga—Yes, they left me alone. Pretty much ceased. If I would see people in the streets, we didn't greet each other. *We wouldn't look at each other; we would just pretend we didn't see each other. Just walk by like nothing, you know.*

Liliana—What about the Norteños?

Olga—Yeah, they don't care. Pretty much they left me alone. . . .

Liliana—'Cause you didn't kick it with them either?

Olga—'Cause I didn't kick it with them no more, 'cause I was a girl. Even the girls, they would leave me alone. It [was] kind of like the word got around, you know? What had happened between me and my sister, and how it like went down and stuff. So it kind of went around to my benefit where they isolated me from all, *from everything, you know, even from what the varrio was, from what the color was, from everything.*

Liliana—So they didn't try to recruit you either?

Olga—No, nothing. Nothing. *I mean the word travels along,* really fast. *I got a job, now I'm working, never worked, I'm being responsible, so, going to Job Corps. So, it's like, "Okay, this girl is trying to do things right, let's leave her alone."*

Liliana—So, okay. So there are some gang membership requirements. Being jumped, wearing the colors, being down, sort of like a number of things to get in. And there's a number of things to get out? . . . and maybe go get a job?

Olga—That would be drop out, get jumped out, too, if you're gonna leave the varrio, leave the varrio forever. That needs to happen. "I'm going to get a job and start a family and then I'm just going to hang out." No, you cannot just hang out, no contact, no nothing. You know. Another. . . .

Liliana—No colors. . . .

Olga—No colors. . . . Really not claim, not claim no more. Not associate, do not associate.

Liliana—Would Norteños approach you and ask you what you claimed?

Olga—No, because my appearance and everything changed about me. I wasn't dressing how I used to. I wasn't associating or going to places. . . . See, I knew the places where I could go and couldn't go.

Liliana—Both for Sureños and Norteños.

Olga—Uh huh, for Sureños and Norteños. So like I told you, I pretty much was job, school, home, job, school, home. And I did that for years. So when [they] don't see a face anymore, they just think two things: "Well, she's not claiming no more, she's cleaning up. Let's leave her alone. Why do we even look for her? There's all THESE that we need to deal with!" *See what I'm saying? So, that's pretty much what happened to me.*

Here we see that "Por Vida," the Sureños' claim about gang membership being "for life," really is not the case. Might there have been a sense in which Olga's gender, level of involvement, family status, and knowledge of the gang's business worked in her favor, as seems also to have happened for Eréndira? Would the more hard-core males, those having done prison time, perhaps with undisclosed and unaccounted for crimes, expect more resistance from their "down" homies than Olga did? From her story, it sounds as though even gang members can accede to a version of the dominant narrative of the American dream: Work hard, stay clean, stay out of trouble, and you too shall be left alone if you choose to leave the gang. Olga's homies and the enemy alike, the people who had previously supported her identity as "Little Giggles," now acquiesced as she acted toward inhabiting a story that held currency in mainstream society.

As the previous voices attest, the process of leaving the gang—a de-gangification, so to say—is often not a single, one-time event; rather, it is a gradual extricating from the gang through practices that run the opposite of those to which the women have become habituated. The difficulty for some of these women lies in unlearning old habits as well as learning new habits, in avoiding the ruts in favor of the unexplored trail. As the saying goes, "Better the Devil you know than the Devil you don't." The gang, both despite and because of its familiarly devilish ways, provides a painfully interdependent familiarity to counter the differently painful confusion that these women face when they attempt to compose a new plot twist in their story.

GRACIA

Independence from the gang often seems illusory because if there is one thing they know very well, it is how to inhabit a gang, especially for those in Gangs of Family, as was the case for Gracia. The decision to leave, although laudable, requires support that may be beyond the women's linguistic horizons, so that this new storytelling habit manifests in a series of starts and stops, much like a smoker's well-intended repeated failures to quit smoking. For Gracia, betrayal also appeared in a first draft of her story of disinhabiting the gang. In Chapter 12, "Betrayal," and to some extent in Chapter 7, "Of Colors and Names," she denounced her homies for not backing her up on several occasions when she and her children were in danger and her homegirls for attempting to "get with" her boyfriend. Her yarn of gang glamour began to tatter, yet she needed a new one—one to cover her tattoos, her very own Norteña claim—one that must be cut wholesale from a text yet unwoven, unfamiliar, and uninhabited.

Gracia—And so, that's where I made up my mind, I was done. I was done. [. . .] From that day on, that's when I started deciding that I wanted to live life differently and that I didn't want to be in gangs no more. Of course I had to fight my way out of gangs, I couldn't just get out.

Liliana—So, they, the tattoos represented an identity that you were trying to disassociate yourself from and you saw what challenges it posed, not only for your identity, but for your trying to go straight. I don't know, I mean, is there a term for that? Drop-out, or quit the gang, leave the gang? Is there a term that is used for this, among gang members, when they refer to somebody who's out of it?

Gracia—Oh, yeah. If you get out, what are you called? You're either called a "drop-out" or you're called every name in the book. Or someone that, I've been called either a "drop-out" or "ranker" . . . someone that "isn't down with us no more," or "she's scared." I could just be called a whole bunch of names, any name you can think of. I don't remember being called too many names, because back then it was just a drop-out. So it was either a drop-out, or kids nowadays I hear them say um, like, "She's a punk, she couldn't hang with them" [rocks head side to side], or she wasn't tough enough or she ain't down, she was never down, and you know, she couldn't hang with . . . being a Norteña, and she didn't have the real stuff of what it took or whatever." They could say whatever they want, but most of the time it was either a drop-out [sic].

Liliana—And when you, when you, did you share your transition to other people? Did you say, "You know, I'm getting out" or "I feel endangered"?

Stories of horrific jumping-out beatings engendered this book; yet now I am seeking commonalities to verbalize one's intentions of leaving the gang. Although people may intend to do something, often we lack a script or set of instructions to present our wishes or intentions to others. Here I am inquiring about the content of specific storytelling acts: The act of quitting the gang speaks volumes, and a gang member going through the process of disinhabiting is saying something polysemic, but specifically, what does one say when one wants to get out? In war, a surrendering party waves a white flag. In gangs, is there an equivalent marker or an acceptable script? What could one of these women say to her homies that would make them understand or just accept her excuse for wanting out? It strikes me as ironic that the term "drop-out" is used because so often gang members have already dropped out of school and other aspects of a law-abiding society prior to joining a gang. When employees quit, get fired, or get laid off at a company, sometimes an "exit interview" is conducted, mostly for the purpose of retrieving company property such as keys from the employee's possession, but also to ascertain the reasons the employee quit, if that indeed happened. Resignation letters and lay-off notices are de rigueur in some organizations, and often there is a protocol and specificity in wording. On Facebook, one can discretely "unfriend" someone. While driving, we use our turn signals; while moving out of a relationship, aren't there at least "Fifty Ways to Leave Your Lover"? ("You just slip out the back, Jack/Make a new plan, Stan/You don't need to be coy, Roy/Just get yourself free.") What do gangs do instead of or in addition to the ritual beating of jumping out? How does one signal one's intentions to disinhabit a gang . . . and live to tell it?

   Gracia—I just didn't want to have any part of it no more, 'cause I was really straightforward. I wasn't going to hide how I felt and wasn't scared of anybody so I just told them, "I don't want to be down with this no more, you guys are fake, you guys are phonies" [laughs]. And they'd get mad. Oh! They'd get pissed off, "Well, what do you mean we're fake? We're the phonies? You're the one that's getting out, the one that started all this; now you don't want to be part of it?" And they would call me all those names, "punk" and a whole bunch of bad words and stuff. So I started pointing out "I had kids to take care of and when this happened, you weren't there. And when I wasn't there you were trying to get with my man!" And so I started you know naming all sorts of stuff they did to me, I was like, "So what? I'm supposed to stay loyal to you guys, and you? Behind my back you guys aren't loyal to me? Nope! It doesn't work like that."
   So I had to fight, fight my way out. Yeah, every time I saw them, we'd fight. We walked down the street, if we were on a bus, we'd fight. They didn't want me in the neighborhood anymore if I wasn't going to be a Norteña, and I had an attitude of "Well, I live here! Where am I supposed

to go?" You know, so I had like a big reputation so, I was one of the best fighters in the neighborhood, where I was called "Little Loca Boxer," that was my nickname. I even had to fight a girl for that name, 'cause we both had the same name but we both lived in the same neighborhood. We lived on this side of the neighborhood and she lived on this part of the neighborhood, by Overfelt School. So, we had to fight to keep our name. Of course, I won, so that name stuck with me, and even trying to get out the gangs, I still wanted to hold up my reputation as being tough, being one of the best fighters and not be scared of no one. And so, I think that could have been why I fought so much . . . it's because I wasn't willing to let anybody um, punk me or try to put me down or scare me or make me run. So I had to keep standing up for what I had believed in, and that was me being the toughest girl and nobody was gonna get me down.

Gracia's gang moniker—"Little Loca Boxer"—gave her standing in the gang, yet it also prevented her from leaving the gang easily, for scholastic achievement and careers are not earned and kept by one's physical prowess and fighting skills. Therefore, Gracia needed not only a new set of habits away from the gang but a new nickname! Of course, she had precious little need for one outside the gang, but the actions that her gang name imposed kept her tethered to it despite her protestations to the contrary. The disinhabiting process came in starts and stops, as she engaged in rethinking her gains vis-à-vis her investments in that lifestyle, and she tried to do things differently by doing the same things that had led her to form and later lead the gang. Thus, fighting her way out of a group whose main purpose is to fight posed a practical paradox for her: Being tough identified her as a leader while inhabiting the gang, yet being tough had different significance and limited her storytelling possibilities as she attempted to disinhabit the gang.

Gracia—And I started thinking like that: "It's my life, my decision, not hers, not his, not the gang group, the gang lifestyle; it's me, it's me, it's Gracia who's going to take care of Gracia, it's Gracia who's going to get Gracia to where she needs to get to in life, it's Gracia who's going to support her family and provide the best care and love that I possibly can. Not the homeboys, not the homegirls, not the color red, not the Norte living style." It was me, me, it all bottomed down to me. So that's how it's been from then on.

Her stories lived and stories told—in short, Gracia's social worlds—were at odds as she tried to inhabit the demands of a future, unknown world while disinhabiting her association with the gang, painfully familiar to her. Enmeshed in gang habits, Gracia's main source of income was drug dealing, which led to her arrest after selling dope to an undercover police officer. Her jail experiences are detailed in Chapter 9, "Time Served!" When she came out of jail, the struggle to author a new identity continued.

Gracia—Well, then that's when I . . . just stopped hanging out with the same old people. I stayed away from everybody, even some family members. It took me keeping distance from family members. Because again, back to my family members, they played a major part, because either they were using drugs, selling drugs, or they were into gangs. So being around that was, and of course, that's all I knew, it was really easy to go right back into it. So keeping my distance from some family members, friends, people I knew, helped me keep my head straight and helped me realize that I could do it, I could make changes in my life and that there was people out there willing to help me because I. . . . When I heard about the Clean Slate Tattoo Removal Program, that's when I really started thinking deeper about how to get out, how to stay out. That's when I started advocating for myself and, and, and I met Juan and there was another lady, Christine, who helped my husband and me go through Clean Slate Tattoo Removal Program.

Because, again . . . I had family members all the way when I was a baby all the way up, I had family members now that uh, three of them, one has already been sentenced to life in prison and two of them are fighting it. And so, of course I had Dad who, who's in and out of prison, he gets in trouble one more time, that's his third strike, he's gone for a long time. I have a brother, if he gets in trouble. I have tons of family. . . . I've lost family members to gang violence. Last year, I had a cousin who was shot in the face and died. He protected his cousin, I mean his brother from getting shot. I mean, they're Norteños . . . my cousin wasn't a Norteño, he WAS a Norteño, but he was slowly, little by little, trying to get out of it because he was gonna become a father and he knew the great responsibility of being a father and because he didn't have a father role model in his life, he had really made up his mind then that he was not going to give his son the life that his dad gave him by not being there for him. So that's what his dream was, to be the best father that he could be. He went out, partied with his brother, they came home, and the Sureños followed them and they got off and exchanged some words and they went to shoot his younger brother and he jumped in the middle and got shot in the face and his life ended. So, when I say, that was all in my family, you know, the drug using, Dad's now been put away for life, the gang-banging, everything.

236

So that's . . . there was really no positive role models, no resources or way out to get out. So I had to get it from other means, from other persons.

The inexorable pull of Gangs of Family habits, the destructive legacy of unavoidable and excruciating family violence, drug abuse, and normalized dysfunctionality all led Gracia, as it does many women attempting to gain independence from a gang, to face enormous challenges in playing a societal deck stacked high against her due to her being so unfamiliar with the practical, lived experience of doing something else instead of being in a gang. Her saving grace was the encounter she had in jail with religion because it was through her church contacts on the outside that she sought the opportunity to acquire a new identity, a new look, and a new relationship with her husband (as detailed in Chapter 13, "The Narrative of Redemption"). Initially, she inhabited independence from her family as a necessary step to clean living. The removal of her tattoos allowed her to become an inter(in)dependent authority of new stories that led her to transcend gangs.

LUPE

Other chapters elaborate on the potential that some stories of betrayal (Chapter 12) and religious encounters (Chapter 13) hold for a gradual exit out of a gang. As evidenced in Lupe's storytelling, the trajectory out of the gang can be sinuous and sporadic and incorporates recognizing the downside to La Vida Loca, redemption, and betrayal as vestibules into the habituation of transcendence.

Lupe—So, that's what happened for the next two years . . . you would think that after I got stabbed that my life would get better . . . that I would start to make some changes, and I think that really deep, deep down inside I really was like trying to find myself, I enrolled in college. . . .

. . . it was my last year of high school, which it was difficult 'cause I was a senior, so I missed a lot of school, I was in the hospital, I had to do summer school and catch up on credits. I graduated, and then I began to try to find myself, kind of like in a journey to improve my life. I went straight from high school to San José State . . . I don't know what I was thinking, I was not prepped for college, was not prepped at all, but I had some good friends in the community, I was very involved in the Chicano community, so I had some people who mentored me, were there even when we were going through the whole retaliation, they were trying to mediate between us, so there was a lot of community involvement as well, trying to help us, to guide us, and they helped me get into college, but being addicted, I was addicted to drugs and not having a clear vision and purpose in life I gripped, and I would end up from college in San José State, I was like one of the first Cholas there, I looked around I looked like a sore thumb, sticking out of the whole campus . . . because of the way I looked, because I dressed a certain way, people would look at me kind of strange. I didn't belong there, maybe I was lost . . . so I got really discouraged and I went to . . . I would end up in downtown San José, walking around, meeting up with friends and homies and partying, and eventually I dropped out of State.

Liliana—So you weren't in any kind of treatment for . . . ?

Lupe—No, I didn't enter any kind of treatment, no . . . it's interesting that, because I was, people saw me and saw the potential for a young leader, even though it was negative, in a lot of ways they saw a lot of positive in me that I was able to lead and a lot of young people would listen, so I ended up getting a good job right out of . . . cause I was doing Speedy every summer, the Speedy jobs, so I started working at [a community-based social services agency], I worked there. . . . I believe this was the end of my senior year . . . after the stabbing, because I was trying to better myself, get myself together, so I started working, I got stabbed in January, so I started working in the summer at [the agency].

So, I'm working and they ended up liking me so I stayed on board full time. So, I developed a youth resource for them, I did some Barrios Unidos kind of work, bring gangs together . . . but again . . . because of the addiction and . . . but I wasn't open about it. . . .

So, I hid my drug use from them really well and people didn't know I was addicted. So, I'd go to work and do all that and after work I'd go home and . . . and get high then go to work. . . . But eventually it catches up with you. From that work I went to working at a treatment program, working as a youth counselor, and I remember I was talking to clients about PCP . . . and one day a mother came in about her daughter and they were discussing the problems and the girl looks at me and she says, "What about her eyes? Look at her eyes! They're all glossy!" . . . talking about me as a counselor. And boy! That was like a ton of bricks just hit me across the head . . . 'cause it was like someone was confronting me, indirectly . . . and I felt like crawling under the table. . . .

Lupe described at length the positive influence that a particular religious organization had on her process of getting and staying clean and sober, which is detailed in Chapter 13, "The Narrative of Redemption." Now we return to her discussion of the relational spaces she had to inhabit in order to fully disinhabit from the gang.

Lupe—I was still working at this treatment program, but now I was able to be effective because I could be honest with people about . . . I was bound . . . I was addicted and I had to learn to live a new life, I had to make new friends. I had to stop all of my connections with my old friends and dealers, my network, people who were selling drugs to me. This was family to me. It wasn't just people: it was my "familia" that I had to stop associating with because I now, I wanted to live a new life and I was nineteen years old. I had to relearn. I had to unlearn and I had to relearn. Because when you're in a gang, you lose your morals, you lose your self-respect, you lose your faith, you lose everything. It's such a degrading lifestyle, it's all a façade, but inside, you're deteriorating, in all aspects of your life. So, I had to rebuild all of that.

And my parents had brought us up very well and taught us very well, but I lost a lot of that in the gang, in the drugs, so I started to rebuild it in a sort of . . . now I was able to reach out, and that was kind of like being in a mission in my life to help others, and that's all I've done in the past twenty . . . I'm coming up on twenty-five years of my spiritual birthday; it is in March. That's all I've done: service to others, be it drugs, gangs, domestic violence, sexual assault, I've been working on all those aspects. Today I work as an outpatient drug counselor. I also work with victims of gang violence, so I work with family members, 'cause I know firsthand what that feels like and the pain. . . .

The support resources that at first eluded Gracia in her quest for a new identity were laid before Lupe to no avail. Her duplicity helped her win the battle of keeping her job but also brought her to lose the battle being fought within her to invent a new story. The leadership qualities that, ironically, many gang members display—and that, in Lupe's case, many supporters in her activist community hoped to redirect—did not emerge at first. Members of her network of supporters were willing to assist, yet a crucial piece, invisible even to herself, derailed their most concentrated efforts: her pernicious drug habit. In order to get off drugs, she had to recognize the necessity of disinhabiting not just a gang but an entire lifestyle and her identity, as enabled by members of her drug addiction network. Although there are many programs—both lay and religion-based—that aim to help people leave gangs, the Victory Outreach Church is said to be among the most effective (Montano & Cottrell, personal communication, September 21, 2007) in helping people stay out once they get out (see Chapter 13). This effectiveness carries vital significance in Lupe's story of not merely leaving the gang but finding solace in a life without dependency on drugs and beyond the gang habits that engendered it.

Although gang-involved women may leave the gang for a variety of reasons, drug abuse and violent relationships are much harder to disinhabit. As we see in the following section, for Marisa, pregnancy provided her a meaningful punctuation mark with which to transform her story of disinhabiting not so much the gang as the attendant lifestyle habits previously mentioned.

MARISA

I remind the reader about the peculiarities of Marisa's story, which permitted unique storytelling abilities; these peculiarities derived from the arrangement she had with her brother to earn money as his drug runner, but only as long as she continued earning good grades in school.

Marisa—I always had to do my schoolwork, I had to. If not, I wasn't going to be able to go out with him. He wasn't going to give me any money, any opportunities to make money. That was the deal. And sometimes I wonder if that wasn't the deal, I wouldn't have made it that far in school, you know what I mean? Sounds like a shitty way to get somebody to go to school, but there's not very many people I know who have been involved in gangs who can say they're high school graduates. That makes me kind of proud.

Despite their deal and despite her brother's refusal to give her drugs, Marisa nonetheless developed a dependency on drugs that eventually led to homelessness. She sought and received treatment several times, relapsing each time. Yet when speaking about how she was in another round of hitting rock bottom due to her drug abuse, Marisa identifies her pregnancy as the dénouement for cleaning up and inhabiting transcendence:

Marisa—And um, I didn't . . . don't want my daughter to grow up like that. So, I . . . I remember one day sitting down with my brother, 'cause there was a point where he got clean, and um, I told him that I was pregnant and he told me to get help. So I got help again. I got clean one more time and I have a little girl. She's a year now. And after, after that, that whole selling drugs, and wanting to hang out and be in the streets, and be a part of . . . being friends with these people who probably don't give a shit about you anyways, you know what I mean? They're probably just hanging out because you're helping them . . . you're probably bringing . . . what's that word I'm looking for here? . . . it's convenient for them because you have what they want, that type of thing. I just let that go.

My husband was in prison when she was born, but things have been really good since then. You know, I got myself into college, we have our own place, things . . . I know that, uh, I've seen people that I used to hang out with that I know from like my brother, from my brother's 'hood and things like that, they're still doing the same old thing. And probably because they don't have any hope or because they don't have anything to look to. And I tell them, "You don't have to feel like that, never, because there's so much more life to live. There's so many things out there."

The trajectory of Marisa's life reads like a success story, and she knows she is the author. Education was initially the condition her brother imposed on her in the world of drugs and gangs, yet by protecting her education, he worked to ensure it could become Marisa's meal ticket in the law-abiding world. The next chapter provides more depth and detail on how the change in Marisa's self-concept helped her transcend. Her pregnancy helped her get clean, and her daughter, her relationship with the child's father, and her schooling helped her inhabit an inter(in)dependent space vis-à-vis the gang. Such are the markers of her transcendent story.

DISCUSSION

Of these six gang-involved women—Eréndira, Florencia, Gracia, Olga, Lupe, and Marisa—only Gracia and Lupe encountered resistance from their fellow gang members when they decided to make the move out of the gang. Both Gracia and Florencia became pregnant and had children while still actively inhabiting the gang. Gracia had to fight her way out, which, paradoxically, had been why she formed her own gang, so this made her suspect: It was plausible that they thought she was bluffing and was just fighting them to start a rival gang. Fighting also was one of the reasons that Gracia cited for wanting to leave, whereas Florencia's drug abuse lowered her standing in the gang. Lupe's defining moment was a stabbing that gave her license to leave, yet the separation was not a clean-cut, one-time event but a protracted process of disinhabiting. Notably, out of the six, only Lupe was not pregnant during her gang involvement or gang disinhabiting. Olga was not pregnant either when she left the *varrio*, but she had three daughters as her husband's gang involvement continued and her own drug use worsened. For Eréndira and Marisa, pregnancy afforded a novel situation from which to author a new story that needed to be told to help them sever their gang ties.

From these stories, I confirm the notion that it is possible to leave a gang and that the myths about what gang members have to do in order to leave, such as being killed or having to kill someone in your own family (Decker & Van Winkle, 1996; Klein, 1971), in the case of these women are only that: myths.

To keep people from being able to decide to leave, gangs tell their members that they must perform some heinous act such as killing someone they love, or that they must be "jumped out," a beating purportedly even more brutal and extensive than the jumping in. Granted, on joining a gang, nobody gives new members a welcome orientation where they stipulate the conditions of membership, as one might receive if one were to join a health club. There is no cancellation policy, there is no money-back guarantee, and there is no guarantee! There is only a penalty for early withdrawal, and it is in the gang's interest that the penalty remain secret or that it be exaggerated, for even the act of discussing how one might exit the gang might raise some gangbanger eyebrows. Although the allure of gangs for youth includes protection, prestige, and purpose, by joining a gang, many youth become even more endangered. Gang-involved youth can expect not only to perform violence but also to endure it at the hands of members of rival gangs as well as their own. Despite the pervasive violence, gangs give youth a sense of belonging—in essence, fictive kin that function as an ersatz family—by privileging the story of "having their back" or providing protection.

Moreover, the powerful influence of gangs on their members resides precisely in the "Por Vida" story that not only carries a silencing element but also foments an unspeakable story where no one knows for sure what it takes to get out. Although many youth know others who have gotten out (Decker & Lauritsen, 2006), they also know the vicious attacks that their peers are capable of perpetrating on rivals; they can very well imagine themselves being the target of a similar fate. They have no one to turn to for justice; they only know retribution. Therefore, the story of retribution as a consequence of leaving the gang enjoys privilege among others for its being unimaginable. In this sense, the story of "Por Vida" thrives in the streets and in the neighborhoods, where stories of former homies' successfully leaving the gang might languish for lack of novelty appeal. Although the inherent dangers of leaving a gang cannot be ignored, neither can they be allowed to remain the single reason given for staying in the gang. None of the research associates consulted for this book even mentioned it, for they had other, more practical concerns. In the concluding chapter of this book, I discuss strategies for practitioners in helping youth story their way out of gangs.

Gang entry is often as slow, protracted a process as is an exit from it. But just as gang members are persistent in their recruitment of new youth to their ranks, so intervention models must display this quality of tenacity if they are to succeed (Jackson, Bass, & Sharpe, 2005). Although gang membership may be considered an individual choice, the alternatives available to youth faced with this choice are few at best and misguided at worst. The effects on a young woman's life of gang involvement are portentious. Storytelling toward transcendence is equally fateful; the difference lies in whether the storyteller has access to linguistic resources with which to transform a potential tragedy into a fulfilled autobiography.

15

Transcending Gangs

Margie, Elisa, Angela, Marisa, and Olga

The stories of young women who avoid gang involvement could provide significant insights to academics and practitioners in developing or enhancing programs for gang avoidance, prevention, and abatement. This chapter is not intended to evaluate or assess the effectiveness of such programs, but rather to illustrate how the particular set of research associates who were consulted for this book story their experiences of disinhabiting and transcending gangs or of staying away from them altogether. Here, I also provide some commentary about my own research trajectory pertinent to practitioners who work with gang-involved and gang-impacted youth, as well as some suggestions and strategies culled from the stories intended to enhance practitioners' skills and researchers' approaches in addressing the needs of gang-impacted and gang-involved youth. Three basic models are examined, in this order: (a) "Gangs-of-Family involved, not looking to get out," (b) "Gang-involved in the past, experiencing different ways to disinhabit," and (c) "Never involved, despite significant gang-impact."

From qualitative data, researchers find "considerable evidence that youth in gangs will avoid delinquent and violent behaviors when acceptable alternatives are available and unlikely to call their honor into question" (Hughes, 2005, p. 107), a point that should encourage community-based organizations and social service agencies as well as municipal, county, state, and federal government funding sources to continue providing sound and safe alternatives for at-risk youth. My concern in this chapter is to seek answers for questions such as: How do these young women sidestep the pitfalls that many of their peers seem unable to avoid? What linguistic resources are available to them so that they can tell a story of avoiding the gang involvement that others seem to embrace? The research associates whose stories are included here in this "never involved, despite significant impact" model are Elisa and Angela.

Moreover, as I discussed in the previous chapter, the process of disinhabiting a gang is not always a one-time effort, so getting out is but one step in the process of transcending. What different resources— financial, emotional, cultural, educational, political—do gang-involved women need after they have declared that they want out? Helping someone who fell, was pushed, or jumped into an icy cold lake and almost froze to death requires different resources and efforts than helping someone stay dry and warm during a rainstorm, for the story-telling resources of gang-involved women are markedly different from the stories of those who are merely gang-impacted. I classified this group of women as "Gang-involved in the past, experiencing different ways to disinhabit." The challenges encountered by Marisa and Olga in transcending gangs are included in this set.

Most important, I believe significant insights can be gleaned from the stories of women who are still actively involved, not just for what they say but for what they do not, cannot, or will not say about their gang habits. Therefore, the special case of Margie—who, at the time of the interview consultation, had no intention of leaving the gang and whom I classified under the model of "Gangs-of-Family involved, not looking to get out"—should provide a relevant place to start this discussion. Therefore, I discuss Margie's story first and then follow it with the stories of two women who managed to avoid gang involvement despite being gang-impacted, and two others who overcame many challenges of disinhabiting.

MARGIE

Margie was the only one of the 13 research associates whose stories make up this book who actively inhabited a gang at the time of the interview consultation. I offer her story here as a point of departure, as counterbalance, and as a sample of the target population I believe some readers of this book will want to reach: the gang-involved Latina who needs to author a new story beyond the gang habits.

It is plausible to assume that those who find it most difficult to renounce the gang lifestyle and habits may be the most hard-core gang members. On the one hand, if even someone who is so "down" (see, for an example of this contrast, the story of Florencia) can offer a testimony for transcending the gang, therein lies the hope that she can actually do so. On the other hand, different women encounter different challenges, whether because they believe the gang lifestyle is rewarding, do not know another way of being outside the gang, or believe the gang provides them with what they need. Margie was one such storyteller, for she seemed ensconced in the gang habits, unable (or unwilling?) to envision either an alternative future for herself or a coherent description of her current gang habits. What follows is a composite of my various attempts during the semi-structured interview to guide her storytelling into a reflection on the future.

Liliana—If you were to stop gang-banging, what would you miss the most?

Margie—I'm still an active gang member, that's never going to change. I might change the way I act or change the way I do things, but I'm never not going to be a gang member, like I can't do it. I'm deep into it. I don't know what it's like to not be in a gang. I don't know what I'll miss about not banging, it's engrained in my head, it's the only lifestyle I know and that's the only way I'm going to live, I have not known any other way, so I wouldn't know what I'd miss.

Liliana—About banging Norte, what do you like the most?

Margie—I don't know, I really don't. . . .

Liliana—What other ways do you think people find to get out?

Margie—I am not trying to get out, so I don't really know. I'm not too worried about it.

Liliana—What would you say if one of your friends told you she didn't want to bang anymore?

Margie—I would not go after them, because I already know there would be people after them.

Liliana—What about other ways that women use to get out of gangs, like religion? What do you make of that? Does it make sense?

Margie—It does not make sense to me to get out because of having a relationship with God. I think about God, at times, when I need him. I don't believe in that, hearing voices. God does not do much for me. My mom brought me. I'm not spiritual . . . I don't want to speak about that.

Liliana—How else can one live a life that's not so painful . . . is it a normal part of life? . . . So much pain?

Margie—I don't worry about emotions. I'd just probably end up breaking down or something. . . .

Liliana—What do you see yourself doing five years from now? If I meet you five years from now, what will you be doing differently? What will you be doing the same?

Margie—I'll just go with whatever comes to me.

Liliana—What will you do to make it happen?

Margie—I don't worry about the future; don't think too much about it. I might not be here next day. It's got so bad I got my graveside paid for and my stone already engraved, got my coffin picked out and everything. I got my will written; I've done that since I was fourteen, just because I didn't think I was going to make it until eighteen. I paid for everything myself, and I got life insurance. Everything is taken care of, just waiting for when the day is going to come that I got to go. Whatever gets me gets me.

Liliana—Do you have the sense that something is going to happen?

Margie—No.

Liliana—What makes your story unique?

Margie—I couldn't tell. . . .

Although it may seem unconventional to follow this line of inquiry, recall that my reasons for doing so were guided by an interviewing method known as Circular Questioning (CQ), which I discussed in depth in Chapter 3. Using that explanation of CQ, I now offer a set of hypotheses for Margie's reticence. My attempted moves to positively connote are briefly exemplified in Margie's section of Chapter 10, "Mother'hood." In the current discussion, I was attempting to hypothesize that, if she were able to re-contextualize her gang experience to find security in her relationships with others beyond the gang, she would find it easier to leave the gang.

So, how could CQ have worked with Margie? Although I have no evidence from the answers she gave, I can hypothesize that my questions might have resulted in a seed being planted to think of herself beyond the gang. How could my efforts to help her generate a different story not yield some progress? Because I only had 1 hour with her; because the purpose of the consultation was to hear her story, not to intervene; and because other limitations on her part stonewalled my attempts at circularity, namely, the silencing element that gangs impose on their members. In terms of secrecy on the part of prisoners generally, and residents of a halfway house specifically, Wieder (2001) has provided an insightful analysis of the "convict code" that guides their behavior. Essentially, this pithy phrase not only describes a sociological phenomenon, a demand to "not be a snitch," or a situation of paucity of information like the one I encountered with Margie, but also points to the very shadow we are trying to shine a light on. My experience with Margie confirms Wieder's argument that the "convict code" proves instrumental in creating, maintaining, and transforming a particular type of meaning among individuals who wish to maintain secrecy about aspects of their lives. Even when I asked Margie descriptive questions designed to highlight the connectivity of the gang as a system, such as, "What do you like the most about banging Norte?", or reflective questions intended to conceptualize change, such as, "What will you miss the most when you stop claiming Norte?", the implacable force of her gang's equivalent of the "convict code" kept her from being able to describe connections or reflect on the possibilities for change in her life. By doing this, I hoped to elicit some kind of story-starter about the space she inhabited with the gang and to inquire about her own storytelling powers to move toward independence or even inter(in)-dependence. I was curious to see whether she saw the gang as a stifling or an inspiring force or both, to see whether she recognized the paradox, and to see how she managed to transcend it, whether she recognized it or not. As Milan Kundera (1981) observes, a "method of organized forgetting" (p. 22) is necessary for someone in power to deprive someone out of power of her or his identity and conscious-ness. Latinas like Margie, who have seldom been in power, face not just a forgetting of their identity and consciousness but an absence of the component integral for their creating and nurturing: fulfilling rela-tionships. Moreover, the pain that Margie chooses not to feel lest she break down brings to mind Gergen's (2009) notion of pain as a rela-tional achievement: "When we express our pain we are engaging in a culturally prepared performance. We are not reporting on the state of the psyche, but acting within a tradition of relationship. That is, we are engaging in an action that has achieved its intelligibility from a history of co-action" (p. 128).

What strikes me the most about Margie's story is its lack of hope. What would the future be like for women such as Margie if she could turn herself in to the authorities and stop looking over her shoulder—stop running away from the law and find a place where she could get drug and alcohol treatment, job training, sex and parenting education, psychological counseling, and other services to help her learn new and healthy patterns for being and acting in the world? What if she could eventually be reunited with her son? How can she reconcile the difference between experiencing gangs as a lifestyle that one chooses and gangs as a way to live that one is born into? I believe her (lack of) storytelling skills and my inability to elicit them present the primary challenge to her inhabiting a different space beyond the gang. As I observed earlier, the gang functions as a silencing force, dictating what she can or cannot say.

More specifically, Margie's relational experiences in the gang as a primary meaning-making context create her understanding that being in the gang requires her to be silent on many aspects of her life. Despite my prompt, she is unable to imagine not only a different future—one beyond the gang—but any future at all. This silencing occurs to such an extent that her storytelling skills fail her even when asked to describe what she enjoys about her present. Is it the case that her skills have atrophied or that she never developed them at all? How could she envision another reality when she has experienced no reality beyond the gang and her notions of self and personhood developed in gang habits? Further, the fact that she has already planned her own funeral but cannot figure out a way to obtain legitimate employment implies her acceptance of the idea that gang membership is not for life but for death. It comes more easily to plan for her death than it does to plan for her life. That death is imminent is not a revelation because she most likely has seen people in her life die gang-related deaths at an early age. Therefore, paying for all the funeral expenses fits into her self-concept of someone who takes care of things, who leaves no worries for others, and who believes she has no other story to tell about what makes her uniquely human. To help such a unique story be told, perhaps we could take a cue from writer Ursula K. Le Guin (1989):

> In the telling of a story, reason is only a support system. It can provide causal connections; it can extrapolate; it can judge what is likely, plausible, possible. All this is crucial to the invention of a good story, a sane fantasy, a sound piece of fiction [but] we cannot ask reason to take us across the gulfs of the absurd. Only the imagination can get us out of the bind of the eternal present, inventing or hypothesizing or pretending or discovering a way that reason can then follow into the infinity of options, a clue through the labyrinths of choice, a golden string, the story, leading us to the freedom that is properly human, the freedom open to those whose minds can accept unreality. (p. 45)

Because Margie deeply inhabits the gang, she cannot tell a story about the meaning of being a Northener, and through her silence, she embodies loyalty to the gang. The untold story also demands her silence, and in this silence she inhabits dependence.

On theorizing about the matter of Margie's gang-imposed silence, I now would like to refer to the Japanese concept of dependence. Doi (1990) explains the notion of *amae* among Japanese that, among other uses of the term, characterizes parent–child relationships. In the practice of *amae* in Japan, parents indulge their children to a large extent because the latter are totally dependent on the former; as children age, *amae* wanes but does not end entirely and then finds a reverse expression in the children's honoring their parents as they age.

Returning to Margie, who became a mother at the age of 11, we might say that she experienced little to no *amae*, for what indulgent parent would send his 7-year-old daughter to sell drugs to earn money to pay bills? *Amae* is a good form of dependence in which children are made to feel entitled, whereas Margie's dependence on the gangs excludes *amae* by dictating loyalty to her Gang of Family but not providing the initial seeds for it in her infancy. In fact, this form of dependence denies her any vision of herself apart from the gang. Margie had planned and prepaid for her own funeral at the ripe old age of 18. Doi, a psychiatrist, might argue that Margie lacked *amae*, which prevented her from developing a healthy *jibun*, or self. Schizophrenics, whose awareness of self is abnormal, have a "latent desire for *amae* but no experience of relations with others involving *amae*" (Doi, 1990, p. 20). Granted, this work is not intended as psychoanalysis nor is Margie Japanese. Although these concepts are culturally deeply felt among Japanese, in the Mexican culture, children who are indulged are called "*consentidos*," which translates literally as "someone felt with," indicating the emotional affinity that a parent may have for one of her or his offspring. This characterization often is not limited to parents who are indulgent (*consentidores*); grandparents, aunts and uncles, godparents, neighbors, and even teachers have their "*consentidos*"—youth with whom they identify and whom they sponsor, spoil, indulge, and favor. It is common for a young person to acknowledge that she or he is the "*consentida/o*" of a certain adult. For example, Olga, in recounting her husband's reticence to move in with her and his demand that the newlywed couple move in with his mother, described him as being a "momma's boy." Had she been speaking Spanish at that moment, she would most likely have said, "*El era el consentido de su mamá.*" By contrast, a person who is ill behaved is said to have no mother— "*no tiene madre*"—and the same is said among Mexicans of someone whose extremely cruel actions are beyond the pale, unthinkable for someone with a proper upbringing. The point of this extended discussion and contrast between what Doi identifies as something uniquely Japanese, as *amae*, and what I am theorizing here as being uniquely Mexican, as "*consentir*" (typically by one's mother), is to argue that

Margie was deprived of this benefit, thus her sense of self is challenged to the point of not being able to tell a story of her life.

How could Margie tell a story that she has no idea how to live? The story Margie could be guided to tell using CQ places her as being relationally connected to the well-being of others (*amae/consentidora*); she could be guided to recognize the need to reject death in order to continue being a good mother and caregiver. In this untold story, she would be acknowledged as a young mother who has hopes and aspirations for her son (who becomes her own *consentido*) and would be guided to think of some aspirations for herself as well. It would portray her as having the wherewithal to quit drugs and alcohol and eventually find or create enough meaning-making resources to effectively pay her debt to society, turn her life around and away from jail, and make a clean break: in other words, to disinhabit the gang and, in so doing, to transcend it.

TRANSCENDING AFTER DISINHABITING

In Chapter 14, "Disinhabiting the Gang," we saw how women utilized an event to punctuate their exit from the gang, although several of them recognized that it was not a one-time effect. Habits are hard to break. How can women who have made the decision to disinhabit the gang manage to transcend? Marisa and Olga have stories that could inform practitioners on how to support their efforts in making a clean and definitive break from the gang habits.

MARISA

Beyond the gang habits, transcending also means finding a different life course; it means taking pieces and parts from one's previously told story and using those, along with some new ones, to reinvent a new self, a new sense of purpose, and, most likely, a new "lived happily ever after." Marisa had a lot of this in place to accomplish the new story, the peculiarities of which entail reconfiguring aspects of her ethnicity into the new story with which to position her new self. In contrast to Margie, who lacked the relational anchors to transcend the gang, Marisa's unique experience in the Gangs of Family provided such anchors. Marisa's relationships with her brother (she was his *consentida*), her deceased father, and the father of her daughter paralleled her evolution from the gang habits into transcendence. Curiously, in all her storytelling, Marisa invoked few relationships with other females, good or bad. Here she discussed how she met her partner while she was still involved in the gang and then described their joint disinhabiting of the gang and inhabiting of mother'hood (or rather in their case "parent'hood") instead:

Liliana—How did you meet?

Marisa—At the bus stop, to be honest.

Liliana—. . . and so, how, how did you then come to . . . you know . . . hang out . . . ?

Marisa—Well, he . . . I gave him my phone number, he called me. We hooked up one day, I had dope, he had some dope, we partied, and then, after that, that's about the time when I stopped going home, started hanging out, you know, on the streets. After that we were just together. He was a . . . to be honest, we weren't together that long before I got pregnant. And yeah, I got pregnant, we were together for a few months and he went back to prison and, um, I had a beautiful baby girl.

Liliana—And did you go see him?

Marisa—[Shakes head] No, I refused. I refused to take my child in there. I know that, as a child, I went in there one time with my mother to see my dad and it's no place for a child. It's up to him to stay out and see his kid, 'cause I'm not gonna . . . you know. I'll send him pictures, sure, but it's different. It's one thing to see them in pictures and it's another to hold them in your arms. So, it's up to him. Sounds kind of . . . shitty, but sometimes a woman has to put her foot down and that's where I draw the line.

Liliana—So kind of like your brother drawing the line, you get the grades. . . .

Marisa—Yeah, kinda. . . .

Liliana—. . . but in this case, you're not asking him to do something . . . illegal. . . .

Marisa—. . . illegal . . . yeah [laughs] I'm just asking him to be a father. . . .

Liliana—. . . and he's up to the challenge.

Marisa—Yeah, uh hm. So, they say actions speak louder than words with everybody, so . . . we'll see . . . take it . . . you know, take it one day at a time.

Staying clean and sober, transcending the gang habits, and inhabiting a new story became more accessible for Marisa through education. She explained that, while she inhabited the gang lifestyle, the betterment of her people meant to protect the drug business by keeping a low profile, being creative in the distribution of drugs, and protecting themselves. Beyond the gang habits, she developed a social consciousness that helped to give new meaning to the phrase "the betterment of my people."

Marisa—To me the betterment of our people means to go get an education. As far as being Latina, a lot of people say "You can't make it!" It's a white world, as far as apparently, you know. . . . There's not a lot of good jobs out there for Latinos, especially Latino women, and I plan to make it as far as I can, you know, to show them that we can, I can do this. This was our land before it was theirs. That's the way I look at it, and I'm here to take it back. If I can do it, then that just shows someone who's younger than me "Oh, look where she came from. She did it, I can do it too!" That's how I, you know, that's why I want to. And for, uh, you know, my people, all the things we went through as far as . . . even back to . . . well, I took [. . .] this Chicano Studies class and just like reading how we came from like the Mayan area and the Tolteca area, and everything that they went through, from how Hernán Cortés went, and just everything we've been through, to now, why would I, why should I allow myself as being this, you know, Mexican-American woman, to let my people down like that? That's how I feel, you know. I've always been really in touch with my culture. I want to, you know, I want to make somebody out there proud of me. My father just passed away last month and I don't . . . I couldn't see myself going back to that 'cause he is watching me now.

Although Marisa kept in touch with her homies, they did not challenge her transformation. On the contrary, they supported her transformation, especially her brother. Interestingly, she distinguished herself from them in that she internalized the transformation:

Marisa—. . . they knew that I needed to take a step back, and they all understood. They still do, and I must say that, you know, they're happy to see me do well.

Liliana—Who? Your homies? Your family? Who's happy to see you do well?

Marisa—Just you know, people that my brother knows. Homeboys that I went to school with. Homegirls that I knew from school or the street, things like that. Or I'll walk into an AA meeting and I'll see somebody I used to party [with] or something and they're doing well and I'm doing well, they're happy to see me doing well. But they're still caught up in the whole prison system and things like that. They're only going to meetings because they have to, because somebody told them they had to be going to meetings. If you knew me back then, I was just a snot-nosed kid. To be really honest, that's all I was: a snot-nosed kid who knew how to count money, you know, weigh dope, bag it up and sell it, pretty much.

Liliana—If you think about it, what are those skills good for to you now?

Marisa—. . . A business degree! I want to own my own business and make money. I ran into one of my homeboys at my father's funeral and he hugged me. Him and my brother have been friends since I was five years old. He's clean now, he's doing really good and he hugged me and he told me "You grew up to be a very beautiful woman!" and I wanted to cry, you know. It felt good to hear that, especially since he's hot stuff too! [Laughs.] You know? It felt good to hear that from somebody who knew me since I was nothing telling me, you know, be happy for me and telling me that I'm beautiful, that I have a beautiful family.

Liliana—. . . how did your consciousness of, you know, being a Capitol Park Norteña, how has it evolved in terms of you? "The Other," the enemy . . . who are they now? Does it matter? Do you care?

Marisa—Not anymore!

Liliana—And . . . so, who are you now? Who's Marisa?

Marisa—I'm a mother, I'm a mother and a wife and a very strong independent woman who has goals in her life and is working to achieve them. And I want to be able to show, you know, show people that there is more to life out there, there is. I never want to be told that I'm a sellout, that I'm a dropout, that I'm this, that I'm that. I'm just someone that wanted to do something different with my life and I chose to go out there and get it. 'Cause I'm sure there's plenty of people out there who are still doing, you know, in the gangs and drugs and stuff, that want something better but don't know how to go out there and get it. I was never afraid to ask for help and I'm still not. I think that's what really puts me aside from the rest of them.

Unlike Margie, Marisa knows what makes her story unique, recognizes the value of it and the role that others play in it, and hopes to serve as an example for others to search and achieve their own storytelling potential. Marisa's relational self has morphed from a destructive and destructing one into a creative one that generates possibilities, one that, although it relies on the approval and encouragement from others who *consienten* her, also positions her to motivate the next generation. She inhabits inter(in)dependence.

OLGA

In contrast to Margie, who was still active yet said she was no longer using drugs and alcohol, and to Marisa, who left the gang lifestyle because of her pregnancy, Olga's drug abuse intensified long after she had left the gang and after she became a mother of three daughters. Leaving the gang and leaving the La Vida Loca lifestyle behind sometimes happens simultaneously, yet Olga's story challenges the notion that inhabiting the gang can be the lowest point in a person's life. Olga's longing for home and not finding it in the gang may have led her out of the gang proper, but the "emptiness," as she calls it, brought her to inhabit an equally disempowering and destructive space: depression-caused addiction, which is detailed in Chapter 13, "The Narrative of Redemption." After answering a circular question about what it would have taken for her to stay in school, she detailed the loneliness she felt that drove her to inhabit the gang her brother and sister had formed. Olga and I began the research consultation speaking Spanish, and more than halfway through the 3 hours we spoke, we switched to English mixed with Spanish expressions (see Appendix A). Here *italics* signify that English was spoken.

Liliana—So what do you think would have made it okay for you to wanna stay in school? Because that's the thing that everybody says, "Stay in school, stay in school!" But it's not a matter of, "Oh, do I want to go to school?" You know, it's not a simple choice. . . .

Olga—Yeah, yeah. What probably would have made me stay? Maybe if I would have felt like . . . in my case, it was a lot of I felt people just didn't care. Like I was just nothing, you know. Like there was no interest.

Liliana—Like your family?

Olga—Oh, family, teachers, like I said, the only reason I went to the varrios was 'cause I found that there. At school I wasn't finding it. I mean, teachers never took the time like, "Are you okay?" And I know it's not their job; they're there to teach. But I think sometimes teachers should, a lot of these teachers would take time and get into kids lives, a lot of the time, that's what they want: people to get into their lives, you know? "Why are you doing that bad?" You know, you're showing them that you care. You're showing them that there's some hope. And when there is no one doing that, well, *"So what? They don't care! I don't care! So what"?* So, it was easy for me to make that decision. *But I think if I probably would have had like somebody there to encourage me, a counselor, even a teacher, somebody there you know, pushing me,* that *I could do it, "What are you doing? What are you getting involved in?" I probably would have talked and I probably would have. . . . That's probably what I needed at that point.*

Liliana—Somebody to show some warmth and some humanity.

Olga—Yeah, some humanity that I mattered to them, *you know, that they cared. I think that probably would have made me stay.*

Liliana—But how could you not? What kind of resources did you have available . . . ?

Olga—[Animatedly] *. . . and you know, that is so different because, like I told you, there was ten of us. Only three of us chose to live that lifestyle. My other brothers and sisters chose to go to school and get an education, get married and have families. To this day, there's, let's see . . . to this day, let me see . . . my sister, my brother, there's four of us, now me, I'm including myself now, we're still married to the same person we married, and our kids are already grown up. We could say we have a good relationship with our spouse which we never had no example of a good relationship with a spouse, not through our families or even our spouse's families, you know.*

Liliana—It's very hard.

Olga—Yeah, it's very hard because we had no idea what we were getting ourselves into and yet, we all married young. The only one that married at nineteen, at twenty, actually at twenty-one, was my older sister. Other than that, all of us got married seventeen, eighteen, seventeen, eighteen, or we got together with our spouse you know, at seventeen. So, you know, the, the odds were great, the odds of us not making it and just turning out like my parents were great. But I know because of my end, my end, God intervened, in my life.

Liliana—So what do you think helped the other seven hold it together?

Olga—Hold it together? [Looks quizzical] *They focused, the focus, they put the focus outside the family and chose influential friends, good friends. I think that influences, like the people you're surrounded with, you know, family that they did have good families and that they were able to be exposed to that. I think that helped them make the right choices and stay away from, you know, going the wrong way.*

Liliana—Well in your case though, you had your friends who were Norteñas. Was there a possibility for you to have friends who were not affiliated? I mean, you know, with kids who were, were nothing?

Olga—Yeah, there was a chance but I just felt that I couldn't relate to them. I felt like they were nerds, I felt like they thought they were too good. . . .

Liliana—. . . because they were not affiliated?

Olga—. . . because they were not affiliated, or I felt like they were snobs. You know, we probably didn't have the same kind of clothes. And I think though that's our mentality. It's not society or anything, it's one's mentality. Because my sister that is a year older than me, we went to school together but yet she chose friends that weren't gang members. You know, that was HER own mentality! You know, my younger brother the same. You know, he went to school, he chose to be in football, be in sports, get involved that way. He actually used to tell us, "You guys are no good, you have Cholo friends!" You know, and we would argue and fight between me and him because of what he would tell me, you know.

Liliana—He was invalidating you . . . ?

Olga—Yeah, so you see I think it's own self, it's like your own mentality, who you choose to hang around with, who you choose to be cool with, or hang with, you know and now like with my daughters, I have one. . . .

Liliana—How old are they?

Olga—Sixteen, fourteen, ah, she'll be fifteen next month in February, eleven, four, and four months, the youngest one. *So I look at them and they know what we went through. I've never gone into details about my life. My husband is more OPEN to details* [makes sweeping motion with right arm above her head].

Liliana—Is he kind of braggy about it?

Olga—He's kind of braggy about it. You know, me no, it's pretty much if they ask questions and then maybe I'll tell them, if I choose to. But I try to tell them you know, "You guys, your upbringing is totally different from mine. I had freedom. I was young, I was eight, seven, you know, we were playing outside until two in the morning." I tell them, "I was out drinking, my mom wasn't home. That's how I was brought up, I didn't have a mom or a dad that are here, that love you guys, that are here for you, that go to your school meetings, that are into everything. . . ." You know, but they have to make their own choices too. So I tell them, "You guys have to make your own choices." And they're all different. My fifteen-year-old hasn't been in school for the past year. She's made a lot of wrong choices herself, with a lot of the people that she's chosen to hang around with. And it's not the people that you blame, it's one's choices. She's understanding that now. She'll be sixteen this summer. My oldest one is in Bible school right now. She took a year off from high school to go to Bible school and draw closer to a relationship with the Lord, because her in her own strength, she knew that she could probably get diverted into other things being in high school, exposed to a lot of things, so she just went back after the break. My fourteen-year-old is struggling in school a lot because she wants to do the cool thing, so I just bear with her, try to encourage her. My eleven-year-old is looking at everybody and her sisters saying, "I'm not going to make the choices that they made. I'm going to be in school and I'm going to do this." And my four-year-old, she's jumping around being happy with her toys. So, yeah, I've learned that everybody chooses what life that is good to turn to. But it's never too late, because even me, when I made that choice at sixteen, close to seventeen, to leave the gang. It was a rude awakening, and I'd seen that there's another life out there. Another style of life that I could actually live, that I could belong to and have a sense of peace. It feels good when you get your first paycheck and you know that you worked for it, you know. It feels good you know to. . . . Now, this is where I am; try to help the kids.

Despondency and choices appear as points on a continuum that anchor Olga's story of what led her, one of her brothers, and one of her sisters to start the gang and what kept the other seven siblings away from it. Other points along the continuum include poor school attendance and, consequently, performance; feeling a lack of connection—not being anyone's *consentida*—not just in her birth family, but also at school; and lacking good role models for initiating and sustaining healthy relationships. Ultimately, her story transcends the gang through a relationship with God. Yet, while the narrative of redemption may be invoked as the last step in her struggle to disinhabit the gang, this discussion exemplifies how she came to conceptualize gang transcendence as a complex, multipartite, and idiosyncratic process. In hearing her condition positively connoted and being asked circular questions (e.g., But how could you not? What kind of resources did you have available . . . ? So what do you think helped the other seven hold it together? Was there a possibility for you to have friends who were not affiliated?), Olga made systemic connections that helped her recognize her own agency, the choices that others made, and how seven of her siblings managed to focus on establishing friendships with noninvolved youth and avoided La Vida Loca. Despite their parents' troubled relationship, some of the siblings—including her—managed to stay together with their partners.

The transcendence in Olga's story also depends on the notion that she knows it is being reconstructed: If she knew then what she knows now about gangs, if she had had the nurturing that she sought, she might not have become involved. In this way, she tells a story that was not lived. Although she points out the circumstances that led her to inhabit a gang story, she also acknowledges the better choices her siblings made. Moreover, she is hoping to guide her five daughters to create a concept of self that does not depend on the gang like hers did, to make better choices to inhabit a different story. Finally, transcendence in her story emerged from the pivotal moment when she moved beyond lamenting what could not have been and toward what can be lived. Transcendence in Olga's case implies not just disinhabiting and staying out herself but helping her five daughters and other youth stay out and away from gangs altogether through the work she does in her church by ensuring they all feel *consentidas*: special, relevant, wanted, unique, and cared for.

TRANSCENDING BY AVOIDING THE GANG: ANGELA AND ELISA

This final set of transcendence stories comes from research consultants who described their efforts and challenges in staying out and away from the gang. These are gang-impacted young women who either tell a retroactive story of sidestepping the gang landmines of drugs and being challenged to pick sides or describe the challenges that their situation poses for them: living in gang-impacted neighborhoods and having gang-involved relatives and friends. While Angela clearly invokes the narrative of redemption to anchor her transcending story, Elisa fashions a story of resistance to the indignities of gang harassment to provide an alternate strategy, one that helps the young women she works with empower themselves so that they can be their own *consentidas*.

ANGELA

Angela and I met in 1999, and we have kept some irregular contact since then. In an informal conversation during which I shared some details about my work with gang-impacted and gang-involved Latinas, she told me that she had had some brushes with gangs in her youth (the complete description can be found in Appendix A, "The Storytellers"). A few weeks later, I approached her to ask whether she would be willing to talk with me about such experiences, and she agreed. I provide this brief explanation because the following transcript might seem more like a conversation among friends than a research interview. We were talking about the role her family played both in her being attracted to the gangs initially and later as a protective shield against the gang allure. In this particular excerpt, I was asking about how she managed to not become involved. As elsewhere, English is indicated with *italics*.

Liliana—And do you think that what helped you to not get further involved was that you had a base at home . . . ?

Angela—Yes.

Liliana—. . . in your family for that, right? Then, when you started to distance yourself from them, what happened?

Angela—Nothing.

Liliana—Nobody bothered you? Nobody called you? They didn't miss you? They didn't say, "Hey! Where are you? Why do you hide?" Did they look for you?

Angela—Dr. Rossmann, something very . . . interesting happened to me when I was young. My parents never forced me to work. I wanted to, and a friend had a stand in an indoor swap meet, *I don't know if you know about this. I was thirteen years old and wanted to work. So she told me, "Come help my mom and she'll pay you by the day." That's also what helped, that I always wanted to work, so at thirteen I started to work in that little stand, and one day I just went to mind the shop. And the next day, I caught an American stealing and I became very popular there, and they always wanted to hire me on the weekends. Then what helped me was the fact that I started working at thirteen, because it was in the exact stage when I was involved with those people. I started to occupy my mind with positive things. I started to work, I started to work at thirteen and at that stage, my family . . . my father had a heart attack and almost died. I was thirteen. It was a stage during which I think certain things happened in my life that guided me toward a better road. Because maybe if I hadn't started working, and there weren't any Christian principles in my family, because when my father got sick was when he changed. I think that I would have decided to take completely opposite paths in my life.* When they talk about children in sports, involved in the community, it's very true. And in my case, *it helped me to be a little, to find more ambition in life. To work, to get ahead, was totally. . . .*

Liliana—. . . and it helped you, for example, in that you weren't in the street anymore? You weren't just doing nothing. You had something to do and they like left you alone?

Angela—I was busy. I didn't want to be with them, what happened is that I now was busy.

The story of Angela choosing the path of righteousness has clear and anchoring punctuations: Through her sterling efforts of protecting her employer's property, she became the *consentida*, and she had something to do. During the same time, her family had a near tragedy, and she had the wherewithal to become mindful and to opt at the age of 13 for a path of goodness.

Liliana—How did you end up hanging out? Did you get together at school and then in the street or would you go to each other's houses?

Angela—After school, where the bus picked us up. I would tell my dad that it picked us up later and since he worked, he'd pick me up later, like a half an hour, forty-five minutes. But that was a long time!

Liliana—Yes, of course, and what would you do then?

Angela—That's when they'd get together, and I remember the one time they started passing the weed, I knew that the base has a lot to do, Doctor, I knew that it was wrong and I didn't take it. Since then, I've never tried it. I don't want to try it. Then, the base has a lot to do with it, the environment.

Liliana—So, after school is where you had a window of opportunity. . . .

Angela—Oh, yeah! I believe that it's when the greatest window of opportunity. It wasn't like, "*Can we come over to your house?*" My parents didn't want to let me go. They were very strict, but they didn't notice that when they least thought, it would be the moment I'd take to make mischief. How sad, but that's how it was.

I'm struck by the apparent contradiction in her story, not because I expect consistency across stories, but because I wonder if she sees contradictory strands—those between having a strong family base that helped her not take the drug and being sufficiently duplicitous to come up with ways to stall her father's pickup time so she could hang out with the girls, of whom she knew they would not approve. Moreover, I am curious to see how she reconciles the contradiction, if at all.

Angela—*I totally know what you mean. Dr. Rossmann, I was a lost child. If my influence in the negative side of being in these gangs, surrounded . . . would have advanced itself more, in that stage, my ambition, my aggressiveness . . . would have advanced in the negative. It would have turned negative, because I have a strong personality. I learned to get angry quick and not let anybody say anything to me. This aggressiveness was constructed during that time frame when I was so* [slaps back of right hand on palm of left] *hit so many times. It was like a thin line before going completely negative because I could have gone to the degree of killing someone, Dr. Rossmann. I remember when I was violent when all this was going on in my life and all this confusion, I got my fist and I hit the window and I punched it through, I was so angry.*

And when you're that young and you do something like that, that was a negative sign, "Where are you going to?" So, you know my anger started getting uncontrolled, I was not controlling my anger. . . .

No one for Angela to be *consentida* by, fear, loneliness, and now anger: a volatile combination that could have easily destined her to perpetuate violence on her peers and her own family had she continued on that path. The person I have known and who is sitting across from me now is anything but violent or angry, so I have to ask what is different in her life now.

Liliana—So how do you control it now?

Angela—Well, I don't really have it that much like I used to. When I was young, I was just angry, but what I'm saying is that I could have done worse. I am nervous that maybe I could have killed someone, with the anger that I learned to have when I was that young.

Liliana—Because you watched your parents, because you got pushed out? Where do you think it came from?

Angela—You know, now that I think about it because I hadn't thought about it the way I am now, it's I think it started growing up and seeing that in the household and then having this group of friends use that anger negatively . . . when I was little I didn't use it negatively, I was scared. And then when people were violent towards me, I just felt like a victim the same fear that I had before. That is, when my father spanked me, you were afraid, when they fought, you were afraid, when it turned the other way around, I used it against other people.

Liliana—Yes, and what interests me, among other things, is that pivotal point, right? Of change, of decision, of when one comes to a moment and says "this road is not good for me, there are other paths and I know how they go." How does one realize there are other paths, because there are people who don't know, people who don't have, who can't. Then, in what way can one help them to invent, to imagine those paths to be able to make the decision? That's what intrigues me. That is the interrogation, among the people who do this work. I barely scratch the surface.

Angela—Do you think that it's because there isn't anyone that can inspire them to do something positive? That there's only the negative? Because they did that to me, Dr. Rossmann. I started seeing negative things about *drugs, killings, stabbings, it scared me, but my bully side, that side that I didn't want people to walk into me and still, it went through high school with me.* Like *I had this "chola"* [makes angry face] *kind of. . . .*

Liliana—"Create name for yourself and take a nap." In Spanish, the dicho or saying is: "Crea fama y échate a dormir."

Angela—*What does that mean?*

Liliana—That you already had the reputation for being in charge.

As Angela's story progresses, the elements of fear and loneliness sublimate into anger and aggression and, from these, into faith and success. The little girl, fearful of a violent home life, gives off the scent of fear to the Cholas in her school. As she pursues the need to escape by switching schools, she transforms herself into the one who either harasses or puts others in check. But a close encounter with taboo substances, combined with the opportunity to be accepted (*consentida*) for her courage, and the aftermath of a near-tragedy at home, help her not only renounce the bully role but manage through inter(in)-dependence to transcend her role of bully to student leader to college graduate to now a successful businesswoman and mother. Although her parents' relationship was marked by violence and alcoholism (see her story in Chapter 5, "Family Violence"), Angela's actions in transcending the gang were inter(in)dependent, a joint achievement with her parents' transcending their own relational challenges.

ELISA

There is a peculiar way to describe young Latinas who, although they live in gang-impacted neighborhoods, do not become involved: They are called "nothing." Elisa was "nothing" vis-à-vis the gang, but in her own eyes she was a soccer player, and in the work she did she helped girls find a path that might start with being "nothing" but geared them toward making something of themselves. When we met, she was a youth and family specialist at one of the community service agencies where some of the observations, research consultations, and interviews for this book took place.

Liliana—I'm interested in understanding this phenomenon of girls in, out, and around gangs. That it seems to me sometimes the lines are blurred, but maybe not, because I don't know much about what goes on. How would you say, from your perspective, is there a distinction that is made, in order to provide the services? For example, if there's a girl who's in a gang, does that girl require more attention, or more hours, and who decides that she's in a gang? Does she have to say "I'm in a gang"? Is there some sort of tattoo or mark or, you know, there's no certificate that they get, like they got when they graduate from this gang? So you could say that this is an alternative gang? Let's start with how. . . .

Elisa—I think like you said, just being in this community, it's like you are surrounded by gangs. For example, right here in every single street, there is a gang. It's either Norteño or Sureño. There's three centers, a mile away and each one has a gang in it. Those are close, but within, like in different corners, there's different gangs. So kids want to come out, and they want to play, so no matter what, you have a friend who is in a gang, or is involved in a gang, you have a neighbor that is in a gang. You know what I mean? They're all involved in certain ways. There's different levels. Like there's girls that are just wannabes. There's girls that are just friends with them, there's girls that are in it. You can't tell, but it's like living in this community, you are forced to pick a side. You know how, if kids want to come out and play, like they want to come to the Center, just for coming into the Center it's like you're choosing to go with the Sureños because you're going to that Center. You're choosing to be their friend. So you choose to what center you want to go to, but once you go to that center, you are . . . that's what you'll become. It's like when I came here for the first time and I played, I was nothing. I was a soccer player. But when I would go to school, and they said, "Oh, my God, you go to that Center. Oh, well, you kick it with all of the Sureños, you cannot talk to them," you know what I mean?

Liliana—To be in a gang means. . . .

Elisa—Usually the kids that are in a gang are kids that don't have parents, no parent involvement at all, kids that have a lot of problems at home and kids that are looking for attention. So usually, the kids that are really deep into it are the kids that are always in the streets, that don't have a home to go back to. The kids that are wannabes are the kids that just come out from four to seven and want to kick it and then go home.

Liliana—They have supervision?

Elisa—They have supervision. So they're only behaving bad during those three hours and then they go back home. But the really, really bad kids are the ones that have no supervision at all. Don't have any parents to go back to, that don't have anyone that tells them "don't dress like this, don't wear that, don't say that." Those are the bad kids.

Liliana—Those are the ones that get involved. . . .

Elisa—Yes, those are the ones that they say, "He shot someone," they don't care because they don't have that person that's going to tell them, "Why did you do that?" They don't care if they go to jail because they don't have that parent that's going to cry if they go to jail. You know what I mean? Most of the kids, when they come here is like, "I'm going to do this, I'm going to get this certificate for my dad, because he works really hard." They don't have anyone to work hard for. If they want to behave bad, then they behave bad. And that's mostly the kids we have to deal with the most. They're fewer, but those are the kids that control all the kids. Like in class, normally I have twelve girls. If that one girl comes into class and one girl does not have any supervision and is a hard-core gangster, she will destroy my class. She will not let me lecture, she will not let me do anything. [Gets teary-eyed.] Girls are so afraid of her that they won't even pay attention to me, because whatever she says, that's what they do, you know what I mean? So I think that's how a gang is. . . .

What Elisa is describing is a young person who is not *consentida*; a child who has never been made to feel relevant. Among the various gang-prevention and intervention programs I have observed and learned about, the notion that each individual is a person of relevance regularly features prominently in the curricula. I am not "discovering" anything new here; what I am proposing is that this notion be centered on the culturally embedded concept of *consentir*.

Liliana—And what happens when if a girl decides . . . that she wants to stand up, that she won't listen. . . .

Elisa—She would probably . . . she'd probably kick her butt, after . . . so they would probably fight. So, if this one girl doesn't want to do that, she'd probably turn seven girls against her and they will just stop talking to her or after class, they would just jump her. That's what would happen.

In Chapter 7 ("Of Colors and Names"), Elisa tells a powerful story about the consequences she suffered by wearing the wrong color at the wrong place and time. Although she knew the parameters of gang membership included wardrobe considerations, she chose to be the one to stand up. I am curious as to how she first got the notion that there were sides to choose, despite the fact that she has made the poignantly existential choice not to choose either side.

Liliana—You grew up here, and you said you saw them as your friends. Can you recollect a moment when this notion of "gangs" became known to you? When you start knowing that there were sides to choose and. . . .

Elisa—I think it was . . . not when I was in middle school. I wasn't affected in middle school. But as soon as I was an eighth grader, I realized like "there's gangs, there's sides, you know, that you have to choose" and it's like, like I said, it's a Hispanic thing, it's not like you unite. So I had girls that were Mexican but they were Chicanas that were my friends and there were Sureñas. Like I said, I'm nothing, so I talked to them [signals with one hand], and I talked to them [signals with the other hand]. The first time I realized was because my friend [gets upset, teary eyed] got together with a Norteño, and it was all about Norte and I didn't understand. Um, there was an incident that, okay, we went to visit her at her boyfriend's house and that's where all the gangsters hanged out, outside in the yard. It's weird because like I didn't know what was going on, but they were looking everywhere, like all the time. It's like they were chillin', just having fun, but looking all the time, you could not be sitting down having fun. And like. . . . And um, all of a sudden, like from the corner, they saw a car coming and they were all like, "C'mon, let's run, run!" The car comes and he starts like shooting, so we were all inside the house. That was the first time I realized, "Oh, my God! This is dangerous!" You know what I mean? And like we didn't know anything about that, but I realized like in ninth grade. Like I never went back to that house, but after that, it was just in my mind, there's a sign where you have to go.

Liliana—So you spoke earlier of the kids that are in danger of banging are the ones without supervision, does she fall under that category?

Elisa—No, because she was the girlfriend, she met him through her brother . . . and like she really liked him and all of that. But after three years, like after her mom told her, "You know what? That's not the good thing, that's not the good guy," like I said, if you have that parent that's going to be with you, that's going to tell you that's not the right place. Of course like us humans, we're going to make mistakes. We're gonna fall, but we're gonna get back up again. That's just part of life, but after three years, she found out, know what I mean? That's not the guy for her. Like she let him go and um but it was because of her parents, because they told her, "You know what? That's not the right way to go."

Liliana—So she's not with him now?

Elisa—Yeah, she's nothing.

This is a brief tale of a girl who became "nothing" because her parents looked after her, gave her advice, steered her away from negative influences, and were her *consentidores*. To advance my theory further, let us return to Gergen (2009) for a moment to contrast his ideas of "multi-being" to Doi's concept of *amae*. Doi (1990) claims that *amae* emerges as an infant becomes aware of others—beyond the mother—whose potential and willingness to *amaeru* (to be indulged or *consentido/a*, in Spanish), is undetermined, yet

> [*amae*] works to foster a sense of oneness between the mother and child. In this sense, the *amae* mentality could be defined as the attempt to deny the fact of separation that is such an inseparable part of human existence and to obliterate the pain of separation. (Doi, 1990, p. 75)

In a similar vein, Gergen (2009) writes that the first-time mother and her newborn infant represent an "icon of harmonious coordination [where] the mother and child are closest to a relationship unlinked to other relationships" (p. 159). Yet, fast-forwarding to the teen years, the same mother and child are "now each deeply immersed in relationships other than with each other" to which they bring not only "residues from long and numerous histories of relationships" but more immediate residues of current relationships. "They are fully embedded, relational beings" (Gergen, 2009, p. 160). The parents of Elisa's friend were able to invoke that "icon of harmonious coordination" by focusing on their daughter's well-being and confronting head-on the "residues" of her relationship with her Cholo boyfriend. *Consentir* in this sense means more than just to indulge, but to remind this girl of her origins, of her worth as a human being, and of the expectations that not only the parents had for her but that she should have for herself.

Liliana—. . . what do you see as a way out of it, individually and as a community?

Elisa—Honestly, first I think it's a phase. When you're in high school, you're looking for an identity, like soccer, and dance class and gangs, you're looking for an identity. Like, to be honest with you, the kids that are in a gang are the kids that are lost, the kids that don't know where they're going. They're finding their own group and their identity. Honestly, some of the girls I've had in class, they have been Norteñas and they have been Sureñas. So, it's not like they . . . are just looking for somewhere to go. I see some girls that when they were in middle school, they were in that corner and they were Norteñas and they were like saying all this stuff and then they moved to this corner [signals in opposite direction] which is Sureño and they became Sureñas. So I think they're looking for an identity, they're looking for something, they're looking for themselves. And normally, like I'm telling you, it's the kids that don't have the parent. They're just looking for themselves, they're looking for, they want to find who they are and what they believe in, I don't know, like usually . . . I don't know what would be a way out of it. Maybe things like us educating them, like "that's not the right thing, that's not like what you're supposed to do," which is hard, because they've just been to school for six hours and how can you expect them to come here two more hours? It's just hard. . . .

I venture to argue the following: The pain of separation that Doi identifies as the genesis of *amae*; the pain that, according to Gergen, gains meaning solely relationally; and the pain of not belonging that Olga and now Elisa invoke—all these pains merge into a need for being *consentida/o*, of seeking a relational connection with anyone with whom one can "be oneself" and not worry what they will think, and of being unconditionally accepted without judgment, of finding a home. As we saw in Chapter 13, "The Narrative of Redemption," some of the gang-involved women in this book have found a home in Christ. But this does not work for everyone: Margie made it very clear, at the time we spoke anyway, that God and religion would not be a viable influence on her. Elisa and others who work with gang-impacted youth recognize this and manage to *consentir* them without invoking a religious conversion. In her closing words, Elisa provides a well-known and almost trite yet effective safeguard through which to transcend the gang: parental involvement.

Liliana—. . . So, what would you say would be your biggest concern? The thing that, if you could change, you would, about this phenomenon of gang-related behavior? You came to work here because obviously you want to make a difference, so what would you say is the biggest challenge for you?

Elisa—. . . The biggest challenge? [Sighs.] I think that just keeping kids out of the streets would be the biggest thing and, like I said, parents are the biggest thing because it's what keeps them going straight. If we could just get them to come to classes and understanding themselves, because what they're trying to do is identifying and not all kids that start in a gang end up in a gang, but like having them get educated, having them realize like maybe they're going through a phase, but like that's not the right way to go, understanding themselves. For example, my class—teach them that, you know, they are who they are and they don't need to be someone else to be effective. So, maybe education, I would say, educating them.

Liliana—To end on an upbeat note, what are the things that, when you look around, your work, your family, your community, your friends, what are the things that uplift you?

Elisa—Just in general or like in the girls?

Liliana—Yeah, in your family, I guess, specifically with the girls in gangs, gang-related, girls that are in, out, or around gangs. But if you're having a hard time pinning it, you can zoom out, but if you can talk specifically about the girls. . . .

Elisa—To me, it's just seeing them, for example, and the girls, to me it would just be seeing them grow and realize, you know what I mean? That they're bigger, that they can do better things, that they don't have to be Sureñas, that because they're Hispanic, they can't go to college; they can do anything they want. And um, in life, I think just growing. Achieving my goals, not just staying as a Hispanic, or as a Sureña, but like growing and maybe going to college and maybe next year the university and becoming something of myself to show that Hispanics are not just people that stay low but that grow, that become something in their lives, that are not just gang members, are people that want to educate themselves and go in professions, and want better for their families and their communities. I think that would be my thing. . . .

Liliana—You designed the programs?

Elisa—This program was already made, but I make the classes according to what I think that they want to learn. So, how I see the girls, what they need is how I make the class to fit them, for them to grow.

Liliana—So they have some input . . . ?

Elisa—Yeah, whatever . . . like, in the check in, when they're checking in and something that they say "Oooo," and it's a topic of drugs, I HAVE to make sure I put in the drugs in there. Because it's always a topic, or there's always a topic of sex. I always put in a sex topic, yeah.

In the group that Elisa led at the community services agency, all young women checked in—said their name and told something good that happened to them that week—ate a meal, had a lesson and activities, played games, and took home something they made. Each young woman's relevance in life, or at least at the Center, was evident from the moment each young woman stated her given name, not her gang name if she was gang-involved, and continued as they were engaged in participating fully in all the activities at the Center, whether they claimed or not.

Liliana—How would you know that what you do is working?

Elisa—. . . what I do is working? Usually, is when they come up to me, or usually when we start there's girls that don't want to come to class or that [others] have to make to come to class or that never want to talk, but after two or three classes they start talking, they start letting me know what they feel. The start, or at the end, they say "Oh, I want to share, I want to share!" They raise their hand and they say, "I want to tell you that I learned this and that I want to become this." Or just when I'm walking in the hallways, they come up to me and say, "Oh, the mayor went to my high school today and he said this." It's like they're paying attention. They want to learn. They're not only trying to come and tell me about their messed up [lives], but about the good things that they have in their lives, or that they're learning in their life, so I see that as working.

Elisa might see her work as being a youth and family specialist, yet what she is doing is giving girls the tools necessary to tell a story of transcendence: that, despite the lack of parental involvement—often this is because the parents are undocumented and working three jobs to make ends meet, might be illiterate or non-English-speaking, or at times themselves lost to a chemical dependency—the girls have options, and Elisa is one among many people who help them learn about such options as well as help them pursue them.

For those who are gang-impacted, the gang provides a distraction of the multiple marginalities (Vigil, 1988), a place like the home that often eludes them, a feeling of belonging they have never had. Although the rules may seem straightforward to them, let us not forget that they are children and adolescents whose brains have not developed the capacity to make such momentous and life-impacting decisions. But what of the youth who end up gang-involved despite the fact that they have both parents with economic means to provide for their needs? As stated previously, the mere presence and active involvement of parents may be a necessary but insufficient condition for transcending the gangs.

Elisa remarks that parents and professionals like her point out to youth that being attracted to gangs may be a "phase" some kids go through. I propose that transcending gangs is not a once-in-a-lifetime event. Note how the emphasis is on the gerundized noun "transcending," to signify ongoing transformation. In keeping with Gergen's (2009) idea of humans as multi-beings whose relational residues co-create notions of self, a gang-involved Latina is not just defined by the particular stage in which she finds herself—gang-impacted, gang-involved, or ex-gang member—but by her compounded life experiences with those with whom (not to whom!) she relates. We might come to think of these transitions in terms of phases, rites of passage, or liminal periods during which she has no identity.

LIMINALITY, PERMANENT LIMINALITY, AND TRANSCENDENCE

The concept of liminality was identified by van Gennep (1909/1972) as one of three essential stages in rituals that demarcate the passage of time. The preliminal stage has a separating function, during which the person being initiated relinquishes her or his prior patterns and practices. In the liminal stage, there is a suspension of heretofore accepted norms and rules, yielding to a temporary, often painful, arrangement of order, action, and response by all involved. This disjointed phase, sanctioned by some convener or celebrant, functions to eliminate connections to the past, to suspend the identity of the one being initiated as she or he performs a series of tasks or tests designed to determine fitness to cross a veritable threshold leading to the final, postliminal stage of reintegration where new connections will be established under the new identity.

Turner (1969) expanded on liminal beings as those "betwixt and between the positions assigned and arrayed by law, custom, convention, and ceremonial" (p. 94). Their liminality determines their identity during their passage from one form of identity to another through a cultural ritual, often behaving passively or humbly, implicitly obedient, and unconditionally accepting of arbitrary punishment.

The ritual of being jumped in a gang can be explained as this state of liminality. If a group of individuals is subject to the same painful ritual, its members develop intense bonds with each other without individual identity markers or hierarchies, known as *comunitas* (Douglas, 1984). They renounce their previous connections, separating themselves from their family and from law-abiding society. Once the rite is completed, they emerge as different beings, with the intended identity of those on the other side; in gang terms, the new name and the new tattoos determine their gang-banger identity.

Potentially, individuals could remain liminal permanently in any of the three stages should these become structured (Szakolczai, 2000, 2009). The identity of transsexual men has been depicted as permanently liminal as they seek to establish a stable identity after a transition period (Booth, 2011). Once they identify either by self or others as being transsexual, these men embody a perpetual betwixt and between given how others respond to them under this new guise.

In the case of some of these gang-involved Latinas, the preliminal separating stage often occurs in a vacuum of structure to begin with, as discussed in Chapter 5, "Family Violence," and so they may have little or nothing to renounce in their previous life. Unlike the separation that occurs during *amae*, as discussed previously, the gang-impacted girl may be ambivalent about separating from her family of origin—if one is present to begin with—due to the multiple marginalities she encounters (Vigil, 1988). In many rites of passage, the pain and violence incurred during the liminal stage are endured precisely because these excruciating experiences are so limited to this particular stage. By contrast, in situations of family violence, physical or psychological pain is, if not a permanent, at least a common situation, not to be relieved—and certainly exacerbated—by gang membership. Moreover, in the postliminal phase, the gang-involved girl does not achieve full re-integration as her new membership and new identity end up separating her from the norms of law-abiding society, multiplying her previous marginalities.

For our purposes, those who were gang-involved chose to identify themselves as having been active in a gang in order to enlist others into the same de-gangified identity. But gang involvement, while significant for a woman's identity, is not the only aspect that impacts it. I concur with Booth (2011) that perpetual liminality has the potential for increased visibility, yet it comes at a cost to all these women, whether in the "not looking to get out" model, like Margie, "involved in the past, experiencing different ways to disinhabit," like Marisa and Olga, or "never involved, despite significant gang-impact," like Angela and Elisa. As discussed in Chapter 6, "Tattoos and Identities," for women like Florencia, who chose to keep her gang tattoos, their perpetual liminality is embodied and deeply felt. For others like Gracia and Eréndira, who chose to cover or remove their tattoos, their perpetual liminality may be optional. Transcending gangs thus implies an ongoing identifying, relying on the past, and engaging the present to create a story of inter(in)dependence for the future.

16

Conclusion

The Story of Esperanza

REVISITING THE PROMISED GAINS

The questions pursued in this chapter are: Do you, the reader, believe the time and effort spent reading this book up to this point have been worthwhile? Are you better off from reading this book than you were on page 1? Have I, along with my research consultants, given you an insightful understanding of the communication processes by which Latinas get in, get out, and stay out of gangs? I hope so because that has been my goal all along. I would like to spend the first part of this chapter revisiting the learnings from each of the themes in this story of stories. In the second part, I return to the Story of Esperanza that began in the Introduction. The main goal is to envision a story of hope and possibilities for gang-impacted and gang-involved Latinas.

"GETTING IN" IS HALF THE PROBLEM

The eternal question "Why do girls join gangs?" may not have been definitively answered, I humbly accept, although this was not my goal in Chapter 4. What I believe the stories of "Inhabiting the Gang" have rendered is not necessarily to support previously conducted research about risk factors; rather, what I believe the storytellers have accomplished is to illuminate the lived experiences behind such factors. Their race, the low levels of education achieved by their parents, their lives of poverty, the lack of at least one parent, and their early sexual activity might have been predictors of gang entry, but their stories illustrate their distinct, idiosyncratic, and complex communicative processes for inhabiting the gang.

    Several stories vividly described the allure that gangs held for them, in terms of the perceived prestige that gang membership brought

(Lupe), as well as the persistent lack of safety, and thus need for "back up," in their neighborhoods (Eréndira and Gracia). In some cases, the inhabiting process was gradual and almost prefigured by violence at home, either between the parents (Olga) or against the children (Florencia), although gang entry often signifies increased violence exposure. Inhabiting gangs seemed like a logical conclusion for those in Gangs of Family (Margie and Gracia).

A key concept I advanced with respect to inhabiting the gang is the notion of "ersatz family," to illustrate how these girls turn to the gang as a substitute to provide for those functions that most families typically serve but that they lacked: food and shelter, identity needs, moral guidance, and emotional support, as poignantly told by Olga. In one of the stories of "Inhabiting the Gang" (Marisa), gang membership was peripheral to the higher motive of dealing drugs. All the women storied a void in their lives that, at the time, was easily filled by their inhabiting a gang, regardless of whether it actually improved their lives, and that all but one of those involved now recognize it did not.

VIOLENCE BEGETS MORE VIOLENCE

So accustomed are these girls to seeing or experiencing violence that the prospect of being jumped in is not as unattractive for them as it would be for others, and thus not a deterrent but a rite that is seen as a badge of courage. Being jumped into the gang pales in comparison to being sexually abused, and Florencia provided an agonizing account of her own family molestation that she directly credited with landing her in a gang. "Torture" was how she described her experiences of violence in the home.

Although being in a gang may lead some to feel temporarily empowered against the forces of violence in the home (Florencia and Olga), on the streets (Eréndira), or at school (Angela), the violence encountered within the gang is not considered liberating by any of them. What I hope this chapter highlights is the urgency with which, if we are to reduce or eliminate the entry of Latina girls in gangs, we must look into their situations of violence in the home.

MARKED FOR LIFE IN A GANG AND BEYOND

Not all tattoos are created equal because gang tattoos mark the bearer as a member of a certain class that carries great stigma. As we learned from Gracia, Florencia, and Eréndira, at the time they may have thought that their decision to join a gang was as irrevocable as their tattoos. In Chapter 6, "Tattoos and Identities," we learned that, although tattoos gave them a certain status and prestige in the gang, some of these women found, painfully, that the tattoos mark them for the rest of their lives, even if they are covered (Eréndira), removed (Gracia), or undisturbed (Florencia). There are other perspectives on tattoos: Teresa was warned by her gang-involved mother to avoid getting any tattoos, although the mother had several gang-related tattoos herself; and Marisa briefly stories tattoos as a business opportunity. But the story of Chakira gives us an unusual perspective, for gang tattoos played a pivotal role in the apprehension and incarceration of her gang-involved brother. Her knowledge about tattoos is detailed and exhaustive, and the fact that, at the age of 16, she understood the tremendous risks that inked skin poses for the bearer makes this more remarkable. Tattoos tell a story in and of themselves—a story that is not conducive to the bearer's face needs nearly as permanently as the tattoos themselves.

COLORED EXPERIENCES

What a difference a color makes in one's wardrobe choices if one is gang-impacted and even more so if one is gang-involved! While the research consultants may have experienced color differently depending on their level of involvement or lack thereof, every single woman who storied gang colors in Chapter 7, "Of Colors and Names," was painfully aware that colors are a force to be reckoned with in their daily lives, in their neighborhoods, and in their fashion choices. Sporting red or blue could be the easiest way to show support for one side or another. Colors also are the easiest markers of gang identity to disavow, although gang-involved girls run the risk of being labeled a "ranker" if they cover or avoid colors. Although some schools prohibit students from wearing either red or blue, a Sureño claim is easier to hide in jeans and other attire. Color alone is not considered an indicator of gang membership or even of gang sympathizing; it must be combined with other garment styles for it to gain signification. Women whose stories were included in Chapter 7 found colors useful to distinguish friend from foe (Daniela and Eréndira); recognized how colors exposed them to harassment, violence, and threats (Elisa, Florencia, and Chakira); and acknowledged the futility of supporting a color (Teresa, Gracia, and Marisa).

(BARELY) LIVING CRAZY

One does not need to join a gang to live a lifestyle characterized by abuse of alcohol and drugs, multiple sex partners, crime (petty or otherwise), and violence, but gang membership makes the presence of all these elements almost a foregone conclusion. The stories in Chapter 8, "In la Vida Loca, 'You Get Up to Get High,'" describe living crazy gang experiences ranging from bullying (Angela) and frequent and heavy drug use (Eréndira, Lupe, and Florencia) to fights and other types of violence (Olga and Margie) and sexual promiscuity (Marisa). Waxing nostalgic when recounting their exploits in La Vida Loca frequently played a role in these stories, although in the end, all the women regretted having been involved in such dangerous, deviant, and dehumanizing activities. That violence in the home prefigured such experiences should give us a reason to work toward comprehensive approaches that attempt to reduce violence and other harmful lifestyle habits in the lives of gang-impacted Latinas as well as society in general.

JAILHOUSE BLUES AND REDS

Living crazy often leads to incarceration and, in Chapter 9, "Time Served!," those who were gang-involved storied more propensity to lose their liberty early and often. Religious influences in prison planted the seed for the disinhabiting process for some (Gracia) but not all. Lucha, who was not gang-involved, found prison extremely distasteful, yet at the same time she storied her identity as resourceful, savvy, and, most importantly, repentant. For some of these women, being able to find a community of their own in prison also played a role in disinhabiting the lifestyle (Lucha), if not the gang itself (Gracia). How, then, to explain the difference between those for whom incarceration deterred them from further involvement (Eréndira and Gracia) and those who were not only still gang-involved but also uninterested in disinhabiting the gang (Margie)? What else would be needed to sufficiently "reform" them into disinhabiting from the gang? To begin answering these questions, I have explored the notion of storytelling toward transcendence. In the end, the real stigma derived from serving time precluded these women's disinhabiting attempts because being convicted felons kept them from finding work (Lucha and Margie).

THE GANG-INVOLVED MOTHER

To reiterate, gang membership is not necessarily conducive to early motherhood, just as having a child is not necessarily conducive to disinhabiting the gang. In Chapter 10, "Mother'hood," we saw the peculiarities of being a mother while involved in the gang/*varrio*/*barrio*/'hood, and thus I use the term "mother'hood" to encompass such peculiarities. For some (Eréndira and Marisa), their story of pregnancy and mother'hood ran contrary to their story of the gang, so pregnancy was viewed as a godsend in leaving the gang. This was not so for others (Gracia and Florencia), who initially viewed pregnancy and parenting as impeding their gang lifestyle, although losing custody of their children eventually punctuated their story of disinhabiting. Ultimately, mother'hood challenged each woman differently: On the one hand, the youngest mother (Margie) had no plans to leave the gang, whereas on the other hand, the mother with the most children (Olga, with five daughters) had left the gang years before her first pregnancy but found tremendous obstacles to disinhabiting the lifestyle.

LOYALTY AND RESPECT

The notions of loyalty and respect play an important role in stories about gang involvement, although the women whose voices animate Chapter 11, "Loyalty and Respect," recognize that gangs have their own unique way of establishing such norms. Here I also expanded on the notion of the ersatz family and how gang members provide the loyalty that one might expect from one's blood relations (Florencia). Because the gang often substitutes for these functions, the definition of loyalty and respect specifies narrow terms. The loyalty in these women's stories points to a toggle function: Either you have or you don't, either you are loyal or a snitch, either you back us up or you rank, and either you honor my relationship with my man or you don't. But as other themes in their stories begin to converge, it becomes obvious that the stories about the loyalty they expected (stories told), the loyalty they provided (stories lived), and the loyalty they obtained (storied unheard) could not be reconciled (Gracia, Eréndira, and Lupe). In some cases, respect seemed equivalent to loyalty, but safety trumped loyalty. For Eréndira, hiding her gang colors was not intended to show disrespect, and thus disloyalty, but to show good judgment in avoiding attack. Furthermore, although it may strike the reader as inane that someone would take to fisticuffs for being the subject of a look of disdain, in the case of the gang-impacted Angela, such disdainful looks were considered disrespectful and threatening, and they warranted putting someone "in check," that is, roughing them up to remind them that, in the gang, subservience is a form of respect. Last, loyalty and respect for the color must remain in the Gangs of Family, otherwise this provides sufficient excuse for the gang-involved (Margie) to turn on members of her own family. In summary, I stress that stories about gang loyalty and respect are sometimes contradictory and living in contradictory stories creates tension. We first need to embark on a dedicated attempt to understand the communicative patterns and practices that concepts such as loyalty and respect take among gang-involved and gang-impacted youth. Perhaps then we could see whether such storytelling tension can be relieved by telling a supra story, one of transcendence.

BETRAYED INTO DISINHABITING

The very reason given for inhabiting a gang—the search for back-up and support in an ersatz family—transforms into feelings of disappointment when that back-up is withheld, which turns into feeling betrayed. Having bought the gang lifestyle and habits wholesale, these women found that their lives were threatened by the gang (Lupe) or family or friends turned on them (Eréndira and Olga). Despite the fact that at one time they had been in a position of authority and leadership in the gang (Florencia and Gracia), the gang's code of loyalty and respect contained exception clauses when their mother'hood or drug abuse meant they were unable to perform their gang duties as expected. Betrayal, although painful to recount, acted as prologue in their story of disinhabiting. In particular situations, although betrayal is not specifically identified as a precursor to the narrative of redemption, it functions as an enthymeme to suggest that the gang's promises of back-up are a mirage, a "false doctrine" (Olga), and a "bondage" (Florencia). Thus, these promises intimate that enduring betrayal from the gang members should be expected because betrayal proves instrumental in the women's transcendent storytelling. Betrayal, loyalty, and respect are topics that could have been discussed further in this book. I invite readers to pick up where I left off and to offer ways to understand these from the communication perspective.

SANCTUARIES FROM THE GANGS

As a person with nontraditional spiritual and religious beliefs, I found it extremely challenging to comprehend the stories of women who found God or Christ and believed that "he" led them away from the path of gangs. This book is not about me; how I view my research consultants and their stories is, rather, the concern. Yet I now hold enormous respect and appreciation for those whose lives have been transformed, whose redemption stories played a pivotal role in their transcending gangs. Betrayal, although not explicitly referred to by those who story it, loomed in the background as an enthymeme in corresponding stories of redemption.

In fact, faith in God was not just invoked as a way out of a gang but also as something that was credited for the birth of a child (Eréndira and Marisa) or that helped the women (Angela and Olga) heal their family interactions. Faith and the corresponding religious habits also provided a much-sought-after sanctuary where women (Gracia, Olga, and Florencia) found the acceptance, respect, and support they had sought in the gang unsuccessfully. Taking the religious path out of a gang assuaged their fears that the gang members would hunt them down for leaving the gang (Lupe); surprisingly, gang members accepted a person's religious transformation as a valid reason for wanting out. In the end, the storytellers acknowledge that the ersatz family the gang provided was a mirage and affirm that the members of their church gave and give them unconditional love and acceptance, thus setting the stage for transcendence.

MANY PATHS AND MANY CHALLENGES
TO DISINHABITING THE GANG

No single method or approach for leaving the gang predominates in these stories. The women whose stories are included in Chapter 14, "Disinhabiting the Gang," retrospectively weave previously discussed strands into their yarns of disinhabiting the gang, such as incarceration, betrayal, mother'hood, and redemption. Their stories also highlight the dangers associated with living a gang lifestyle and how much better off they are now than before. One of the points I made in Chapter 14 is that stories by women who have left the gang serve as cautionary tales for those who are gang-impacted and interested in joining a gang, as well as for those currently involved in a gang. Any single story by these survivors carries significant persuasive power, in that it provides examples of how to do something perceived as impossible or risky. While the lore among gang members might stress that once in there is no way out, the stories these women live and tell provide useful insight into how they have quit the gang habits and gone on to live healthy, happy, and productive lives. All of them are careful not to oversimplify the process, and many invoke a variety of reasons for quitting the gang habits, although a single event may be credited for their disinhabiting in some cases. When asked directly, none of them seemed to know a term that could be used to describe their disinhabiting the lifestyle of gangs. Perhaps in our work to help people find their way out of addiction and violence, we could be sufficiently playful with language to create a new term for their condition. This term might allow them to further own the courageous and difficult process of restorying their lives and ease their transition into a new identity beyond the gang.

TRANSCENDENCE AND INTER(IN)DEPENDENCE

Disinhabiting is a crucial step toward transcendence, yet it is not sufficient to inhabit inter(in)dependence. In Chapter 15, "Transcending Gangs," I aimed to critique my own research trajectory vis-à-vis the professionals involved in helping youth get out and stay out of gangs. My concern was to provide useful insights to address the needs of gang-impacted and gang-involved youth. To accomplish this goal, I developed three basic models of gang involvement: (a) "Gangs-of-Family involved, not looking to get out" (Margie); (b) "Gang-involved in the past, experiencing different ways to disinhabit" (Marisa and Olga); and (c) "Never involved, despite significant gang impact" (Angela and Elisa).

From these stories, and culling from psychoanalysis of Japanese behavior, I highlighted the notion of *consentir* among Latina culture. This practice of endearing, indulging, and favoring a young person—or rather, its lack in their lives—pervaded the reasons storied by those who transcended gangs by either disinhabiting (Marisa and Olga) or never inhabiting them in the first place (Angela and Elisa). In one case where transcendence had not yet occurred (Margie), the concept of *consentir* or being *consentida* is conspicuous for its absence. I argue that for any one of the research consultants, the ability to inhabit inter(in)dependence rests heavily on being taken into account, on having someone look after her, on enduring life's vicissitudes ensconced in a supportive community, and on feeling that her life and her work have a significant impact on the lives of others.

HOPING AGAINST HOPE

At the end of Chapter 1, "A Story of Stories," Esperanza and Soledad, the allegorically named, fictional, gang-impacted and gang-involved sisters, are at El Club de las Quince when news breaks of a gang-related stabbing nearby. Here follows the continuation of that story, followed by my justification for envisioning it this way.

MEANWHILE, BACK AT EL CLUB . . .

Franky comes running in from the street, out of breath, to tell Esperanza, Soledad, Caridad, Fe, and all the others that a boy from the neighborhood has just been stabbed behind the convenience store. He is a 16-year-old who claims a Sureño *varrio*, and although he is alive, he has lost a lot of blood and also possibly an eye. A group of girls hears this and runs to tell Malena, his girlfriend. Malena is "nothing," but many of her friends have been trying to get her and her boyfriend to begin claiming Quince. Malena leaves with three other girls, and the older girls at the front desk insist they wear yellow or white shirts to avoid being jumped.

Esperanza, now joined by Soledad, watches all this with a mixture of surprise and trepidation. This is neither the first nor the last color-related stabbing they know of to take place in their neighborhood, but they wonder how a shirt of a particular color can protect someone from attack. The girl at the counter then turns to them and says, "It's probably safer here than out in the streets, but if you want to leave, you should also put on something yellow or white. They'll leave you alone if they see you're a peacemaker." Esperanza is not about to leave and turns to Soledad, who seems to know both Malena and her boyfriend. The stabbed boy is friends with "El Chulo," and Soledad knows him as "Narco," but at El Club they refer to him as Marco.

Planning and carrying out regular activities under such circumstances, even at El Club, is a bit of a challenge, so the staff decides to focus on the matter at hand. They gather the youth in various small groups, and, after a moment of silence for the injured boy and his family, they give them a chance to find out what facts are known about the stabbing. The youth are also asked to repeat the Quince pledge of nonviolence and are reminded of their peacekeeping duties: to pay attention to the potential for fights, to talk to youth in the streets and at school who might be hit up, and to remind them that no one bothers those who claim Quince, especially if they wear yellow or white. The staff reminds them that belonging to Quince means something beyond the XIII–XIV, Sur–Norte, Blue–Red dichotomy.

The two sisters see the same series of events unfold and yet make different sense of them. Soledad thinks there is no way the attack on "Narco" can go unanswered and is hoping to find out how his homies will respond. She leaves El Club alone, hoping to run into someone who knows "El Chulo" or "Narco" to back them up. Esperanza, however, goes into a room they call "The Sanctuary" as Fe and an older girl lead a group of youth in a prayer for Marco. She finds Octavio, and, as she heads home, she takes a leaflet about a workshop for making drinking tumblers out of wine bottles that is taking place at El Club next week.

When they get home, Junior is on his cell phone, telling someone that he can't go out and hangs up. Esperanza realizes he's "ranking" and notices that he is not wearing any blue but does not say anything to him about it, only mentioning that Octavio wants to stay outside "kickin' it" with some neighborhood boys. Junior goes outside to tell him to come see his new phone app. Octavio dismisses him, but Junior talks to him and his friends, and eventually the two brothers go inside their small courtyard to look at the cell phone. Esperanza tells Junior what happened at El Club and that Soledad is still missing. Junior takes Octavio to find her. Although Esperanza, Soledad, and Octavio ate at El Club, Esperanza looks into the bag of food she got at El Club for something for Junior to eat. Her mother will be home in a couple of hours and will also bring some food home, but the quality and quantity are never reliable. She looks at the pictures on the tumbler-making leaflet, and she envisions the cupboard filled with such tumblers, wondering if she will have one to give to her father when he crosses the border again from Mexico. Esperanza goes to the calendar on the kitchen wall and writes an X by the date of the workshop. As she does that, she realizes that today is Soledad's 15th birthday and hopes their brothers find her soon and bring her home safe.

THE STORY OF HOPE

Although I have never met a girl who had the life experiences of Esperanza, there are many like her somewhere, expected to be, if not involved in gangs like Soledad, at least impacted by them like Esperanza. El Club de Las Quince does not exist . . . yet. What does exist are girls as young as age 7 who need help to guide their identity development so that they stay away from gangs. I have chosen to create this artyfact (a story cobbled together out of bits and pieces of stories, segments of observations, parts of secondhand accounts, and moments of informal conversations) to propose that programs to help young Latinas get out and stay out of gangs—to disinhabit and transcend gangs—need to be mindful of the existing rules and norms in the neighborhoods where they operate. The notion of colors, tattoos, tags, and gang signs are so deeply felt by youth in gang-impacted neighborhoods that it makes sense to co-opt them in the formation of a gang-cum-social club that will give the girls something beneficial to belong to. Moreover, the profound influence of religious organizations in helping people quit and stay away not just from gangs, but from drug and alcohol addictions altogether, must not be underestimated. Although participation in a religious group cannot be expected to function as a panacea to all gang-involved youth, it must be examined for what it does offer in order to extract its most promising features and apply them to lay programs.

In this manner, I extend a humble invitation to professionals working with gang-impacted youth, and specifically Latinas, to incorporate the insights I gained from listening to the stories of the girls and women consulted for this book. This work is meant neither as a to-do list nor as a magic wand that, if waved in a timely and skillful way, can safeguard a girl from evil. This is not an insider's look, for my contact with gang-involved and gang-impacted youth is quite limited in comparison to those who live and work with them over the course of years. It is not meant to take an "outsider knows best" approach, for many of the suggestions here are already being practiced with good results. Specifically, I do not mean to present my suggestions as new approaches when we all know that versions of these have been in practice for many years, with good results.

Rather, the following is a collection of theory-based extrapolations that I hope will serve as a bridge between what has worked in a variety of settings and a specific aim—namely, to help young Latinas transcend gangs regardless of their level of involvement. Of course, these suggestions must be read in the context of the contemporary political and economic climate, in which they may appear not to be fundable despite the fact that the choice not to fund them could well be more costly in the long run. Yet I argue they are more than pie-in-the-sky solutions to very real challenges. Mostly, these suggestions are also presented in the form of an imagined future that focuses less on the destructive and challenging aspects of gang-impacted neighborhoods and more on the already existing and potentially engaging, generative, healthful, and supportive aspects of such communities. I begin with very general suggestions and examples to those working at the neighborhood level, continue with what might be useful to those working with groups, and conclude with specific ideas for those working at the one-on-one level. I end with what I hope could serve as a beginning for girls like Esperanza—and, more important, for girls like Soledad—to be able to author their own story of transcendence because, as Cronen (1995) poignantly remarks, "the telling of a story is part of a lived story" (p. 46).

CO-OPTING THE HOOD

Those who work with youth living in gang-impacted areas are all too aware of the gangs' power to bring youth under a locally cohesive identifier of neighborhood loyalty and belonging. A name, a symbol, a slogan, and a raison d'être, *amaeru*, or being *consentidas* are what some of the girls and women I spoke with longed for and, unfortunately, found in the gangs. As Patterson and colleagues (2008) express it, "to the degree that people understand new strategies, their ability to make their own life better grows exponentially. To the degree that people understand the forces that are already influencing their behavior, they are more empowered to choose their response" (p. 21). The City of San José, California, has funded the highly regarded Mayor's Gang Prevention Task Force, which teams the Parks, Recreation, and Neighborhood Services Department with the Police Department and local community-based organizations (CBOs) into a tripartite approach to gangs: prevention, intervention, and suppression. A variety of CBOs are designated as Bringing Everyone's Strengths Together (B.E.S.T.) agencies focusing on youth services. The "weed and seed" approach and the Graffiti Removal Program are helping to reclaim neighborhoods from crime and blight to return them to the control of the residents. Additionally, programs such as the Tattoo Removal Program (mentioned prominently in Gracia's story in Chapter 6) have been instrumental in helping people transcend gangs. Taking a page (or many) from their playbook, it is important to ask what more our gang-impacted communities would need in order to realize their potential as aesthetically pleasing, safe, economically vibrant zones of community and individual empowerment.

Let us support the inception or continuation of social movements designed to create and maintain community gardens and cooperative markets that carry locally grown produce and other foodstuffs, like those found in Mexico and other Latin American countries. Not only are these stores familiar to recent immigrants, but they also replicate movements in more affluent areas to buy local, fresh, and organic. The idea of the community garden that sells its own produce comes from a newspaper story (Rogers, 2011) about a Transition Assistance Program at Camp Pendleton in Oceanside, California, that offers tuition assistance to combat veterans for a course in sustainable agriculture taught by a former Marine. What would our communities be like if such opportunities were offered to inner-city youth? To people exiting prison? The key to strong communities lies not in providing handouts but in providing opportunities for empowerment—a hand up. Determining who is ready to provide them, who will take advantage of them once they are established, and, more important, who will fund them compounds the task before us.

Coupled with this would be measures to satisfy the need for a strong identifying force, something that the residents can rally around together—not against an enemy, but around a core set of beliefs, commitments, or ethos. For example, I live in a neighborhood known for its palm-lined streets. It was developed in the 1930s; as in many older neighborhoods in the City of San José, vintage homes are ubiquitous. Unique to my neighborhood are its particular historical characteristics, the efforts by some residents to restore historic pillars at the main entrances, and social activities such as a Fourth of July children's parade, barbecue potluck, and fireworks watching; Friday night porch parties in the summer; and a seasonal palm or Christmas tree display on front lawns, plus a holiday potluck. The palm tree is the tacitly acknowledged unifying symbol. The neighborhood is not without its disputes, such as one between those who see the role of the neighborhood organization as solely for historical preservation and those who see it as more all-encompassing and hence as sponsoring the aforementioned activities, along with a neighborhood watch. Yet in real-estate promotions, the neighborhood is described as "highly coveted." Although this type of community identity is not exclusive to middle-class, mostly white neighborhoods, in those neighborhoods where poverty and need reside, so do other priorities, like those multiple marginalities faced by Esperanza's family. Pride in one's neighborhood is an important place to tap the potential for transformation. A unifying neighborhood symbol or name not only helps but is sometimes instrumental in that process: witness the many "*varrios*" whose name includes the *barrio* whence they come. How, then, to turn the pride that *varrios* instill in their members into pride for a *barrio*? The different spelling here is allegoric of the difference in intent. Loyalty and respect for one's neighborhood is an area ripe for further study.

WHITE SHIRTS AS PEACEKEEPERS

Troops wearing blue helmets in war zones signify the presence of United Nations Peacekeeping Forces. Although the original charter establishing the UN does not specifically address peacekeeping, this aspect of its role has become one of the most prominent ones in recent years (United Nations, 2008). There are five specific duties of the UN peacekeeping forces: (a) conflict prevention, which entails keeping disputes from escalating; (b) peacemaking, related to addressing conflicts in progress and moving them toward peaceful resolution; (c) peacekeeping, focusing on assisting in the implementation of agreements achieved by the peacemakers and working together to lay the foundations for sustainable peace; (d) peace enforcement, which authorizes the application of a range of coercive measures to restore peace or respond to threats to or breach of the peace, however fragile; and (e) peacebuilding, tasked with strengthening capacities for conflict management to reduce the risk of (re)lapsing into conflict and with creating the necessary conditions for sustainable peace (United Nations, 2008).

The idea of the "White Shirts" in Esperanza's story is modeled after the UN Peacekeeping Forces' guiding principles of consent of the parties, impartiality, and nonuse of force except in self-defense. Some of these preventive and interventive activities are often performed by staff of CBOs who work with gang-impacted and gang-involved youth. One of the times I was observing a group of girls at a CBO, a stabbing incident occurred similar to the one I described in Esperanza's story. The staff responded in a similar fashion, except that the pledge of nonviolence was not performed, and the prayer occurred spontaneously and was not staff-led. The Institute for Peace and Justice (2011) features several versions of the Pledge of Non-Violence on its website (http://www.ipj-ppj.org/Pledge%20of%20Nonviolence.html), and finding the appropriate pledge among these can serve as an integral element in gang transcendence efforts. Specifically, the Youth Group Pledge of Nonviolence reads:

> Making peace must start within ourselves and in our youth group. Each of us, members of (GROUP NAME), commit [sic] ourselves as best we can to become nonviolent and peaceable people.
>
> - To Respect Self and Others: To respect myself, to affirm others and to avoid uncaring criticism, hateful words, physical or emotional attacks, negative peer pressure, and self-destructive behavior, including abuse of alcohol and drugs.
>
> - To Communicate Better: To share my feelings honestly, to look for safe ways to express my anger and other emotions, to work at solving problems peacefully, and to encourage an open system of communication throughout the group.

- To Listen: To listen carefully to one another, especially those who disagree with me, and to consider others' feelings and needs as valid as my own.

- To Forgive: To apologize and make amends when I have hurt another, to forgive others, and to keep from holding grudges.

- To Respect Nature: To treat the environment and all living things with respect and care and to promote environmental concern in our faith community.

- To Recreate Nonviolently: To select activities and entertainment that strengthen my commitment to nonviolence and that promote a less violent society, and to avoid social activities that make violence look exciting, funny or acceptable.

- To Act Courageously: To challenge violence in all its forms whenever I encounter it, whether at home, at school, at work, or in the community, and to stand with others who are treated unfairly, even if it means standing alone.

- This is our pledge. We will check ourselves monthly to keep our promise to build a more peaceable youth group.

"Eliminating violence, one youth group at a time, starting with our own."

Although Esperanza was quizzical and Soledad skeptical about whether a peacemaker designation such as a white shirt—or in the case of the UN Peacekeeping Forces, a blue helmet—can actually protect someone from attack, I believe that there is plenty of evidence that gang-involved youth do not live completely outside the bounds of society (Fazila, 2004), and that they understand and, as in the cases of Lupe and Elisa, come to respect the decisions by some youth to involve themselves with religious or sports groups rather than gangs. Why not add peacemaking to that mix? To wit,

> The fact that multi-dimensional United Nations peacekeeping operations enjoy a high degree of international legitimacy and represent the collective will of the international community gives them considerable leverage over the parties. This leverage can be used to build and sustain a political consensus around the peace process, promote good governance and maintain pressure on the parties to implement key institutional reforms. (United Nations, 2008, p. 24)

The White Shirts depicted in the story of Esperanza would be neutral parties, in the sense that they would not intervene unless they had the consent of the conflicting parties. It would be imperative to establish that theirs is a peacemaking and peacekeeping group, and that their success is based on recognizing individuals as relational beings (Gergen, 2009) and understanding the devastating effects of intolerance (Gruwell, 1999). This would ensure their buy-in to the process. Oftentimes parties in conflict are tired of fighting, but having done it for so long, they lack the necessary capacities to do much else. One of the main objectives in peacekeeping is to learn and understand the local characteristics in order to help ensure that the parties remain engaged and thus committed to the process. In terms of impartiality, the White Shirts would not take sides, but they would be committed to a peaceful resolution of the conflict by being trained in peer mediation techniques, specifically, the empowerment model of transformative mediation (Baruch Bush & Folger, 2005). Their training could also include an adapted form of the Comprehensive Conflict Coaching (CCC) Model (Jones & Brinkert, 2008). Theoretically grounded in the communication perspective and social constructionist in orientation, the CCC model assumes a systems orientation in order to understand conflict. Although it is not intended to function linearly, implementing the model could begin with (a) discovering the story; (b) exploring the story from the perspectives of identity, emotion, and power; (c) crafting the best story; and (d) enacting the best story—all of which could include building capacities for communication skills, conflict styles, negotiation, and other Alternative Dispute Resolution processes (Jones & Brinkert, 2008). Models such as the CCC could equip gang-transcending youth to better meet the challenge to take action when parties contradict the peace process and at the same time ensure that they maintain good relations with all sides so as not to compromise their image of impartiality. With time, their deeds would become known for their successes, like the UN peacekeeping operations described earlier.

The third guiding principle of the UN peacekeeping operations, that of nonuse of force, is indicated but only the first part. Although the second part, "except in self-defense or in defense of the mandate," may be very effective for UN Peacekeeping Operations, I do not believe it would work for a peacekeeping group of girls. Perhaps their self-defense could come by using camera phones, through which they could take pictures and post them to social networks like Twitter as a deterrent, although this in itself might expose them to risk and retaliation. I do not presume for a minute that just by wearing a white shirt a youth would be immune to attack or even free from being "hit up" to reveal her or his gang claim, which they all are presumed to have. Instead, what I am inferring is that, given the stories I heard from some of these girls and women, the knowledge and determination of those who do not back down from an attack—not in defiance of the other but in defiance of the situation—will give them confidence, and the other will eventually desist in their harassment. Word travels fast in the 'hood, and co-opting it toward peace requires unity around peacemaking signs and symbols, patterns and practices, words and deeds. El Club de las Quince, with its XV claim and White Shirts, is invented to signify what a peaceful alternative to gangs might look like, using some of the gang iconography—colors, roman numerals, tattoos, preparative work, initiation rituals, and so on.

FAITH IN WHAT WORKS

The name of the character Fe, who prays with and for gang-involved and gang-impacted youth, is allegorically intended to reiterate the enormous power of faith and religion in quitting not just gangs but drug and alcohol addiction. As mentioned previously, I came to this notion quite skeptically and cynically because I could not reconcile the fact of hard-core gang criminals with the notion of their religious conversion. I did not believe that individuals who have committed vicious attacks on others could be redeemed in law-abiding, God-fearing society just by accepting Jesus Christ as their savior. That is, until I met one. A former member of Nuestra Familia prison gang now acts as a "street preacher," in the words of the police sergeant who introduced me to him, and who remarked that religious organizations (namely, Victory Outreach) have the highest success rate of any 12-step program in the city of San José (W. Montano, personal communication, September 27, 2007).

What works? From the stories by the women who inform this book, this is what they found in religion, specifically, Christianity: unconditional acceptance; not fictive kin but an ersatz family that is concerned for their well-being and that checks in on them early and often; protection from attack and retaliation by gang members through the development of an identity of a religious person; the promise of commitment and the elimination of the fear of betrayal; and a group of former addicts and gang members who know the situation and can attest to the difficulties in leaving but also to the "false doctrine," as Olga called the gang lifestyle. A good part of Victory Outreach membership is made up of such individuals and their families, as well as people who work to keep youth out of gangs by giving them what they lack at home:

structure, support, accountability, identity, and responsibility. Moreover, to join this group (VO), there is no need to "put in work" by committing crimes, injuring others, or consuming and selling illegal substances. What is there not to like?

Plenty, in many cases. Lest the previous paragraphs be seen as an effort to proselytize, let me clarify my intent. That religious conversion works for some is indisputable, and that it works for everyone is not so clearly established. My point is rather to invite a systemic analysis and critique of such gang-transcending efforts and to adapt them into a lay format, such as what Lafontaine, Acoose, and Schissel (2009) suggest to guide youth to imbue their lives with meaning beyond the gang or, as Percy (2003) has shown, to help youth take advantage of opportunities to develop a sense of competence. My suggestion is twofold: (a) to examine the role of Christianity with an eye toward pragmatism, and (b) to stress that adapting what it offers into an ecumenical or even a nonreligious format is not meant in the spirit of political correctness or disdain for religion. It is intended to ensure that a multipronged effort is developed so that no one who hopes to transcend a gang is left behind because the religious aspects of a certain program do not work well for her or him.

STORYING LIVES, STORYING TRANSCENDENCE

Another inspiration for the gang-transcending potential of Las Quince comes from the work of Mimi Silbert, founder of the Delancey Street Foundation in San Francisco (Patterson et al., 2008). Before working and living together at Delancey, the former gang member clients have been operating under the code of the street: care only about yourself and don't snitch on anyone. At Delancey, these are reversed so that everyone there is required to look after and be responsible for someone else's success and is expected to identify and confront others on their violations of the house rules, thus enforcing a culture of support and accountability.

Skeptics of the notion that improved self-esteem can lead to empowerment do not typically account for (a) the damaging effects on young minds of always being on the losing end, and (b) the double jeopardy encountered by marginalized youth, especially those youth whose only talents seemingly lie in misbehaving (Fazila, 2004). Self-esteem that routinely praises youth for simple accomplishments is not only misguided but often caricaturized as white middle-class, liberal denial of the competitiveness that is needed to make society stronger (Buchholz,

2011). A segment of the population that seldom, if ever, hears words of recognition and praise, especially within societal structures like schools, is going to try to find it whence it comes most easily: the gang. So, efforts to boost the self-esteem of gang-impacted youth would not be wasted altogether, especially if these efforts go beyond disingenuous praise for its own sake and tie the recognition to actual lived events. As Zander and Zander (2000) point out, oftentimes those who appear most disengaged are those who have the most to contribute and by focusing on engaging them we open up tremendous possibilities for growth.

Yet there is a second component that the staff at the Delancey Street Foundation also considers vital to set the conditions for empowerment: entrusting the most recently arrived clients into the care of their most immediate predecessors. This strategy places the previous novices in an expert position, responsible for the successes of their charges, and this act alone brings tremendous satisfaction because it becomes scaffolding for climbing out of dejection and into self-sufficiency by enacting the phrase "each one teach one." That is why Caridad, Fe, and Franky are tasked with welcoming Esperanza and Soledad and with ensuring that they find El Club hospitable. They want to involve them in activities that will not just keep them occupied and off the streets where they can be hit up by the Cholas, but activities that will help them stay in school (tutoring), gain new skills and stay healthy (video editing, exercise), possibly yield income (organic gardening, arts and crafts), and lead to transcendence (storytelling, peacekeeping, and mediation). On the power of stories, Patterson and colleagues (2008) have this to say:

> A well-told narrative provides concrete and vivid detail rather than terse summaries and unclear conclusions. It changes people's views of how the world works because it presents a plausible, touching, and memorable flow of cause and effect that can alter people's views of the consequences of various actions or beliefs. (p. 59)

The play that Soledad has an opportunity to join in the fictional story is based on this notion—specifically, on the compelling force of the play titled "The Duke of Earl" that members of the Victory Outreach have staged in the past and that was mentioned by Florencia in her narrative of redemption story. This play depicts the life of a gang-banger from his youth of longing to belong to something bigger than himself, through his addiction, and culminating in his redemption through Christ. Victory Outreach members admit that this story brings audience members, regardless of their interpretive and meaning-making resources, to empathize directly with the experience itself, as powerfully as if they were acting or even living the story themselves. And yet, a word of caution is required here, for Soledad has an untold (perhaps untellable) story about mother'hood. The playwrights' group she has the opportunity to join should not place too much pressure on her to "tell her story" unless during counseling she is guided to objectify and externalize her situation (Freedman & Combs, 1996). For as Freedman and Combs (1996) remark, "people are born into stories; their social and historical contexts constantly invite them to tell and remember the stories of certain events and to leave others unstoried" (p. 42).

And if it turns out that Soledad is involved in a gang ("down"), Besag (2006) offers strategies for working with bullies, and specifically girls in gangs, such as identifying the rewards Soledad receives from being in the gang and matching these with more appropriate tasks and rewards, and developing tangible and sought-after skills like video production and graphic design. Additionally, the communication and leaderships skills that many gang-involved girls exhibit, as attested to by many of the storytellers in this book, but specifically by Florencia and Gracia, can be redirected toward positive aims, such as public speaking, directing and/or acting in plays, and ultimately transcending the gang through storytelling because, as Cronen (1995) poignantly remarks, "the telling of a story is part of a lived story" (p. 46).

Last, in the County of Santa Clara, the Three Principles Division of the Department of Alcohol and Drug Services has been involved in training projects at alternative schools that help "staff and students recognize the common sense and goodness within them, and recognize the same resource in each other" (Maldonado, personal communication, January 16, 2008). Their successful strategy is based on the psychological notion of the Three Principles—Mind, Thought, and Consciousness—so that each person understands his or her role in creating a unique personal reality from thoughts that dictate how they view themselves and the world. This realization helps them see how they behave in the world, and then they can create more compassion for others. With more compassion, students begin to understand more clearly that people around them are not enemies and that everyone is simply reacting to their own version of reality based on past beliefs and habits of thought. Approaches that utilize the Three Principles might resemble or replicate their success in improving attitudes among all players, positively shifting the culture of the school or group, increasing school attendance even when rival gang members are also attending, decreasing gang violence and vandalism, and overall improving human relations and communication (Maldonado, 2008).

FROM SOLITUDE, HOPE

Esperanza wakes as Junior and Octavio half carry, half drag Soledad into the apartment. She is crying, her blue tank top, covered in blood, is ripped, and her hair is disheveled: She has been in a fight. The siblings help her clean her wounds. Octavio wants to know who did it. Junior says it doesn't matter, what matters is that she's home safe. Esperanza combs Soledad's hair, and when she's finished, she hands her a clean shirt. Soledad looks at the shirt and begins to smile, but doing so hurts her swollen mouth. She reaches for it to put it on. The shirt is white.

—To the Esperanzas and Soledads in our communities

Appendix A

The Storytellers

Angela, Chakira, Daniela, Elisa, Eréndira, Florencia, Gracia, Lucha, Lupe, Margie, Marisa, Olga, and Teresa

The voices of the women interviewed for this project encompass many similarities and differences. The purpose of this chapter is not to establish these but to merely introduce the women, their backgrounds, where and how I met them, and the themes that emerged from each of their stories. Here the women are listed in alphabetical order by the pseudonyms I gave them, and these summaries provide basic information about each that became relevant as their stories emerged in the various themes. Here follows my summaries of the lives of the storytellers: Angela, Chakira, Daniela, Elisa, Eréndira, Florencia, Gracia, Lucha, Lupe, Margie, Marisa, Olga, and Teresa.

ANGELA

I knew Angela through my work and only casually learned about her previous peripheral gang involvement one day when I was describing my project to her. When she intimated she had some gang experiences, I asked whether she would be willing to be a research consultant for my project, and she agreed. We met in my office and the videotaped interview lasted almost 2 hours. It was conducted in Spanish, with a peppering of English. For the purposes of this book, whenever she or I spoke English during the interview, it is signified in *italics*. Although her experiences date from the time she was 11 years old and into her teens, when we spoke she was in her early 30s.

She described family strife in the form of her parents' physical and verbal fighting, often in her presence, which made her feel lonely. Because her half-siblings were all much older, she was, in effect, an only child born to both of her parents. Neither parent used drugs, although her father drank heavily and had been drinking when most of the fights occurred.

Angela's exposure to gangs began while she was in middle school in Southern California as she was bullied by her classmates. Although these were gang-involved girls, and although it happened approximately 20 years ago, these gangs did not fit neatly into the Sureño–Norteño dichotomy endemic to most gangs in present-day San José, California. Nonetheless, the bullying that Angela endured included physical assaults. To avoid exposure to such dehumanizing treatment at the hands of her gang-involved peers, she switched schools. At her new school, she then became friends with girls who were gang-involved, and she became the bully to others. She served as the enforcer in situations, such as when it was known that another girl was saying things about her group; she would "put her in check" and demand respect by way of threats of physical violence. She was never jumped into a gang but wore Chola-style clothes. She described an event in which her friend stabbed someone and another event in which a neighbor boy who was gang-involved was shot and killed with impunity by Marines from the nearby military base. As she became exposed to more violence and drugs, she understood the implications of her actions and began to distance herself from the girls in the gang.

Coupled with this distancing, her father suffered a massive heart attack when she was in her teens, and her family life improved because both her parents became more involved in church. She joined them at church, got a job, and stayed away from gangs altogether. Angela's leadership skills were harnessed in the workplace as she continued working and going to school. She was unmarried and had a 4-year-old son. She had a college degree and was a successful businesswoman. "Family Violence," "In la Vida Loca," "Loyalty and Respect," "The Narrative of Redemption," and "Transcending Gangs" are the themes (and chapters) that capture her story.

CHAKIRA

This young woman was 16 years old at the time we spoke and attended the young women's group session at a community center. She came to the center to "stay out of trouble" and participated actively in the weekly group sessions that I observed for a period of 4 months. On one occasion, the group session leader took the girls outside to do an exercise on gender identity, and, on returning indoors, the group ran into several heavily tattooed gang members displaying their Sureño loyalties with colors and hand signs. They were positioned to the side of the entrance because they would not be allowed to enter the center in such attire. Seeing them, Chakira remarked in Spanish "¡Ay si, muy gangsters!" loosely translated into, "Oh, yeah! They're ever the gangsters!," but they paid her no mind.

On learning about my project, she expressed interest in being the "first" to be interviewed, although her friend Daniela beat her to it. When explaining the research project and the consent form to this interview subject, she understood it was the beginning of the interview and began speaking about how women are victimized in the gang. The interview was conducted mostly in Spanish, but we both switched between Spanish and English. In the transcript, when either one spoke English, it is notated in *italics*.

Chakira was born in the United States, although both her parents were born in México. Her father had worked in landscaping and small electronics manufacturing. Her mother had worked in big-box retail stores and fast-food restaurants. Although they were still living together, she explained that there wasn't "much love between them anymore," but she did not speak about violence at home. She had an older sister who was in medical school and worked in the health care field, a younger half-sister, and two brothers. The older sister and the older brother were born in México, and the remaining three siblings, like her, were born in the United States. The older brother had been incarcerated 2 weeks prior to the time of the interview for an undisclosed crime, and the younger one was beginning to dabble with gangs, although he was also involved with a dancing crew that, while it seemed to transcend colors, still had animosity and fights against other dancing crews. The older brother was "down" with Sur, so this made her suspect to being sympathetic to Sureños. As the little sister of a known Sureño, she must negotiate this ascribed identity regardless of whether she interacted with Sureños, Norteños, or those who were "nothing." She had been involved in fighting against Norteños and seemed quite knowledgeable about gang symbolism, such as gang names and insults, numbers, tattoos, and colors. Given this, I designated her as "gang-impacted" because she neither had been jumped nor had active involvement in a gang, yet her experience belonged to the Gangs of Family.

About her older brother's incarceration, she made it clear that her family disapproved of his gang involvement, and that all of them, including her brother, used his jail sentence as a cautionary tale for Chakira to stay away from gangs. When we spoke about what the future held for her, she hoped to become a veterinarian or an architect. Chakira's story appears most poignantly in the themes of "Tattoos and Identity," "Of Colors and Names," and "Betrayal."

DANIELA

Daniela was 15 years old when we spoke at the center, which she attended for after-school programs during the year. She was in ninth grade and had been attending the center for more than one and a half years when we spoke; her friends told her about the programs, and that motivated her to start coming. This was the first interview at the center for me, and I assume for her, too, so we both spent some time orienting ourselves to each other. I asked her some general questions about her life, background, family, and so on, and then she steered it to the topic of gangs on her own when discussing problems at school. Although we spoke mostly in Spanish, we both switched between English and Spanish. The transcript shows the English translation, when necessary, in *italics*.

Daniela was born in the United States, although both her parents were born in Michoacán, México. She lived at home with her mother, her older sister, her older sister's infant daughter, and her younger sister. As I found out later in the interview, her father had left the family when they went to México for a visit, staying back. She volunteered that, during that visit to México 5 years prior, she did not like it.

Fights seemed to be Daniela's primary experience of the gang, although she hinted at not being in a gang but just "liking the color" blue. One fight was initiated when the other girl issued a derogatory insult to her friends, who claimed Sur; the second was when a girl who "kicks it Norte" accused Daniela of stealing her boyfriend. There was a third fight, one with a girl who had moved away and whom several of her friends had antagonized, but this girl's gang membership or peripheral affiliation was not made clear. She felt safe in her neighborhood from being harassed to choose a side. Yet she fought when her Sureños friends were disrespected. As part of her identity, Sur signified loyalty, although to what she did not make clear. On the weekends, she went to parties with her friends, where they would encounter fights with Norteños or other Sureños from different crews, cliques, or sets.

Aside from fights, other activities that occupied Daniela and her group of friends included talking about their problems at school and coming to the center to "group" and discuss topics that they could not talk with their parents about. She said she was not alone in being unable to talk to her mother about issues like sex. She had an older sister who got pregnant at 16, dropped out of school to care for her own daughter, and worked at the time at a fast-food chain restaurant. Her sister's experience made Daniela realize that early motherhood is indeed difficult, and she decided she would not have a child for at least 5 years, when she turned 20. Daniela did not have a boyfriend when we spoke, nor was she looking for one, finding herself freer without one and not needing "to watch him" so that he would not cheat, and she agreed with me when I uttered the classic *dicho* (saying) that is a favorite of all women—whether single and not looking, or single and pretending not to be looking—in México: "*Mas vale sola que mal acompañada*" ("Better off alone than in bad company"). However, on one occasion after the interview when I observed the group, when the girls were chatting before the session started, the gossip was about whether Daniela was pregnant. It turned out she wasn't . . . at least not that time.

Daniela's mother had been caring for her three daughters for the last 5 years, since her father had stayed behind when the family had last visited México. It had been a hard life, although at the time of the interview, the mother received public assistance. Daniela also took care of two young children on the weekends to earn spending money.

We discussed a bit more about parties, rules, consequences, and her mother's reaction to her suspension from school for fighting. I specifically wanted to know whether her mother was aware of her being "around" the gang, and this is how Daniela brought up the subject of gangs. Her mother took away her computer privileges for a while, which she missed for not being able to go on MySpace, fix her profile "to express" herself, and meet and chat with her friends. She volunteered that her profile was about love, and next to her picture there was a quote that read, "You never know what you have until you lose it and when you lose it you can't get it back." This is a story about being a typical teenager in the first decade of the 21st century, who uses technology such as MySpace for social networking.

Daniela's notions of the future were equally undetermined, although she knew that fighting would get her in trouble at school and passing her tests at school would help her in her senior year. She did not want a job like her mother's, who has a sixth-grade education, or like her sister's, who went up to ninth grade. Both from her sister and from a close friend, Daniela knew about the hardships of single motherhood.

Because she had not been jumped into a gang but was friends with gang members, I consider Daniela "gang-impacted," although if her association with them became known to law enforcement, she might be "validated" as a gang member due to her fights about gang-related insults and against other gang-"validated" youth.

Daniela's story is indicative of the theme "Of Colors and Names."

ELISA

Elisa was born in the northern Mexican state of Chihuahua and grew up in the neighborhood in which one of the centers where I conducted some of the interviews was located. She started coming to the center for after-school programs at the age of 12, at 18 she began working there as recreation staff, and at 20, as a Youth and Family Specialist, she became the group facilitator. Her group's focus was to speak to the girls about gangs: to stay out if not yet involved and to get out if already involved. She held great hope for the girls in her group, hoping to provide them in their weekly sessions with the attention and guidance she surmised they missed at home and felt was necessary to steer the girls away from the gang lifestyle. She attended the local community college and was hoping to transfer to San José State University. Due to this peripheral exposure to gangs, Elisa falls into the category I devised titled "gang-impacted."

Elisa speculated that it was a privilege for youths to attend the center and that only about 10% of them were obligated by their parole officers to attend some kind of program to keep them off the streets. Elisa explained that, in that particular neighborhood, there were three centers within a mile of each other and that two of them were known Norteño hangouts, whereas the center where she met her group was thought to be Sureño, and she lamented that, by coming to one center or the other, youth such as herself become associated with that particular color or gang. Discussing the differences between gang impact and involvement, she stated, "So, not everybody is in it, but somehow they all know someone. Somehow they all are. . . ." Although she told a riveting story about her own brush with gangs (in Chapter 7, "Of Colors and Names"), she also expressed in no uncertain terms that, as a soccer player, she was "nothing," meaning she was not affiliated with either side. Despite this non-claim (meaning she claims no affiliation with any gang), Elisa is nonetheless gang-impacted in the taxonomy I offer for the mere fact that she resides in a neighborhood with gang presence. Her voice is present in "Of Colors and Names" and "Transcending Gangs."

ERÉNDIRA

I was introduced to Eréndira through my contact at a local church that ministers to gang-involved youth and adults. I phoned her, and, after a couple of attempts, I managed to meet with her. I picked her up at her home and we went to lunch. She was wearing Bermuda-length denim pants, a feminine blue polka-dot blouse, and glitter and sequined turquoise-blue ballet slippers. These seemed like typical Sureño colors, for she disclosed she had been jumped in a Sureño gang, but when I asked her specifically about it the second time we met, she was dismissive of their significance. However, while riding back in the car near her home, she pointed out a pregnant woman who was claiming Norte by wearing a burgundy sweatshirt (presumably someone she knew), and Eréndira remarked how the woman in question was endangering not only herself but also her unborn child.

Both times we met, she brought along her 6-month-old son, "Angel." She was articulate and curious about my work, which I had previewed to her over the phone. We started speaking English, but when she told me that her mother was from México and I told her I was, too, we switched to Spanish and continued in it, except for a few occasions when we chose to switch to English for convenience; namely, when the words are hard to translate or unknown by either one of us in Spanish, such as "Juvenile Hall" and "probation," or idiomatic expressions such as "have my back." In the transcript, her and my usage of English is notated in *italics*.

In the car and at lunch, it was not possible to tape the conversation or to take notes. I wrote an account of our conversation after I left her, and a week later, when we met to tape the interview, I asked her to review it for accuracy and completeness. She began her story by telling me that she grew up in a single-parent household. Her mother crossed over from México (Michoacán) into Arizona when Eréndira was 2 months old. Her father was not much of a presence or influence in her life, which left her feeling sad and angry. Her mother was emotionally available, but she was often working hard to support her, so she did not have much contact with her either.

Eréndira started doing drugs at 11 years old, and soon after she was jumped and joined a Sureño gang. She was always getting into fights for reasons as simple as being looked at the wrong way. She said she had a "short fuse" and every provocation was met with her ire and full physical force, which she thought came from being angry at her father for abandoning her and her mother, and which she meted out to others who disrespected her. "If you let them walk all over you, they won't respect you. If you fight back, they leave you alone," she said. These fights got her into trouble, which at first was minor: She was suspended for a few days or sent to Juvenile Hall for three nights.

Eventually, these violent events caught up with her and she was expelled from one school and transferred to another. Her drug use and her gang involvement were a puzzle to her teachers, many of whom counseled her by pointing out that she had the potential to make a difference in her life. She consistently got good grades, but her fights with other girls, mostly Norteñas, not only kept her from staying in school and graduating but also landed her in various correctional facilities, among them Juvenile Hall and "The Ranch," which is what juvenile rehabilitation facilities in Santa Clara County are colloquially called. At one time, she and her friends even managed to smuggle drugs into The Ranch. She had been on probation off and on since the age of 12 and on house arrest three times. On two occasions, she managed to cut the ankle bracelet, but the third time she kept to the terms of her sentence.

On the way to the interview, in the car, she spoke eloquently about the falsehood of division between gangs; how they all fought over the same thing, engaged in the same violence, took the same drugs, got hit by the same bullets, and shed the same blood. It was an enlightening and insightful story, which I was unable to tape or write down, so once she was on camera, I managed to get her to re-create it.

Eréndira's story of gang involvement eloquently gives voice to most of the themes in this book: "Inhabiting the Gang," "Tattoos and Identity," "Of Colors and Names," "In la Vida Loca," Time Served!," "Mother'hood," "Loyalty and Respect," "Betrayal," "The Narrative of Redemption," and "Disinhabiting the Gang."

FLORENCIA

I met Florencia at her house for the research consultation, which was conducted in English, although she said she spoke both English and Spanish. I told her to speak freely about her background, her family, her entry into the gang, her experiences within it, the role of women in gangs, and, of course, how she got out. I did not have to ask her much more after that because she spoke on all those topics and many more for more than 3 hours.

She was born in Texas and was the youngest of three children. Due to extremely violent conditions at home, her brother, 11 years older than her, left home and became gang-involved at the age of 14, while her sister, who was 14 years older than Florencia, left for the military at the age of 18. Her parents separated and got back together several times, sometimes at the insistence of her older sister. In between, her father's alcoholism and brutality toward the mother and children, coupled with her mother's own partying, left her not only lonely and vulnerable but extremely angry. Starting at about 7 years of age, Florencia suffered sexual abuse. She did not specify the perpetrator, but hinted that it was someone known to her family, perhaps even a family member.

She always hung out with people who were older than she was, and although she had few but good female friends, most of her friends were males. At a young age, she was involved in a Norteño gang, although she did not specify her age or whether she was jumped in. Her justification for being in a gang was to avoid being victimized by being strong and to have back-up. At first she was involved in petty crimes, but soon she began to use drugs like marijuana and methamphetamines ("crank" or "crystal meth") and eventually crack, cocaine, PCP, and heroin. As her influence grew, she became a "shot-caller" and was mostly involved with men as partners in drug dealing, partners in sex, or both. At age 13, her friend introduced her to a 25-year-old man who had just been released from prison, and she soon became his partner and was pregnant by him. Their daughter was born with severe disabilities due to spina bifida and hydrocephaly. She had hoped her love for her daughter would help her get clean; instead she began her deep descent into the gang lifestyle, characterized by heavy drug use and, most significantly, drug dealing. She spoke at length about her gang exploits and the crazy life she led.

Eventually, her recurring memories of childhood sexual abuse led her to a drug overdose and she was hospitalized. After her hospitalization, her mother took her to see a drama at a church about the damaging effects of the gang lifestyle. During and after the performance, Florencia strongly identified with the characters, which led her to begin the process of leaving the gang by becoming a Christian. She subsequently married a man who had been deeply involved in a Sureño gang, and they now have three children, in addition to her older daughter, now in her teens. They are the pastors of a church that focuses on keeping youth away from gangs and also helping them get out of gangs if they're already in. She was in her mid-30s when we spoke. For her substantial experiences in the gang lifestyle, Florencia exemplifies the gang-involved classification I designated. Her voice is heard in stories about "Inhabiting the Gang," "Family Violence," "Tattoos and Identity,"

"In la Vida Loca," "Mother'hood," "Loyalty and Respect," "Betrayal," "The Narrative of Redemption," and "Disinhabiting the Gang."

LUCHA

Lucha and I met and spoke twice. The first was informally, in private, where I explained my project to her and tried to answer any questions she might have, mostly to reassure her that I was not connected to law enforcement. The second meeting was formal and was videotaped. Before the first meeting, one of the staff members of the drop-in center for homeless youth where I met her warned me that Lucha was a "big talker" and that she would say anything I wanted to hear. I thanked her politely, not knowing what to say or do, but reminded myself that all qualitative research projects, especially those involving subjects who are on the margins of society, present researchers with many challenges of veracity that are beyond our reach.

Her story begins on the note that her father, a drug dealer, died when she was 5, and that her mother, who was incarcerated many times, belonged to the Nuestra Familia prison gang. Her father came from the southern Mexican state of Michoacán, and her mother was born in Texas.

When Lucha was 12 and her mother remarried, she became homeless and continued to take care of her siblings. She parted with the gang and thus became alienated from her other extended family. She had several tattoos, none gang-related, although on one of the days we spoke, she wore red basketball shorts and mentioned as a sort of pet peeve not ever wearing blue.

She expressed many strong opinions about the differences between Sureños and Norteños, between Mexicans and Mexican Americans, and between Mexican Americans and whites, mostly focusing on the paradoxical elements of her identity. Although as a youth she worked in the fields, following the crops with the seasons with her family, and hence her Norteña legacy, she was the first in her family to graduate from high school. She had spent the previous summer in jail for an undisclosed felony.

The topics that Lucha talked about ranged from purchasing a used car from a man from México (using the Spanish pronunciation of the country), having "beer money with wine taste" to describe her extravagant tastes in contrast to her poor finances, and her relationship with her African-American boyfriend to her efforts to go to school and get a job, her challenges in doing that due to with her felony conviction, and how much more difficult it is for Mexicans to get back on their feet and go "legit" because of the lack of opportunities. She had an outstanding debt to the county for two of her court cases and for traffic tickets nearing $10,000, so she took out a loan to pay some of it off, but the loan company was a scam and she lost $500.

She repeatedly exemplified her self-sufficiency and her can-do attitude and spoke kindly of farm workers, most of whom she proclaimed are Mexican and know how to care for the land. Had her Gangs of Family legacy been enacted, she would have been in the category of gang-involved. But because she stayed away from the gangs themselves, if not the lifestyle, under the taxonomy outlined in this book she falls under the category of gang-impacted. Her story is found in the themes of "Family Violence" and "Time Served!"

LUPE

Lupe, the oldest women I spoke to, was born in 1961. I met her through a contact on the Mayor's Gang Prevention Task Force in San José. She was an active member of a Victory Outreach church that ministers to gang-involved and gang-impacted people, as well as people with drug and alcohol addiction.

Lupe's father came from Zacatecas, México, and worked in maintenance; her mother came from San Antonio, Texas, and was a homemaker. Her involvement in gangs began before her teen years, although her parents tried to provide a healthy home environment. Her siblings and Lupe became acquainted with new neighbors who had moved to San José in the 1970s from Los Angeles and were gang-involved.

The gangs in those days were not aligned with either Norte or Sur, but congregated in "*varrios*," or neighborhoods, and included a number of low-rider sets. She ran with the men in the gangs, some of whom were boyfriends to her, handsome and strong, but in the end all of them were verbally and physically abusive to her. Lupe and her homegirls did not participate actively in any gang-related activities such as drug dealing, drive-by shootings, or thefts; fights with other gangs, however, were unavoidable. Lupe's story also included information about her advocacy work for Chicana/Chicano causes that took place during the latter years of her involvement in the gang and that continued after she left the gang. At a New Year's Eve party when she was 17 years old, she was the victim of a gang-related stabbing that almost killed her. As a result, she encountered problems with the gang and the police, as she was thought to know the perpetrator. Although she left the gang after the stabbing, she did not really abandon the lifestyle concomitantly because she remained addicted to alcohol and PCP even while she was trying to stay in college. What with taking drugs and feeling alienated from her campus peers for being Latina, she eventually dropped out but managed to get and keep a job in a social services agency that provided services to the Chicano community. Here she helped organize resources for youth and eventually became a drug and alcohol counselor. She struggled with her addiction during those years until her conversion to Christianity at the age of 19.

Although Lupe still had not finished her college education, she continued her work in addiction counseling and had been clean and sober since 1982. She was single and had two grown children: a daughter and a son. Her gang involvement story is detailed in the themes of "Inhabiting the Gang," "In la Vida Loca," "Loyalty and Respect," "Betrayal," "The Narrative of Redemption," and "Disinhabiting the Gang."

MARGIE

Margie was the only woman who was still active in a gang at the time of the research consultation. I met her at a drop-in center for homeless youth. She was 18 years old when we spoke and had a 6-year-old son who was being cared for by her stepfather. The videotaped interview lasted 1 hour, and at the start she asked me not to film her face because she was wanted by authorities in another county for an undisclosed crime.

I began the interview by asking her general questions about family, being Mexican, immigrants, gangs, and her future. I asked her to speak freely on any of these topics, and I told her I would ask questions to clarify or elaborate. The methods for girls and women to enter gangs vary: Some are jumped in, others are sexed in, and still others have no need for either because they belong to the gang by virtue of having been born into it. Although Margie inhabited the Gangs of Family in this way, and she associated with gang members through her drug dealing, she nonetheless was jumped into a Norteño gang when she was 14 years old. She quit school about the same time.

The conversation was terse and not sophisticated despite my efforts to engage her about difficult topics such as the brutality and pain associated with gang membership, normalized dysfunctionality, and motherhood at an extremely early age, as well as coping with her current homeless situation. At times she seemed unwilling or unable to answer many questions or to speak on other topics.

Nonetheless, she revealed that she was born in the United States and expressed tremendous disdain toward Sureños, specifically in two instances. The first one was when we were discussing the possibility of her son joining gangs. She said she wished he wouldn't, but if he decided to, she would be there for him. When I asked whether she would still support him if he joined a Sureño gang, she emphatically said no. The second time was when she told a story about a cousin of hers who had joined a Sureño gang and how Margie had broken into her cousin's house and beaten her.

I believe that, although Margie spoke to me for an hour, revealing a great many intimate details about her life, her story of her gang experiences remains untold. The gang serves as a silencing force demanding secrecy about its actions: As an active member of a gang, Margie's habits prohibited her from talking about what goes on in the gang. Even those aspects of her life that did not relate directly to her gang involvement, like her family background and her plans for the future, were difficult for her to articulate. She storied her life in the context of self-sufficiency, yet paradoxically her identity depended on the gang as primary meaning-making resource. Because she had been on her own for a while, the need to provide for her family prefigured her actions in the gang, such as drug dealing and fighting. Although she had become emancipated, and thus was independent from family connections, she remained dependent on the gang to play the role of ersatz family.

Margie took a pragmatic stance about her situation, grown out of a self-concept of someone who takes care of things, in order to dismiss unstated concerns about whether she could remain clean and sober, why she did not hold a "legit" job, or why she was hiding from the law. Her confidence in staying clean extended to having confidence in her friends, whom she believed would not pressure her to stray by offering her the crack pipe. She even offered a candid assessment of the conditions inside prison walls, yet she was resigned in knowing that in the future she would have to be reincarcerated as a way to "get cleared."

When I asked her about the possibility of leaving the gang, she was unable to envision any type of future beyond the gang, but she offered that she had made her own funeral arrangements at the age of 14. Margie unequivocally belongs to the gang-involved category that I devised to distinguish levels of exposure to and participation in gangs. Margie's story is found in "Inhabiting the Gang," "Family Violence," "Time Served!," "Mother'hood," "Loyalty and Respect," and "Transcending Gangs." The decision to include her in this last theme, although she had not yet transcended according to my taxonomy, is to identify her as the target class for efforts to help Latinas leave gangs.

MARISA

Marisa was a client at a drop-in center for homeless youth where I was allowed to recruit interview subjects. I met her once and we spoke for about an hour, almost entirely in English. One of the center's staff had promoted my interviews as "a chance to tell [their] story" about gangs and being Latina. Marisa was offered a $20 gift card as an incentive to be interviewed. I wanted to avoid too direct an approach to asking about her "gang" story, and I also wanted to give interviewees the opportunity to highlight other aspects of their life beyond the gang. Therefore, I presented them with some themes and let them talk freely, interjecting when I believed I needed to pursue something further. Marisa eagerly answered my questions and provided many unprompted answers to questions I had not even asked.

Her grandparents came from the Mexican states of Zacatecas and Jalisco; both parents were born in the United States. She was the youngest of three children, all of whom were U.S.-born. Her father was a heavy drug user during her childhood, and her parents divorced in her early childhood. When she was 10, the father sobered up and tried to return to the home, but the mother had already remarried. Her older brother left the home and had a family of his own with four children by the time he was 20. The middle brother became involved in Norteño gangs by way of selling drugs, and Marisa became a drug distributor for him at the age of 10.

The brother would make arrangements for her to deliver drugs after school, which she carried in a lunch box. She would deliver the box to the designated home, where the customers would take the box into another room, take the drugs out, and put the money in. The brother would give Marisa money on the condition that she stayed in school and brought home good grades. The mother was oblivious to this because Marisa didn't spend her money extravagantly. Because she had her own money, she began using drugs, mostly crystal meth, at age 15. The brother bought her a car, clothes, and make-up, but never drugs, she assured me.

When her drug use got the better of her, her father urged her to get help. She attended a treatment center for adolescents and graduated from high school there. But back in town, she soon found her way to the old homies and the drugs, if not to the drug dealing. Her brother refused to give her the drugs that he himself was selling and using, so she avoided him. Her mother had "washed her hands" of Marisa before she went away, so she ended up homeless.

Fortunately, as she told it, she became pregnant and decided to get clean. She had a 1-year-old daughter and was living with the girl's father when we met, but when their daughter was born, Marisa's partner was incarcerated, and she refused to bring the infant to visit him in jail. The birth of her daughter helped her transform her life because she saw the child's life as a "gift from God." She was also attending a local community college and hoping to transfer to UC Berkeley to pursue Chicano Studies or some other social science degree.

Although Marisa did not join the gang, her experiences around the gang had remarkable characteristics, in that she was enlisted at a young age as a drug distributor. Her "good girl" image provided the appropriate cover at school and with law enforcement. Yet she shared experiences in common with other gang-impacted Latinas: alienation due to a felt lack of belonging, inattentive parents, and poor body image. Her brother and his homeboys and homegirls fulfilled many of her needs despite the fact that this fulfillment was through participation in illegal activities.

A take on this part of Marisa's story might go something like this: She possessed a talent for inconspicuousness, which was recognized early on by her brother the businessman, and she was rewarded for it. While distributing drugs, she was expected to remain unscathed by the gang lifestyle by getting good grades. Yet the money only went so far in providing her satisfaction. Her choices of relationships brought her, if not calamity, at least not the emotional fulfillment she expected. Although she had the money, drugs, looks, position in the gang, and feminine charm to command better treatment, she allowed circumstances to occur that she later recognized as having diminished her sense of well-being.

Despite its early idiosyncrasies, Marisa's story now takes a familiar turn as she described the pivotal role her pregnancy and the birth of her daughter had in the process of independence from the gang lifestyle. The fact that she never was jumped in or tattooed, and that her mother, father, and brother all disapproved of her drug use, also may have contributed to her being able to story a different course for her life. However, because of the drug dealing and usage, as well as access to and knowledge of weapons, her collateral participation in gang fights, and her exposure to many sexual partners, I have classified her as gang-involved rather than gang-impacted. Marisa's story of paradoxical gang involvement is found in "Inhabiting the Gang," "Of Color and Names," "In la Vida Loca," "Mother'hood," "Loyalty and Respect," "The Narrative of Redemption," "Disinhabiting the Gang," and "Transcending Gangs."

OLGA

I met Olga through a contact with Victory Outreach, where she and her husband were the pastors of one of the churches. They have five daughters, and Olga was in her mid-30s when we met at her church for the research consultation. The interview began in Spanish but gradually switched to almost entirely English. I denoted where the language shifts occurred by italicizing when she or I spoke in English.

Olga was born in Zacatecas, México, and at the age of 2, her parents brought her to live in the United States, along with her older brothers and sisters. Fights, drinking, and partying characterized her earlier memories of family life at around 7 years old. Although eventually her parents divorced, they continued living together for a number of years. To escape such an unstable environment, the siblings took different routes: The oldest sister went to college, whereas the oldest brother and another sister took to the streets to look for "a safe place"—an ersatz family that would support them emotionally and financially. They also sought a safeguard from the obstacles set before underprivileged immigrant youth, such as discrimination and harassment. Therefore, in the gang, they also found Sureño "back-up" against Norteños in school who picked on them.

Olga's story of why she got involved in gangs resonates with so many others: the lack of a firm family structure. Although both parents were present and worked hard, their own lifestyles made at least some of their 10 children feel irrelevant and unappreciated, to the point that they sought relevance and appreciation in the gangs. Olga is one among several research consultants whose stories hint at the notion that, more than fictive kin, the gang functions as ersatz kin for many youth, insofar as it actually replaces a dysfunctional, neglectful, or nonexistent family in economic, emotional, and moral terms. An interesting detail of Olga's story touches on issues of racism and discrimination felt by immigrants that also contribute to their choosing the gang lifestyle. Another question pertains to the difference between Olga and her gang-involved siblings and the other siblings who chose a different lifestyle away from the gangs.

Once involved in the gang, the siblings became well known in the streets as their gang evolved into the largest Sureño "*varrio*" in San José, and, as a result, the harassment and the threats worsened. At age 12, Olga's friends at school were mostly Norteñas; on seeing this, her 17-year-old, gang-involved sister invited her to inhabit their Sureño *varrio*. At about the same time, her brother was stabbed by a group of Norteños, and this event served as the deciding factor. At 14, Olga asked to get jumped in the *varrio*, but the siblings declined, telling her that they all knew she was faithful because she was always around. At school, she would be approached by her former Norteña friends and occasionally attacked, yet she never did "back down." Seeing this, others who were also victimized by Norteños took inspiration from her and began forming other Sureño *varrios*.

The gang lifestyle for Olga implied skipping school—eventually dropping out, sleeping all day, hanging out and partying all night with the homeboys and homegirls, and fighting to protect the *varrio*'s reputation, among other activities. Yet La Vida Loca didn't sit well with Olga because she began questioning the benefits of being in the gang versus being at home. Rather than weighing the (dis)advantages of supporting a group whose main purpose was to fend off attacks from the enemy, Olga's misgivings came from seeing the actions of the people within the gang. Although she was protected by her siblings, who looked after her in fights and even prohibited her from using drugs, she disapproved of the way their addictions made them foolishly aggressive, to the point of picking fights unwarrantedly within and outside the gang. Also appalling to Olga was the brutal treatment that women in the gang received from the men, and the fact that many of these youth, including her own sister, were having children at a young age, for whom they were incapable of providing care. Around the same time, one of the homeboys to whom she was attracted became incarcerated. In fact, the reputation of the *varrio* improved the more people went to and came out of prison; the homeboys proved their gang mettle this way, and being tough was the currency not only of prison but also of the streets. Unfortunately, that toughness carried over into their own kind, and many girls, women, and infants ended up right where Olga had been in her own childhood: without a safe place to call home.

All these factors coalesced, resulting in a fight Olga had with her sister that led her to distance herself from the gang. For some time, Olga was literally homeless, spending the night at the airport terminals (which would become unthinkable after 9/11) and wandering around all night through industrial and warehouse areas. To her good fortune, another sister uninvolved in the gang helped her get a job. At 17, Olga began working at a temp agency, trying to right her ship, but her boyfriend, out from prison on a weekend pass, was shot and killed. This gave her gang-involved sister an excuse to call her and make amends; thus, they reestablished some of the strength in their previous bond. Despite the fact that the sister remained gang-involved, Olga's further attempts to withdraw from the gang were tacitly accepted by her former homies. By no longer claiming or wearing blue, by having a job, and by changing her self-presentation artifacts (or lack thereof), the possibility to disinhabit the gang was established.

Although Olga managed to leave the gang, she did not leave the lifestyle behind entirely. Another former homeboy and sometime-boyfriend who was on the verge of deportation managed to convince his parole officer that he was engaged to Olga and so—at the age of 17—she married him to help him remain in the United States. They had three daughters, but he remained active in the *varrio*, despite his parole obligations. Olga encountered many difficulties reconciling her new role as mother with her role of provider, in addition to the challenges of being married to a verbally abusive gang-banger. She then also began abusing drugs and alcohol heavily. The couple separated several times; during one such separation, he overdosed, and at the hospital, Olga—now 22—was roped into reestablishing the relationship. Her husband had learned about the ministry to gang members of Victory Outreach, and he begged her to attend the church together: This pivotal moment transformed their lives, their marriage, and their future.

When I spoke with her, Olga was in her early 30s, and she and her husband had five daughters and ran the outreach programs at one of the churches. Their lives were dedicated to helping gang-impacted youth stay away from gangs and to helping gang-involved youth leave the gangs. Olga had found a home at last.

The arc of Olga's story places her squarely into the category of gang-involved. Her story helps illustrate the themes of "Inhabiting the Gang," "Family Violence," "In la Vida Loca," "Mother'hood," "Betrayal," "The Narrative of Redemption," "Disinhabiting the Gang," and "Transcending Gangs."

TERESA

Teresa claimed not to be gang-involved, although both her parents had been involved in gangs at one point or another in their lives, with different negative consequences for her. When we spoke, she was 20 years old and had a job at a small fast-food chain restaurant. The day we spoke at a drop-in center for homeless youth where she occasionally went to receive health and social services, she was upset because they had just told her at work she did not need to come in, thus cutting her weekly hours by 6. She was concerned about earning enough money to make the rent.

About her father, she knew little and told even less: Suffice it to say that she wasn't fond of him because of his criminal and drug-dealing activities. Her mother's side of the family came from Del Rio, Texas, so she referred to them as "Tejanos." Her maternal grandparents had moved all 11 siblings, of whom her mother was the youngest, to San José, California, to work in the canneries. Her grandfather was a decorated World War II soldier, and after the war, he worked in construction and purchased a "nice house," where Teresa grew up.

Although her mother graduated from high school, she "banged Norte" and gave birth to Teresa when she was 20. Teresa admiringly described her mother's loyalty and dependability, on the one hand, and her "crazy" ways of fights and gangs that were found right in her own neighborhood, on the other. Her mother got jumped in a gang "'cause that was around, it was a sense of security," in Teresa's words. Teresa's story highlights the devotion and admiration she expressed about her mother despite the troubles Teresa encountered living with her.

Even though Teresa was around Norteño gangs because of her mother's involvement, and members of her family in her same age group were involved, Teresa somehow managed to stay out of the gangs. Interestingly, although she did not deny that she would engage in violent behavior, she articulated emphatically that violence would not be something she had to do because she was in a gang, but because she felt individually that she had to do it.

Teresa seemed quite willing to express her knowledge about gang history and lore, as well as her own aunt's participation in the "Chicano Power movement . . . the LA riots, she was in all the marches and she was in the Brown Berets." Despite this background, Teresa spoke derisively about the Chicano movement and focused instead on the inanity of "disrespect," how people take it too seriously and how pride can be deadly. Teresa's idea of respect drew from a code of individuality, which she believes should emanate from within. Her rules for respect were that it should not be expected, only insofar as a person first should provide respect for self, without exceeding it by being proud.

In discussing colors, she talked about gang colors almost as though they were an aesthetic choice, but she took offense when others assumed she was a Norteña on the occasions when she wore red. She had been taking care of her younger stepsister since Teresa was 9 and even took care of her own mother when her mother was in an abusive relationship with the father of Teresa's stepsister. This man, who was not in a gang but dealt drugs nonetheless, was described as "the scum of the earth" for hitting her mother and Teresa. Despite this, she felt more fortunate than her younger sister because the younger child had experienced their homelessness and emotional abuse as an infant, unlike Teresa, who was older when such events ensued. She claimed that being exposed to gangs, drugs, guns, and other such deviance did not have as negative an effect on her as being exposed to domestic violence the way her stepsister had been as a young child. Yet Teresa took it in stride: She did the best she could in the face of her mother's depression caused by her abusive relationship. From her abusive step-father, Teresa suffered physical and emotional pain, but the need to care for her mother and sister helped her manage the emotional pain.

She acknowledged using marijuana since the age of 12 and drink-ing since 14, the latter becoming a problem that she overcame. Teresa got her first job at 17, had never gotten fired, finished high school, and then attended junior college to become a clinical medical assistant but ended up dropping out.

As mentioned before, when we spoke, Teresa was preoccupied with the news that her work hours at a fast-food restaurant would be reduced; her preoccupation was due mostly to the fact that she had just taken over the rent of a house. She later revealed that the house had been rented by the family of one of her aunts, who had gone to prison. Having a house, as opposed to an apartment, made her feel mature, more responsible, and more settled, and she hinted at it several times before I managed to ask her directly to tell me the story about the house. She used the opportunity to return to a story about being a responsible woman, the strength of females in her family, and to make a connection with popular notions of Mexican and Mexican-American families in the U.S. entertainment media.

Rather than being a mere platitude, Teresa's favorite slogan was, "I've always been my own person, done my own thing, I've always been about what benefits me and the people around me." This and other pithy life lessons helped her navigate an uncertain and unforgiving sea of vicissitudes she had encountered in her life. Teresa's tangential expo-sure to crime and the gang lifestyle in her childhood, and as a 20-year-old through her extended family, shaped her identity of being a fighter, a doer, a person who got things done, and someone mature beyond her years who knew how to avoid trouble and who held it together. Teresa gladly traveled the nontraditional trails that had been blazed by her female relatives. Teresa's story about her gang impact is included in the themes of "Tattoos and Identity" and "Of Colors and Names."

Appendix B

Glossary of Common Gang Terms

The following list is a partial compilation of terms and concepts meaningful to the gang-impacted and gang-involved women, as well as to law enforcement officers and the professionals at community-based organizations (CBOs) with whom I spoke as part of this book. I have by no means attempted to create a comprehensive lexicon of gang-related terms; if one were to exist, it would almost instantly become obsolete because some of these terms can be short-lived, region- or gang-specific, and multipurpose. The terms and concepts range from individual words to phrases that function as nouns (n.), verbs (v.), adjectives (adj.), or adverbs (adv.). In short, this modest attempt is an invitation to others to add, revise, challenge, delete, or otherwise improve. One such vocabulary was written by Harris (1988), and this is my attempt to expand on it. All errors and omissions are mine alone.

Angel dust—(n.) the hallucinogenic drug phencyclidine hydrochloride (PCP).

Back down—(v.) to run away from a fight, to surrender. Opposite of "back it up."

Back it up—(v.) to support a gang or color, as in "she backs up blue." To stand up for the gang, to defend its name, to put in work to support it, such as "ratpacking" or assaulting rival gang members, and to keep the business of the gang secret. Usage includes "I got your back" or "I have your back" to mean "I support you." See by comparison "Down" and by contrast "Back down," "Leva," "No good," or "Rank out."

Back-up—(n.) support against attacks. Preventive moves against harassment.

Bang—(v.) to be a gang member, a gang-banger. To run around with gang members.

Barrio—(n.) traditional spelling for "neighborhood." Also see "Varrio."

Brincar—(v.) infinitive form in Spanish for the verb "to jump." To beat a prospective gang member by the gang members. See "Jump in." Also, to attack an enemy.

Buster—(n.) an insulting term by Sureños for Norteños.

Carnal—(n.) a relative or a sibling-like friend, from *carne*, Spanish for "flesh."

Chapetes/Chapetas—(n.) an insulting term by Sureños for Norteños.

Cholo/Chola—(n.) a gang member. Also, a style of dressing with oversized clothing, sagging pants, or creased khaki pants of specific brands (Ben Davis, Dickies, etc.).

Claim—(v.) to voice loyalties to a gang, as in "Those girls claim Norte."

Clique—(n.) also "clica" or "clicka." An alternative term for gang. Sometimes used to refer to all-girls groups with little to no involvement in crime or illegal activities but engaged in fights with other cliques. See "Crew" and "Set."

Coyote—(n.) a person who helps others cross the border illegally, a smuggler of people.

Crack—(n.) a crystalline form of cocaine broken into small pieces and smoked.

Crank—(n.) a street name for methamphetamine, also known as "crystal," "crystal meth," or "meth."

Crew—(n.) an alternative term for gang. Sometimes used to refer to members of a dancing troupe with little or no involvement in crime or illegal activities but engaged in fights with other crews. See "Clique" and "Set."

Dirt—(n.) crimes, gang-banging, as in, "We did a lot of dirt in those days."

Dissing—(v.) disrespecting someone, saying bad things about a person.

Dots—(n.) a tattoo consisting of three dots to signify "La Vida Loca" or entry into a gang. Also a tattoo with three dots on one hand and one on the other to signify a Sureño claim; four dots on one hand and one on the other signify a Norteño claim.

Down—(v.) to be heavily involved, supportive, and loyal to a color. One who is faithful to the gang, dependable, ready to follow orders, or trustworthy. Usage: "He's down." Contrast with "Leva" or "No good."

Farmeros—(n.) Self-ascribed term for Northerners, Norteños. In recognition of their farm laborers' origins, they sometimes use the stylized black eagle of the United Farm Workers flag in their gang symbols and tattoos.

Feria—(n.) money.

Gang-banger—(n.) a gang-involved person, a member of a gang.

Gangs of Family—(n.) condition of being (assumed to be) a gang member because one's family member(s) is (are) in a gang. A legacy of sorts.

Gringo/gringa—(n.) a white or Caucasian person; a light-haired, fair-complexioned person; also an American-born person of Mexican descent. See by comparison "Güero/Güera" and by contrast "Pocho/Pocha."

Güero/Güera—(n.) (pronounced "way-roh" and "way-rah") blondie; a light-haired and fair-complexioned person. See "Gringo/Gringa."

Hard-core—(adj.) a deeply involved gang member. One involved with drug-dealing and committing serious crimes, most likely having been incarcerated for such.

Hellah—(adj. & adv.) a lot. As in "I accumulated hellah traffic tickets" or "This party is going to be hellah good!"

Hit up—(v.) to demand to know someone's gang affiliation.

Homeboy/Homegirl—(n.) a fellow gang member, a trusted peer.

Homie—(n.) shortened form of "homeboy" or "homegirl."

Hood rat—(n.) a woman involved in or impacted by a gang who has many sex partners; a promiscuous woman, or a woman who engages in sexual activities in exchange for drugs.

Hunting—(adv. & v.) picking fights, as in "They went Buster hunting," to mean Sureños went to pick a fight with Norteños.

Jack, jacking—(v.) stealing, as in carjacking; also, to mug people and steal their valuables.

Jaina—(n.) pronounced like "hyena," a woman.

Jale—(n.) pronounced "hah–lay." From the Spanish verb *jalar*, meaning "to pull." Literally, "a pull"; a "job" to be performed, a gig.

Jump in—(v.) ritual group beating to accept new gang members. See "Jump out."

Jump out—(v.) group beating to dismiss one member from her/his former gang. Typically, it is a longer and more vicious assault than "jumping in."

Jumping—(v.) assaulting rival gang members. See "Ratpacking."

Kick it with—(v.) to spend time with, hang out, as in "I kick it with Sureños."

Known associate—(n.) a term used by law enforcement to refer to individuals who, although not yet "validated" as gang members, nonetheless are known to associate with such.

La Eme—(n.) m., "the M," in English. The name of a prison gang affiliated with the Mexican Mafia.

Legit—(adj.) legitimate, formal. As in "Rosa left the gang and got a legit job."

Leño—(n.) a log; a cigarette laced with PCP.

Leva—(n.) a snitch, an untrustworthy person. To "be on the leva" means to be distrusted, to be suspected of being a "narc" or a "rata."

Life—(n.) lifestyle, the gang lifestyle. Also, a life sentence in prison.

Loco/Loca—(n. & adj.) under the influence of drugs. Also sometimes used as one of three parts in a gang's name, as in "Varrio Sur Locos."

Mad-dogging—(v.) staring at someone with disdain; typically a precursor to a fight among gang members.

Mexican Mafia—(n.) The name for a prison gang, often associated with Sureños.

Mule—(n.) a girl or woman who is used to carry drugs or guns. Someone who does a gang member's bidding or runs errands for them. A person in a low position.

Narc—(n.) a police informant; alternately, an undercover police officer conducting narcotics investigations.

Narco—(n.) Spanish slang for drug dealer, short for "narcotraficante."

No good—(adj.) In bad standing with the gang members, not to be trusted or undependable. Synonymous with "on the leva."

Norcacas—(n.) a derogatory name for Norteños by Sureños.

Norputos—(n.) a derogatory name for Norteños by Sureños.

Nothing—(adj.) not affiliated with either gang, as in "Loverboy's girlfriend was nothing."

Nowhere—(adj.) a response by a "nothing" when being "hit up," asked where she or he is from—in essence, what gang she or he claims.

Nuestra Familia—(n.) "Our Family," in English. The name for a prison gang, often associated with Norteños.

O.G.—(n.) Old Gangster. Often referring to a gang's founder, or someone who has been incarcerated and is now respected as a sort of gang elder in the *varrio*. See "Veterano."

Paisa—(n.) a person from Mexico; a shortened form of *paisano*, fellow countryman. Sometimes used as a derogatory term for Sureños.

Paño—(n.) a bandana, kerchief. Norteños wear red paños while Sureños wear blue paños.

PCP—(n.) the hallucinogenic drug phencyclidine hydrochloride, also known as "angel dust."

Pistol whip—(v.) to hit someone with a gun to intimidate them.

Pocho/Pocha—(n.) an American-born person of Mexican descent, see also "Gringo/Gringa."

Por Vida—(adj.) Spanish for "For Life," often seen in gang tattoos or graffiti to demonstrate lifetime commitment to the gang lifestyle, most often in Sureño nomenclature.

Punked—(v.) getting harassed, being assaulted, being overpowered, or being outdone by someone inferior.

Put someone in check—(v.) to warn a person to show respect.

Quinceañera—(n.) a large party to celebrate a girl's 15th birthday; commonly celebrated among Mexican and Mexican-American families, Quinceañeras are not at all exclusive to gangs.

Ranch, the—(n.) Colloquial term for one of the juvenile rehabilitation facilities in Santa Clara County, California.

Rank, rank out—(v.) to not back up, to hide or deny one's gang affiliation, especially when being "hit up."

Ranker—(n.) a drop-out, someone who has left the gang, who did not "back it up" or did not claim the gang when being "hit up." Used derogatorily.

Ratpacking—(v.) assaulting rival gang members, see "Jumping."

Rata—(n.) "Rat" in English. A snitch.

Raza—(n.) Mexican people, dark-skinned people, used to signify solidarity among them.

Rifar—(n.) to bang or to claim a color. Mostly used when speaking Spanish or Spanglish, as in "Ella rifa blue," to mean "She supports Sureños."

Sancha—(n.) term used to refer to a woman who is not the main sexual partner of a man; a mistress.

Scrap/Scrapa—(n.) an insulting term by Norteños for Sureños.

Set—(n.) an alternative term for gang. See "Crew" and "Clique."

Sexed in—(v.) a woman's initiation into a gang by requiring her to have sex with several gang members.

Shisty moves—(n.) dishonest behavior, as in diluting drugs and selling them as pure.

Shot-caller—(n.) a leader in a gang. One who calls the shots, who assigns tasks to its members.

Throw signs—(v.) to make letters with hand signs to refer to a given gang. See "Tirar."

Tirar—(v.) In Spanish, to throw, referring to the act of making hand signs to signify the letters of the gang. Can be performed as recognition of one's homies, instead of a fight, to start a fight, or as a parting shot after vanquishing an opponent. Also typically seen in pictures where each gang member will make one letter and two or three members together make up the gang initials.

Validated—(adj.) a term used by police to refer to a person who has been identified as belonging to a gang from a "totality of circumstances," including pictures (see "Tirar") with validated gang members or "known associates," from gang-related tattoos, from self-claims, from being arrested in the company of validated gang members or known associates, and from possessing gang paraphernalia and wearing gang attire and gang colors.

Varrio—(n.) misspelling of *barrio*, a street, a neighborhood; used by gang members to refer to their gang's name, as in "Varrio Sur Vatos."

Vato—(n.) a boy, a young man. Short for *chivato*, a kid goat.

Veterano—(n.) an old gang member. A veteran. See "O.G."

Vida Loca, La—(adj.) the crazy life; running with gang members. Using and dealing drugs.

Wannabe—(n.) a girl who aspires to be in the gang but has not yet been accepted or treated as a member by the gang.

Y.A.—(n.) also C.Y.A., California Youth Authority. The former name for the Department of Juvenile Justice of the State of California.

References

Archer, L., & Grascia, A. (2006). Girls, gangs and crime: Profile of the young female offender. *Journal of Gang Research, 13*(2), 37–48.

Armitage, J. S., & Dugan, R. E. (2006). Marginalized experiences of Hispanic females in youth-based religious groups. *Journal for the Scientific Study of Religion, 45*(2), 217–231. Retrieved January 10, 2008, from http://onlinelibrary.wiley.com/doi/10.1111/j.1468-5906.2006.00302.x/pdf

Armstrong, M. L. (1991). Career-oriented women with tattoos. *Journal of Nursing Scholarship, 23*(4), 215–220.

Atkinson, M. (2002). Pretty in ink: Conformity, resistance, and negotiation in women's tattooing. *Sex Roles, 47*, 219–235.

Atkinson, M., & Young, K. (2001). Flesh journeys: Neo primitives and the contemporary rediscovery of radical body modification. *Deviant Behavior, 22*, 117–146.

Baruch Bush, R. A., & Folger, J. P. (2005). *The promise of mediation: The transformative approach to conflict.* San Francisco: Jossey-Bass.

Bazan, L. E., Harris, L., & Lorentzen, L. A. (2002). Migrant gangs, religion, and tattoo removal. *Peace Review, 14*(4), 379–383.

Becerra, R. M., & de Anda, D. (1984). Pregnancy and motherhood among Mexican American adolescents. *Health and Social Work, 9*(2), 106–123.

Beckford, R. (2004). *God and the gangs.* London: Darton, Longman & Todd.

Bellah, R. (1970). Christianity and symbolic realism. *Journal for the Scientific Study of Religion, 9*(2), 89–96.

Bellah, R. N., Madsen, R., Sullivan, W. M., Swidler, A., & Tipton, S. M. (1985). *Habits of the heart: Individualism and commitment in American life.* New York: Harper & Row.

Besag, V. E. (2006). *Understanding girls' friendships, fights and feuds: A practical approach to girls' bullying.* Berkshire, UK: McGraw-Hill.

Booth, E. T. (2011). Queering queer eye: The stability of gay identity confronts the liminality of trans embodiment. *Western Journal of Communication, 75*(2), 185–204.

Braunberger, C. (2000). Revolting bodies: The monster beauty of tattooed women. *NWSA Journal, 12*(2), 1–23.

Brotherton, D. C., & Barrios, L. (2004). *The Almighty Latin King and Queen Nation: Street politics and the transformation of a New York City gang.* New York: Columbia University Press.

Buchholz, T. G. (2011). *Rush: Why you need and love the rat race.* New York: Hudson Street Press.

Bursik, R. J., Jr., & Grasmick, H. G. (2006). Defining and researching gangs. In A. Egley, Jr., C. L. Maxson, J. Miller, & M. Klein (Eds.), *The modern gang reader* (pp. 2–13). Los Angeles: Roxbury.

Campbell, A. (1984/1991). *The girls in the gang.* Oxford: Basil Blackwell.

Campbell, A. (1987). Self definition by rejection. *Social Problems, 34,* 451–466.

Campbell, A. (1995). Female participation in gangs. In C.R. Huff (Ed.), *Gangs in America* (pp. 163–182). Newbury Park: Sage.

Carleton, R. A., Esparza, P., Thaxter, P., & Grant, K. E. (2008). Stress, religious coping resources, and depressive symptoms in an urban adolescent sample. *Journal for the Scientific Study of Religion, 47*(1), 113–121. Retrieved March 28, 2008, from http://web.ebscohost.com.libaccess.sjlibrary.org/ehost/detail?vid=6&hid=115&sid=57acf37e-c906-4d16-914b-cafb97acee27%40sessionmgr7

Carroll, L., & Anderson, R. (2002). Body piercing, tattooing, self-esteem, and body investment in adolescent girls. *Adolescence, 37*(147), 627–637.

Cepeda, A., & Valdez. A. (2003). Risk behaviors among young Mexican American gang-associated females: Sexual relations, partying, substance use, and crime. *Journal of Adolescent Research, 18*(1), 90–106. Retrieved February 20, 2008, from http://jar.sagepub.com

Chesney-Lind, M. (1993). Girls, gangs, and violence: Anatomy of a backlash. *Humanity and Society, 17*(3), 321–324.

Chesney-Lind, M. (1997). *Female offenders: Girls, women, and crime.* Thousand Oaks, CA: Sage.

Chesney-Lind, M. (2001). What about the girls? Delinquency programming as if gender mattered. *Corrections Today, 63*(1). Retrieved June 9, 2008, from http://web.ebscohost.com.libaccess.sjlibrary.org/ehost/pdf?vid=6&hid=114&sid=929270dd-04cf-4699-8851-b5992dd778f1%40sessionmgr3

Cohen, G. (1969). The delinquency of gangs and spontaneous groups. In T. Sellin & M. W. Wolfgang (Eds.), *Delinquency: Selected studies* (pp. 61–111). New York: Wiley Press.

Cooper, L., Anaf, J., & Bowden, M. (2006). Contested concepts in violence against women: "Intimate," "domestic" or "torture"? *Australian Social Work, 59*(3), 314–327.

Cronen, V. E. (1995). Coordinated management of meaning: The consequentiality of communication and the recapturing of experience. In S. J. Sigman (Ed.), *The consequentiality of communication* (pp. 17–65). Hillsdale, NJ: Lawrence Erlbaum Associates.

Curry, G. D. (1998). Female gang involvement. *Journal of Research in Crime Delinquency, 35*(1), 100–118.

Curry, G. D. (1999). Responding to female gang involvement. In M. Chesney-Lind & J. M. Hagedorn (Eds.), *Female gangs in America: Essays on girls, gangs, and gender* (pp. 133–153). Chicago: Lake View Press.

Decker, S. H., & Lauritsen, J. L. (2006). Leaving the gang. In A. Egley, Jr., C. L. Maxson, J. Miller, & M. W. Klein (Eds.), *The modern gang reader* (pp. 192–205). Los Angeles: Roxbury.

Decker S. H., & Van Winkle, B. (1996). *Life in the gang: Family, friends, and violence*. Cambridge, UK: Cambridge University Press.

de la Rouchefoucauld, F. (1678/2009). *Reflections; or sentences and moral maxims*. Project Guttenberg. Retrieved September 23, 2011, from http://www.gutenberg.org/9/1/0/9105/.

De Tocqueville, A. (1969). *Democracy in America* (Trans. G. Lawrence). New York: Doubleday.

DeMello, M. (2000). *Bodies of inscription: A cultural history of the modern tattoo community*. Durham, NC: Duke University Press.

Doherty, K. T. (1998). A mind of her own: Effects of need for closure and gender on reactions to nonconformity. *Sex Roles, 38*, 801–819.

Doi, T. (1990). *The anatomy of dependence: The key analysis of Japanese behavior* (Trans. J. Bester). Tokyo: Kodansha International.

Douglas, M. (1984). *Implicit meanings: Selected essays in anthropology*. London: Routledge.

Fagan, J. (1993). The political economy of drug dealing among urban gangs. In R. Davis, A. Lurigio, & D. P. Rosenbaum (Eds.), *Drugs and community*. Springfield, IL: Charles C Thomas.

Fazila, B. (2004). "I want you to see us as a person and not as a gang member or a thug": Young people define their identities in the public sphere. *Identity, The Journal of the Society for Identity Formation, 4*(1), 39–57.

Freedman, J., & Combs, G. (1996). *Narrative therapy: The social construction of preferred realities*. New York: Norton.

Gadlin, H., & Ouellette, P. A. (1986/1987). Mediation Milanese: An application of systemic family therapy to family mediation. *Mediation Quarterly, 14/15*, 101–118.

Garot, R. (2007). "Where you from!" Gang identity as performance. *Journal of Contemporary Ethnography, 36*(1), 50–84. Retrieved January 30, 2008, from http://jce.sagepub.com/cgi/content/abstract/36/1/50

Geertz, C. (1973). Thick description: Toward an interpretive theory of culture. In C. Geertz (Ed.), *The interpretation of cultures: Selected essays* (pp. 3–30). New York: Basic Books.

Gerbner, G., Gross, L., Morgan, M., & Signorielli, N. (1986). Living with television. In J. Bryant & D. Zillmann (Eds.), *Perspectives on media effects*. Hillsdale, NJ: Lawrence Erlbaum Associates.

Gergen, K. J. (2009). *Relational being: Beyond self and community*. New York: Oxford University Press.

Goffman, E. (1967). *Interaction ritual: Essays on face-to-face behavior*. New York: Pantheon Books.

Goodkind, S. (2005). Gender-specific services in the juvenile justice system: A critical examination. *Affilia, 20*(1), 52–70. Available at http://aff.sagepub.com/cgi/content/abstract/20/1/52

Green, G., South, N., & Smith, R. (2006). "The say that you re a danger but you are not": Representations and the construction of the moral self in narratives of "dangerous individuals." *Deviant Behavior, 27,* 299–328.

Gruwell, E. (1999). *The Freedom Writers Diary: How a teacher and 150 teens used writing to change themselves and the world around them.* New York: Random House.

Hall, E. (1963). A system for the notation of proxemic behavior. *American Anthropologist, 65,* 1003–1026.

Harris, M. (1988). *Cholas: Latino girls in gangs.* New York: AMS Press.

Hawkes, D., Senn, C., & Thorn, C. (2004). Factors that influence attitudes toward women with tattoos. *Sex Roles: A Journal of Research, 50*(9–10), 593–605. Retrieved February 22, 2008, from http://find.galegroup.com/itx/start.do?prodId=EAIM

Horowitz, R. (1983). *Honor and the American dream: Culture and identity in a Chicano community.* New Brunswick, NJ: Rutgers University Press.

Horowitz, R. (1990). Sociological perspectives on gangs: Conflicting definitions and concepts. In C. R. Huff (Ed.), *Gangs in America* (pp. 37–54). Newbury Park, CA: Sage.

Hughes, L. A. (2005). Studying youth gangs: Alternative methods and conclusions. *Journal of Contemporary Criminal Justice, 21*(2), 98–119. Retrieved June 9, 2008, from http://ccj.sagepub.com

Hunt, G., & Joe-Laidler, K. (2006). Situations of violence in the lives of girl gang members. In A. Egley, Jr., C. L. Maxson, J. Miller, & M. W. Klein (Eds.), *The modern gang reader* (pp. 244–257). Los Angeles, CA: Roxbury.

Hunt, G., Joe-Laidler, K., & MacKenzie, K. (2005). Moving into motherhood: Gang girls and controlled risk. *Youth & Society, 36,* 333. Retrieved February 22, 2008, from http://yas.sagepub.com/cgi/content/abstract/36/3/333

Institute for Peace and Justice. (2011). *TAP–Teens Acting for Peace Pledge of Non-Violence.* Retrieved April 9, 2011, from http://www.ipj-ppj.org/TAP%20Archives/tap/pledge.html

Jackson, M. S., Bass, L., & Sharpe, E. G. (2005). Working with youth street gangs and their families: Utilizing a nurturing model for social work practice. *Journal of Gang Research, 12*(2), 1–17.

Joe-Laidler, K., & Hunt, G. (2001). Accomplishing femininity among girls in the gang. *British Journal of Criminology, 41*(4), 656–678.

Jones, T. S., & Brinkert, R. (2008). *Conflict coaching: Conflict management strategies and skills for the individual.* Los Angeles: Sage.

Jordan, J. (2007). *Pascal's wager: Pragmatic arguments and belief in God.* London: Oxford University Press.

Kegan, R. (1982). *The evolving self: Problem and process in human development.* Cambridge, MA: Harvard University Press.

Kempf-Leonard, K., & Johansson, P. (2007). Gender and runaways: Risk factors, delinquency, and juvenile justice. *Youth Violence and Juvenile Justice,*

5(3), 308–327. Retrieved January 30, 2008, from http://yvj.sagepub.com/cgi/content/abstract/5/3/308

Klein, M. W. (1969). On group context and delinquency. *Sociology and Social Research, 54*, 63–71.

Klein, M. W. (1971). *Street gangs and street workers.* Englewood Cliffs, NJ: Prentice Hall.

Klein, M. W., & Maxson, C. L. (1989). Street gang violence. In N. A Weiner & M. E. Wolfgang (Eds.), *Violent crime, violent criminals* (pp. 198–234). Newbury Park, CA: Sage.

Kosut, M. (2006). Mad artists and tattooed perverts: Deviant discourse and the social construction of cultural categories. *Deviant Behavior, 27*(1), 73–95.

Kundera, M. (1981). *The book of laughter and forgetting* (Trans. M. Henry). New York: Penguin Books.

Le Guin, U. (1989). *Dancing at the edge of the world: Thoughts on words, women, places.* New York: Harper & Row/Perennial.

Lafontaine, T., Acoose, S., & Schissel, B. (2009). Healing connections: Rising above the gang. *Journal of Gang Research, 16*(2), 27–55. Retrieved July 31, 2010, from http://www.ncjrs.gov/App/publications/abstract.aspx?ID=248654

Lesser, J., Anderson, N., & Koniak-Griffin, D. (1998). Sometimes youth don't feel ready to be an adult or a mom: The experience of adolescent pregnancy. *Journal of Child and Adolescent Psychiatric Nursing, 11*, 7–16.

Lesser, J., & Koniak-Griffin, D. (2000). The impact of physical or sexual abuse on chronic depression in adolescent mothers. *Journal of Pediatric Nursing, 15*(6), 378–387.

Lesser, J., Koniak-Griffin, D., & Anderson, N. (1999). Depressed adolescent mothers' perceptions of their own maternal role. *Issues in Mental Health Nursing, 20*, 131–149.

Luke, K. P. (2008). Are girls really becoming more violent? A critical analysis. *Affilia: Journal of Women and Social Work, 23*(1), 38–50. Retrieved January 30, 2008, from http://aff.sagepub.com at San José State University.

MacIntyre, A. (1981). *After virtue.* London: Duckworth.

McLean, G. (1991). *Cities of lonesome fear: God among the gangs.* Chicago: Moody Press.

McNamee, S., & Gergen, K.J. (1999). *Relational responsibility: Resources for sustainable dialogue.* Thousand Oaks, CA: Sage.

Mendoza-Denton, N. (2008). *Homegirls: Language and cultural practice among Latina youth gangs.* Malden, MA: Blackwell Publishing.

Mifflin, M. (1997). *Bodies of subversion: A secret history of women and tattoo.* New York: Juno Books.

Miller, J. (1998). Gender and victimization risk among young women in gangs. *Journal of Research in Crime and Delinquency, 35*, 429–453.

Miller, J. (2000). *One of the guys: Girls, gangs, and gender.* New York: Oxford University Press.

Miller, J. (2006). Getting into gangs. In A. Egley, Jr., C. L. Maxson, J. Miller, & M. W. Klein (Eds.), *The modern gang reader* (pp. 43–59). Los Angeles: Roxbury.

Miranda, M. (2003). *Homegirls in the public sphere*. Austin, TX: University of Texas Press.

Molidor, C. (1996). Female gang members: A profile of aggression and victimization. *Social Work, 41*(3), 251–257.

Moore, J. (1991). *Going down to the barrio: Homeboys and homegirls in change*. Philadelphia, PA: Temple University Press.

Moore, J. (1994). The chola life course: Chicana heroin users and the barrio gang. *International Journal of Addictions, 29*(9), 1115–1126.

Moore, J., & Devitt, M. (1989). The paradox of deviance in addicted Mexican American mothers. *Gender & Society, 3*(1), 53–70.

Moore, J. W., & Hagedorn, J. M. (1999). What happens to girls in the gang? In M. Chesney-Lind & J. M. Hagedorn (Eds.), *Female gangs in America* (pp. 177–186). Chicago: Lake View Press.

Moore, J. W., & Hagedorn, J. (2006). Female gangs: A focus on research. In A. Egley, Jr., C. L. Maxson, J. Miller, & M. W. Klein (Eds.), *The modern gang reader* (pp. 192–205). Los Angeles: Roxbury.

Nash, B. (2011). Letters: Are our horses helping our kids? *Modern Arabian Horse Magazine, 3*, 16.

Osterud, A. K. (2009). *The tattooed lady: A history*. Golden, CO: Fulcrum Publishing.

Padilla, F. (1992). *The gang as an American enterprise*. New Brunswick, NJ: Rutgers University Press.

Palmer, C. T., & Tilley, C. F. (1995). Sexual access to females as a motivation for joining gangs: An evolutionary approach. *Journal of Sex Research, 32*(3), 213–217.

Patterson, K., Grenny, J., Maxfield, D., McMillan, R., & Switzler, A. (2008). *Influencer: The power to change anything*. New York: McGraw-Hill.

Pearce, W. B. (1989). *Communication and the human condition*. Carbondale, IL: Southern Illinois University Press.

Pearce, W. B. (1994). *Interpersonal communication: Making social worlds*. New York: HarperCollins.

Pearce, W. B. (2008). *Making social worlds: A communication perspective*. Malden, MA: Blackwell Publishing.

Pearce, W. B. & Cronen, V. E. (1980). *Communication, action and meaning: The creation of social realities*. New York: Praeger.

Pearce, W. B., & Pearce, K. A. (1998). Transcendent storytelling: Abilities for systemic practitioners and their clients. *Human Systems, 9*, 167–185.

Percy, M. S. (2003). Feeling loved, having friends to count on, and taking care of myself: Minority children living in poverty describe what is "special" to them. *Journal of Children and Poverty, 9*(1), 55–70.

Post, D. (1990, Spring). Interindependence: A new concept in relationships. *Lesbian Ethics, 4*(1). Retrieved March 11, 2008, from http://www.feminist-reprise.org/docs/interindependence.htm

Poumele, S. (2007, September 25). *Workshop on gangs*. Washington United Youth Center, San José, CA.

Puzo, M. (1969). *The godfather*. New York: G. P. Putnam's Sons.

Reiss, A. J., Jr. (1988). Co-offending and criminal careers. In M. Tonry & N. Morris (Eds.), *Crime and justice: A review of research* (Vol. 10, pp. 117–170). Chicago: University of Chicago Press.

Rescher, N. (1985). *Pascal's wager: A study of practical reasoning in philosophical theology*. South Bend, IN: University of Notre Dame Press.

Revolutionary Communist Party USA. (2002). Brave resistance at Pelican Bay SHU: Prison hunger strike against supermax torture. *Revolutionary Worker #1176*. Posted November 24, 2002. Retrieved June 11, 2008, from http://rwor.org/a/v24/1171-1180/1176/pelican.htm

Rogers, R. (2011). Military: Going green harvests employment for vets. *The North County Times*. Posted January 7, 2011. Retrieved January 16, 2011, from http://www.nctimes.com/news/local/military/article_689cfd59-be49-51de-9ac3-04a54c1b6206.html

Rossmann, L. C. (2002). What if we asked circular questions to transform controversial issues? Possibilities for the classroom. *Exchanges*. Available at http://www.exchangesjournal.org/print/print_1065.html

Rossmann, L. C. (2004). Remembering the Alamo: Cosmopolitan communication and grammars of transcendence. *Human Systems 15*, 31–42.

Rubin, H. J., & Rubin, I. S. (1995). *Qualitative interviewing: The art of hearing data*. Thousand Oaks, CA: Sage.

Scharffs, B. G. (2004, February 6–7). The autonomy of church and state. *Brigham Young University Law Review*. Retrieved March 11, 2008, from http://findarticles.com/p/articles/mi_qa3736/is_200402/ai_n9474012

Schneider, D. M. (1980). *American kinship: A cultural account* (2nd ed.). Chicago: University of Chicago Press.

Schneider, D. M. (1984). *A critique of the study of kinship*. Ann Arbor: University of Michigan Press.

Scott, K. Y. (1991). *The habit of survival: Black women's strategies for life*. New Brunswick, NJ: Rutgers University Press.

Selvini Palazzoli, M., Cecchin, G., Prata, G., & Boscolo, L. (1978). *Paradox and counterparadox: A new model in the therapy of the family in schizophrenic transaction*. New York: Aronson.

Servaes, J. (1986). *Cultural identity and the mass media in the third world*. Seoul: International Broadcasting Society.

Shaw, B. (2004). *Schoolgirls out of school: The education of girls in the gang*. Unpublished dissertation, University of Utah.

Smilde, D., & May, M. (2010). *The emerging strong program in the sociology of religion: Social science research council working papers*. Retrieved January 7, 2011, from http://blogs.ssrc.org/tif/wp-content/uploads/2010/02/Emerging-Strong-Program-TIF.pdf

Spergel, I. A. (1990). Youth gangs: Continuity and change. In M. Tonry & N. Morris (Eds.), *Crime and justice: A review of research* (Vol. 12, pp. 171–275). Chicago: University of Chicago Press.

Sutherland, E. H. (1934). *Principles of criminology* (2nd ed.). Philadelphia, PA: J. B. Lippincott.

Szakolczai, A. (2000) *Reflexive historical sociology*. London: Routledge.

Szakolczai, A. (2009). Liminality and experience: Structuring transitory situations and transformative events. *International Political Anthropology, 2*(1), 141–172.

Thornberry, T. B., Krohn, M. D., Lizotte, A. J., & Chard-Wierschem, D. (2006). Antecedents of gang membership. In M. W. Klein, C. L. Maxson, & J. Miller (Eds.), *The modern gang reader* (pp. 30–42). Los Angeles: Roxbury.

Thrasher, F. M. (1927). *The gang*. Chicago: University of Chicago Press.

Tomm, K. (1985). Circular interviewing: A multifaceted clinical tool. In D. Campbell & R. Draper (Eds.), *Applications of systemic family therapy: The Milan approach* (pp. 33–45). London: Grune & Stratton.

Turner, V. (1969). *The ritual process: Structure and anti-structure*. Ithaca, NY: Cornell University Press.

United Nations. (2008). *Peacekeeping operations principles and guidelines*. New York: United Nations Secretariat. Retrieved June 10, 2011, from http://www.peacekeepingbestpractices.unlb.org/pbps/library/capstone_doctrine_eng.pdf

Van Gennep, A. (1909/1972). *Rites of passage*. Chicago: University of Chicago Press.

Varriale, J. A. (2008). Female gang members and desistance: Pregnancy as a possible exit strategy. *Journal of Gang Research, 15*(4), 35–64.

Vigil, J. D. (1988). *Barrio gangs: Street life and identity in Southern California*. Austin: University of Texas Press.

Webb, S. (2007). *Tattooed women*. Atglen, PA: Schiffer Publishing.

Wieder, D. L. (2001). Telling the convict code. In R. M. Emerson (Ed.), *Contemporary field research: A collection of readings* (pp. 76–88). Prospect Heights, IL: Waveland Press.

Wittgenstein, L. (1953/2001). *Philosophical investigations*. Boston: Blackwell Publishing.

Zander, R. S., & Zander, B. (2000). *The art of possibility: Transforming professional and personal life*. New York: Penguin.

Author Index

Subject Index

Lightning Source UK Ltd.
Milton Keynes UK
UKOW03n1339200314

228515UK00001B/61/P